Kate Colquhoun's previous works of non-fiction were shortlisted for the Duff Cooper Prize 2004 and longlisted for the Samuel Johnson Prize 2003. *Mr Briggs' Hat* was shortlisted for the CWA Non-fiction Dagger Award. She writes for several newspapers and magazines, and appears regularly on national radio and television. She lives in London with her two sons.

'A fascinating, meticulously researched book, full of period detail. Colquhoun's success in weaving together a series of complex topics is no mean feat and an even greater achievement is to have presented them clearly and simply'

Katie Waldegrave, *Spectator*

'Kate Colquhoun has a complicated and fascinating story to tell. She has researched the case well, reading the original trial transcripts and contemporary newspaper reports in addition to the many previous accounts of the Maybrick case'

Catherine Peters, *Literary Review*

'Kate Colquhoun's account of the Maybrick case is brilliantly detailed – her knowledge of the uses and misuses of poison would put that of many pharmacists to shame'

Rachel Cooke, *Observer*

'With deliciously dark elements of addiction, deception, torrid adultery and poison, this is the riveting true story of a sensational Victorian trial of 1889 ... Colquhoun's writing has a wonderful slow burn to it, and until the final page, she keeps us guessing: guilty, or not guilty?

Bookseller

'[Colquhoun] builds an almost unbearable tension into the events ... This book is much more than a real-life murder mystery. Colquhoun has researched her subject thoroughly and presents a forensic account of the facts as known ... Colquhoun spins a tale rich in detail and atmosphere, and her meticulous research never overshadows her obvious talent for storytelling'

...le, *Herald*

Also by Kate Colquhoun

Mr Briggs' Hat

Taste: The History of Britain through its Cooking

The Thrifty Cookbook: 476 Ways to
Eat Well with Leftovers

A Thing in Disguise: The Visionary Life of
Joseph Paxton

DID SHE KILL HIM?

A Victorian Tale of Deception, Adultery and Arsenic

KATE COLQUHOUN

ABACUS

First published in Great Britain in 2014 by Little, Brown
This paperback edition published in 2015 by Abacus

1 3 5 7 9 10 8 6 4 2

Copyright © Kate Colquhoun, 2014

The moral right of the author has been asserted.

All rights reserved.
No part of this publication may be reproduced, stored in a
retrieval system, or transmitted in any form or by any means, without
the prior permission in writing of the publisher, nor be otherwise circulated
in any form of binding or cover other than that in which it is published
and without a similar condition including this condition being
imposed on the subsequent purchaser.

A CIP catalogue record for this book
is available from the British Library.

ISBN 978-0-349-13856-5

Typeset in Sabon by M Rules
Printed and bound in Great Britain by
Clays Ltd, St Ives plc

Papers used by Abacus are from well-managed forests
and other responsible sources.

MIX
Paper from
responsible sources
FSC   FSC® C104740
www.fsc.org

Abacus
An imprint of
Little, Brown Book Group
100 Victoria Embankment
London EC4Y 0DY

An Hachette UK Company
www.hachette.co.uk

www.littlebrown.co.uk

For
D, F & B

... it is too painful to think that she is a woman, with a woman's destiny before her – a woman spinning in young ignorance a light web of folly and vain hopes which may one day close round her and press upon her, a rancorous poisoned garment, changing all at once ... into a life of deep human anguish.

George Eliot, *Adam Bede* (1859)

I want a happiness without a hole in it ... The golden bowl ... the bowl without the crack.

Henry James, *The Golden Bowl* (1904)

Contents

THREE

Author's Note

The detail of this story and all italicised speech is taken from primary record, including Home Office documents, contemporary newspaper accounts, American archives, court transcripts and Florence Maybrick's emotionally charged memoir.

I have chosen to quote sparingly from a number of letters written by Florence and printed in earlier books about the case despite the fact that the originals have since been lost; there is no reason to believe they were not accurately quoted and they give us rare glimpses into her state of mind. Endnotes indicate where this is the case.

Although I have stuck rigorously to contemporary sources, the reconstruction of history inevitably remains to some extent a work of imagination.

Wednesday 7 August 1889

She had not expected them to be so quick and when the call came her pulse was still fast, her mouth dry.

She heard the key turn in the lock. Felt, rather than saw, the door swing open. Gathering her black skirts in one gloved hand and rising uncertainly from the wooden bench, she stepped out into the corridor, turning towards the stone staircase, ignoring the wardress's offer of support.

She can hear, now, the murmur of many voices from above, the shuffling of feet, throats being cleared. The very air seems to shiver with significance. Taking each step slowly, she fights to compose her features and to calm her breathing.

Five feet, three inches tall, alabaster pale beneath a fine black veil, the slender young widow has never seemed more fragile as she emerges into the open body of a packed courtroom. Turning through a hip-height gate to her right she enters the dock, taking her seat once again towards the railings at its front. Her small hands rest deliberately in her lap. Two female prison guards are close behind, one on either side.

She woke at dawn and it is now almost ten to four in the afternoon. The stooping judge re-enters through a door directly in front of her. She is the focus of the room's attention as she looks up at him, her eyes fixed and unflinching. To Judge Stephen's left a dark curtain ripples before being drawn to one side. Twelve black-coated men file into the jury box. It has taken them just forty-three minutes. She wonders whether any of them will dare to turn towards her. She is determined not to look away.

Dust motes dance in the light slanting from the windows before a cloud blots out the rays. Blown by a sharp wind, raindrops scatter against the glass skylight above her. There are seconds, then, of silence.

She hears the clerk ask his final question.

She straightens her back in the chair, feels the bare board beneath her feet, tries to raise her chin.

It is time.

ONE

CHAPTER 1

March 1889

Whenever the doorbell rings I feel ready to faint for fear it is someone coming to have an account paid.

The pen had hovered for a moment above the letter while she considered.

When Jim comes home at night – she continued in her neat cursive script – *it is with fear and trembling that I look into his face to see whether anyone has been to the office about my bills.*

*

In one of Liverpool's best suburban addresses, Florence Maybrick was lost in thought as she sat in a silk-covered chair before the wide bay window. The parlour was almost perfect: embossed wallpapers offset red plush drapes lined with pale blue satin; several small tables, including one with negro supports, displayed shiny ornaments. A thick Persian carpet deadened the tread of restless feet.

A letter recently addressed to her mother in Paris lay beside her. It contained little of the chatter of the old days – the reports of balls and dinners, of new dresses, of renewed acquaintances or the children. Instead, despite her effort to alight on a defiantly insouciant tone, it charted a newer reality of arguments, accusations and continuing financial anxiety.

In a while she would call Bessie to take it to the post. For the present her tapering fingers remained idle in the lap from which one of her three cats had lately jumped, bored by her failure to show it affection.

Today, the twenty-six-year-old was wonderfully put together, her clothes painstakingly considered if a little over-fussed. Loose curls, dark blonde with a hint of auburn, were bundled up at the back of her head and fashionably frizzed across her full forehead. Slim at the waist, wrists and ankles, but with softly voluptuous bust and hips, she was all sensuousness, with large blue-violet eyes that made her irresistibly charming and aroused protective instincts in men. Yet a lack of angle in the line of her jaw conspired against Florence being a beauty, and a careful observer might even have noticed a peculiar detachment about her, for the young American was impressionable and egotistical, worldly but not wise.

Her glance lingered on the Viennese clock on the mantelpiece and slid across the cool lustre of the pair of Canton porcelain vases. Through the broad archway, early spring blossoms had been gathered into cut-glass vases and set on the Collard & Collard piano. Further down was the dining room with its Turkey carpet, leather-seated Chippendale chairs and sturdy oak dining table spacious enough for forty guests.

Each of these formal public rooms opened on to a broad hall where double doors led to steps and a gravel sweep that snaked out towards substantial gates set into walls draped with ivy. At the back of the hall a dark-wood staircase rose to a half-landing where a stained-glass window scattered coloured drops of light about the walls and floors. A narrower set of stone steps went down to the flagged kitchen, servants' dining room, scullery, pantry, china and coal stores and the washroom with its large copper tub.

The parlour fire smouldered. Occasionally a log resettled with a gentle plume of ash.

Outside, beyond lace-draped French windows, lawns reached down towards the river, covered by a layer of thick snow that muffled the memory of happier summers. A pair of peacocks high-stepped – screaming at the cartwheeling flakes – past shrubberies, flowerbeds and summerhouses, round a large pond and through the thickest drifts lumped over the long grass in the orchard. The chickens ruffled their feathers against the cold; in the kennels and stables the dogs and horses breathed white into the cold air. A fashionable three-seated phaeton was locked away in its shed, protected from the encroaching white.

Upstairs, on the first floor, was the Maybricks' substantial master bedroom with its adjoining dressing room containing a single bed. Next door to it was a large, square guest room and, further along the corridor, a night nursery for the two children – seven-year-old James (known as Sonny or Bobo) and Gladys, who would soon turn three. A linen cupboard was at one end of the landing and a lavatory and bathroom at the other, along with a separate 'housemaid's closet' with a large sink and shelves. On the second floor were lower-ceilinged rooms, a day nursery where the children took their lessons and three smaller bedrooms shared by the female staff – a cook, housemaid, parlour maid and the children's nurse.

Battlecrease House spoke of prosperity and stability, proclaiming Florence and her solid English husband – twenty-four years her senior – to be an ambitious couple attuned to the envy game. It was a private, family space but also an assertion of their conformity to conventional taste and morality, a stage for the formal dinners and whist suppers that oiled the wheels of society and business. As Henry James' Madame Merle noted, *one's house, one's furniture, one's garments, the books one reads, the company one keeps – these things are all expressive.*

One half of a substantial, squarely built building divided into two separate homes, Battlecrease had been James' choice. Next door lived the Steels: Maud and her solicitor husband Douglas. Over the road was the Liverpool Cricket Club, its spacious grounds ensuring that the plot was not overlooked – that it was private if not remote. Turn left from the driveway and narrow Riversdale Road soon joined broad Aigburth Road with its clusters of small shops: grocers, butchers and several chemists. Turn right instead, cross the bridge over a little railway line and the road ended with a fine view of the slate-grey Mersey, an expanse of river and sky raked by slanting light and bracing winds. On the far bank were the tree-studded hills of the Wirral.

Right on the border of the southern suburbs of Aigburth and Grassendale, the district was all fresh air, birdsong and a slow pace of life. Yet it took only half an hour to reach the heart of the robust city by train or carriage and servants and workers could easily grab a penny seat in the tram running down Aigburth Road.

Just five miles away, Liverpool – the principal city of Lancashire and known as 'the Port of Empire' – might have been another world. As the nation's second most important city, goods and passengers crowded the shipping basins, warehouses and factories that lined the six miles of its industrialised shore. Mercantile ambition and civic power had triumphed here: wrought-iron lamp-posts stood sentinel on the corners of the main streets and grand new classical structures graced the city centre, including St George's Hall (1838), the Walker Art Gallery (1874) and the County Sessions House (1884). For a swelling bourgeoisie clamouring for cultural pastimes there was a thriving Philharmonic Hall and Society, as well as an ever-growing number of theatres, concert and music halls, libraries and various other improvement societies.

Six hundred thousand souls called it home. A system of over two hundred horse-drawn trams ran on tracks down the centre of arterial roads and from its five railway termini lines radiated to the north, south and east. Streets had been re-developed for shops that offered the latest Paris fashions and everything an aspiring couple could need in order to make their lives appear 'just so'. There was Lewis's – one of the earliest department stores – as well as auction houses and salerooms. There was a thriving city press and W. H. Smith's red carts dashed across the roads, piled high with the latest newspapers. Overwhelmingly, there was noise and action: the shriek of trains pitted against the rumble of coal wagons, the tramp of policemen's boots, the whir of machinery, the clatter of horses: what the *Liverpool Review* described as the *roar of the great caravansary*.

Alongside the city's elegant late-Georgian districts Victorian terraces had multiplied and a string of urban parks, punctuated with developments of pretty detached villas, proclaimed the gentrification of the suburbs. By comparison, along the line of docks that described Liverpool's western margin the smell of seawater mingled with the tang of creosote, sweat and smoke. Past tall stone buildings and warehouses bursting with tobacco, cotton and spices, an assortment of vehicles swerved through dense traffic. Extending for miles, the tall masts of boats pricked at the sky – their rigging slapping fractiously in the wind – while above them lowered the broad funnels of the transatlantic steamers delivering immigrants to England or waiting for the flood tide to transport passengers to the New World.

By the late 1880s other English ports were beginning to compete, but about a third of all the country's business and almost all of her American trade still passed through Liverpool. As a result, alongside its middle-class entertainments, its concert halls and hospitals, the city was pitted with sugar refineries, iron and brass foundries, breweries, roperies, alkali and soap works, cable and anchor manufactories and tar and turpentine distilleries. Neighbouring collieries fuelled its industry. Canal and rail links with nearby Manchester boosted its wealth.

Liverpool's connection with America's Southern cotton growers was so close that the city had supported the Southern states during the American Civil War, hoisting Confederate flags on its public buildings. Cotton was the king: around six million bales arrived each year from America's Atlantic and Gulf ports, accounting for almost half of Liverpool's imports, destined for the forty million spindles and half a million looms of the Lancashire cotton mills. Bundled in the heat of the cotton fields, it was unloaded in a city where, during the autumn and winter, river fog slicked the cobbled streets and drizzle diffused the light from shop windows as pedestrians turned their shoulders to the squalls blown in from the sea.

The great industrial city was powerfully exciting, providing the opportunity to accumulate significant wealth and offering numberless chances for improvement. Yet its renaissance was rooted in the dirty profits of the slave trade and the place still had, for all its self-regard, its ambition and its pride, a rotten underbelly. Slums straggled back from the waterfront; ragged, malnourished and deformed children swarmed through shambolic rookeries and courts where forty families might be forced to share a single water tap and latrine, and where filth seeped into the walls. Regardless of the City Corporation's vigorous attempts at slum clearance and the fact that it was the first both to appoint a Medical Office of Health and to establish district nurses, the bustle of commerce masked a city of extremes. Under the surface of thrusting progress, beneath the skin of propriety and manners, vicious poverty, a violent gang culture and physical suffering persisted. *I had seen wealth. I had seen poverty*, Richard Armstrong would write in 1890, *but never before had I seen streets ... with all that wealth can buy loaded with the haunts of hopeless penury ... the gaunt faces of the poor, the sodden faces of the abandoned, the indifferent air of so many who might have been helpers and healers of woe.*

Battlecrease House and suburban Aigburth were financed by the profits of this industrial trade but they stood apart from its poverty, providing protection from the distressing shadow of material want, the city's stench as much as its noise and speed. Attuned to the distant boom of the ships' blasts, to the ebb and flow of the mighty river that reflected and magnified the light, the only complaints here were from the mournful seagulls whose pulsing cries seemed unceasingly to stitch together the land, sea and sky.

*

Sitting in the Battlecrease parlour that Saturday morning, 16 March 1889, Florence felt suffocated. It was too quiet. The nursemaid, Alice Yapp, had the children. James was in the city fussing over his deals. Mrs Humphreys, the cook, was preparing lunch. The young maids – Bessie Brierley and Mary Cadwallader – were tucking, polishing and tidying, putting to rights the nursery, straightening the upstairs rooms, quietly moving down corridors as they completed their chores.

Across the hall were a less formal family morning room and James' study, the three doors of which were always locked. Inside it were comfortably deep leather chairs and shelves containing reference books: his dictionaries and encyclopaedia, newspapers and business journals. On the walls hung engravings that poked fun at the institution of marriage. The room was an approximation of a gentleman's club, a place for James to entertain male friends and to keep wine, liquor, cigars, cards and poker chips. Redolent with the odour of tobacco, cluttered with various bottles of pills, potions and tonics, it was his sanctuary, tidied only when he gave the maids permission to go inside.

The study signalled loudly that James Maybrick's time, his space and his choices were precious, that in the pursuit of his very public, commercial role his decisions and appetites took precedence. Constrained by far narrower conventions, the job of his youthful wife was to contribute to the moral guardianship of the nation through the proper upbringing of their children and the generally emollient influence of her virtuous femininity. She was expected to derive personal fulfilment from within the margins of her marriage, her children and the management of her domestic sphere. As Oscar Wilde's Lord Goring put it: *a man's life is of more value than a woman's. It has larger issues, wider scope, greater ambitions. A woman's life revolves in curves of emotions. It is upon lines of intellect that a man's life progresses.*

Obsessively testing out the reflecting powers of her mirrors, indolently fond of second-rate love stories, Florence Maybrick's life was, by comparison with James' and even her staff's, stagnant. She may not have railed, even privately, against the social code that required her to suppress too much individuality but nor did she quite manage to involve herself in the practical concerns of the drawing room, nursery or kitchen. James set the agenda. He, mostly, saw to the hiring of new staff and gave orders around the house. He, born and raised in Lancashire, supplied their circle of friends.

While his life was centred on the external world, her efforts were concentrated on concealing her growing loneliness while burnishing the appearance of respectability. Looking the part – her silhouette exaggerated by tight skirts, protruding bustles, high-necked shirts, frills, feathers and furbelows – Florence managed effectively to ensure that their lives appeared unblemished. Yet something was not quite right. The glaze of the Maybricks' carefully constructed world was beginning to crackle. Submerged beneath the apparent harmony of her mildly Southern drawl and their prettily cohesive marriage lurked the deeper dangers of broken promises, curdling disappointment and growing discontent.

CHAPTER 2

Expectations

Anthony Trollope, a novelist who put the importance of marriage at the centre of so much of his work, wrote some time around 1873 that a man seeks a woman's hand *because she has waltzed stoutly with him, and talked pleasantly between the dances*. The risk, he suggested, was all on her side since he would *take her to his sphere of life, not bind himself to hers. She, knowing nothing*, took *a monstrous leap in the dark*, and everything changed.

Florence had taken a great leap.

She had been born in September 1862 in the prosperous Southern seaport of Mobile, Alabama. Carrie Holbrook, her adventurous, full-lipped mother, was from a socially elevated New York family and had snapped up William Chandler, a banker and one of the most eligible Southern-states bachelors, at the outset of the Civil War. Taking Mobile society by storm, she soon won a reputation for partying fast and late, ruffling so many feathers by her incursion that when Florence's father died she wasted little time in gathering up her two young children and leaving the sweeping bays of the Gulf of Mexico. Within a year Carrie had married Frank DuBarry, a dashing

Confederate officer whom she may have originally met in Mobile several years earlier. The match led to conjecture and gossip, and when DuBarry soon died of battle wounds while on board a blockade-runner the fact that his widow insisted he be buried at sea rather than returned to land raised eyebrows all over again.

Carrie Holbrook Chandler spent the following years travelling between New York and the European cities of Paris, Cologne and St Petersburg. Her son Holbrook and daughter Florence received interrupted, patchy educations, and were perhaps unaware that their mother existed on the very margins of scandal. By 1880 Carrie was middle-aged, loud, large, ebullient and, once again, single, having been abandoned by her third husband, a handsome but profligate Prussian army officer called Baron von Roques. Florence was just seventeen when, that spring, she and her mother boarded the SS *Baltic* in New York and set out for Liverpool.

James Maybrick was also on board. Still a bachelor at forty-one, somewhere above medium height, with slightly grizzled sandy hair and heavy-lidded grey eyes, he had a fine-boned face – almost hawkish at some angles – and wore drooping moustaches over an emphatically firm mouth. His coats were admirably fitted and, according to his contemporaries, he was educated, interesting, stiff-backed, generally popular and as tenacious as a bulldog. Some said he was fond of wine, women and horses, and though he was only a handful of years younger than the Baroness he pursued her daughter throughout the ten-day voyage – making Florence laugh, paying her constant attention and effectively concealing his tendency to pessimism, his quick temper and his obsessions about his health.

Their ship had been built in the early 1870s and was already old-fashioned, yet its first-class cabins were comfortable and its dinner menus ran to multiple courses. Days aboard an ocean steamer were particularly conducive to the growth of sudden friendships and theirs were filled with a series of social events that included dances, concerts, masques and cards – providing, as everyone understood, endless opportunities for partying and flirtation. James played the courtship game with confidence: sixteen months later he and Florence were married at Christopher Wren's St James's Church, Piccadilly. It is unlikely that either she or her mother knew that the Maybrick coat of arms, bearing the motto *Time Reveals All*, had been hurriedly ordered from the College of Arms just weeks before the ceremony.

It is possible too that the fast-talking Baroness exaggerated the truth about Florence's fortune. Substantial where her daughter was delicate, forthright and worldly where the girl was tentative and quiet, von Roques was financially straitened. Later, some would wonder whether Florence set out deliberately to ensnare James, asking whether the Southern belle's feelings had been genuine. Had she been flattered by the attentions of a handsome, apparently rich older Englishman who professed to offer her a position within the Liverpool elite? Did she marry to gain independence of her mother? Was she coaxed, bribed or simply naïve, an unwitting hostage in a dance of mutual deception choreographed by her mother and a man old enough to be her father?

Apparently incompatible by age and upbringing, the union of the Mobile ingénue and the stiff English cotton broker was, at any rate, fashionable. Seven years earlier the impulsive love match between Jennie Jerome of Brooklyn, New York, and Lord Randolph Churchill, third son of the Duke of Marlborough, had unleashed a flood of matches between American girls fixed on the romantic image of the old-world and rather dour Englishmen in need of new-world cash. Well-off American mothers with pretty daughters of marriageable age were beginning to flock to Europe, lured by the example of the engagements announced in the society columns of the papers.

James, having lived for a while in Virginia, was used to American girls but the majority of his family and neighbours were not and his new wife was conspicuous not only by her youth and accent but by so many small differences. He had been born and raised in Liverpool, one of five sons of a respectable engraver-turned-parish clerk who were all privately educated at a local boarding school to take advantage of the county's industrial flourishing. The eldest, William, was by 1880 a shipping clerk in Manchester and the fourth son, Thomas, was the manager of a packing business. James was the second-born, particularly close to Michael – two years his junior – and Edwin, the baby of the family born thirteen years after James. These three bachelors formed a mutually reliant triangle.

When James and Florence married, Michael was forty, six foot tall, powerfully built, blond and distinguished. Known to his family as 'Blucher', he was considered the cleverest, was organist to the Grand Lodge of Freemasons and had started to make his fortune as a successful baritone singer and composer of popular songs. Fame had begun to make him inscrutable and a little arrogant so that some old family friends privately carped that Michael had already booked himself a tomb in Westminster Abbey. Put simply, having moved south to London he had outgrown the city of his birth. Whether or not he considered his new sister-in-law to be an adventuress, he made it clear that he had little time for the frivolous, apparently inconsequential young bride of his much-loved sibling.

From the start, Florence found Michael uncomfortably cold and domineering, but James' youngest sibling, Edwin, made up for it by being charming. In his early thirties, equally tall, with wavy black hair, pale skin and deep brown eyes, Edwin enjoyed a reputation as the best looking of the Maybrick brothers. He was junior partner in James' Liverpool cotton business and he was good company – so much so that when he was not in America he accompanied Florence to the parties and dances they both loved. Indeed, perhaps because Edwin was closer in age to Florence than James and because the two were so often seen together, knowing looks were exchanged in the conservative parlours of the city's suburbs though James seemed broadly unconcerned. It may even have suited him that his young brother kept his wife happy by paying her attention. Only once, at a formal dinner, did he appear rattled by their friendship: hearing Florence wonder aloud how different her life would have been had it been Edwin instead of James on the SS *Baltic* he had reddened, clenched his fist and dropped his knife. It took only seconds, one guest noted, for him to suppress his sudden rage, recover himself and project once more the impression of smooth equanimity.

Beyond her new husband's immediate family, Florence's social circle was made up of those with whom James did business or had grown up and chief among these last were the Janions. Mrs Janion – Domilita – was an elderly Chilean whom James and Florence would soon ask to stand as their first child's godmother and her three daughters were regular visitors to Battlecrease. The eldest, Matilda Briggs, was separated from her husband and now lived with her own two daughters at her brother Richard's house on the edge of Sefton Park. Nearer James' age than Florence's, Matilda could be overbearing, advising him on what coats to wear, suggesting what might be most appropriate for dinner, failing to appreciate that her intrusive confidence made Florence feel inconsequential and sidelined. It could not have helped that Matilda was also said to have once been in love with James, nor that she and her younger sister Constance – Mrs Hughes – were thick as thieves and more or less intimidating. Only the youngest Janion girl, Gertrude, was unmarried and fun; the same age as Florence, she did at first become a friend.

*

Almost exactly forty weeks after their wedding the Maybricks' son was born. The pair were lodging with Richard Janion and Matilda

Briggs and it was not always easy, perhaps, for Florence to feel herself being judged by Matilda, for whom marriage and motherhood were neither new nor joyful. It may therefore have been with some relief that when the baby was about three months old Florence began to organise the packing of steamer trunks in anticipation of returning to America. In Norfolk, Virginia – a town of fifty thousand building its post-Civil War recovery largely on the strength of its cotton trade – she and James would properly establish their first marital home in a country and among people she understood.

Two years later, in the late spring of 1884, believing his business to be on more solid ground and hankering again for Liverpool, James moved them back, leasing from Matilda Briggs a pretty stucco villa called Beechville in the prosperous suburb of Grassendale. Renting was not unusual: in fact, for most middle-class Victorians, house ownership was less important than occupying the sort of property that signalled status, so that only around 10 per cent actually bought their homes – the rest signing three- to seven-year agreements that allowed them to trade up or down as their circumstances changed.

At Beechville, Florence and James put down English roots. In the summer of 1886 a daughter – Gladys – was born and, for a while, things seemed comfortable and settled. The Maybrick phaeton was pulled by a pair of satiny black horses sporting brass-buckled harnesses, managed by a groom immaculate in his uniform. Each Sunday James and Florence rode out together into the countryside, to all appearances unified, polished and carefree. Florence laughed, teased and sang on a whim; she was nicknamed 'Birdie' by acquaintances and 'Bunny' by her fond husband. They entertained and accepted hospitality, smiling and gracious, a couple radiating reliability.

By the time Gladys was beginning to form her first words, though, both were struggling with the effort of concealing their escalating difficulties. For a start, James had discovered soon after their marriage that his mother-in-law was in need of a financial prop. Pursued for debts she had run up with her estranged husband, the Baroness repeatedly asked him for small loans which she then failed to repay. After six years he was exasperated by her lies but continued to hope that Florence would profit from income generated from some land she had inherited in America. Then, his patience thinning, he began to demand that the Baroness repay money taken without authorisation from his wife's inheritance trust. By 1887 relations were so sour that James made almost no effort to conceal his bitterness that Florence's promised fortune had turned out to be little more than a meagre annuity.

He was enraged by stories that the Baroness had broken her word countless times and that she was said to have destroyed the faith even of her closest friends. He was equally antipathetic towards Florence's brother Holbrook, furiously accusing him during one particularly difficult period of having hidden the fact of their limited means while he was courting Florence – insinuating that he had been swindled. Forbidding Florence from talking to her brother or mother about their private affairs, James for a while refused to allow her to receive their letters and permitted her to write to them only at his dictation. To him, everything about his wife's unconventional little family had become unpleasantly different, from their conversation to their manners and – it seemed – their probity. He wanted to keep them at arm's length. For his part, Holbrook came to the conclusion that his brother-in-law had turned out, dismayingly, to be both *a bully and a brute*.

These resentments added to Florence's isolation and, compounding it all, a general economic slowdown was adversely affecting James' business, putting them both under pressure. In October 1887 Florence wrote to her mother that their assets were reduced to fifteen hundred pounds, with just five hundred safely in the bank. Edwin was in America, charged with investing a thousand pounds in Galveston cotton in the hope of trading it at a profit. Fearing the venture would fail, Florence

confessed that James' business had made only £125 in the previous five years. She believed they were close to ruin. As their
capital dwindled she had, she wrote, tried to persuade James to
rent a cheaper house but, on the contrary, he had his eye on the
lease for Battlecrease. *I am utterly worn* out, she complained,
*and in such a state of overstrained nervousness that I am hardly
fit for anything.*

Florence particularly loathed the fact that James had borrowed
money from Matilda Briggs, yet her disinclination to rein in
her own spending only made things worse. To each side of her
husband's exclusive Liverpool club, the Palatine in upmarket Bold
Street, were shops that offered the kind of expensive fashions and
jewellery she found endlessly appealing. Her wardrobe rustled and
shone with surah silk jackets, evening dresses designed to emphasise her spider-waist, light grey silks trimmed in dark purple velvet
or Brussels lace. Side by side with her precious letters and the bits
of remaining jewellery that were carefully stored in the drawers
of her dressing chest were fans, cosmetics and scents, pin-tucked
blouses in the latest styles and kid gloves and silk stockings rolled
in tissue paper. Stacked high in boxes in the corner of the dressing
room were fine Milan straw hats with curling feathers, felted wool
toques and small-brimmed bonnets with ruched ribbons and
fine veils.

Obsessed by presenting a faultless appearance, Florence was as
vain, impatient and tiresomely self-absorbed as a spoiled child.
She ran up bills at photographic studios, confectioners, station-
ers and purveyors of furnishings and china, but shopping was not
her only failing. Matching James' love of the track, she had also
made a number of disastrous wagers. Horse racing was all about
the flash of money – sleek animals, trophies, prize funds and
grandstand prices – and technology had changed the nature of
race-day gambling. Betting shops and racing newspapers all
relied on the telegraph for stable gossip, starting prices and
results, and anyone with access to a post office wire service could

place a bet without even being present at the course. Thus Florence had accumulated substantial secret debts.

Hiding the extent of these liabilities even from her beloved, if unreliable, mother, Florence was clearer sighted about their household expenses and regularly tried to convince James to make changes so that they could live more economically. He disagreed. *He says it would ruin him outright*, she wrote to the Baroness, *for one must keep up appearances until he has more capital to fall back on ... The least suspicion aroused, all claims would pour in at once and how could Jim settle with what he has now?* In other words, if the Liverpool cotton network caught wind of Maybrick's business difficulties, he would be sunk. Broking – taking a gamble on the price of commodities – involved a series of deals underpinned by gentlemen's promises: the merest whisper of financial insecurity could puncture the precious bubble of mutual faith on which businesses like his survived and, since success depended on credit-worthiness, reputations were fiercely guarded. James understood that a projection of domestic affluence underpinned vital assumptions about his professional reliability.

Thus, three years after returning to Liverpool, things were so tight that he allowed Florence just seven pounds a week for housekeeping – around half the amount recommended by one contemporary household manual for the running of a more modest home than their own, occupied by a couple with just one child and three servants. The insufficiency fed a growing discontent on both sides. If James had married for money he had been mistaken and if he had painted a rosier picture of his financial status she, too, had been deluded. Together they were trapped in the late-Victorian cult of money articulated by Oscar Wilde's Sir Robert Chilton: *what this century worships is wealth. The God of this century is wealth. To succeed one must have wealth. At all costs, one must have wealth.*

The two-decade age gap between Florence and James began to

seem unbridgeable as 1887 threw up continuous challenges. In
April Holbrook died in Paris of tuberculosis. Then James and
Florence's little boy caught scarlet fever as it raged through the
city: the rest of the family decamped to Wales, leaving Florence
alone to nurse the boy through six gruelling weeks while the
cook set down meals beyond a curtain hung outside the nursery
door. Finally, towards December 1887, Florence discovered that
James had been maintaining a long-term mistress. She never said
how she knew – perhaps she came across accounts or bills that
gave the game away – but the sure knowledge of her husband's
calculated, long-term infidelity dealt a final, shattering blow to
her girlishly romantic dreams.

CHAPTER 3

One Man's Poison

Painfully aware of the growing distance between them, Florence and James each worried about the future. Endlessly fussing over his health and fearing that his family would be penniless in the event of his death, James arranged two life insurance policies: five hundred pounds with the Scottish Widows Fund and two thousand with the Mutual Reserve Fund Life Association of New York. In both cases he assigned his wife as the beneficiary. Then in early 1888, despite Florence's growing concerns about their rising debts, he moved them all into Battlecrease House.

In her extensive new home, in the seventh year of her marriage, Florence felt grand but unmoored. She breakfasted in bed, strolled indolently about the garden, rearranged her wardrobes, petted the children and read American romances with Old-South plots whose evocations of dust, heat and scandals were the absolute antithesis of her cold, very proper English world. When she was sick of rattling around in the big house she changed and took the carriage into Liverpool, sometimes returning with James. By now the couple rarely strolled together in the garden and when they did it was never arm in arm. She no longer fondly counted his grey hairs and he no longer bothered to tease her, as he used to do, about non-existent holes in her stockings.

At formal dinners and dances, dressed in low-necked, short-sleeved gowns, Florence was as poised as a statue, openly admired. Small diamonds clasped tightly around her throat sparkled as she waited in the hall to receive their guests and their pretty compliments while James blustered about the price of cotton and asked after wayward sons. Both relied on the appearance of calm, on the proficiency of their cook and the assistance of the maids, who stood smartly to one side. Buttoned into their Sunday best, the children were brought downstairs by the ramrod-straight nursemaid and were briefly shown off before being whisked smartly back upstairs.

Social obligations designed to cement bonds with the city's mercantile elite meant that Florence and James rarely spent more than two evenings a week at home alone. Florence had developed an easy familiarity with many of James' colleagues. She flirted, leaning – sometimes – just a little too close, patting them on their heads, putting her fingers under one's chin, resting her hand on another's knee. Occasionally she laughed just a bit too loud. The effort of it all could be exhausting and Florence was beginning to realise that she might make plenty of acquaintances in her adopted land but no really intimate, lasting friends.

And so she played her wifely role, alive to the social part assigned to her, while remaining a foreign element, a cuckoo in the Liverpool nest. In this she was not alone, for the truth behind many of the fashionable Anglo-American alliances of the time was that even New World heiresses were rarely wholeheartedly accepted by the conservative societies into which they married. Consuelo Vanderbilt was said to have wept throughout her marriage to Viscount Mandeville, the Duke of Manchester's heir, in 1895 and the Duke was contemptuous of the *little American savage entering his family*. Endlessly portrayed as lively, talkative and vibrantly energetic on the one hand, vulgar and lacking in morals on the other, American girls often found the myriad rigid social conventions of England – beyond the allure of its fine buildings and landscapes – simply stifling.

English men and women took for granted things that shocked or made new American wives miserable, or were horrified by things the Americans did quite innocently. Some found New York women particularly forward, lacking in the female duties of grace, fragrance and passivity, and British in-laws certainly often considered American girls too exaggerated for their tastes. Unpractised in the pretences and compliances of her Liverpool milieu Florence was, to some, a blast of fresh air. To others, her difference rankled.

She may not even have been aware that within visiting distance were at least two other young American women also suffering in the social chill of the seaport city. Florence Schieffelin had recently married Bruce Ismay the shipping magnate, who would one day build the *Titanic*, but she already understood that *she had sacrificed her life for a drab Liverpool suburb with a man she no longer recognised*. Ismay immersed himself in work and she felt alone and homesick, an outsider constrained to conceal her wretchedness at the tedium of her life, making up for it by purchasing everything that was most up to date. Ismay's business manager Harold Sanderson had also married an American girl, Maud Blood. Poor Maud also found it hard to fit in.

James' business associates were friendly but his brother Michael, on his rare visits north, could be frostily impolite and James had turned out to be faithless and morose. Florence felt lonely and fragile; she felt let down. Love had not, as it did in her trashy novels, revolutionised her life or lasted, rapturously unchanged. The snobberies, rivalries and relative torpor of her Liverpool life had begun to feel insufferable; marriage had turned out to be a disappointment, made up of a succession of cloying, empty days.

Like so many contemporary literary heroines, Florence was

waiting for something to happen, something to lift her from the solitude and dreariness of her life, to erase its ennui and halt her deepening unhappiness. Restless, she found it almost impossible to concentrate on their daily lives.

Even in the good times it had become obvious that almost nothing about the management of her home came naturally to her, despite the advice of ladies' domestic magazines or the frequent, uninvited counsel of Matilda Briggs. Household manuals aimed at bourgeois wives regularly warned against slatternly cooks, made suggestions about how to counter a housemaid's impudence and cautioned mistresses to be on the alert for rebellions in the form of sulks, answering back or turning a deaf ear to bells. But the effects of industrialisation, by making alternatives to domestic work more easily available, meant that it could be as hard to persuade staff to remain as it was to find them in the first place and Florence had discovered at first hand that old-fashioned deference could no longer be taken for granted.

Mixing familiarity with apparent civility, able to leave without notice, cooks, maids and nursemaids had more power than ever before and they knew it. At Battlecrease the upstairs and downstairs maids were forever changing; Florence could hardly keep up. Currently, Bessie Brierley and Mary Cadwallader – a Shropshire girl nicknamed 'Gentle Mary' – were both even-tempered and good-hearted but Florence rarely issued an instruction. The fact that she was neither competent nor engaged enough efficiently to organise their daily chores meant that the two girls sometimes idled about their work or lingered in the kitchen catching up on gossip with the cook.

There, at least, Florence was comfortable. Mrs Elizabeth Humphreys had supervised the kitchen for the Maybricks when they lived at Beechville and in October 1888 James managed to persuade her to return after a short break. Her presence made Florence a little more relaxed. Unlike the girls who scuttled around corners or who broke off conversations as she approached, Mrs

Humphreys never felt like a threat. She fussed over James with herbal teas and with the stewed fruit and baked apples that he believed to be good for his liver and she happily prepared the plainer dishes he demanded whenever he believed that his health was in decline. Rather than countering every suggestion with an alternative – like Matilda or her sister Constance – Mrs Humphreys agreed with her mistress that soles and chickens were better for James' indigestion than joints, cheese and sardines. She was a constant and gentle soul, calm and patient but also competent enough to provide for the flashy dinner parties that Florence seemed, increasingly, to enjoy. In short, Humphreys was both friendly and reliable, and she got on with her work without the need for direction.

Florence's greatest difficulty was with the children's nursemaid hired a year or so earlier, when Gladys was just a few months old.

James had taken on Alice Yapp, a young woman from a large Shropshire family who had worked in a previous household alongside Mary Cadwallader, but who had none of that maid's easy familiarity. Instead, with her largish nose, downward-sloping eyebrows and prepossessing air Yapp neither looked jovial nor exuded warmth. Although almost exactly the same age as Florence, more than a decade of looking after the children of wealthy suburban families had given her a slightly pinched air and Florence had reprimanded her several times for being decidedly too stern.

Insisting on being called Nurse Yapp, the young woman in charge of the children was stricter than anyone Florence had encountered during her own upbringing. Once ready for bed, they were not allowed to romp or play. Always neat and clean, they were drilled in their table manners and the little boy was slapped sharply if he tilted his bowl to get at the last bits of his breakfast porridge. It was the kind of efficiency and capability that ranked high in James' estimation, but Florence worried, especially about Gladys, who seemed to be receiving too little warmth and who was often left to cry alone in her room.

Unconvinced that Alice Yapp would ever care deeply for her children, Florence had tried to encourage warmth in the girl without much luck, and she felt uncomfortable. She had the impression that Yapp poked about the house when she was out; she felt watched and judged; and she was acutely conscious that the nursemaid hardly bothered to mask a latent antipathy towards her. Florence found it hard to know how to counter Yapp's hostility – she was always hurrying the children in and out of rooms, off to walks, into meals or marching them up the stairs to bed. She seemed to Florence rarely to smile, to be both impudent and resentful. More, Yapp's resilient disregard deepened Florence's growing sense of her own uselessness.

*

On the morning of 31 December 1888, as rain coursed into the gutters and the clouds sank so low that the sky muffled Battle-crease House, a violent argument erupted – almost certainly about money – which ended with James stamping his foot and tearing up the will in which he had made his wife his sole legatee and trustee for the children. Dramatically tossing the papers aside, he taunted Florence that he intended to settle the bulk of his fortune on the children, allowing her only the third she was due under the law. He had gained less financially from their marriage than he had hoped; he would not allow her to profit in the event of his death.

Florence watched the scraps of paper flutter to the carpet, one or two drifting under the card table, others bursting into flame as they spun into the fire. She did not stoop to gather them up, determined to wait for James' temper to burn itself out rather than react. She felt the ground to be shifting uncertainly but was resolved not to fall. Later, trembling at her desk, she communicated it all in a letter to her mother. Feigning unconcern she scribbled that *I am sure it matters little to me as long as the children are provided for ... my own income will do for me alone.*

It was bluster. Perfectly aware that her mother would not be able financially to support her, Florence must also have appreciated that £125 a year drawn on her grandmother's heavily mortgaged property in New York would be, under any circumstances, an insufficient safety net. However much she pretended or tried to reassure, it was apparent that her marriage had settled into something unexpected and uncomfortable. Frustrations, suppressed, had become lodged into the corners of their lives. Sometimes she gasped with the ache of it. The effort of concealing the fact that their marriage was disintegrating was beginning to wear her out.

*

On dull days the river and the sky joined to form an apparently impenetrable grey veil while the smell of the sea was a constant reminder of risk, profit and loss, emphasising the reality that her native country was drearily distant. James was increasingly bilious and self-centred. Fine dresses alone were no longer enough to hold his attention and, along with their financial difficulties, his general pessimism cast a pall. Taking it in turns with Edwin to make regular cotton-buying trips to America, he left Florence to stew in the suburbs.

Contributing to the strain of it all, she had noticed and was worried by peculiar habits that seemed to be undermining James' health and contributing to the shortness of his temper. Naturally prone to gloom about his business prospects and to general hypochondria, he had for years been an inveterate self-medicator. If conversation turned on an illness or a new disease he worried about contracting it. If he heard of a new, efficacious medication he hastened to try it out. Bottles and vials, boxes and packets cluttered Battlecrease's rooms; the drawers and shelves in his study and dressing room were littered with pills and liquids. Price's glycerine bottles, bismuth, mixtures of brandy and physic, boxes of crystals, gargles, borax and soda mint tablets cluttered the surfaces. In his desk was a case containing a syringe as well as a bottle of belladonna and packets of potash and phosphori pills. Dispensed by chemists in Liverpool and Virginia, many of the bottles were empty but for sticky brown sediments. Several were labelled 'Not to be Taken'.

Exercised continually by real and fancied ills, a serial complainer of aches or of vaguer symptoms that came and went, dyspeptic, James was – according to most who knew him – endlessly asking the chemist to prepare him tonics. The family physician, Dr Richard Hopper, from his grand consulting rooms in Liverpool's Rodney Street, had variously diagnosed a derangement of the liver, an irritable digestive system and nervous disorders that acted negatively on Maybrick's gut. Forty-six years old, Irish-born Hopper was serious and cautious, a compact figure with sharp features and short black hair just beginning to grey. During one consultation James had showed him a bundle of prescriptions from New York – all aphrodisiacal tonics in which strychnine was the chief ingredient – admitting that he used arsenic as an 'anti-periodic' or general prophylactic against disease.

In response, the doctor warned James against taking poisons, yet he knew that many of these toxins were used widely both in prescription and over-the-counter medicines. In particular, pick-me-ups known as nerve tonics had become increasingly popular during the nineteenth century, touted as effective in fortifying the nerves against malaise or undefined illness, and Dr Hopper prescribed them just as readily as the rest of his profession. Indeed, he was typical in finding no contradiction between his advice to James and his advocacy of solutions known to include strychnine or arsenical solutions like nux vomica.

When Florence came to express her concerns about her husband to Richard Hopper during the summer of 1888 he already knew about James' predilections. What Florence wanted to know, though, was whether it was possible to discover exactly what her husband was taking. Frantic about his vacillating health, she told the doctor that she believed that *he takes some poison or strong*

medicine that he is very reticent about, and I am sure it will do
him harm as he is always worse after it. As a result, when Hopper
was next at Battlecrease he made a point of taking a quick look
in the dressing room that opened off the master bedroom. Casting
his eye over the many potions and pills, he did notice some
dangerous phosphoric acid but either he forgot or he decided not
to question James further about it. He may simply have concluded
that his patient was self-dosing against the general effects of
advancing age or to enhance his sexual performance away from
home; certainly the doctor seems to have overlooked the fact that
James' habit might be causing or contributing to his neurotic
irritability. When, later, he did raise the subject with his patient,
Maybrick was not pleased. Taking his medical business elsewhere, he
effectively sidestepped both the physician and his wife.

Florence was not alone in noticing James' appetites. Among
his friends, he alternately boasted about taking poison and denied
it, becoming adept at changing the subject whenever he felt uncomfortably challenged. If Edwin, as his business partner, wondered
whether the addiction contributed to their shaky financial position he chose to do nothing.

By the spring of 1889 Florence had become desperate. James
complained constantly of headaches and of numbness in his hands
and feet. It was difficult to separate reality from hypochondria.
When, in early March, the twenty-eight-year-old doctor from
nearby Garston – Dr Richard Humphreys – came to Battlecrease
in order to treat the children for whooping cough, she broached
the subject again. Interrupted nights had stretched her to the limit.
Desperate for support, she confided in the young doctor, telling him
about James' strange powders and her deepening fears that he was
killing himself.

Once more it was futile. Failing to recognise the depth of her
concern, Dr Humphreys brushed Florence's anxieties aside. If
James should suddenly and inexplicably die, he joked, *You can*
always say that we spoke about it.

CHAPTER 4

The Marriage Question

Florence thus had much to think about that morning as she sat in her parlour watching, distractedly, the snow settle, hearing it dislodge every so often from gutter or branch with a soft thump. As the silence in the house thickened she was making up her mind whether to abandon caution.

Shaking herself, then, out of the reverie into which she had fallen, she rose from her chair, deliberately picked up the letter addressed to her mother and made for the hall. It was a quarter to ten in the morning. She would go to the post office herself.

Collecting her cape and bonnet, she stooped to remove her soft slippers before pushing her small feet into stout outdoor boots. Then, pulling the door closed, she stepped down onto the driveway, walked through the gate, turned left and, skirting the ice-edged puddles while bending her shoulders slightly into the sharp wind, arrived at the junction of Riversdale and Aigburth Roads.

She had no intention of simply asking for a stamp that would get her letter to France. Conditioned by the example of her mother and her taste in romantic novels to believe that personal fulfilment came in the form of a handsome man, Florence had determined to break free of the constrictions of her married life. When she reached the post office counter she therefore handed a message to the clerk and paid for it to be cabled to Flatman's Hotel in London's West End. Her wire enquired, on behalf of her sister-in-law Mrs Thomas Maybrick, whether a bedroom and sitting room would be available for a week from Thursday 21 March – five days hence. Turning on her heel, heart fluttering, Florence then flounced back through the door.

A storm was rising. The wire had been sent and, as she waited at Battlecrease for a response, every door sent banging by the wind and every creak of the boards made her start. Each branch that snapped outside set up expectations of footfall on the drive and the telegraph boy's knock. All her calculation, all her will, were harnessed to the affectation of indifference during luncheon and the remainder of Saturday afternoon. James perused the newspapers from an armchair in his study; Gladys toddled around after her older brother, both trying to evade the strictures of Nurse Yapp's supervision; the cook and the maids kept to the warmth of the kitchen. Florence tried uselessly to concentrate on a novel. If her husband passed by the morning room, throwing out the occasional question, she answered him gently. Distractedly, she rearranged the cushions. Then she stared out the window.

At length, the hotel wired that rooms were available but a letter of confirmation did not arrive on its heels as Florence had expected. Throughout Sunday she fretted. Then, as soon as James left for his office on Monday morning she wrote to them at greater length. Mr Flatman's eventual, fuller answer then set in train a flurry of animated organisation. On Wednesday Florence wrote again to announce that her sister-in-law was planning to arrive the following afternoon, at around four o'clock. She was at pains to be absolutely clear: *Mrs Maybrick hopes she has not confused Mr Flatman by writing for her sister as his letter*

*gives her the impression that he expects both herself and Mrs T.
Maybrick whereas it is only the lady and her husband who are
coming to town.*

She did not intend, of course, for the Thomas Maybricks to
enjoy those rooms. Telling James that her godmother required
nursing, relying on the likelihood that he would not object, she
planned instead to set off for London by the morning express on
Thursday 21st. At the last minute, though, there was a hitch. As
she finalised the details of her packing, another letter arrived
from the hotel: the rooms would not, after all, be free until
Friday.

It was too late to change her plans. Rushing off a note, Florence advised Flatman that her relatives would spend a night with
friends in town before checking in on Friday afternoon. It complicated things, but she was determined. Thinking ahead, she
penned instructions for the hotel to prepare a private dinner for
Friday evening, *consisting, say, of soup Fish Sole Mutton cutlets
Duckling and Green peas and new potatoes Cheese & celery &
Dessert. Of course if the above is more than Mr Flatman can
manage with the other dinners to provide he must reduce the bill
of fare. Dinner about 7.15.* Spinning out her deception, she
added, *Mrs Maybrick has taken upon herself to make the
arrangements for Mrs T. Maybrick as the young lady is not very
experienced.*

Still the shifting details of her arrangements would not settle.
Another wire arrived, communicating that there had been a
mistake: the rooms would be available on the 21st after all. It
made things simpler. And so, that Thursday morning, Florence
left for Lime Street station, ignoring the arch expression on Alice
Yapp's face as, dressing case in hand, she turned to instruct the
nursemaid to be sure to redirect her mail to the Grand Hotel,
London.

Arriving in the capital, Florence took a hansom from Euston
station to the corner of Henrietta Street and Chapel Place, just off

Cavendish Square and in the centre of the West End, an upper-middle-class residential district favoured by physicians, surgeons and solicitors. One of the most fashionable modern department stores, Marshall & Snelgrove, occupied an entire block where once there had been seven separate shops. Opposite it was the tall, narrow building of Flatman's Hotel. Taking her portmanteau and small bag from the cab, the head waiter guided Mrs Maybrick inside and then upstairs to her suite of rooms.

Her choice of hotel, the place where most cotton men from Liverpool, the Continent and America stayed when in London, was foolhardily indiscreet. If she were recognised – and with her feathered hats and striking clothes she was hard to miss – or if she bumped into any one of their acquaintances, it could cause uproar.

*

Three days later – early on Sunday afternoon – Florence checked out of Flatman's Hotel. Fresh from one of the most audacious acts of her life, she did not plan to return to Liverpool in a hurry. She would remain in London for much of the following week, staying with friends in Kensington. She had arranged to dine at the Café Royal with James' self-important brother Michael and would return home on Thursday 28th in time for the Grand National the following day. In the steeplechase's fiftieth anniversary year, the Prince of Wales was coming to Aintree and a great crowd was anticipated – she had already picked out exactly what she intended to wear.

Florence also planned to seek the advice of a firm of London solicitors, hoping they would help her to arrange for a divorce from James on the grounds of his infidelity. On the first of her evenings in London she had dined with John Baillie Knight, a childhood friend, confiding in him *that she was in some great trouble ... that she had come to London to see a solicitor relative to a separation from her husband, that she could not live with him any more on account of him keeping this woman ...*

that he was cruel to her and had struck her. In the absence of father or brother, she had been desperate for Knight's advice about who to consult.

Victorian marriage laws had been changing, beginning with the 1857 Divorce Act, which aimed to protect the property of deserted wives. In 1870 and again in 1882 the Married Women's Property Acts were designed to allow women control over the money and property they owned prior to their marriage, while other new legislation enacted during the 1870s allowed them certain rights of appeal for the custody of children and legal protection against abuse. Yet Florence was still in a difficult position. It would be two more years until the current law, allowing husbands the legal right to their wives' bodies without consent, would be changed. More alarmingly, a double standard was enshrined in the Divorce Act so that a man needed only to demonstrate that his wife had committed adultery while she, in addition to his faithlessness, had to prove cruelty, desertion or worse: rape, buggery, incest or bestiality. Even then the process was expensive and divorced women could expect to be socially excluded. Hardest of all, if Florence managed to arrange for a separation there was no guarantee that she would be allowed to continue to live with her children.

Asking for a divorce painfully confronted the status quo. Victorian women like Florence were expected to be strong in the management of their staff but weak and passive as wives, to mask intemperate feelings and to balance independence of mind with the reality that they were subjugated both in law and by convention. Encouraged by the popularity of Dickens' novels, the ideal of the home and family had become central to middle-class society: manuals, etiquette guides and didactic fiction all reinforced notions of submission and self-effacement. Unsurprisingly, then, wives who did not present themselves as models of chastity, philanthropy and morality risked being judged as depraved or even mad.

If there was a deep-rooted flash of American independence within her spirit, Florence had learned that England expected her to mask it. Transplanted, separated by an ocean from the intimacy of her immediate or extended family and her childhood friends, she was isolated by her marriage and her nationality. Nothing suggests that she was mentally or socially alert enough to have taken an interest in the ideals of the emerging feminist movement but there is nothing, either, to indicate that she did not chafe at her confinement within an idealisation of domestic morality. Discovering that James pursued a parallel life with another woman, that his faithlessness was neither temporary nor short-term, simply made all the rest of their difficulties insupportable.

Her husband's broker friends had noticed and sometimes commented on his wife's flirtatious ways: there had been gossip about the obvious friendship between her and Edwin Maybrick, and a certain amount of idle chat about other men. At the end of 1888 a Liverpool cotton broker had written to his American supplier that a dangerously attractive, thirty-eight-year-old bachelor called Alfred Brierley seemed *to have the inside track* with Mrs Maybrick's affections. Brierley was also involved in the cotton business; his office was just a stone's throw from James' and the two were well acquainted. If James heard the rumours, this correspondent worried that he would *plug* the younger man *full of lead*.

Was it simply that, youthful but married to a man twenty-four years her senior, Florence unconsciously flexed for individual satisfaction separate from being a wife, mother and daughter? Was her coquetry an innocent demand for attention? She hovered between the old world and the new, between marriage and infidelity, conservatism and rebellion, domestic ineptitude and the competence of women like Matilda Briggs. However frank she allowed herself to be with her London solicitors about her personal affairs, they advised her to write to her husband and dictated to her the terms on which she should ask for a separation in consequence of James' adulterous connection with another woman. She should ask him to move out, they said, allowing her to continue to live at Battlecrease with young James and Gladys.

When she did eventually travel back to Liverpool, Florence must have mused on the fact that hers was not the only vexatious failure of a marriage and that she was not the first woman to be required to feign respectability. The previous year, an outspoken novelist called Mona Caird had published an essay on marriage in the radical *Westminster Review*. Critical of the women who sought its 'bondage', she had argued that matrimony was an outmoded social form that imprisoned women in sexual and social subjugation. The essay made Caird the most infamous feminist in England because, while her views might have been expected to interest only a small group of intellectuals and political thinkers, the *Daily Telegraph* – most successful of the middle-class newspapers – reacted with alarm. Struck by the idea that the institution of marriage was a failure, it asked its readers to comment and during the summer of 1888 was overwhelmed by twenty-seven thousand responses – proof that Middle England had been caught up in a widening debate.

The dilemma of whether it was possible for love and desire to survive marriage was not new: *there is*, wrote Trollope in 1860, *an aroma of love, an indefinable delicacy of flavour, which ... is gone before the church portal is left, vanishing with the maiden name, and incompatible with the solid comfort appertaining to the rank of wife*. He knew as well as anyone that marriage could work against self-definition, describing his heroine Alice Vavasour's *vague idea that there was a something to be done, a something over and beyond, or perhaps altogether beside that marrying and having two children. If she only knew what it was.* Concerned about his characters' dilemmas, Trollope was in real life – like most of his class and generation – conservative: Alice could not be *so far advanced as to think that women should be lawyers and doctors*; her ambitions to be *useful* are therefore limited to an aspiration simply to be the wife of a politician.

Born of an explicitly feminist agenda, the 'marriage question' explored by the *Daily Telegraph* brought unsettling new ideas to the breakfast tables of the bourgeoisie, aggravating existing discussions about the complexities of the female lot. Women were expected to be pure: female adultery constituted a social danger, not least because it threatened certainties about inheritance. Further, some wondered what would happen if women demanded faithfulness from their husbands and there were others who feared for their own positions if 'virile' women began to aspire to a life without marriage. It was complicated: social gains had created a new set of expectations among some women but they remained economically vulnerable and educationally limited. As a result, the Women's Movement was thus less interested in the right to vote or the virtues of marriage than in the importance of creating opportunities for women to achieve independence and self-actualisation through work, giving them a chance to break free of patriarchal control.

*

Heading home, hoping for liberation from her unhappy marriage, nursing a thrilling secret and, perhaps, promising herself that she would not need to conceal her true feelings for much longer, Florence prepared to take up again the mantle of a dutiful wife.

She needed to summon enough caution to steer a narrow path through the dangerous waters of a marriage suffused with the unspoken challenge of estrangement. The greatest threat to her domestic survival was that her trip to London would make her feel important and inviolable, mistress of her own destiny and answerable to none. Still only twenty-six, she needed to find the strength and art to fight her emotional struggle in the shadows and on tiptoe, to summon the restraint necessary to preserve the cool lustre of appearances, allowing the turbulence of her situation to work itself out while dropping subtle anchors to prevent it from sweeping her into oblivion.

In her conversations with James she must sidestep his pessimism about business, ignoring his constant predictions of future failure, his refusal to get to grips with their domestic expenses and his endless, wearing fears about his health. In her dealings with the staff and with their friends she must focus on looking, talking and moving as if she had not a care in the world.

In all this, Florence might have been the very model for the growing literary interest in the disenfranchised woman suffering within the confines of marriage, succumbing to society's double standards while struggling to find a way to be true both to herself and the requirements of her milieu. It was a theme that twisted particularly at the heart of the many contemporary novels charting the invasion of the 'dollar princesses'.

In Henry James' hands, American–European matches were often snares, part of a great social game founded on the need for money and in which public performances concealed a complicated tissue of pretences, masking profound, often silent, sadness. Focusing on the social and emotional strains that flexed within these glossy liaisons, James worked them into the core of *Portrait of a Lady* (1880) and returned to the idea repeatedly over the next two decades. Other novels, including Sherwood's *A Transplanted Rose* (1882), Harrison's *The Anglomaniacs* (1890), Atherton's *American Wives and English Husbands* (1898) and, later, Edith Wharton's *The Buccaneers* drew on the same refrain: cracked marriages in which the overwhelming female requirement was patience. Even the heroine of Atherton's novel, despite loving her chilly English husband, longed to *get away from him,* [to] *be Herself for a time ... She wanted her individuality back, that was the long and short of it.*

In just a handful of years a very modern fictional heroine – Kate Chopin's Edna Pontellier – would suddenly, urgently want something to make her feel alive and separate, freed from the listlessness of her existence. In fiction like this, love – or infatuation – could be potent enough for women to walk away from their families and to demand separate lives. Outside the pages of novels, most women stayed put, feeling both trapped and tormented. Some, like Maggie Verver in Henry James' *The Golden Bowl* (1904), maintained a dignified exterior despite the agony of a faithless spouse, giving in to the restrictive standards of society. But the effort required to survive such a vertiginous balancing act was corrosive: sometimes Maggie had to stuff her handkerchief in her mouth and *keep it there, for the most part, night and day, so as not to be heard too indecently moaning.*

Henry James emphasised that, in her humiliating powerlessness, Maggie's only possibility of success was to keep her frustrations covert and to work within the established rules. It remained to be seen whether Florence could perfect a similar pose.

CHAPTER 5

Racing

At Aintree on Friday morning all the well-dressed ladies wanted tickets to the Grand Stand, hoping to rub shoulders with royalty, but Florence's friend Gertrude Janion had not come and some of their party speculated that the two women had fallen out over Alfred Brierley. Even the Maybricks' cook had heard that the debonair young cotton broker had been paying attention to the youngest Janion girl and, earlier in the year, it had seemed that Florence was trying to help things along. All laughter and energy, she and Gertrude had one day burst into James' Tithebarn Street office and asked his bookkeeper, George Smith, to find Brierley's address in the directory. Before Smith could find it, though, James had returned. Flustered, Gertrude beat a hasty retreat from the building, leaving Florence to cover their tracks as she whispered urgently to the clerk that *it didn't matter and ... they did not want Mr Maybrick to know*.

The Brierleys and the Janions were old family friends: Alfred, the sixth of ten children, had been a boarder at Seafield House School in Lytham St Annes along with two of the Janion boys – products of mid-century Lancashire prosperity when money from trade was plentiful enough to buy a private education. Florence's mother would later say she believed that Gertrude had set her cap at Alfred and that both the older Janion girls, Matilda and Constance, encouraged the match. Brierley's interest, though, had waned and he seemed currently to prefer the company of Florence – a fact that might have accounted for Gertrude's absence from Aintree that day.

At Florence's side instead was twenty-six-year-old Christina Samuelson who had, along with her husband, first met the Maybricks towards the end of the previous year. Bumping into them again at the Palace Hotel, Birkdale after a race meeting, the four had played whist. It had been a long day, irritations had flared and Christina had lost her temper, throwing down her cards and storming upstairs. Florence had interceded, soothing the rumpled feathers of her new friend by reassuring her that she too sometimes 'hated' James.

Under cheerful skies, Florence and Christina now joined the Aintree crowds while sleek horses in their owners' colours paraded from ring to racecourse and conversation ranged across form, fashion and bets. Fine carriages circled the ground and omnibuses, carts and trams delivered pleasure-seekers from the railway station. Bells rang to signal the start of races, dense hordes strained to get to the stands or massed around the track palings. Touts mingled with pickpockets and stable scamps; well-turned-out men and elegant ladies raised field glasses or unpacked picnic hampers. Groups eddied around tents selling alcohol while ragged boys squeezed to get to the front. By mid-morning, the murmurs and shouts of a vast throng of disparate classes combined into a confounding din as excitement thickened.

Race succeeded race. Energies flagged. James, usually buoyantly attentive in public, was becoming irate. Having foolishly forbidden Florence from leaving his side, he glared as she returned from the Grand Stand on Alfred Brierley's arm. Several years earlier Brierley had lived for a season in Savannah,

Georgia in order to learn the business of cotton exporting and he and James' Alabama wife behaved towards each other with an easy familiarity. Indeed, the contrast between Brierley and Maybrick was marked. Six feet tall, the younger man was slender, broad-shouldered, with reddish blond hair, an oval-shaped face and strikingly white teeth. He had mournful blue eyes, thick brows, a long nose and a closely clipped beard worn in a jaunty point just below his chin, unlike James' old-fashioned drooping moustaches. Brierley's features were animated, he smoked cigars, drank brandy and wore – in contrast to James' sombre black frockcoat – a flamboyant brown checked suit, a thin ribbon tie rather than a traditional cravat and a round-crowned hat with upward-curling brim in place of the traditional black silk topper. Brierley had a fine commercial reputation coupled with a character said to be lively, earnest, and just a little bit flash.

Some thought that James' jealousy that afternoon was fuelled by some sharp insinuations about the nature of the friendship between Florence and Brierley voiced by Constance Hughes or her husband Charles, both irritated that Brierley was paying more attention to Florence than to Gertrude. Whether this is true or not, James was unable to conceal his obstinate rage and flung a rash of stinging words at his wife in front of their friends. Appalled and humiliated, she bit her lip and suppressed a rising fury. Then, when the races were over and James prepared to return home on horseback, Florence decided to get her own back. Making sure that her actions spoke as loudly as his words, she caught Brierley's arm and hung on to him as they turned towards the omnibus. Under her breath – but not so low that her companions could not hear – she seethed that she would *give it to* [James] *hot and heavy for speaking to me like that in public.* Whether or not Brierley quite caught the full implication of what was going on, no one apparently noticed.

*

Florence was still in a temper when she arrived home at around seven o'clock, walking straight up to the nursery where Nurse Yapp had the children. About ten minutes later James joined them, taking little Gladys fondly onto his knee. Florence left the room. Not a word had been spoken. The strain between the couple was at concert pitch.

At about half-past seven, once James had closed the heavy doors of their bedroom behind him, a quarrel erupted and, however private they believed their words to be, raised voices soon caught the attention of the servants. On her way to collect the children's supper things, housemaid Bessie heard the commotion, paused on the threshold of the room and then hurried on. Alice Yapp, standing at the nursery door the better to hear it all, distinctly understood James to be shouting that *the scandal will be all over the town tomorrow*. Stepping forward, she waited for more until she was startled by the sound of the bedroom bell ringing, loud and insistent. Bessie hurried past, knocked at the door of the master bedroom, entered and received James' orders to summon a cab. Then she practically flew back downstairs in her haste. Yapp did not move. Moments later, the master-bedroom door opened again and the two came out, unconscious of her presence as they descended the stairs to the hall. Yapp lingered, then crept towards the balustrade and leaned over, listening as her master's voice rose to a wail, his words *Florrie, I never thought it would come to this* echoing through the hallway.

Whether or not James had got wind of Florence's business in London, whether his pride had been piqued by advice to watch out for his wife or whether he was fired up by the day's racing, by drink or by medicine, he seemed not to care that their private disharmony was being witnessed by his staff. Nurse Yapp remained on the landing. Bessie stood by the front door, listening for the cab. The kitchen maid Mary Cadwallader had called to Mrs Humphreys about the rumpus and both had come up from the kitchen and were watching from the foot of the main stairs.

Florence was still wearing her race bonnet. Her dress was disordered and some buttonholes were torn. She had been hit. One eye was beginning to swell slightly. She was weeping.

James' fury, the scene playing itself out in the hallway, would burn itself into the memories of the four who watched it, yet Alice Yapp and Elizabeth Humphreys would disagree over one detail. According to the children's nurse, her mistress had decided to leave the house and James was beside himself about it, threatening *by heaven, Florrie, be careful: if you once cross this threshold you shall never enter the house again.* The cook had the opposite impression: that James had ordered his wife to leave, that he followed her about the hall, raving and stamping *like a madman – waving his pocket handkerchief over his head*, telling her to take off her fur cape before quitting the house, warning her to take nothing with her that she had not bought herself.

Galvanised by the tears, the scuffle and the sight of her young mistress being ejected from her home, Mrs Humphreys intervened, stepping forward and begging her master to calm down. Reminding him of the proximity of their neighbours, she implied that, if he continued, their reputations would be lost.

Don't send the mistress away tonight, she suggested. *Where can she go? Let her stay 'till morning.*

Meanwhile Yapp hurried down and asked Florence to come upstairs to see the baby. Florence did not move. Taking control, Yapp put her arm around her waist and pulled her towards the foot of the staircase, past the hissing gas jet burning beneath a glass globe on its finial, up ten steps to the first bend, turning to reach the first floor. Reassuring and coaxing, Yapp then made up the single bed in the dressing room attached to the principal bedroom and put her mistress to bed.

Downstairs, the cook noticed that James had become *so exhausted that he fell across an oak settle in the hall and went quite stiff.* Unable to make out whether he was drunk or in a fit, she left him, sent the waiting cab away and locked the front door. Then she bustled upstairs to check on her mistress. By the time she came down to finish closing up the house James had roused himself and seemed intent on spending the night in the dining room. The emotional explosion had served, momentarily, to invert the order of things: cook, maids and nursemaid each endeavouring to restore calm and draw a veil over the dishar-mony. Re-establishing quiet, they turned down the lamps, pulled doors closed and checked the windows before withdrawing. Something had fractured. It remained to be seen whether it might be mended.

*

The next day, before he left for work, James managed to per-suade Florence to return to their bedroom. So far as the servants were concerned, things were being patched up. Last night's indecorous scene was to be forgotten.

When she was sure he had gone Florence called for the gig and drove straight over to the tall townhouse where her son had been born seven years earlier. With no other friend on whom to rely, she was turning to Matilda Briggs for help. Her bruised eye was painful, but since wife-beating was tacitly accepted if it sprang from 'aggravation' on the part of the wife, and if it didn't go too far, no great fuss would be made about her face. Anyway, she was hoping for more lasting advice. Matilda had managed to procure a deed of separation from her husband without giving up her children; she knew first-hand about the failure of modern marriage and, living comfortably with her brother, she had almost miraculously managed not to attract the disfavour of her social circle.

Matilda had often cowed Florence but she was the only one whom she could ask for practical assistance. Though the older woman argued forcefully against the idea that Florence might leave James, Mrs Briggs at least agreed to accompany his young wife, first to organise a private letter box so that she could receive her mother's letters without his interference and then to consult James' former physician, Dr Richard Hopper.

An hour or so later – having discovered that the post office had no boxes available – Matilda and Florence made for the south-eastern edge of the city centre, to Rodney Street with its graceful Georgian houses rising over several storeys, decorous with wrought-iron railings, balconies, gleaming brass footplates and glazed fanlights. The 'Harley Street of the north', most of this street's residents were doctors, dentists or chemists and Hopper occupied one of the most substantial buildings at No. 63. Coincidentally, the rooms rented by Edwin Maybrick were at the other end of the same street.

Stepping past impressive entrance columns, the women were ushered into the doctor's rooms. Hearing her story and noting that Florence's livid bruise proclaimed a real grievance, he united with Matilda Briggs in trying to dissuade Florence from the course on which she seemed so determined. Instead of a separation, Dr Hopper suggested that he try to affect some sort of reconciliation.

The letter dictated by Florence's London solicitors had clearly not been sent to James and now these two older counsellors diverted her from her intention to visit a set of Liverpool lawyers. She returned home. Dr Hopper arrived later that afternoon, joining Florence and James in the parlour where he tried to get at the reason for the couple's violent argument, questioning James closely and encouraging him to admit that he was furious with his wife for going off with a man at the racecourse *contrary to his expressed wish*. James professed himself intent on patching things up. Florence resisted. An extraordinarily frank discussion ensued during which James told Hopper that *they had ceased to have sexual intercourse for three months* and Florence repeated what she had said that morning: that she felt *some repugnance* towards her husband, that *she could not bear sleeping with him and did not care to have any more babies*. She came clean about some of her debts. Finally, she submitted to the two men's desire that she agree to remain married.

The next day – Sunday – Matilda visited, but where the doctor had soothed, her impolitic behaviour enervated. Listening to James while he told her all about the unpleasant quarrels and the process of patching them up, Matilda gave Florence the impression that she was signalling her allegiance to her older friend. Resentments convulsed. The servants were once again aware of voices raised to shouts and heard their mistress deny – as she threw open the parlour door and marched up the stairs – that she had ever invited anyone to Battlecrease without her husband's permission. Once in her room, overcome with emotion, Florence sank to the floor.

Finding her in a heap, Mary Cadwallader raised the alarm. James took the stairs at a gallop, saw his wife prostrate and dropped to his knees. Trembling with concern, his fury forgotten, he barked at Mary to go and get the neighbourhood physician.

Everyone's nerves were in tatters and no one seemed to be properly in control. James' emotions swung violently between suspicion and devotion. Florence was hysterical. Mrs Briggs felt it her duty to take up the domestic reins and remain in the house but, behind her capable front, she was so tense that she went up and down the stairs to the kitchen, bothering the cook with repeated requests for a little beer. By about nine in the evening she was tipsy and had borrowed one of Florence's dressing gowns though, as it was much too small for her, she appeared *half undressed* and embarrassingly wild when young Dr Humphreys did arrive so that he asked the cook with some horror who on earth 'that woman' was.

*

Dr Hopper returned the following day. Florence was in a state again. This time, one of her mother's London friends, Margaret

Baillie, had stirred things up. Believing that Florence had lied to them all about staying at the Grand Hotel during her recent visit to London, Margaret had written to Florence's mother who now demanded an explanation. *I cannot understand your movements*, wrote the Baroness. *I thought you were there with MB. It was ridiculous to have your letters addressed to the Grand when you were not there.* She closed with hopeful caution: *Your conduct has been indiscreet but I cannot think that you have done wrong.*

The problem was that James had read this letter before passing it to Florence and his jealousies were reignited. With her ill-laid plans fraying at the edges, Florence had taken to her bed in agitation.

By the time Richard Hopper arrived there had been time to dream up an explanation. She had stayed, she said, with her sick godmother who was consulting Sir James Paget, one of the leading surgeons of his generation. This godmother preferred to live in lodgings and to dine at the Grand. It was absurd, but the story seemed to work: James did not demur. Hurrying on, Florence then revealed the full extent of her debts, admitting that she had pawned some of her jewellery and borrowed from moneylenders in order to help her struggling mother. None of it was entirely clear – first she admitted to twelve hundred pounds, but then revised the figure to five hundred – but by the time James finally left the room, apparently appeased, he had agreed to sort out all his wife's financial indiscretions.

Before Hopper had the chance to follow James downstairs Florence called him back. Afraid that something was *not quite right internally*, she asked him to examine her. Hopper declined, recommending that she make an appointment to see one of his colleagues instead. Subsequently he would remember her request and wonder whether Florence had been trying to tell him that she thought she might be pregnant.

*

When the well-intentioned Dr Hopper left Battlecrease after his third visit on Tuesday he believed that the Maybricks were perfectly reconciled for the sake of their children. As far as he was concerned, James had put his suspicions aside and Florence was reassured about her future as his wife. It did not cross his mind that it might all be a pretence.

James' mistress had not been mentioned during their negotiations. Yet it transpired that it was not simply the folly or extent of Florence's debts that now threatened the marriage. James had let slip to Florence that he did not believe her stories about London and that he had placed an advertisement in the papers asking for information about where she might have stayed and with whom. Desperately concerned that the game was up, she scribbled several long letters to John Baillie Knight begging him to cover for her, describing the violent quarrel and expressing her continuing hope that James would agree to a separation.

Despite appearances to the contrary, it seems that Florence was still hoping to escape her marriage. Retaining both her children and her home would depend on two things: on James remaining ignorant of what she had done in London and on his agreeing to settle her debts.

Had she remained calm, withdrawing to the morning room and faultlessly playing the role of wronged wife and dutiful mother, she might have managed the situation to her advantage.

She could not do it.

CHAPTER 6

Dangerous Potions

The truth was that Florence was too infatuated with Alfred Brierley to feign indifference. Both she and her husband were emotionally volatile. James had already proved that passion could be the enemy to 'behaviour' and now Florence could not help herself from writing to Brierley, speaking of her feelings for him and of her fear that James knew.

Brierley, on the other hand, was beginning to appreciate that their indiscreet flirtation at the Grand National had been fool-hardy, even dangerous. He may not have been the unfeeling cad typically present in Florence's romantic fictions, but it did turn out that his affections for her were shallow, based – he would later admit – on *only the pleasure of the association for the time being*. Waking up to the reality that to pit himself openly against a senior cotton man for the affections of his young, foreign wife would constitute a social and commercial disaster, Brierley's inter-est had begun very rapidly to cool.

Replying to Florence's impassioned note, he therefore encouraged her to control her feelings and to hold her nerve. He prevaricated: *I was willing to meet you*, he wrote, *altho' it wd have been very dan-*

gerous ... I should like to see you but ... we had better perhaps not meet until late in the autumn. Then came the blow. *I am going to try and get away in about a fortnight and I think I shall take a round trip to the Mediterranean, which will take 6 or 7 weeks.* Horrified by the possibility of being dragged into a scandal, Brierley calculated that an extended trip would buy him time. He may even have hoped that, during these long weeks, Florence's ardour would diminish or die. *And now, dear, Goodbye*, he closed, *hoping we shall meet in the autumn.*

The realisation that the dapper young man for whom she was in danger of jeopardising her own reputation might desert her in favour of a pleasure cruise threw Florence into a hiatus. On Saturday 6 April, a week after taking her sorrows to Dr Hopper, she left Battlecrease and made for Brierley's city lodgings at 60 Huskisson Street.

With her clearly blackened eye proving how dramatic things had become, Florence told Alfred about James *beating her and dragging her about the room.* She might have begged him not to go abroad, complaining about the tepidity of her life, her loneliness and the lack of reciprocity in her marriage. Did she also urge him to help her to escape its stifling limitations?

Whatever she said, it made no difference. Brierley was resolute, telling her that they should neither meet nor correspond and urging her to resist temptation. Whether Florence left that handsome man's rooms distraught, confused or appeased, she could not have known that it would be the last time the two would ever meet alone.

*

Three days later James left Liverpool for London, planning to stay with Michael in his Regent's Park rooms and to begin the process of sorting out Florence's debts. He is unlikely to have savoured the prospect of dealing with moneylenders and may have anticipated the kind of scene described by so many contemporary novelists – a rickety table covered with dirty papers, a squalid room filled with bits of filthy, chipped crockery full of twists and wisps of paper, for Florence had signed double-fanged documents, foolishly agreeing to a crippling interest rate of 60 per cent. In so doing, she had plunged her husband into the wretched shame of being supplicant to sly-eyed rogues who demanded to be treated with civility.

James was experienced enough to tough out the humiliation. Characteristically he also made sure that he had time while in the capital to consult his brother's physician, Dr Fuller, to whom he repeated his usual complaints about pains in the head, numbness in the right leg and an irrational fear of becoming paralysed. Considering that *there was nothing the matter* beyond *a disordered digestion*, Fuller issued three prescriptions: Plummer's liver pills containing antimony (a toxic element similar to arsenic), an *aperient* or mild laxative and a tonic of nux vomica containing 0.125 per cent strychnine.

The remedies were designed to stimulate appetite and to purge; they were not overtly dangerous – indeed, by comparison with other nineteenth-century potions they were fairly innocuous. James had not told the doctor about his unorthodox medicinal habits and, even if he had, Fuller would probably still have stuck to his recommendations despite the fact that they contained irritant toxins that had the potential to do more harm to James' digestion than good: the laxatives were likely to have contained mercury compounds that could ulcerate the mouth and antimony, used as a vomitive, could lead to dangerous dehydration. Like Dr Hopper, Fuller was a perfect example of the late-Victorian physician: his knowledge, compared to the previous generation, was immeasurably advanced, yet medical practice remained somewhat confused and, often, careless.

Fuller also advocated that James take Fowler's Solution, a proprietary medicine with a prized place in almost all middle-class Victorian bathroom cabinets. Invented in the late eighteenth century, it contained a solution of potassium arsenite with a drop of lavender and, while the popularity of other remedies waxed and waned, its reputation as a cure-all steadily increased so that by the late nineteenth century it was being taken for anaemia, rheumatism, typhus, syphilis, morning sickness, diabetes, parasites, rickets, lumbago, snake bite and more generally as a prophylactic against infectious disease. In small doses Fowler's Solution was said to stimulate circulation and weight gain, temper depression, increase sexual prowess and cure stomach problems and there were plenty of imitations – including Pearson's, Donovan's and Bieto's – each of which also contained arsenic in various quantities. In fact during the 1880s arsenic was considered so medicinally valuable that one practitioner suggested that *if a law were passed compelling physicians to confine themselves to two remedies only in their entire practice, arsenic would be my choice for one, opium for another.*

The Victorian pharmacopoeia contained plenty of readily available treatments based on noxious compounds. The trick with Fowler's was to regulate the doses in order to control the side effects: twelve drops taken three times a day was considered effective for an adult and contained around 0.18 of a grain of arsenic. Get the dose wrong, and it might result in burning eyes, tender gums, skin rashes, painful inflammation of the nerves in the arms and legs, indigestion, impotence, vomiting, a coated tongue or general anxiety and depression. Most doctors believed that tingling in the extremities or the onset of nausea indicated that the drug was working. In reality, any of these symptoms were likely to indicate the beginning of a dangerously toxic reaction.

Since James' spirits generally soared or plummeted according to his daily well-being, he was cheered by Dr Fuller's positive diagnosis of his health. What the doctor, like several before him, had failed to recognise was his patent's reliance on the tonic effect of poisons and the consequent, cumulative weakening of his mental and physical health.

*

Meanwhile, in Liverpool, Florence was again battling with an inquisition from John Knight's aunt. Margaret Baillie wrote that she remained unsatisfied that Florence was telling the truth.

Initially pacified by the Baroness von Roques's explanation of her daughter's whereabouts in London, Margaret now communicated that, while she was wary of meddling, she believed Florence had told so many lies that she was now *doubtful of the truth of anything that you had said when circumstances looked adverse to you. We are plain people*, she admonished, *and accustomed to believe absolutely what is told us.* Florence's *want of accuracy* had thrown her and her sister into a state of anxiety she found almost impossible to describe. Margaret was troubled and wanted it understood that she would not be pacified by patently empty explanations. What, she wanted to know, was really going on?

The ripples caused by Florence's fabrications were spreading and she was frightened that if James encountered the Baillies in London they would say something to re-awaken his suspicions. Catching up the heavy train of her tight skirt, she pulled it to one side in order to sit at her writing desk. Things were precarious. Alive to Brierley's unwillingness to stick with her through the unpleasantness of a divorce she realised that, rather than pressing for a separation, she must change direction and convince James to cleave to his marriage. Otherwise she might be destroyed.

My own darling Hubby!, she began to write. Had he managed her debts? Had Blucher helped? She had, she wrote, had *a terrible night of it* during which she had longed for, but resisted taking, a sedative. She wheedled – *I will be brave and courageous because* [you think] *I may yet be a comfort* – and she grovelled, admitting *the depth of disgrace to which I have fallen, for now that I am down, I can judge better how very far above me others must be morally.*

As she tried to convince her 'Jim' of her contrition, of her despair that she would ever regain his esteem, Florence's writing became increasingly erratic. She promised to live a life of submissive atonement for his and the children's sakes and she pleaded *please, darling, put me out of my pain as soon as you can ... tell me the worst at once – and let it be over ... Darling try to be as lenient towards me as you can for notwithstanding all your generous and tender loving kindness my burdens are almost more than I can bear.* Professing love, she asked for his compassion and forgiveness, signing herself *your own loving wifey Bunny.* As an afterthought she scribbled in the margin in pencil *the children are well. I have been nowhere and seen no one.*

Was this emotional letter simply an expression of self-recrimination, of regret and concern that they would be bankrupted by her financial stupidity? Or was it the result of dread in the face of impending ruin? Florence was scared. If Margaret Baillie's interference exposed her she faced the possibility not only of losing James' protection but of being separated both from her children and her good name, of being cast out of Battlecrease with nowhere to turn but to her impoverished mother in Paris.

When James returned from London two days later his office clerk, Thomas Lowry, thought he was in unusually good health and spirits. Others heard James proclaim he had never felt so well in his life, and when he went back to London a few days later to complete his business he made a point of calling on Dr Fuller to tell him so. Agreeing that his patient's dyspeptic symptoms seemed dramatically to have reduced, Fuller altered his prescriptions, suggesting sulphur lozenges and a couple of tonics: one for the stomach containing an innocuous mixture of glycerine and peppermint water and the other for the nerves made with sweet spirits of nitre, nux vomica, *cascara sagrada* and camphor.

*

It must have seemed to Florence that she was on firmer ground. James appeared happier both about his health and their reconciliation. He no longer demanded to read her letters and he said nothing further about the prospect of a separation. Things were settling and she relaxed enough to confide in the cook that her husband's difficulty in covering their domestic expenses would soon be eased by an increase in their income. Things were still tight – she asked Mrs Humphreys *to economise all* [she] *could without stinting* – but the future looked less bleak. Now Florence could anticipate with pleasure both Edwin's imminent return from America and a masked ball to which they had been invited at the end of the month. James had already agreed to her suggestion that Edwin should escort her there. It was what she needed to take her mind off things.

Absorbed in planning her costume for the ball, Florence veered between excitement and disdain for Liverpool's parochialism, writing to her mother that she hoped for *diablerie, wit and life* though she feared that the city's best would *hardly know what is expected* of it. What thrilled her was the chance to shine, to steal a march on them all: *we are requested to come in 'dominoes and masks' and I should like to know how the former is made and if the latter are not procurable in gauze instead of papier mâché.* What she wanted was the effect described in an article she had recently read about a *bal masque* at the Opéra in Paris. Why should she hide her lovely face if she could part obscure it and still be absolutely *à la mode*?

Like a young girl anticipating her first dance, Florence scrutinised herself in the mirror, touching her skin with the tips of her fingers. She wanted an unblemished complexion yet she could feel the threat of spots – perhaps the result of all the stress of the previous weeks – and so she began to assemble the ingredients needed to prepare her usual face wash. Putting a handful of flypapers into a small basin, pouring over some elderflower water, she left the concoction to steep on her dressing table, covered with a plate and several folded towels to keep out the air and light. After several hours she fished out the limp papers and threw them in the slop pail, added some rose water and glycerine to the tea-coloured solution left in the bowl and then bottled it. The recipe for this face wash had come to her from a New York doctor and, in the past, she had asked chemists to make it up for her, but after the prescription was mislaid she simply got used to doing it herself.

After such a miserable month she wanted to be beautiful. She would breakfast in bed in order to be rested. She would be the most immaculately dressed, the most carefully coiffed and the most sparklingly lovely. She would dance and laugh and flirt and have fun. This masked ball was more than a social event; to Florence it promised a temporary escape from the painful pretences that crowded her days.

*

A fortnight passed. On Thursday 25 April Edwin, fresh from America, called in at the Liverpool offices he shared with James. On the northern margin of the ambitious, money-getting city was the Cotton Exchange Building, known popularly as 'Change, with a cobbled, open-air square – Exchange Flags – in which most of the business took place. Colonnaded on three sides, the fourth taken up by the rear elevation of the Town Hall, the Flags were covered with a white snow of threads from the handling of hundreds of samples, fibres that clung to trouser bottoms, whirled in the breeze and landed on lapels. There was so much of the stuff that smoking was banned.

Liverpool led the world market for cotton. The first financial derivatives, cotton futures, were traded there in the 1700s and during the nineteenth century it had made the fortunes of some of the city's most famous names, including the Rathbones and the Holts. By the 1880s fine houses built with cotton profits peppered the areas around Sefton Park and the southern suburbs.

From Exchange Flags, several narrow passages led away to prosperous streets like Tithebarn Street to the north, lined with tall warehouses and impressive buildings including the Knowsley – a factory converted into suites of offices – in which the Maybricks based their business. This commercial district, a knot of seven streets that made up the original medieval city, was punctuated with the signs of very modern wealth: important front doors, gilded clocks, plate-glass windows and Corinthian columns. Tucked behind Tithebarn Street was the squat, square form of the Albany, a purpose-built office block with a white-tiled courtyard designed to provide steady light to its cotton sampling rooms. A little further east was the three-hundred-foot-wide front of the recently remodelled Exchange station, whose tracks streaked towards Manchester, Blackpool, the Lake District, Leeds, Bradford and Glasgow Central. To the south, Dale Street housed grand new insurance offices and everywhere there were hat shops, gentlemen's outfitters, shoe shops, silversmiths, wine brokers and chemists. Black-clad brokers crowded the streets. The tang of seaweed and mould from the nearby docks hung in the air while from inns and taverns, chophouses and restaurants, the smell of meat, potatoes and beer rose and mingled with the whiff of business risk.

Blown by wind flecked with rain, chased by the spasmic cries of the gulls, Edwin arrived at No. 32 the Knowsley Building from his lodgings in Rodney Street to find James in the process of redrafting his will. He noticed that his brother's hand was shaking as it moved across the blue paper, that he did not seem well and was clearly distressed. James' instructions signalled his intention of leaving everything he owned to his two children, with his brothers Michael and Thomas as trustees.

The furniture I desire to remain intact to be used in furnishing a home which can be shared by my widow and children, but the furniture is to be the children's. I further desire that all moneys be invested in the names of the above trustees (Michael and Thomas) and the income ... used for the children's benefit and education, such education to be left to the discretion of said trustees. My widow will have for her portion of my estate the policies on my life, say £500 with the Scottish Widows Fund and £2000 with the Mutual Reserve Fund Life Association of New York, both policies

*being made out in her name. The interest on this £2500
together with the £125 a year which she receives from her
New York property, will make a sum which, although
small, will yet be the means of keeping her respectably.*

What had happened? Manifestly, something had gone wrong
between James and Florence, something to drive him to ignore
the fact that, under the law, a third of his property belonged to
her on his death. Frustrated that he had gained so little, financially, from his marriage he now requested that his brothers try
to find a way of retaining the capital on his policies while paying
over to his widow only the yearly interest. Florence could be
allowed to remain under the same roof as her children only so
long as she did not remarry. They were uncharitable instructions.
If she came to know of them, Florence would have to hope her
husband would live a very long and healthy life.

It was unclear what had prompted such decisive, emotive
action. Had James decided to maintain a deception for the sake
of his own expediency, a sham marriage within which he could
continue to enjoy the company of his long-term mistress while
cutting off his wife in the event of his death? Had something fundamental altered in order for him now to carry out a threat with
which he had menaced Florence in the past, but done nothing
about? Had he discovered, or had she admitted, something and,
as a consequence, did he anticipate a separation and hunger for
revenge? Was it simply that the extent of her debts had alarmed
him more deeply than he had let on? Or had Michael – in whom
he was known to confide – suggested that James finally cast off
his useless American wife?

Just two weeks earlier James had boasted about his renewed
vigour. He was not, so far as his wife and staff were aware, suffering from renewed ill health. What, then, made him now
contemplate his own death? What caused his hand so decidedly
to shake as he set down the terms of his final testament?

CHAPTER 7

More Like Dying than Living

The next morning Mary Cadwallader received the mail from the delivery boy and took most of it, including what felt like a bottle in a package postmarked from London, straight upstairs to her master's bedroom.

Twenty-four hours later, on Saturday 27 April, James said he felt decidedly seedy, complaining of vomiting and numbness in his legs and telling Mary that he thought he had taken an overdose of the medicine that arrived the day before. Unwilling to remain in bed, he determined to press on with his day's engagements; setting off for Tithebarn Street on horseback, he said that he would ride over later to the Wirral Races.

Florence, left behind, fretted.

Mr Maybrick has taken an overdose of medicine. He's very sick and in great pain, she told Alice Yapp when the children were brought to her after breakfast. The nursemaid merely nodded. It was clear to Florence that, no matter how much concern she expressed, she was powerless to prevent James getting his hands on increasing quantities of strange medicines. When she was sure he had gone, she hurried upstairs and threw the remains of whatever he had taken down the sink.

Thomas Lowry and his fellow bookkeeper George Smith were also concerned when James arrived at the office at around eleven o'clock, looking pale. Leaning heavily against a mantelpiece littered with dozens of bottles and packets from nearby chemists, including Clay & Abraham and Thompson & Capper, James told them that he had had a *most strange experience that morning*, that he had *taken an overdose of medicine ... with strychnine in it*. So frank was he about his physical health that he described being *on the WC for an hour*, adding that *all his limbs were stiff and he could not move*. Both men were used to these stories of aches and pains; both had frequently seen their employer take medicines and heard him discussing various treatments with his clients. They knew that most visitors thought the place resembled a chemist's shop, with its clutter of bottles of all sizes, shapes and colours.

The pain in James' stomach kept up all day; he got drenched at the races, then dined with friends and returned home late. He was shaky. Undressing, he told Florence that during dinner his hands had been so tremulous that he had upset a wine glass. Mortified that his companions might think he had been drunk, he said he still felt numb and dreadfully sick. Although he had been so very unwell in the morning, the fact that her husband had managed to remain out all day suggested to Florence that his symptoms were not severe enough to take fright. She had listened to similar complaints so many times before; he always rallied.

*

Mary Cadwallader came running up the short path of No. 4 Old Garston Road, bumping into Dr Humphreys outside his four-storey Regency terrace just as he was setting off for the Sunday-morning service at nearby St Mary's. Once she had control of her breath, she told him that Mr Maybrick was having a terrible morning of it. Mrs Maybrick asked for him to come.

At nine o'clock that morning James had drunk some brandy, hoping that it would steady his shaking hands. Florence worried. She rang the bell and then, remembering that it was Bessie's day off, went down to the kitchen herself. Encountering Alice Yapp on the landing outside the bedroom, she asked her to *go and stay with master while I go downstairs*. Then, telling the cook that an emetic would *remove the brandy if nothing else*, Florence found some mustard powder in the pantry, tapped some out into a small cup and added water. Without waiting to be handed a spoon, she stirred the mixture together with her finger before taking it back upstairs.

Humphrey [*sic*], she said over her shoulder to the cook, *the master has taken another dose of that horrid medicine. I'll take this up and you follow with another as quick as you can.*

It seemed to do the trick: when Elizabeth Humphreys arrived at the bedroom James was already vomiting. Coming to the door, Florence exchanged her empty cup for Mrs Humphreys' full one, thanked her and hurried back out of sight. An hour later, when there were no signs of improvement, she asked Mary to fetch the doctor.

Although he had often been to Battlecrease to attend the children or Florence, Dr Richard Humphreys had only treated James on one occasion, when he had a slight nose injury. He knew nothing of his medical history and may even have forgotten the concerns expressed about him by Florence a few weeks before.

Arriving at around eleven o'clock, Richard Humphreys went straight upstairs to the main bedroom. James lay in the heavy double bed, which was against the middle of the wall to the right of the doorway. On the opposite wall was a polished chest of drawers beside a wide fireplace. To the right of the door, a tall, carved wardrobe dominated the room and on the far side, beyond the bed, was a single window before which was a small circular pedestal table and Florence's low chair. Her dressing table was positioned on the left of the window; on its right, close to the door to the adjoining dressing room, was a wash-stand.

The doctor listened to James' descriptions of palpitations, a dread of paralysis, a general terror of dying and the fact that he blamed his current symptoms on a strong cup of morning tea. Nothing was said about the medicine sent from London, nor that he might have made himself ill by taking too much of it. Instead James grumbled about having suffered from headaches since the Ascot races the previous summer, complained of a 'dirty' tongue and said that on the previous day he had felt stiffness in his legs, his arms seemed to twitch and he was overcome with the sensation that everyone *looked a long way off*. Finally, he admitted that he knew that some called him a hypochondriac, but insisted that he *knew what he felt*.

The pains in his stomach had gone, but he expressed concerns about his liver and so the doctor examined him externally, finding nothing obviously wrong. Discounting the tea theory, Dr Humphreys believed that his patient had an upset stomach, possibly caused by catching a chill. Asking James what his reactions usually were to nux vomica or strychnine and being told that he thought he was terribly sensitive to both, the doctor advised him to stop taking Dr Fuller's tonics. He should also refrain from solid food for the rest of the day, sipping soda water and milk instead. In addition, the doctor prescribed a digestive physic based on prussic acid – a poison known today as hydrogen cyanide.

By the time Edwin arrived for lunch James was lying on the sofa in the morning room, eager to discuss his symptoms and just about able to join his wife and brother at the table. The cook had prepared him a dish of bread and warm milk. Mary brought it up from the kitchen, stopping to bang the hallway gong smartly as she passed.

James dozed for the rest of the day. By early evening he was hungry and asked for a bowl of arrowroot. Mary Cadwallader began making it and Florence – who had gone down to the kitchen to ask Mrs Humphreys to see to the children because it was Nurse Yapp's evening off – finished it off. Chatting all the while, she stirred together milk, sugar and the arrowroot that would thicken it all into a greyish gruel and then poured it into a bowl. Giving the jug to Mary with instructions to soak it in the scullery sink, Florence then carried the bowl upstairs. Just before dropping the jug into the water Mary, unthinkingly, scooped out a little of the mixture with the end of her finger and sucked it off, noticing vaguely that it was a little darker than normal and that it had a slight taste of almonds. Master wouldn't like it, she said to Mrs Humphreys when the cook came back down from the nursery: everyone knew that he liked his food plain but the mistress had added some vanilla essence to the arrowroot – there was a newly opened bottle still on the side in the larder – and Mary was pretty sure he would complain.

As night fell James started to feel worse again and begged both Florence and Edwin to rub his legs from his hips down. At nine o'clock he began to be sick. There was nothing for it but to tell Mary Cadwallader to run out again for the doctor, but by the time Dr Humphreys arrived back James was better. Now he only complained of the severe pains in his legs, which he described as like the jabbing of knives and forks. Recommending that he drink plenty of water the doctor watched James move his legs himself without any difficulty. Within no time, he was happily sitting up in bed, talking.

Was he still feeling dizzy and fainty? Mary Cadwallader asked solicitously as she showed the doctor to the door, adding – she felt she should – that Mr Maybrick had told her that he had taken an overdose of medicine. Reassuring her that he had complete confidence for a full recovery, young Dr Humphreys slipped out into the night.

For Florence it had been a trying day, juggling the demands of her husband with the entertainment of his brother and the needs of the children. She was worried about James' pallor and his pains, and a little distracted. Spotting Mrs Humphreys as she crossed the hallway, she asked for just one more thing: would the cook warm up a bowl of oxtail soup for her husband? She would come and collect it herself and take it to James in the morning room before they all retired.

Making up a bed for herself in the dressing room, Florence sank into it at just past eleven. The house was still. The shutters were pulled and barred. The fires were dampened and the lamps extinguished except for one left burning low in the main bedroom. The booming echoes of the ships' blasts across the estuary had ceased for the night. The factories and warehouses of the mighty city were mute and dockworkers would not be rising until dawn. At the back of the house, in the night nursery, Gladys breathed softly in her cot and little James shifted sideways, pulling at his covers as he slept. There was no sound from Edwin in the guest room across the hallway. A low rumble from next door told her that James, installed in their solid American walnut bed, finally slept. Only the rogue cry of a seagull and the soft swish of branches outside her window pulled at the edges of Florence's consciousness as she willed sleep to come.

*

During the following morning – Monday – James stayed in bed, penning a long, self-indulgent letter to Michael. It had taken *sheer strength of will*, he wrote, to shake off the feeling of stiff and useless legs on Saturday in order to get to the races and by Sunday *I felt more like dying than living*. He described the twitching in his legs then the stiffness so that *for two mortal hours my legs were like bars of iron stretched out to the fullest extent but as rigid as steel*. The doctor, he wrote, no longer called it indigestion but blamed it on Dr Fuller's nux vomica. *What is the matter with me none of the doctors can so far make out and I suppose never will until I am stretched out and cold and then future generations may profit by it if they hold a post-mortem which I am quite willing they should do.*

Whether or not James chided himself for his habitual carelessness about doses, he had agreed to put Dr Fuller's medicine to one side. Meanwhile, Florence did everything she could to make him comfortable. Up and down the stairs continually, hurrying between the bedroom and the kitchen, ordering and overseeing his food, keeping him warm, she sympathised with his constant and wearing complaints, his shakes, aches, sweats and sickness.

Edwin sat with him for a while and Dr Humphreys returned mid-morning, by which time all James grumbled about was a 'dirty tongue'. He was on the mend. The doctor suggested some coffee, toast and bacon for breakfast and, for luncheon, beef tea – the panacea of the Victorian sickroom – thickened with Du Barry's Revalenta (an invalid gruel with no connection to Florence's erstwhile stepfather), then a little fish or chicken for dinner. In addition, he prescribed Seymour's papain and iridin solution, a mixture designed as a purgative and stimulant for patients with chronic dyspepsia or gastritis. He did not warn his patient that, in large doses, his remedy could cause severe and bloody diarrhoea.

Bustling down to the kitchen, Florence found a brand new tin of Du Barry's in the pantry and took it to the cook, asking her to make it up using some stock and to put it into a brown jar so that James could take it to work. When it was done, Mary Cadwallader brought it up, handing it to James in the hallway just as he was preparing to leave.

*

Florence had hardly returned from a brief walk along Aigburth Road to buy necessities – some more Du Barry's and some face lotions – when James was home again, marching irritably down to the kitchen to tell the cook not to put ketchup in his food again before going back upstairs to bed. Mrs Humphreys shook her head and shrugged off his temper: the food she made had been perfectly plain.

Tuesday, Wednesday and Thursday continued much the same. James ate a bowl of unsweetened bread and milk before deciding whether he was up to business in town or whether he would have work papers sent to the house. Each day, Mrs Humphreys made up Revalenta for lunch and Mary gave it to her mistress in an earthenware jar. Florence generally then wrapped it securely in brown paper and tied it with string, ignoring her husband's complaints about how he loathed the insipidity of the gruel. Edwin had stayed on at Battlecrease. On Tuesday he and Florence had attended the masked ball in Wavertree and on Thursday his presence was a godsend: James forgot to take his lunch into town and, since Edwin was planning to go there anyway, he agreed to deliver it to the office as he passed, sparing anyone else the inconvenience.

April had drawn to a close. The weather was fine. Young men were beginning to congregate at the cricket club across the road and the swifts had arrived, flashing high overhead, diving at flies, screaming with abandon. In the Knowsley Building James' clerks noticed that their employer was paler than usual but knew better than to ask after his health. A new pan had been purchased so that he could warm up the food he brought from home over the fire in his room. The charwoman, Eliza Blucher, washed it out every evening and set it out ready for the next day.

On Wednesday evening, 1 May, James told the doctor that his tongue had cleared and his head no longer ached. He said he would call in to see him when he left work at the end of the week.

On Friday morning he relapsed.

CHAPTER 8

The Slavery of the Sickroom

Apart from James' study, the doors of Battlecrease's many rooms were rarely closed – even the main bedroom door stayed open when he was ill – and the staff, always popping in and out, were constantly meeting their mistress or each other as they went about their duties. Yet the house felt uneasy. In the kitchen, the girls noticed that Mr Maybrick's food sometimes seemed altered, coming back to the kitchen with a slightly different colour or flavour. Often, it was hardly touched. In the nursery, Alice Yapp curtailed the children's games, admonishing them whenever they made a noise. Mrs Maybrick's laugh seemed strained. Edwin had gone back to his lodgings.

When James asked to see the doctor on Friday morning he said that his medicines were disagreeing with him again, but Dr Humphreys felt there was little the matter – especially since Florence, exasperated, burst out that her husband *makes that complaint about everyone's medicine after taking it a few days*. Explaining that his recent prescription was a simple digestive rather than a medicine, the doctor agreed to James' suggestion that he go for a Turkish bath in the hope of sloughing off his malaise. As a result James left for the city an hour or so later, toting – as usual – a jug of invalid food sent up from the kitchen.

When he got home that afternoon he griped about a recurrence of the gnawing pains in his legs and was clearly in so much discomfort that Florence rushed to Bessie to ask for a hot water bottle for his feet. She was troubled. Making James comfortable in the morning room, she hurried downstairs with the intention of making up a glass of beef-juice essence and cold water but then she changed her mind. It would be better, she told Mrs Humphreys, if the cook could add the mixture to some warmed stock. An hour or so later Florence instructed Bessie to get the bedroom ready and James went up, telling the maid when he saw her that he had been sick in the lavatory and that he would like another hot water bottle. He was in bed when she came back with it. Soon after, Florence brought in the children to say good night.

By eight o'clock, her concern had grown.

Mr Maybrick is ill again, she mentioned to Nurse Yapp hoping, perhaps, for a word of support.

It's strange he's sick so long, said the young woman coldly. *I think you ought to send for another doctor.*

Dr Humphreys says it is his liver out of order. But all doctors are fools, said Florence. *They say that because it covers a multitude of sins.* Turning, she went back into the main bedroom.

Florence was probably right to surmise that Dr Humphreys had no firm idea of what was wrong with James, but she brushed off Yapp's suggestion about getting a second opinion because she had no greater faith in any of the rest of his profession. Doctors seemed to her to be by turns expensive, patronising, inconclusive and even dangerously inconsistent. She was almost convinced that James' current illness was caused by the medicine prescribed by the London physician in conjunction with his double-dosing and general hypochondria, but whenever she tried to talk about James' habits with Edwin she got nowhere. Michael and Dr

Hopper were the same. Consequently, she was stuck: simultaneously disinclined to make an unnecessary fuss yet increasingly
fearful of doing nothing.

She was also stung by the hint of accusation in Yapp's words,
by that shimmering sense of unspoken disapproval. To make
things worse, Florence had been unable to persuade James to eat
any of the food Mrs Humphreys had prepared for him. Nothing
she did seemed to work. Exasperated, Florence ate her dinner
alone.

Later, James was sick again. Florence emptied the slops,
straightened his pillows and rubbed his aching limbs with turpentine. When his moans began to frighten her she had the maid
call again for the doctor, who arrived around midnight.

What is making you sick? Dr Humphreys asked.

Cheap sherry put into my luncheon, I suppose, James replied.

It was unlikely that cook Humphreys had added sherry to the
Du Barry's food, but possible that James had tried himself to
make it less insipid. At any rate, he was no longer feeling sick and
was only bothered by the intensity of the aches in his thighs: pain
the doctor ascribed to the massage at the Turkish bath. Discovering that there were some morphia suppositories in the
house, Dr Humphreys introduced one into James' rectum, trusting that the powerful analgesic and narcotic would at least allow
him to get some sleep.

Saturday was worse. When the pain receded, sickness returned
and even a sip of water set James retching. His tongue was furred
and yellow. Florence found it impossible to leave his bedside so
that her horizons were bounded by the bedroom and dressing
room, her hours marked by his protestations about the odd taste
in his mouth or the discomfort in his throat. When the doctor
pressed, there was no tenderness in James' stomach and so he
did not alter his diagnosis, attributing the new bout of sickness
simply to the morphia. He told Florence to give James small
pieces of ice or a damp handkerchief to suck, and to let him wash

his mouth out frequently with Condy's mouthwash but, in an attempt to make the vomiting stop, not to allow him to swallow anything for the time being.

A pricking feeling, like a hair stuck in his throat, made James hawk. For this, the doctor suggested a solution of hydrocyanic acid for which he provided a prescription. But Mary Cadwallader – sent out to get it – had hardly handed the paper to Thomas Wokes, the nearest chemist on the Aigburth Road, before he looked up sharply and said he could not possibly make it up. The doctor, Wokes explained, had forgotten to direct how much water to add. It was a crucial oversight: hydrocyanic acid, sold as Scheele's Prussic Acid, contained 4 per cent of hydrogen cyanide in water; even its vapour was highly poisonous and the fatal dose was just one or two millilitres. Dr Humphreys had meant to prescribe a very dilute mixture commonly used to halt vomiting and alleviate the pain of indigestion. Without the sharp eye of the chemist, a tonic made up to the doctor's partial prescription would have caused James' death.

Hardly was Mary back home – missing the doctor by minutes – than she was sent back out again by Florence to purchase some Valentine's Beef Essence, a small, bulbous bottle of highly concentrated stock whose nutritional qualities were much vaunted. If James could manage to keep this down, the doctor thought, it would help to build up his declining strength.

Drawing the curtains of the sickroom against the bright glare of the May daylight, Florence tried to limit what her husband could get his hands on, telling the staff that all his food and medicine must be given to him by her. She was therefore inexpressibly frustrated to discover that a bottle delivered by the chemist's boy had been taken straight up to the sickroom while she was absent. How could she keep an eye on James if no one would listen to her orders?

The master is very ill, she told the cook.

Holding up her finger and thumb, as if measuring a small

amount, she said that *The doctor says that if he had that much more medicine he would have been a dead man. I've thrown the rest of it away down the sink.*

Despite her best efforts, James could not keep anything down. Thinking that a chicken broth might be better than the bottled beef juice, Florence asked Mrs Humphreys to make some up and put it in a bowl in the larder so that it would be ready whenever it was wanted. That evening she carried a small cup of the broth to the bedroom.

On Sunday Edwin arrived by the one o'clock train and agreed to stay the night. Various mouthwashes, gargles, stomach settlers, malt tonics, oils and pain relievers littered the table at his brother's bedside. More bottles and packets stood on a little table outside the bedroom door. James was able to use the bedside commode but was finding it impossible to move further about the room. He vomited whenever medicine was given to him but – it was odd – his eyes were bright, his skin was clear, his stomach was not tender, he did not have diarrhoea and his temperature was normal. Diluting some Fowler's Solution and leaving it within his easy reach, Dr Humphreys suggested that he take a little each hour. The bottle contained between sixty and eighty doses, or around one twenty-fifth of a grain of arsenic. Keeping her own counsel, Florence came and went from the sickroom with her own gentler remedy: small cups of chicken broth.

By Monday James could eat a little but his throat was now red and the doctor changed his mind about the Fowler's Solution, throwing it into the upstairs lavatory. Believing that infections could be countered by using a chemically treated plaster to produce a blister that would draw infection from the system, he applied one to James' stomach.

Florence needed air; she needed to escape the house, to find life beyond its narrow boundaries. So as not to upset James, she went to the spare bedroom in order to change for a quick trip into town. Meeting Alice Yapp on the landing, she studiously disregarded the nursemaid's insolently obvious surprise, descended the stairs and passed through the front door without looking back. Yapp hung around, watching her mistress disappear. Then, hearing groaning, she pushed the bedroom door further open and went in. James was awake, flushed, moving his head from side to side on the pillow, lamenting the numbness in his hands. Catching them between her own, Yapp began to rub them vigorously.

Later, when Florence came back, Yapp asked her directly: *Why wont you call for Dr Hopper?*

I wanted him to, said Florence. *But he says he won't speak to him, or take what he prescribes for him.*

No, I don't believe that he would, said Yapp.

Was the nurse agreeing with or contradicting her? Florence could not work it out, but she was too tired to take further offence. In an effort to get James to eat something, Mrs Humphreys had made up a different brand of invalid food – Neave's – and it was on the kitchen table waiting to be collected.

The following day, when the blister was opened and its fluid mopped up, James professed himself quite *a different man*, but for the constant pricking in his throat. Florence admitted to Dr Humphreys that she was beginning to find it hard to cope. Maddened by the doctor's apparent inability to make any difference, worried that James was not eating much proper food, she believed that he was weakening rather than getting better, yet when the doctor also suggested that they seek a second opinion she initially refused. Almost as soon as he had gone, though, she changed her mind. Someone more experienced was certainly required. Telegraphing Edwin, Florence asked him to call on a doctor she knew called McShane. Then she went back to James – changing his bed sheets, helping him out of soiled nightclothes and into fresh ones, leaving the laundry basket on the landing for Bessie to collect.

Despite the open window, the sickroom was stale with the odour of James' vomit. Florence's escape to London just weeks before seemed unspeakably remote. At the beck and call of a pallid, grey-haired man who called for her night and day, trying to stick to the letter of the doctor's instructions, this protracted illness was wearing her down. She had become a slave to the sickroom. She was exhausted.

*

Edwin chose to call not for Dr McShane but to send instead for William Carter, who also lived in Rodney Street. In the early afternoon of Tuesday 7 May this respected fifty-two-year-old physician was visiting his patients at the Royal Southern Hospital when he was passed a telephonic message. The first local telephone exchanges opened in large cities like London, Glasgow, Manchester and Liverpool at the end of the 1870s and in 1885 Liverpool had received its first long-distance call, yet telephones were not yet being installed in private houses and it was very rare for a doctor to be summoned by one, so it was with some surprise that Carter learned that he was being pressed by a complete stranger to visit Battlecrease at his earliest convenience. Unable to get away immediately, he arrived there at around half-past five, just as a gathering storm broke violently. Rain fell in sheets. Pouring into the gutters, it splashed from the downpipes and weighed down the plants in the borders until they sagged, forlorn. Pulling up under a sheltering tree, the doctor made a dash for the front door.

Dr Humphreys was waiting in the hall. Shrugging himself free of his coat, the older man passed his sodden hat to Mary. Then the two doctors, strangers to one another, conferred briefly before making for the stairs.

James described his several days of vomiting, the bad taste in his mouth – *as foul as a midden* – his furred tongue, the pricking in his throat and an intense thirst to the two doctors. Dr Carter noted that his throat was dry, red and glazed but that his breath was sweet. Florence's voice rose from the direction of the window, where she quietly sat on a low chair.

His breath is *sweet. It was always thus. But his tongue is so bad*.

It was the first time that the new doctor had noticed the woman waiting patiently for his diagnosis.

Raising James' shirt to press his stomach, causing a little pain due to the recent blister, Carter discovered no other abdominal discomfort; the patient's organs appeared healthy, his temperature was normal, his cramps had passed and his eyes were clear. Maybrick's urine was normal and, on inspection, his last bowel movement was copious and loose: similar, thought Carter, to typhoid stools but without the blood or mucus usually present in such cases. Florence meekly trailed behind the two doctors, following them across the hall to the lavatory, listening to them discussing her husband's evacuations and urine. When Carter finally, peremptorily, asked who she was, she limply held out her hand.

William Carter concluded that James was *a nervous man*. He gathered that the patient was *much in the habit of taking* medicines and that this illness had begun *with a sudden attack of indigestion*. Given that it had commenced after James received a soaking at the races, he concurred with Humphreys' diagnosis of acute food poisoning aggravated by a chill. Both physicians believed that James was recovering and that he would be out of bed by the end of the week. New medicines were directed: antipyrine (an analgesic also used as a tranquilliser) for restlessness and to relieve his throat, tincture of jaborandi (a herbal remedy for diarrhoea) and a few drops of chloride water as a mouthwash.

Florence thought they were wrong.

She did not believe that her husband was improving and, when they were gone, she told Bessie that he was *no better*. She was tense. Alone, she paced the quiet first-floor landing, passing the linen closet, then the night nursery. Turning back towards the main bedroom, her hands trailed distractedly along the edges of the chests against the walls and over the small table on which some medicines were kept, touching the bottles, rearranging them, securing their stoppers. It struck her that, among the clutter of new and old remedies, there were several duplicates and that thick sediment had settled at the base of one in particular. Unstopping the cold glass bottle, tipping it carefully towards the lamp, she slowly poured what she could into a more recently opened bottle, careful not to let its contents drip onto the rug or her dress. Somewhere close, a floorboard creaked. Looking up, she saw Alice Yapp outlined in the doorway of the nursery, watching. Exasperated by her reproachful air, Florence finished pouring and then set down the two bottles and stoppered them before turning back down the corridor towards the lavatory at its far end.

*

After another wretched night Florence refused the cook's offer to sit with James, fearing that *he is quite delirious ... he would not know you.* Instead, when Dr Humphreys arrived at around half-past eight she asked him to telegraph for Mrs Howie, the woman who had attended to her in both her confinements, to come and help. Summoning Edwin back from town – *Jim worse again. Have wired for nurse* – she also sent a note to Matilda Briggs and wired her mother in Paris.

In the midst of it all a letter arrived from her friend John Knight. His aunt, he wrote, was still disconcerted by her lies and now he, too, was feeling irritated. She had made *a mess of it ... and really it was quite unnecessary and still worse most impolitic to tell so many fibs.* He would not, he wrote, *be led into telling any more lies or doing any underhand ... missions. I am quite in the dark now as to what all this mystery is for.* He refused to act as a conduit for her letters. Why would Florence, he asked, risk doing anything to endanger her reputation *at this most critical time?* Meanwhile, he forwarded a letter from Brierley. Although the two had agreed that they would not communicate directly, she had gone back on her promise, writing to Alfred at the start of the week to ask for his support, upbraiding him for planning to go abroad.

Folding it small enough to push into her pocket, Florence determined to read Brierley's note later. Outside in the garden the peafowl strutted and wailed. Inside, wrung out, she was hardly able to find a moment for herself. Mrs Humphreys came to ask for instructions for dinner and James, exhausted after a recent bout of vomiting, asked plaintively for some lemonade. Apart from a mouthwash, the doctors had specifically prohibited all liquids and so, when the cook returned, Florence was forced to say as gently as possible, *but you can't have it dear*. Leaning over, she removed the glass from her husband's reach. His wistful *very well* pulled at her heart.

CHAPTER 9

The Letter

The staff knew only that Mr Maybrick's illness dragged on, that doctors arrived at all times of the day and night and that an atmosphere of watchful anxiety now clung to the house.

When, mid-morning on Wednesday 8th, Matilda Briggs and her sister Constance arrived they refused to wait to be announced and instead proceeded directly upstairs. Hearing the commotion, Florence followed in their wake and caught up with them in the main bedroom, now filled with the rustle of their skirts and the shaking of their bonnets. Their hands fluttered as they fussed at James' bedside, their voices overlapping as they demanded to know what was wrong. Their presence was overwhelming. Ignoring their endless officious questions, Florence pleaded with them to leave her husband in peace, half-coaxing and half-ordering them to *come downstairs and I will tell you his symptoms in five minutes*.

Grudgingly, Matilda and Constance withdrew to the morning room where they rounded on Florence, shocked by what they had fleetingly seen and speaking over one another in their insistence that she should hire more, trained nursing help. Florence was exasperated by their over-mastery of her domain. Curtly she assured them that everything was under control but she did not tell them that Dr Humphreys had already telegraphed for a nurse. Perhaps as a result, Matilda Briggs would not be gainsaid. Determined to bend James' young wife to her will, she took a piece of paper from the escritoire, jabbed the pen into ink and wrote out a wire addressed to the Dover Street Nurses Institution. Handing it to Florence, Matilda insisted that she must arrange immediately for it to be sent.

In Matilda's opinion, the Institution, set up in the 1860s to train nurses for the hospital, the district and for private hire, would alone provide someone of the right calibre.

Florence agreed that she needed the help of a nurse but, despite the fact that she would have to tell Dr Humphreys to abandon their original plans, she failed to explain to Matilda or Constance that she had already made arrangements. Perhaps she was irritated at being told what to do, at being ignored and over-ruled; perhaps she felt bullied and this small rebellion made her feel in control. Or it is possible that she simply accepted the reality that a trained nurse was a better idea than a midwife. Whatever her reasons, her silence ensured that the older women judged her to be at best fuzzy-headed, at worst coldly uncaring.

With her apparently vacuous prioritisation of fashion and fun over the serious business of life, Florence was the very opposite of the women who would soon take control of James' care. Nursing was one of the few professional occupations available to unmarried women who needed or wanted economic independence. The Dover Street Institution provided a rigorous twelve-month nursing education and it set out clear rules for its private nurses: their weekly rate was agreed in advance, travelling and washing expenses were refunded and, if the patient was infectious, temporary quarantine lodgings must be found and paid for. Nurses were forbidden from drinking wine or spirits, were to be given every third night off and must take at least six hours' rest out of the sickroom when working over consecutive nights. Rather than giving them gifts, it was suggested that the families who employed them should make donations in order to finance their work with the poor.

Dover Street nurses were instructed to study the art of patience, to be quiet, watchful, methodical and cheerful, and were trained both to ensure that the sickroom was well aired and perfectly clean and that the patient was given medicine or food with strict accuracy and punctuality. Its reports proclaimed it to be *well known that far more patients die unnecessarily ... from defective nursing ... however devoted or watchful the relative may be*. Thus its rigorously trained nurses fulfilled a twofold function – caring devotedly for their patients while relieving families of the stress of constant caring, allowing them *with an easy mind* [to] ... *obtain the necessary rest*. The reality was that they provided succour for tired families struggling with illness; it was also inevitable that they could put noses out of joint, trotting into the homes of the sick and upsetting both employers and servants with their brusque efficiency.

On the afternoon of Wednesday 8 May, the first nurse, Ellen Gore, arrived at Battlecrease wearing the Institution's uniform of a red-lined dark cloak embroidered with a star emblem. She was stick-thin with a sharp air of practicality. Florence showed her to the spare room before taking her to meet James, who replied to the nurse's questions about how he was feeling with the news that he was *very ill*.

A little later, Gore asked again about the doctors' diagnosis.

The doctors don't know, said Florence. *There is something the matter with his stomach and liver.*

Serious illness was well known to the Victorian household and James' situation illustrated that, for the well off, it was easy to access medical care, though limited knowledge still meant that doctors often failed to make much of a difference and their remedies often made things worse or produced painful side effects. Nursing handbooks advised that the sickroom should be emptied of everything but the bed, a washstand, a chest of drawers for towels and clean nightclothes, and two tables – one by the bed for drinks and medicine and another, larger, for other general medicines and food. With the help of Mary Cadwallader, Florence had done her best to make things ready, washing James and removing all the medicines that cluttered his bedside table, leaving just the photographs and books in ordered profusion.

As Nurse Gore began to make the room her own, pulling James' covers straight, re-positioning the lamp, Florence handed her some medicine she had made up in a small, plain medicine glass. Then she showed Gore the lavatory on the landing in which she had left Neave's food already prepared in a jug along with 'peptonised milk', chicken broth, brandy to restore strength, champagne to help James sleep and his other, regular medicines which, she said, she would bring along to the bedroom at the times they were supposed to be taken. As well as aiding sleep, champagne had a reputation as being excellent for digestion, calming for hypochondriacs and able even to halt vomiting. Mrs Beeton would have recommended, too, a 'strong beef tea'.

Florence's relief at Gore's presence was tempered by the knowledge that James' care would now be overseen by women whose job it was to listen to the doctors and not to her. Indeed, when Edwin heard that the nurse had arrived he quickly told Gore that she, uniquely, should attend to his brother's needs. As soon as she had the opportunity the nurse went downstairs to tell Mrs Humphreys that she would not require anything from the kitchen.

*

The first Michael knew that his brother's condition had worsened considerably was from a cryptic cable sent by Mrs Briggs some time that Wednesday morning: *Come quick. Strange things are going on here.* Hurrying to the station, he took the first express north.

During the afternoon, as Michael made his way to Liverpool, Florence rested on the small sofa in the morning room, unaware of the distrust fermenting just across the hallway. In the parlour Matilda Briggs, Constance Hughes and Edwin (whom Matilda had rushed into the city to find) were waiting for Michael's arrival to shake them out of their indecision. Disquieting ideas, only vaguely articulated, were taking root in their troubled imaginations.

It was started by Alice Yapp. The day before, Bessie had told her about Dr Humphreys's miswritten prescription and the fact that the chemist had described it as *a deadly poison*. Perhaps Bessie had mistakenly given Yapp the idea that their mistress had something to do with it. Certainly Yapp's fancy had made much of the fact, and when Mrs Briggs and Mrs Hughes arrived that morning she had taken it into her head to beckon to them across the plush lawn and to intimate that she thought something was awry. She told them that she had heard Mr Maybrick ask – plaintively, she thought – for his hands to be rubbed and had been shocked by her mistress's refusal, along with the sharp retort that *it never does you any good*. She also repeated Mary Cadwallader's impression that the food coming back from the bedroom looked and tasted different from that sent out from the kitchen. Finally, Yapp said she was under the impression that her mistress was trying to keep the staff away from the sickroom. Small, perhaps inconsequential, impressions had coalesced in her mind into something more substantial, so that while Yapp stopped short of making any specific accusations she left the two older women in little doubt of her fears. This conversation had prompted the hasty summoning of Michael from the metropolitan comfort of his Regent's Park flat.

Now that Yapp began to concentrate on it, other things occurred to her. In particular she wondered about the bowl she had seen on Mrs Maybrick's toilet table a few weeks earlier. Bessie had asked her to come and take a look at it one afternoon. Lifting a towel stretched tight over the top, the nursemaid had discovered a second towel, folded up. Under that was a plate – a kitchen plate – turned upside down. Beneath that, some long, thin, brown papers were soaking, their dye slowly leeching out to tint the liquid in delicate whorls. There were several of them snaking limply in the bottom of the container. Along their edges, clearly printed, were the words 'flypapers', along with pictures of flies.

Putting everything back as she had found it, Yapp had hurried back to the nursery, wary of being caught poking about. Later, as they sat around the table in the servants' basement room, the girls had wondered among themselves what it was all about. Mrs Humphreys thought it probable that their mistress was making a solution for cleaning her silk dresses, but it did not stop them feeling uneasy. They knew – everyone knew after the sensation surrounding Catherine Flanagan and Margaret Higgins in 1884 – that flypapers were poisonous. Flanagan and Higgins had been convicted of murdering Higgins's husband with arsenic derived from flypapers in order to collect his life insurance. Compelling evidence suggested that they had also killed Higgins's ten-year-old daughter as well as Flanagan's twenty-two-year-old son and an eighteen-year-old lodger. Around the time the Maybricks returned from America, the press had run hot with details of the crime and, thrilled by a sensational trial and the women's double execution, Liverpool talked of little else for months.

None of the Battlecrease servants had heard of the benefits of arsenical face washes and they couldn't quite work out what Florence was up to. Clearly there was no effort at concealment – the bowl was in plain sight, the bedroom door was wide open and Bessie said that Mrs Maybrick saw her go into the room to clear up and made no attempt to move it, so it was still there hours later when Yapp went in. None of it made much sense.

Unaware of these speculations Florence – tired out after so many broken nights, longing for support, sympathy and affection – felt utterly alone. In the grip of her reckless infatuation, feeling keenly the grand isolation of Battlecrease, she was obsessed with the notion that Alfred Brierley should not leave town. Knowing that she could not stay away from the sick-room for much longer, she decided to write to him, pleading once more that he would not *leave England until I have seen you once again!* The household letters were currently being brought straight to her rather than to James and so she begged Brierley to reply while his letters would go unremarked. *I have been nursing all day and night*, she scrawled. Able to make neither head nor tail of the doctors' diagnoses, she was losing faith. Nothing seemed to be making any real improvement or bringing James any relief. *He is <u>sick unto death!</u>* she added; *all depends upon how long his strength will hold out.* Her rushed letter covered two pages and was punctuated with emphatic underlinings. She signed it simply *Yours ever, Florrie.*

*

It was about three o'clock on Wednesday afternoon when Florence hurried across the gravel towards the front gate to intercept Alice Yapp, who had just set out with Gladys for an afternoon walk. After a spattering of rain, the air was mild. The last spring blossoms still clung to some branches or spun in light circles before dropping to the path. The trees and hedges were greening; the air held the welcome promise of a warming week. Handing Yapp a small, crisp envelope, Florence asked her to ensure that she caught the afternoon mail.

It was incautious. Was Florence just too tired to care or was she dull to the possible consequences of trusting this letter to the nursemaid? Her imagination already excited, Yapp noted the name on the envelope. Then she passed it to little Gladys to carry and it was perhaps not at all unexpected that, before they were much further down the road, the child should let go, dropping it into a puddle where it spoiled. Yapp might simply have asked for a new envelope at the post office, rewriting the address. Instead, she broke the seal and opened it. Like the plot of a sensational story spilling over into the day's reality, the first word that struck her – *Dearest!* – made her gasp. Momentarily forgetting her young charge Alice Yapp then began curiously to scan the outpourings of her apparently faithless young mistress.

It all seemed, suddenly, very clear: if Mrs Maybrick was involved with Mr Brierley – if she could so transgress – might she not also be something worse: a scheming poisoner intent on harming her husband? Did this truth not make sense of all the oddities Yapp had already noticed? With no intention of posting the letter, Alice grabbed Gladys' plump little hand and turned back towards the house, her thoughts spinning. The intense privacy of Battlecrease, its many-roomed grandeur, its extensive gardens, its suburban separation from the dirty rattle of the city, all proclaimed the respectability of the Maybrick family. Yapp may have felt no particular loyalty to the American wife who seemed more caught up in herself than in her household, but she was nonetheless horrified by the apparent discovery of a deceit that threatened to undermine it all. Was she also melodramatically excited by the power she acquired by possessing that letter? Did she feel vindicated in her indefinable dislike of Mrs Maybrick now that it was apparently grounded in a reality that something was gravely wrong?

It was obvious to Alice Yapp as she made her way back down Riversdale Road, urging Gladys not to dawdle, that something evil was taking place and that she was in a position to have it stopped.

Within moments of arriving back at the house, she sought out Mrs Briggs, Mrs Hughes and Edwin in the parlour, passed the letter to Edwin and then repeated the suspicions she had aired earlier in the day. Confronted by three overwrought women, listening to their wild accusations, Edwin struggled at first to make sense of it all. Scanning Florence's letter to Brierley, he was appalled by its implication of intimacy and deceit but, having always rubbed along well with her, he was inclined to think the

best of his sister-in-law. Yet it also began to dawn on Edwin that
something odd was going on. Yapp's stories about the flypapers
and the chemist's refusal to make up a prescription began to
merge into a horrifying possibility. Listening to Matilda and
Constance's impressions about the severity of James' illness, in
the company of these women whose distrust was so alive, his
own natural inclination to keep an open mind began to falter.

No one thought to reproach the children's nurse for the
extraordinary fact that she had opened and read her mistress's
letter. Instead, they wondered whether Florence could be trusted.
Was she a respectable wife? If not, was she a conniving threat to
James' life? In the minds of these three, nervily anxious for the
arrival of Michael, propriety and good faith were inseparable: if
one was broken, the other could not possibly survive.

In this corrupted atmosphere, Edwin remembered that he had
brought with him a brand new bottle of Valentine's beef juice and
he left the parlour to deliver it to Nurse Gore. His mind racing
over the recent conversations, without pausing to reflect on the
impression his words might have, he instructed the nurse to make
absolutely sure that she was the only one to give food or medicine to his brother. Even Mrs Maybrick, he warned, must not be
allowed to interfere.

He needed to get out of Battlecrease, away from the worried
frowns and waspish nervousness of the Janion sisters. He needed
space to think.

Calling for the carriage to be brought round to the front door,
Edwin decided to go back into the city. He could thus be at the
station to meet the evening express from London and could fill
Michael in as they made their way back to Battlecrease. Edwin
was sure that his older brother would take charge and he was
content to leave it to Michael to decide what to do.

TWO

CHAPTER 10

Strong Suspicions

Michael had never really warmed to the girl James picked up on a steamer coming back from New York. Now, what Edwin told him as they headed out to Battlecrease whipped him into a fever of concern.

It was still light when their carriage skittered into the driveway. Shocked by the contents of Florence's letter to Brierley, Michael was ready to take control. Striding into the house, dropping his coat, bag and hat onto the wooden settle, he bounded towards the stairs and his beloved brother's room.

Not long after, he was back downstairs again, somewhat calmer, having peremptorily instructed Nurse Gore that he believed his brother had not been properly attended to: he wanted not only for her to continue to prepare everything James ate or drank herself, but to taste it before giving it to him. Gore's reply had been heartening: during that afternoon Mrs Maybrick had brought her some medicine intended for James but, the nurse said, she had thrown it down the sink in the housemaids' closet. Wanting to relieve her patient's sore throat, she had then herself concocted a mixture of glycerine and borax from brand new packets taken from the cupboard and the drawer in the wash-stand.

By choosing not to confer with Florence before issuing his commands, Michael signalled unequivocally his intention to take over as head of the household. Florence had followed the brusque intruder into the bedroom. Indignant, frigid, he asked if she would go down with him to the morning room.

Scarcely was the door closed when he burst out: *I have strong suspicions of this case.*

She blanched, replying, *Whatever do you mean?*

Without asking her whether the presence of the nurse or the call for a second medical opinion had been her ideas, Michael criticised Florence for not paying proper attention, accusing her of delaying the process of professional care. At the very least, he spat, she had been negligent and irresponsible, and he believed that she was to blame for his brother's failure to improve.

Michael had lost his self-control, but if Florence was rattled by the force and tenor of his outburst he was astonished by her defiance. Instead of sinking, shocked, into one of the room's several chairs, her shoulders rolled backwards and down. *I have nursed him alone*, she replied. *And who has a greater right to nurse him than his own wife?*

Her eyes did not leave his face. Michael did not agree.

I am not satisfied, he said.

He believed that it was crucial to remove James as far as possible from Florence's care; he insisted that she cease to take any part in it. She was not, he said, even to pass James a piece of ice. Her shocked expression warned him that he had perhaps gone too far.

They stood in silence, each momentarily unsure where the conversation was heading.

Attempting, then, to mitigate some of the bruising effect of his terribly harsh words, Michael affected concern. Florence was not, he said, strong enough to nurse James alone; now that they were all there to share the burden she must get some rest. Saying nothing, the deposed wife turned on her heel and was through the door and into the hallway by the time he delivered his parting words: *I will see Dr Humphreys at once.*

Richard Humphreys had been to the house earlier in the afternoon, introducing himself to Nurse Gore and giving her instructions about James, who was stable, though he continued to complain of the painful pricking in his throat. Returning at about ten o'clock that night, the doctor found his patient comfortably able to eat a little Neave's food and to drink some milk, chicken broth, brandy and champagne. The doctor was not unduly concerned about the tenesmus – ineffectual straining – from which James now suffered: bowel irritation was a common symptom of the chronic dyspepsia that he and Dr Carter had already diagnosed.

When the doctor reached the hallway, intending to make his way home, Michael drew him aside. Impatient with bland medical assurances that his brother was improving, Michael wanted to hint that he thought his brother had been improperly treated. It was an odd, unexpected little speech and, unclear exactly what this domineering man was trying to insinuate, Dr Humphreys might have wondered whether it was the result of a tiring journey north and the emotion of seeing his brother unwell. So far as the doctor was concerned, everything was entirely above board. Taking his leave, he merely agreed to return the following morning.

In the small dressing room off the main bedroom, Florence wrote a brief postcard to her mother before climbing between the sheets of the narrow single bed and pulling the blanket up under her chin. If Michael's outburst had put her on her mettle then she would at least take advantage of the fortifying effect of a full night's sleep, the first she had enjoyed for weeks.

*

Thursday 9 May dawned with a flurry of rain carried on an easterly breeze that nipped at the pale new foliage and scattered whitecaps across the estuary. James was worse: his bowels were loose, his tongue bad, his throat was distressing him and he now felt intense pain in his lower bowel. Dr Humphreys advised him to stop the medicines he had prescribed and gave him an opium suppository.

Going about her business in the nursery, Alice Yapp heard her mistress's light step in the doorway.

They are blaming me, she heard Mrs Maybrick say, *but I have done all I could.*

Yapp was not going to empathise. Without looking up or turning from her chores, she asked sharply, *What? Why?*

If she had intended to make it clear that she did not want to engage in conversation, Florence did not take the hint.

Mr Michael blames me for not having sent for another doctor and a nurse, Florence continued. *Dr Humphreys said there was no need for another doctor and Dr Carter said on Tuesday there was no need for another nurse.*

Was Florence beginning to wonder whether she really had been slow in reacting to the severity of his illness? Or was she being disingenuous, attempting to cover her tracks? Yapp did not want to let her off the hook: *But I suggested to you two or three times to send for another doctor*, she said.

Florence paused.

Well, she countered, *I have done all that Dr Humphreys ordered. I have done all that he told me to do.*

Yapp's silence once again screamed censure. If Florence flinched at the sting, it was only once she had turned away towards the first-floor landing.

The house was full of lowered voices, of whispers below stairs, discussions in the corridors and consultations in the smart ground-floor rooms. The sound of feet rang in the hallway and drummed incessantly on the broad staircase runner. Battlecrease was full of words whose meanings were given subtler edge by widened eyes or cast-down glances. Everyone felt uncomfortable, though no one was entirely sure which rules had been breached, or to what end.

As if in response to Florence's efforts to justify herself both to Michael and to Yapp, the sense of blame grew until it thrummed invisibly through the hallways, lingering at the edges of conversations, trailing in the stern footsteps of Michael as he strode about the place. Evident in the flickering gazes of Yapp, Cadwallader, Bessie Brierley and Mrs Humphreys, blame seemed to settle in the seams of Florence Maybrick's fancy dresses and blouses, fragile and ruinous as an autumn moth.

Elizabeth Humphreys came to ask after the health of her master before ducking back downstairs to the kitchen where a soft noise behind her told her that she had been followed. With Nurse Gore on duty and the brothers closeted in the parlour, the cook could see that her mistress was at a loose end and she sympathised. Indeed, she was moved to see that Florence was battling with the effort of suppressing tears as she began to discuss arrangements for their dinner. Then, still trying not to cry, she burst out: *Well, Humphreys, I am blamed for all this, for the master's illness.*

In what way, ma'am?

Well, for not getting the proper nurses in, or other doctors.

Dropping her head, her shoulders began to heave. Florence was losing her grip.

If I could, she gasped bitterly, *I would turn everyone out of the house this day. My position is not worth anything in this house now that I have been put out of the master's bedroom and not allowed to give him anything.*

It seemed to the cook that there was some truth in this and she listened quietly to Florence's protestations of Michael's spite since the day she married. If only he would leave her house, Florence whispered, she would never allow him back through its door.

I have done my best Mrs Humphreys, and this is the way you get treated.

Then, having momentarily given way to her despair, Florence

steeled herself. Throwing out a last *never mind*, she went back off upstairs, leaving the cook to her own confused impressions of a family spiralling deeper into crisis.

*

Mid-morning, Nurse Gore was relieved by a second nurse from Dover Street, Margaret Callery. Michael, Edwin and Florence lunched together but otherwise held themselves apart. At teatime Dr Humphreys and the city physician William Carter arrived. They had hardly left James' quiet room on their way down to the hallway when Michael, ignoring all pleasantries, demanded loudly, *What is the matter with my brother, Dr Carter?*

Calmly, Carter repeated his opinion: *He is suffering from acute dyspepsia.*

What's the cause?

Dyspepsia arises from gastritis, which means the inflammation of the stomach.

It was not good enough for Michael. He pressed again, *But what is the cause of it?*

That is by no means clear. It is a condition which might be caused by many things, but Dr Humphreys and I have come to the conclusion that your brother must have committed a grave error of diet, probably by taking some irritant food or drink, or both.

Austere to the point of aggression, Michael had gained the morning room ahead of them. Ushering the two doctors inside, he closed the door and rounded abruptly on Dr Humphreys. *Have you told Dr Carter anything about my suspicions?*

Carter was surprised by the sudden turn of conversation and by the edge in Michael's voice. Wondering what was coming next, he noticed that Michael's face was contorted with the effort of controlling his emotions. Then, with growing astonishment, Carter listened to bitter accusations made against their patient's wife, gathering that Michael believed that Mrs Maybrick was giving her husband something on purpose to make him ill.

Drawing a deep breath, Carter counselled caution. It was, he said, *A very serious imputation to make against a wife – and one which I do not think ought to be advanced without very good grounds.*

God forbid that I should lightly suspect anyone, countered Michael. *But if I believe I have good grounds for the suspicion don't you think it is my duty to communicate it to you?*

The doctors stood at an abyss. It had not crossed their minds that James was being poisoned. William Carter took a step back. He was adamant that they guard against mistrust taking root without proper proof. What, he asked, had led to such a dreadful suspicion?

Michael chose not to tell the doctors about Florence's letter. Instead, he outlined his misgivings in the most general terms, including something about there being a lot of flypapers lying around the house, that on one occasion they had been seen soaking in a basin, that James had been well when he came to stay in London but went downhill fast when he returned home, that there had been most serious quarrels and that he had certain proof of Florence's infidelity. This last struck Carter forcibly. He began to pay more attention to what was being said.

Hands in pockets, rocking on heels, the three men consulted. It was their duty, they decided – without mentioning anything specific and without setting off an alarm – to give even stricter instructions to the nurses regarding James' food, drink and medicine. By the time they parted, Michael had the doctors on his side and they had conceded that Florence should be kept away from her husband. Thus they believed they would establish a ring of protection around James and his health would begin to improve.

The suggestion that arsenic derived from flypapers might have been added to the sick man's food set the doctors thinking, since it made sense of his worsening symptoms and the failure of their treatments. Returning to the bedroom, Carter checked the nurse's record card, noting that mild diarrhoea had begun twenty-four hours earlier, with just four loose motions since. Neither the neighbourhood physician Richard Humphreys – not yet thirty and relatively inexperienced – nor William Carter – grey-haired and practised – was concerned enough to administer an antidote to arsenic. They did agree, though, to perform chemical tests on a small bottle of Neave's food and on James' urine and faeces. To help James rest, Dr Carter prescribed sulphonal – an alcohol-derived 'hypnotic' – and a cocaine solution for the pain in his rectum and throat.

Mrs Humphreys saw her mistress just once more that evening. Florence had collected ice from the larder and gave it to the cook to break with a kitchen hammer. Asking for news, Humphreys was told that *He is very much worse. Inflammation has set in.*

Shuddering, she asked, *Do you think he'll pull through?*

Parcelling the crushed ice into a silk handkerchief, Florence met Mrs Humphreys' eyes with an expression of sad defeat. Cupping her hand under the cold cloth as she prepared to go back upstairs, she replied simply:

Never.

*

In the dimmed sickroom, Nurse Callery was irritated by her patient's wife – the kind of woman who got under her feet, who shadowed her across the room, who lingered at her shoulder as she dispensed medicine, endlessly present yet limpidly disengaged. She watched as Florence sat on the edge of the bed, bending over her husband as the two had a muted but emotional conversation. What was going on? The nurse could not hear, but she thought it odd that this young American woman seemed to be enervating and unsettling rather than calming the poor sick man.

At nine o'clock, when Bessie took her up a cup of tea, Florence was in bed in the dressing room. Nurse Callery was rubbing James' hands. Michael was in the bedroom too, standing beside the washstand. Bessie saw him remove a small bottle from the table and slip it into his pocket before bidding them all good night and leaving the room.

Two hours later Nurse Gore came back on duty. Florence wandered in. Ignoring her, Gore collected the bulbous little bottle of Valentine's beef juice from the landing table, tore off its white leather seal, removed the cork and measured two teaspoons into a tumbler of water. Tasting it first, she offered the glass to James before re-stoppering the bottle and setting it down on the table before the window.

He's had it before, but it always makes him sick, said Florence from her position at the end of the bed. Gore nodded silently.

A little later, having managed to swallow some champagne, James fell into a restless sleep. It was after midnight. Florence was still awake and Ellen Gore looked up as she came back into the sickroom, brushing past the small table by the window. The nurse watched obliquely as Florence reached out with her left hand for the meat juice and tucked it into the heavy folds of her skirts before going back into the dressing room and pushing the door almost closed behind her. It rasped gently as it moved over the thick carpet.

Gore did nothing. Minutes later Florence re-emerged and lingered again by the small table. Gore did not take her eyes off her as Florence requested that she fetch some icy water to bathe her husband's head, simultaneously removing her right hand from her side and silently returning the small bottle to the table, then leaving her hand there a while. She seemed to have no idea that she was being closely observed.

Determined not to leave the room, Gore demurred: *But he is sleeping. I can do it when he wakes*, she said.

Florence didn't answer. She went back into the dressing room.

When James woke shortly afterwards she came back into the bedroom. The nurse watched for a third time as, in the night dimness, Florence once more moved the meat juice bottle, this time taking it from the small table and placing it on the washstand in the corner.

Gore made a mental note to discard that bottle and its contents the following day.

CHAPTER 11

Tests

It was with relief that Dr Humphreys greeted Michael on Friday morning with the news that his tests for arsenic in James' faeces and urine and in the Neave's food indicated not even a trace of poison. Even more satisfactory, both he and Dr Carter considered their patient to be showing signs of getting better. Michael's alarm, they thought, had led them all to jump to the wrong conclusion.

The doctors knew that the problem with arsenic was that it did not announce itself by taste or smell, that it was fatal in relatively tiny doses and that, although its symptoms were well-recognised, they were often confused with severer forms of dysentery or food poisoning. All of this made it remarkably hard to identify, augmenting the poison's reputation as a weapon of cunning and fuelling widespread fear of its administration, either accidentally or on purpose.

Growing anxiety about arsenic had for years put science under pressure to develop accurate tests for its detection. At the beginning of the nineteenth century stomach contents might be fed to animals in cases where poison was suspected in order to see if they also fell sick, but it was an inconclusive practice that required unreasonably large quantities of suspect matter. In 1815 Eliza Fenning, a poor servant girl, was convicted of poisoning a family by putting arsenic in dumplings. 'Evidence' against her consisted of the fact that the dough had not risen properly and that the blade of the knife used to cut them turned black. Although Eliza had also eaten the dumplings and was ill as a result, and despite her desperate protestations of innocence, she was hanged.

What was needed was a test able to detect the small amounts of arsenic that could constitute a fatal dose. Several unsatisfactory methods were promoted until, in 1836, a method was developed by James Marsh, a Kent chemist, for detecting effectively the presence both of arsenic and its cousin antimony. Based on the fact that arsenic combines easily with hydrogen to form arsine gas, the process involved the addition of hydrochloric or sulphuric acid to a suspect sample, followed by a small piece of zinc: the reaction between acid and metal generated hydrogen, which bonded with any arsenic present. When the resulting gas was burned elemental arsenic (if present) would condense onto a piece of glass or white porcelain, leaving a dark grey, mirror-like deposit.

While Marsh's test remained the standard method for detecting arsenic until the 1970s, five years after it was devised a German chemist called Hugo Reinsch had published a description of a process that was less sensitive than Marsh's method but simple and quick to perform. This test required simply for a sample to be boiled with hydrochloric acid into which a piece of copper wire or foil was placed: if arsenic were present it produced a grey or black deposit on the copper. The results of a Reinsch test were first introduced as evidence in a British poisoning trial three years later, in 1844.

The success of both tests may have contributed to the 'poisons panic' of the 1840s, since more effective detection bolstered the perception that deliberate poisoning was on the increase. Designed to isolate minute quantities of arsenic from organic mixtures like food or excreta, the results of both processes were famously used in some of the most high-profile poisoning cases of the second half of the century: Marie Cappelle, a young Parisienne forced into marriage with foundry owner Charles Lafarge, was thereby convicted of his murder in 1840 and then in 1857 the tests revealed large quantities of arsenic in the body of Madeleine Smith's lover. In 1859 the pioneering forensic pathologist Alfred Swaine Taylor produced evidence at inquest that stunned everyone by pointing to the fact that Dr Smethurst had murdered his wife: although no poison was actually found in her organs, it was detected in her stools and in some fluid taken from her bowel.

The Marsh and Reinsch tests, then, made the criminal use of arsenic a more precarious business and promised the ascendancy of chemistry over crime. Yet there were drawbacks. First, both tests required a certain amount of skill, as the arsine gas produced during the Marsh test could be fatal. Then, some organic materials – including vomit – could foam when heated, inhibiting the release of arsine. Further, the results for antimony were broadly similar to those for arsenic and, since antimony was used widely to induce vomiting in poisoning cases, further tests were necessary in order to distinguish between them. Opinion also differed about how long the sample and the acid should be boiled together to complete an effective Reinsch analysis – from minutes to hours. Finally, contaminated reagents yielded bogus results: zinc and sulphuric acid, for example, were occasionally tainted by arsenic during their manufacture.

This last disadvantage was famously made evident when Swaine Taylor was forced to admit that his analyses of Mrs Smethurst's samples might have been contaminated by an impure copper foil of a type Taylor had been using for decades. There was outcry. The fact that supposedly rigorous analyses could be fallible spawned public consternation. Smethurst was tried, found guilty and sentenced to hang but in the fracas that followed Swaine Taylor was scorned, Smethurst was pardoned and the public were left with the justifiable impression that, when it came to arsenic and the establishment of deliberate poisoning, the waters were far muddier than they had been led to believe. In the face of all this, the infant science of toxicology struggled for judicial credibility.

Yet it was also known that arsenic continued to be expelled from the body in urine for days after its ingestion. The Reinsch test used by Dr Humphreys was easy enough for a general physician to perform and sensitive enough for James Maybrick's two doctors to feel confident in their assertion that, despite Michael's overwhelming suspicions, arsenic was not the cause of his brother's present suffering.

*

When Nurse Gore went off duty mid-morning on Friday she did not know about Dr Humphreys's tests or their results. Yet the way Michael Maybrick and the physicians behaved towards her patient's wife made her cautious. Before leaving she remembered to tell Nurse Callery not to use the contents of the bottle of meat juice still present among the plethora of other bottles on the washstand. She also remembered that Mrs Maybrick had suggested adding some ice to James' brandy – Gore had declined, believing it a ruse to get her out of the room – and now the nurse wondered whether there might be something odd about the brandy too.

Before leaving for Dover Street, Gore mentioned this concern to Michael, who went straight upstairs to collect the brandy bottle from the table by the window. Unsatisfied that they had got to the bottom of the cause of his brother's illness, he intended to ask Dr Carter to test this too.

Yesterday's stiff breeze had dropped; the pavements were damp but the sun broke, from time to time, through the clouds as Gore walked towards the railway station. The noise, smells and hustle of the city centre would be relief after Battlecrease's

atmosphere, thick with distrust. She had decided not to tell
Michael about what she had seen Florence do with the meat juice
bottle the night before. So very odd was the theatre with the
bottles that she wanted to ask for advice about it from the Lady
Supervisor at the Institution.

*

A short while later, at lunchtime, Gore travelled back to
Battlecrease steeled to report what she had seen. Listening carefully to her story, Michael simply asked her to bring him the
corked, half-full bottle of Valentine's meat juice that Florence
had moved around so oddly. He resolved to give this to Dr
Carter when he returned in the evening.

James' breath was sweet and his eyes were unclouded but he
continued to vomit, to strain his bowels and to complain both of
soreness in his throat and of overwhelming thirst. Despite this,
doctors had expressed their hope that he was on the mend.

Michael and Florence avoided one another. Each had misgivings. Both were vexed, in their different ways, at what they
considered to be James' continuing decline.

Eager to clear his head, Michael pushed through the garden
door. Oblivious to the placid beauty of the gardens, to the chatter
of the disturbed blackbirds, lost in his thoughts, he skirted the
pond and brushed under the apple and pear trees in the orchard.
The house rose up behind him. There was no discernible movement behind the windows on that side – those of the night nursery,
the bathroom on the first-floor landing, or the servants' rooms
higher up. Everything seemed restrained and calm, but he was in
turmoil. Florence's letter to Brierley had spawned distrust but
something else troubled him. Something was not right; he was convinced of it but could not quite put his finger on what it might be.

Michael believed that he had established proper safeguards to
protect his brother yet his foreboding remained as he returned
to James' room. Florence was there with Nurse Callery. To his

astonishment, his sister-in-law was pouring medicine from one smallish bottle into another larger one before affixing a new label. He could not restrain himself:

How dare you change that medicine?! he exploded. *How dare you alter the bottles?!*

It was intolerable to Michael that Florence was once again involving herself in James' care. Muttering something about it being on account of the thick sediment, the small size of the bottle and the difficulty of properly shaking it, Florence put both bottles down. Michael grew caustic. Turning on the nurse, he demanded that she make arrangements for her own replacement. She was dismissed.

As a result, Nurse Wilson – fat and earnest – arrived at Battlecrease around teatime, coinciding with Dr Carter's visit. James, convinced that he was improving and determined that with a little more sleep he would be quite recovered, was sitting up in bed. Carter was not so sure and Dr Humphreys, arriving just behind him, agreed: their patient's pulse was quicker, he was restless and there was a new symptom – his right hand was perfectly white, suggesting the onset of circulatory failure.

Pocketing both the open bottle of Valentine's meat juice and the brandy, Carter agreed to Michael's request to examine them. He said he would come back at midday the following day.

During the early evening James began to weaken. Florence asked frequently whether it was not time for his medicines, apparently desperate to find something to halt his obvious decline. At one point, exhausted, he waved his hands at her as she tried to persuade him to take the medicine prepared by Nurse Wilson, saying, *Don't give me the wrong medicine again.*

Hearing it, the nurse wondered. James' medicines were all in order, so why should he complain about them being muddled?

What are you talking about? Florence soothed. *You have never had the wrong medicine.*

A little later, as James grew increasingly delirious, Wilson heard him say, several times, *Oh Bunny how could you do it? I did not think it of you.*

Was he still worrying about his medicines? Something was upsetting him. Wilson watched Florence by his side attempting to reassure him, soothing his forehead as she said, *You silly old darling, don't bother your head at all.*

The lightness of the young American's tone failed to cover something else. She sounded, thought the nurse, close to despair.

How is the master? How is the master? As darkness fell, the question was asked repeatedly by Alice Yapp, Bessie Brierley, Mary Cadwallader and Mrs Humphreys. It was answered with vague stares and shaken heads.

Michael was under no illusions. He had asked the doctors to warn him if they began to lose hope of recovery and soon after they left on Friday afternoon he summoned James' clerks from Tithebarn Street. Thomas Lowry and George Smith arrived with a bundle of papers. Watching them go into the sickroom with Edwin and Michael, the cook and Mary Cadwallader heard James cry out:

Oh Lord, if I am to die, why am I to be worried like this? Let me die properly!

It looked to the servants as if the brothers were trying to get James to discuss his will. Were they advising him to make last-minute alterations before it was too late?

*

Will you cut me a sandwich and get me a glass of milk? Florence asked the cook flatly as she slumped at the scrubbed kitchen table around nine o'clock.

Everything had been cleared away for the evening. Outside it was dark. In the kitchen it was cool and dim, peaceful and still. Slowly, in silence, as if in a dream, Florence ate. She brooded. Her mouth worked at the bread, her lips circled the edge of the glass, her slim white hand moved mechanically as she fed herself.

It was hard to tell whether, behind that placid exterior, her mind was drained and blank or in tumult.

After a while, when she had finished eating, Florence straightened. Elizabeth Humphreys watched her mistress push back her chair, rise and step out towards the corridor. At the bottom of the back staircase she turned unexpectedly and advanced again, grasping the cook's warm hand: *Thank you, Humphrey* [sic] *for the kindness you have done me,* she said. *Good-bye.*

Leaning forward, she quickly kissed the cook on the cheek.

This time, to the question *How is the master?* she replied, *He is sinking. There is no hope at all.*

*

At three o'clock on the morning of Saturday 11 May, Mrs Humphreys and Bessie Brierley woke to a soft knocking on their bedroom door. In the grainy pre-dawn light, Florence asked Bessie to go and wake Mary Cadwallader. She wanted the two to go to Mrs Briggs's house in Sefton Park. *Tell her*, she said, *that the master is dying.*

Later, Florence met Matilda and Constance at the front door. *It's so sad*, she said.

She was crying. Clasping them both by the arm, she drew them up to the spare room where Michael, sprawled across the sofa, hardly rose to meet them. Pitilessly, he muttered only: *The game is up.*

Swinging round from the south-east to the north-west, wind sent the clouds skidding, forcing the temperature down by ten degrees. A damp chill had settled around the house. Fires were lit. When Dr Richard Humphreys arrived at breakfast-time the house felt airless.

Dr Carter had worked on his tests until midnight on Friday. When he analysed a small quantity of the beef juice using the Reinsch test a steel-grey deposit had appeared on the copper slip, indicating the presence of a metallic irritant. The doctor placed the foil in a test tube and put it in his pocket.

At midday on Saturday, he drove out to Battlecrease. In Dr Humphreys's presence, Michael asked, *Did you find anything in the beef juice?*

It was written all over the doctor's face.

I am extremely sorry to say that I have, Carter replied.

For a moment, no one spoke. Then Dr Carter showed both men the foil, stressing that although it suggested the presence of arsenic his analyses were not conclusive. Advising restraint, he argued that he should perform similar tests on an unopened bottle of beef juice as a comparison and, if the results so indicated, should then give both bottles to the city analyst to re-examine. Carter was satisfied that their efforts to keep James safe had been effective and believed it unlikely that anything noxious had found its way past the nurses – indeed, their discovery of the apparently tainted meat juice seemed to prove it. He did not suggest re-testing James' excreta to make doubly sure; nor did he or Dr Humphreys administer hydro-concentrated oxide of iron – or ferric hydrate – a commonly used antidote in cases where irritant poisoning was suspected.

Agreeing to the plan, Michael nevertheless suggested that Florence should now be banned even from entering her husband's room.

By mid-afternoon James' pulse was weakening and he was delirious. He plucked at the bedclothes, bunching the crisp cotton into limp wrinkles. He had difficulty putting out his tongue and he refused all nourishment. He wet the bed. The doctors suggested applying a solution of cocaine to his anus, followed by nutrient suppositories. The nurse rubbed his hands with nitroglycerine and, when he could manage to swallow, James took dilute brandy, champagne and sub-nitrate of bismuth, a metal resembling arsenic or antimony that was generally prized for its efficacy in countering diarrhoea.

The sickroom was filling up. The two doctors, Michael and Edwin, the nurse, Mrs Briggs and Mrs Hughes waited. Florence, banished, had taken to her bed in the dressing room after scribbling a note in pencil to Dr Hopper. Having once turned to him for marital advice, she wrote of her isolation and begged for his intercession:

I am sure you must have heard of Jim's dangerous illness, she wrote. *No doubt* [you] *feel that I ought to have called you in to see him ... My misery is great and my position is such a painful one ... my brothers-in-law are here and have taken the nursing of Jim and the management of my house completely out of my hands ... you will understand how powerless I am to assert myself ... I am in great need of a friend! ... Michael, whom Jim informed of the unhappiness existing between us last month, now accuses me of being the primary cause of Jim's present critical state ...* [He] *hardly speaks to me. I am neither cheered nor told the worst ... I am utterly broken hearted ... all I want is to die, too.* Attributing Michael's frigid censure to knowledge of her debts, she asked, *because I have sinned once, must I be misjudged always?*

Ask to see me, she begged. *I have not been to bed since Sunday, for although I may not nurse Jim, I will at least be near him to see what is done.*

If Florence hoped with this letter to restore the balance of power at Battlecrease, she had left it too late.

When Dr Carter saw her lying in the dressing room soon after, in what he would later describe as *apparent unconsciousness*, he directed that she be carried to a spare bedroom and that the dressing room should be locked.

At five o'clock in the evening little James and his sister were taken, briefly, to see their father.

Three and a half hours later, fifteen days after falling ill and half way into his fifty-first year, James Maybrick died.

CHAPTER 12

Whipped into a Frenzy

Returning home after James' death, Dr Carter worked late into the night, performing new tests on an unopened bottle of meat juice. He discovered no arsenic. Puzzling, then, over how it had found its way into the opened bottle he examined the contents of that bottle again, trying to see whether he could detect any un-dissolved crystals. Shaking it vigorously, he poured some onto a white plate and carefully searched for particles of the indigo or soot commonly used to colour the poison. He found nothing. Surmising that the arsenic must therefore have originated in a solution derived from a non-powder source, Carter measured the specific gravity of the contents of each bottle and compared them. The results proved his theory: he *found that the specific gravity of that which contained the arsenic was much less than the specimen which contained* none. In other words, the toxic sample was more dilute.

Parcelling up both bottles the doctor delivered them to Edward Davies, the city analyst, at 187 Upper Parliament Street, a broad, wind-raked artery that ran along the western margin of the city and downhill towards the docks. A handful of years earlier Davies had examined the dregs of another suspect bottle and his discovery of a small particle believed to be a fibre from a flypaper had been central to the conviction for murder of Mrs Flanagan. Now he would test the contents of the two meat juice bottles under strict laboratory conditions.

In the flurry following James' death, both Dr Humphreys and Dr Carter overlooked the fact that, apparently, none of the meat extract in the suspect bottle had been given to James, since the nurse had become suspicious immediately following Mrs Maybrick's actions. What now concerned them most was that, if Davies's analyses confirmed their own results, it would suggest that they had missed a trick.

Both agreed that it was currently impossible to sign a death certificate. In due course, if a metallic irritant really was involved then they would be obliged to inform both the police and the county coroner.

*

A. W. Blyth's magisterial compendium, *Poisons, their Effects and Detection* (1884), listed irritant poisons as arsenic, antimony, ergot, digitalis, zinc, mercury, lead, copper, yew and putrid animal substances, and he characterised their several effects on the body as pain, vomiting and purging. Yet Blyth wrote that caution was necessary: arsenic could produce a multitude of different symptoms and its effects could alter according to the form of the poison – solid, vaporous or soluble – along with the state of health of the person affected.

Blyth explained that, in its acute form, arsenic poisoning usually caused death within eight to twenty-four hours. The sub-acute form was far more common and in these cases symptoms might take several hours to appear and death may be postponed for some days. Observable indications included vomiting, a thickly coated tongue, thirst, pain in the abdomen and – usually but not always – diarrhoea. The pulse was likely to be frequent and irregular and, once the poison was absorbed into the bloodstream and thereby into the body's tissue, there was usually muscular weakness, pallor, hollow eyes, perspiration and body odour, cramps in the calves and red, itching eyes. *In certain cases*, wrote Blyth, *there is a curious remission after violent symptoms … the patient rallies and seems to have recovered but the appearance is deceptive for the symptoms recur and death follows.*

Blyth also described slow poisoning resulting from arsenic ingested in small quantities over long periods. These symptoms were more suggestive of general ill health and malaise, including loss of appetite, yellowness of the skin, inflammation of the conjunctive and nasal mucous membranes, sore gums, numbness, convulsions and intermittent fever.

In other words, when it came to arsenic nothing was clear cut. Indeed, British physicians had been arguing not only about its negative effects but also its medical benefits since in 1851 a group of Austrian peasants from Styria were discovered to be consuming up to five grains of arsenic trioxide (well above the presumed fatal dose) several times a week, claiming that it increased their energy and endurance, virility and complexions, that it boosted courage, provided resistance to disease and extended life. Thirty-odd years later Blyth considered there might be some truth in the Styrians' contentions, noting that a little daily arsenic improved the coats of horses and made them plump. Then, in 1885, *Chambers' Journal* published new information about the peasants, explaining that they

> *begin with very small doses and are seized with a nausea and burning pains in the mouth, throat and stomach, and are probably very much more uncomfortable than a boy who has taken his first cigar. But one peculiarity of arsenic-eating is that when a man has once begun to indulge in it, he must continue to indulge; for if he ceases, the arsenic in his system poisons him, or as it is popularly expressed, the last dose kills him. Indeed he must not only continue his*

indulgence, he must also increase the quantity of the drug,
so that it is extremely difficult to stop the habit.

The link between arsenic and vitality was thus suggested, and
its benefits in the pursuit of beauty were discussed widely during
the 1880s. Dilute arsenical solutions were said to clear the complexion, relieving anything from itching to eruptions, dilating the
capillaries to create a 'milk and roses' hue. When John Singer
Sargent scandalised society in 1884 with his painting of Madame
X in a revealing evening gown it was widely rumoured that her
white skin was the result of doses of the toxin. Gradually, the
idea that arsenic was in fact nature's great medicinal secret settled in the public imagination and products like arsenical toilet
soaps and Dr Simms' Arsenic Complexion Wafers appeared, all
of them promising to effect a *beautiful transparency*.

There were few homes devoid of medicines containing arsenic –
Fowler's Solution being the most famous of them all. Despite all
this, the poison had particularly frightening connotations for the
Victorians partly because, as a cheap and copious by-product of
the smelting industry, it seemed to be everywhere – most commonly
in the white-powder form of arsenic trioxide, also known as arsenious acid. Toxic to most plants and all animals with a central
nervous system, arsenic was practically impossible to evade by the
mid-nineteenth century, present in clothes and candles, wallpapers
and lampshades, in confectionery and millinery, fake flowers, concert tickets, toys, beer, cot and boot linings, perambulators and
pants as well as being legitimately available for killing rats, moths
and flies. Copper arsenite was the chief ingredient in the most popular dye of the period – Scheele's Green – which was then used to
colour decorative papers and fabrics. Britannia metal used for
teapots and cutlery often contained arsenic; brass was bronzed
with a thin film of it; 'King's Yellow' and 'Mineral Blue' pigments
were frequently adulterated with arsenious acid, as were several
popular shades of lilac and the ever-fashionable 'French Grey'.

So pervasive was it that, in 1860, the *Lancet* invited its readers to imagine a man living in a cloud of arsenical dust, sitting

in his library on a summer day, his walls coated with arsenic, a suspicious green dust on his books, and arsenical particles floating in the air, filling his air passages, inflaming his eyes, disturbing his digestion and preparing him for dismal and racking pains ... Arsenic haunts us in our walls, in our paper and paints; it fills the air and at times gets into our food ... or adds a fatal charm to our 'Bath Buns' ... Nothing is innocent now in this world ... but colour is no safeguard. For on the table of this unhappy man – arsenic haunted – lies a brown flypaper ... The spectacle of the sacrifice of a hecatomb of flies is particularly attractive to the child standing near; and as the flypaper is pleasantly flavoured with a sweet and bitter essence, child nature will be sorely tempted to suck the said paper ... [which] contains ... amply sufficient to poison a whole family.

Some, like Queen Victoria in the late 1870s, were concerned enough to order suspect wallpapers to be removed from their homes. Newspapers like *The Times* condemned the government for its laissez-faire attitude, suggesting that MPs would rather allow *the slow poisoning of our little ones* than the economic repercussions of trying to eliminate arsenic from a wide range of products. Others remained sceptical: William Morris refused to avoid even the most pernicious pigments, believing the scare to be a *mere folly*. Yet with so much arsenic in the domestic air, it was little wonder that a rest by the seaside could be so beneficial to the middle-class invalid, nor that digestive disorders, redness of eye and odd cramps in the legs resumed as soon as they returned.

Beyond its insidious presence in the home, concern rose throughout the second half of the nineteenth century about the cheap availability of arsenic. The government attempted to regulate. First, in 1851, with an Arsenic Act that required every purchase to be witnessed and then recorded in a ledger and for quantities under ten pounds in weight to be coloured. Then, in 1868, by creating a schedule of poisons limiting the sale of certain chemicals to pharmacies and chemists. The reality, as the newspapers constantly complained, was that arsenic sales often went unrecorded and anyway it could be bought in the form of plenty of household goods sold at the grocer's or hardware store without restriction.

Just as worrying was the fact that there was no requirement to colour large wholesale batches of arsenic, despite the fact that the white powder was easily confused with innocent substances like flour or sugar. Startling stories circulated of real tragedies: of arsenic being confused with the Plaster of Paris used to adulterate peppermint drops; of arsenic being sold as a toothpowder instead of mercury; of babies dying horribly after being dusted with violet powder containing arsenic-contaminated French chalk.

Easily suspended in the kind of puddings and possets beloved of the Victorians – gruel, arrowroot, sago and the like – arsenic, of all poisons, made people most nervous, partly because it gave rise to such various symptoms that they might be confused with other illnesses or merely overlooked. Drawing on this widespread fear, the sinister fictional villains of 1860s sensation fiction – such as Wilkie Collins's Count Fosco in *The Woman in White* (1860) or Lucretia in Edward Bulwer Lytton's *Children of the Night* (1866) – as well as so-called 'wallpaper novels' like *The Green of the Period* (1869) and *Minsterborough* (1876) all suggested that murder could be committed under the veil of accidental domestic poisoning.

In Bulwer Lytton's novel, Lucretia's slow poisoning of Helen was drawn out in descriptions of lassitude and thirst, of consumptive wasting away and an illness that *puzzles the physician by betraying few or none of its ordinary symptoms*. Two decades later, in 1886 – the year of Gladys Maybrick's birth – the first English translation of Flaubert's *Madame Bovary* appeared, scandalising readers with its intoxicating mix of adultery and poison and containing visceral descriptions of Emma's physical anguish after eating arsenic. No one who read this 'dangerous' novel could easily put from their minds the potent descriptions of the sickness that seized her so suddenly *that she had hardly time to draw out her handkerchief from under the pillow ... she felt an icy cold creeping from her feet to her heart ... Her unequal pulse was now almost imperceptible. Drops of sweat oozed from her bluish face, that seemed as if rigid in the exhalations of a metallic vapor. Her teeth chattered, her dilated eyes looked vaguely about her, and to all questions she replied only with a shake of the head.*

Emotive articles, scandalous mistakes, accidents and trials all educated the public in fear and mistrust, deepening society's fear. Then, because upwards of a third of all Victorian criminal poisoning cases involved arsenic, it settled in the general mind as an instrument of violence most suitable for use in private settings, all the more horrible for its resonances of devious intimacy, scrupulous planning and the subversion of the role of the caregiver.

If you feel a deadly sensation within and gradually grow weaker how do you know that you are not poisoned? asked one mid-century newspaper. *If your hands tingle do you not fancy that it is arsenic? How can you be sure that it is not? Your household perhaps is a well-regulated family, your friends and relations all smile kindly upon you, the meal at each period of the day is punctual and looks correct; but how can you possibly tell that there is not arsenic in the curry?*

*

Florence may have suspected her husband of being addicted to arsenic when she tried to discuss his habits with Dr Hopper, Dr Humphreys and Michael. All three had ignored her concerns. An experienced general practitioner, Richard Hopper might, had he considered it closely enough, have accepted the possibility that James' vacillating health and his uncertain temper were due to increased cravings for a poison to which he had become addicted.

Dr Carter was not warned about James' habits. Neither he nor Dr Humphreys – who had been told – considered of their own accord that arsenic might be the cause of his illness. Although James had complained of a painful pricking in his throat, of a furred tongue, thirst, miserably aching limbs and numbness or tingling in his hands and feet, his eyes remained bright and clear and he had no unusual odour, skin eruptions or odd pigmentation. Importantly, his diarrhoea had been relatively mild despite the painful tenesmus that followed it. Until Michael's odd suggestions, both doctors believed that James' symptoms were consistent with those of acute food poisoning or even the onset of cholera. Then, although Carter's tests indicated the presence of arsenic in the meat juice, it was also significant that Dr Humphreys had discovered no arsenic when he performed tests on James' urine.

Around two hours after his death, Edwin, Michael, Matilda and Constance began to unravel. James had complained of being ill endlessly but he had always bounced back. Now the horrible possibility that he might have been poisoned was destabilising. Upstairs, his widow lay apparently unconscious in the spare bedroom. Horrified and excited, it now seemed obvious to them that she was no less than a calculating murderess. Momentarily, the painful tragedy overwhelming them all unbuttoned their restraint and grief, and their active emotions – shock, rage, impotence and confusion – set them all on a fatal trajectory.

Rousing from their initial bewilderment, these four began to reel into an agony of activity. The flurry caught up the staff, spinning young Bessie Brierley, Mary Cadwallader and Alice Yapp in a strange whirligig of orders, instructions and activity. Michael wanted to lock the silver chest to prevent pilfering and he wanted to open the safe. Did he really, suddenly, distrust his brother's servants? Was he looking for another will? Was he merely inquisitive about his brother's private papers or was there something specific that he wanted to find before anyone else became involved?

The problem was that no one knew where to find James' keys.

While James' corpse cooled, Mrs Briggs and her sister began frenetically to search the bedroom chest, dressing table and washstand. Elbows bent, shoulders strained, drawers were pulled open and underwear was pushed aside. Fingers probed past silk stockings, lifted chemises to get into corners and swept aside hairpins to open enamelled boxes. Fists heaved at handles to reveal innocent piles of linen. Wardrobe doors were flung back, hands felt along shelving and feet rose onto tiptoe.

If Edwin looked for the keys in the obvious place – his brother's office – he would have noticed the potions and pillboxes scattered on the windowsill, mantelpiece and desk. Were there also sensitive papers or articles that needed to be removed? Down in the basement, the cook and the maids were wondering what to tidy away and what to discard.

While the Janion sisters rummaged upstairs, Michael deliberated about what else had to be done. Sending for Nurse Yapp, he instructed her to make arrangements to remove the children from the house.

Calling to Bessie for help, Yapp went first to the linen closet to find a case for the children's clothes. It was unlocked and it was dark. Inside was a trunk with the letters F. E. M. painted on its sides. The two girls lifted it out and hefted it into the night nursery. Yapp then whipped upstairs to sort out piles of things to be packed.

The corpulent Nurse Wilson had taken over once more from Nurse Gore when, some time towards midnight, she was with Yapp in the nursery. The nursemaid knelt before the trunk, plucked at its buckles and threw back the lid. In the corner was a rolled-up sheet from which fell a chocolate box and a small parcel. Removing the lid from the box she and Wilson saw that it contained a packet clearly labelled on one side 'Poison' and on the other 'Arsenic for Cats'. The label was torn and the packet was open at one corner. The small parcel was tied in brown paper and it too was partly open, revealing two or three little bottles with their labels scratched off and a balled-up piece of linen – a handkerchief embroidered with Florence's initials. Packing was postponed. Straightening from her position on the floor, Yapp gathered up her latest discoveries and walked briskly downstairs to present them to Michael.

There was enough arsenic in the packet of cat poison to kill them all several times over. Since it was now past midnight, Michael was uncertain how to proceed. Then he decided to call for his next-door neighbour, the young solicitor Douglas Steel, whose advice was to seal up both the parcel and the chocolate box with its contents and to lock them in the wine cellar.

The shadow of suspicion was lengthening.

*

Nurse Yapp's unearthing of the packet of cat poison ensured that feverish concerns had not lessened by Sunday morning. Pulling Gladys and James into their coats, the nursemaid helped them up into the family carriage and waited while the trunk was installed. Michael had forbidden them from saying goodbye to their mother before leaving to stay with their godmother Mrs Janion – mother of Matilda and Constance. As the horses pulled away and the wheels crunched over the gravel, those two women continued to hunt through the house, ostensibly in an effort to find the keys to the safe.

All the while, Michael sat in the parlour, ignoring the clatter overhead, thinking. In the main bedroom, only the wardrobe was locked. Forced open, it yielded nothing of any particular interest. Under the lining paper in a drawer of Florence's dressing table, though, Constance found three letters and a memorandum. She read them and she almost forgot to breathe.

It was not yet ten o'clock when Constance came downstairs to find Michael. Taking possession of this correspondence, he then swept upstairs, demanding that Edwin unlock the door of James' dressing room and that he explore it along with Mrs Briggs. On the floor in one corner there were two boxes, one on top of the other: in the top one was a slouched hat, and underneath it several bottles. In the lower box there was a tall hat, with a glass containing a piece of linen and a small amount of white liquid under it.

Edwin scoured the cupboard and a small fancy table beside it. In the cupboard, steadied by a piece of brass to prevent it from toppling over, he discovered another small bottle, wrapped in a pocket handkerchief. Leaving everything in its original position, he re-locked the dressing-room doors and dropped the key into his pocket.

No one had yet found the keys to the safe.

Pushing open the door of the spare room, entering it, Edwin approached the bed, ignoring the nurse. Bending over his brother's wife, he gripped the tops of Florence's arms and shook her gently, telling her that James was dead and asking her over and over again to tell him where his keys could be found. Momentarily, Florence's eyes opened and met his. Again he asked. She said nothing. Her eyes closed again and her shoulders became heavy as she fell, to all appearances, back into a stupor.

CHAPTER 13

Scrutiny

To the items found in the trunk by Alice Yapp, Michael added the bottles, glass tumbler and cloth discovered in the dressing room that morning. The fervid search of Battlecrease had turned up plenty of poison, providing a means to kill, and he believed that Florence's letters proved the existence of motive. Yet, as his fevered state began to cool, Michael also began to take stock of the consequences of their recent excitement. By casting suspicion on Florence during James' illness he had perhaps believed that they had found an opportunity to be rid of his brother's irritatingly spendthrift young wife, a way to make her return to her mother in Paris or to America. Baroness von Roques was certainly of this opinion: years later she claimed that *the Maybrick brothers ... gave the bottle to Dr Carter simply to get her out of the house and get rid of her. Michael told me if I would call her mad and have her locked up they would drop the case.* The spiral of events, though, ensured that family hostility towards Florence and her family was no longer simply the issue, and Michael was no longer the one in control.

It may never have crossed his mind during that final week that

James was going to die. He had been in apparently robust health when he visited London just a few weeks earlier. Michael's shock at seeing him so unwell – compounded by the intercepted letter – had perhaps led him to react without thinking. Now there was time to consider the consequences of his failure to behave in a more measured fashion and he realised that the police might soon be involved. If so, the newspapers would begin to dig around in the Maybricks' affairs, threatening to expose indiscretions and secrets best kept concealed. Michael realised now that the family's reputation was at stake.

He knew then that he must try to convince Dr Carter to issue a death certificate. Having raised concerns in the first place, and given the doctor several bottles to test, he accepted that it was impossible to erase the brusque conversations of the past three days but he hoped to get the doctor to see things from the family's point of view and so he visited Carter, importuning the doctor to consider their dreadful position, insisting that he help them to escape the difficulties they now faced. With his brother Thomas at his side, Michael pleaded on behalf of the children and their future welfare, for the sake of Florence – *the unhappy woman* as he called her – and the good name of the family, articulating his dread of the odious possibility of scandal.

Carter shook his head. Awkward and trying as all of this was, there really were only two things to be done: to wait for the analyses of Edward Davies and, if necessary, to refer the matter to the authorities.

Unused to being gainsaid, Michael continued to bully and to cajole by turns but he failed to divert the physician from his course. Carter simply promised to communicate with him the very moment he heard the results of the laboratory tests.

*

Returning to Battlecrease in a fury, Michael marched into the spare room where – ignoring Florence – he addressed Nurse Wilson:

Mrs Maybrick is no longer mistress of this house. As one of the executors I forbid you to allow her to leave this room.

Later, Florence – in something of a daze – asked to see her children and was coldly informed that they were no longer in the house. Shocked, she said nothing. Adrift on a sea of suspicion, confined to the spare room, she was denied access to her belongings, her family or her staff. Visitors were turned away and Michael's intransigence set the tone for all those around her, turning the already rigid nurse into a guard apparently fashioned from steel.

Just one caller made it past the front door. Responding to the letter she had sent him on Saturday morning, Dr Hopper insisted on attending to Florence on Sunday afternoon. He would later record that she was suffering from *a sanguineous discharge which might have been a threatened miscarriage* and that she told him that she had not had her monthly period since 7 March. If his suspicion was right, if she was pregnant, it may have explained her lassitude and her extreme exhaustion that seemed to go beyond mere grief.

Dr Hopper did not positively establish whether Florence was pregnant or miscarrying and he mentioned nothing about it to the nurse or to the rest of the family. Had he done, would Michael have been baffled? Did he know that his brother and his wife had not slept together for months, or would he have believed that Florence was carrying his dead brother's child?

Michael was ignorant of Dr Hopper's surmises and his certainty that Florence, like so many villainesses of popular fiction, was corrupt and subversive continued to grow. Rather than pity her, he believed that her mask had fallen – that there was no longer anything about her worth saving.

*

Later that afternoon the city analyst reported to Carter that he had completed both Reinsch and Marsh tests on the Valentine's meat juice taken from James' bedroom. In his estimation the bottle had contained around a grain of arsenic. Since it was now half-empty, Davies made the assumption – which no one thought to contradict – that James Maybrick had swallowed around half a grain of the poison.

Davies believed that between two and three grains of arsenic constituted a fatal dose, while other experts thought it nearer five. Beyond this, the fact that arsenic had been detected meant that the young Garston doctor, Richard Humphreys, was obliged by law to inform the authorities.

James had been dead for little more than twenty-four hours when, around nine o'clock on Sunday evening, Richard Baxendale – local Inspector of Police – arrived at Battlecrease. Five feet eight inches tall, heavy-set and with a swarthy complexion, hazel eyes and thick brown hair, Baxendale had been a farm labourer before joining the force at twenty-three and was now, a quarter of a century later, a seasoned officer. There was plenty of crime in Liverpool and its outlying districts and much of it was domestic, yet it was rare to be called to a grand house following a death: violence, in his experience, rarely brushed against the fringes of a middle-class household. Baxendale appreciated that he would need to tread carefully.

Once Michael had given him an outline of recent events, Edwin took the Inspector upstairs to see the body. Drawing the key from his pocket, he unlocked the door to the dressing room and pointed out the two boxes on the floor, the bottle and handkerchief propped up in the far end of the cupboard and another bottle in the chest of drawers, nestling under some articles of clothing. The policeman made note of the fact that a small box concealed inside one of the bandboxes contained five small bottles – all corked – and a glass with some white liquid and a rag. Gathering them all up, he decided to take them home for safekeeping.

The next day Inspector Baxendale returned with Isaac Bryning, Superintendent of the Police for the county of West Derby, a stout, six-foot-tall, fifty-three-year-old man with a balding head, grey whiskers, sharp eyes and a reputation for *energy and intelligence in detection, coupled with sound good character*. Once a factory weaver, Isaac Bryning ran a tight ship; he was an adept detective and he knew Aigburth intimately, having policed the suburb for the previous twenty years.

Battlecrease began to resound with the loud tramp of boots and the banging of doors behind retreating backs. A police enquiry had begun, turning the Maybrick home inside out. Official tendrils were unfurling, corners were probed, invasive questions were asked and looks were direct and unshifting. Fulfilling Michael's worst fears, everyone and everything was coming under uncomfortable, unavoidable observation.

Visitors continued to be turned away while ordinary household items were shuffled about. More things were given to the police: bottles collected by Mrs Briggs; the letters found in Florence's dressing table and the one that Nurse Yapp had been asked to post; the packet of cat poison and the other items from the trunk that had been sealed and locked in the wine cellar. The staff remained downstairs and each was interrogated. Medicines and tonics were amassed from side tables, from ledges in the lavatories, from James' office, from the bedrooms and the dressing room. Each item was numbered and listed by the police before being taken away.

Superintendent Bryning asked Dr Humphreys to take certain samples and supervised the doctor's collection of water from the upstairs-landing lavatory, the S-bend in the same room's sink and the pipes in the housemaids' closet. Outside, the two men lifted the drain cover in order to extract some sediment and liquid. All these were placed into separate jars before being sealed, labelled and delivered to the city analyst.

Arrangements were made to take a statement from Nurse Yapp, who was still away with the children. The police questioned Drs Carter and Humphreys and the nurses Wilson, Gore and Callery. They pieced together a chronology of events, noting the various times of professional visits, the altering symptoms of the dead man and the medicines and treatments prescribed. They visited the two chemists within walking distance – Wokes and Hanson on Aigburth Road – and carefully examined the records and accounts of each shop. Then they wired for information to be sent to them from Flatman's Hotel in London.

*

The county coroner, informed of the suspicions surrounding James Maybrick's death, had immediately ordered a post-mortem and the grisly business had to be addressed. At half-past four on the afternoon of Monday 13 May Humphreys and Carter were joined at Battlecrease by a third doctor. Alexander Barron, Professor of Pathology at University College Liverpool, lived, coincidentally, in the same building as Edwin at No. 31 Rodney Street, though the two men were apparently unacquainted. Invited by Dr Humphreys, Barron would assist in the dissection and observation of James Maybrick's internal organs; the two doctors would dictate their findings to Dr Carter, who agreed to involve himself actively only if his opinion was required on a debated point.

Not unusually for the time, they used James' bedroom for the autopsy. Superintendent Bryning and Inspector Baxendale stood silently to one side, watching intently and listening to what the medical men had to say. Oblivious to the murmur of their voices, to the wielding of the scalpel or to the saws that would expose her late husband's brain, Florence continued to lie insensible in the room next door.

Forty-four hours after death, rigor mortis was well advanced; lividity over the lower limbs and the back of the groin confirmed the reported time of death. James' body was fairly nourished, its features were calm and, raising the eyelids, the doctors noted that the pupils were equal and not dilated. Slight decomposition about the abdomen had commenced. A blood-stained discharge from the anus marked the sheet on which the body lay and, when they turned it over, a great effusion of dark liquid flowed from the corpse's mouth.

Making a longitudinal incision down the chest, drawing back the abdominal walls, the doctors exposed the bowels, stomach and intestines, removing and bottling the dark-brownish stomach contents. If James Maybrick had been poisoned, they might expect to find most damage in his digestive tract, so they looked closely for the glistening of arsenic crystals adhering to the stomach walls. What they saw was *moderately diffuse . . . red blotches* and some intensely infected *vermillion red* patches around the stomach, though its middle portion was free from discolouration. Here and there they also noted a number of small brilliantly red dots known as petechiae. Close inspection of the bowel and rectum revealed a *rose blush* in some portions, indicative of infection.

The dead man's lungs were healthy though one contained some blood-stained fluid. The heart appeared normal but for a small clot in the right ventricle. The liver, kidneys, spleen and brain showed no obvious abnormalities; however, the gall bladder appeared *much enlarged*. When James' tongue was removed they saw that its mucous membrane was blackish. The source of the pricking sensation about which he had continually complained seemed to be a minute ulcer on his epiglottis, about the size of a pinhead. His oesophagus was, in its lower portions, unnaturally olive-brown in colour, dotted with several livid spots and swollen; its mucous membrane was notably gelatinous, with an unnatural texture resembling frogspawn.

Once they had been inspected and described for the report, his organs and viscera were returned to his body though portions of each had been collected and placed into stone or glass jars which were then covered with muslin and sealed. A small two-ounce bottle was used to contain some bile from the gall bladder. These, plus a sample of the liquid that came from his mouth and the fluid contents of his stomach, were given to Inspector Baxendale.

Along with all the other items already taken from the house, they meant that Edward Davies was going to be very busy indeed.

By the time the doctors were ready to lay down their instruments and remove their aprons, all three were agreed on the cause of death: an irritant poison, which had set up considerable congestion and inflammation of the stomach and intestines. Exactly what that poison was, though, was unclear – for while there were evident, pathological changes to James Maybrick's intestines and while his tongue was inflamed and thickened, several other symptoms indicative of arsenic poisoning were not present: there were no crystalline particles adhering to the stomach wall, no inflammation of the heart or lungs and no shrinking of the bladder. Arsenic was known to have a corrosive effect, raising blisters and inflaming skin and membrane, yet the petechiae that might be expected to be evident throughout the intestines were only present in a handful of places and these could simply have indicated an infection occasioned by bad food.

Poisons expert A. W. Blyth wrote that it was possible for there to be no changes to the stomach or intestines in cases of arsenic poisoning, though it was rare. The different effects in the dead body, he wrote, like the symptoms it produced in life, could be *widely divergent*. It was accepted, too, that the poison was eliminated from the body relatively quickly, through the purging action of vomiting and diarrhoea and also in urine, bile and sweat. The fact that James' urine was free of any trace of arsenic was an indication that his illness was food-related but, unable to reach an absolute conclusion about the exact cause of death, the three post-mortem doctors agreed that it was now going to be a question of chemistry rather than pathology.

*

By the time Inspector Baxendale began delivering samples to analyst Edward Davies the following day, Michael Maybrick had given the Inspector Dr Fuller's London prescriptions. During the remainder of the week Baxendale would concentrate his attention on the office at Tithebarn Street, removing bottles from the mantelpiece and from locked drawers, the jug used to carry lunch into work and the pan in which it was warmed. Dozens of products ranging from the innocuous to the clearly dangerous were boxed up for testing: half-empty spirit bottles, preparations from Clay & Abraham chemists, spirits of sal volatile and a small bottle of pills labelled 'Poison'; there were tincture of podophyllin, belladonna, and phosphori pills, four packets of borax and several bottles of scent.

At Battlecrease, Baxendale's younger colleague Sergeant James Davenport – a striking, red-faced figure with well-oiled black hair and a bushy black beard – poked about in cupboards. In the linen closet he turned up a bottle of light liquid with no label, also a dressing case belonging to Florence that contained a small quantity of white powder and six white pills. From her dressing table he took lotions, laudanum and boxes of unlabelled crystals and from the pantry he carried off a bottle of vanilla essence. The sitting room, the spare room and the lavatory were picked over, revealing morphia bottles, more stained handkerchiefs, quinine pills, nux vomica solutions, Price's glycerine, corn plasters, pill boxes, soda mint tablets, toothpastes and several empty bottles smeared with sediment.

In total, close to 120 items derived from almost thirty different chemists were collected from unconcealed spaces in the house. Florence's dressing gown and the nightshirts worn by James during his final illness were added to the mounting pile until the list ran to over eight carefully handwritten pages.

Every bottle, box, packet and stain would be tested, painstakingly, for poison.

*

On Tuesday 14 May, as the police got on with their investigation, an inquest into the death of James Maybrick opened at the Aigburth Hotel, a public house just a short walk from Riversdale Road.

An inquest's function, unaltered for centuries, was to enquire into the truth of an unusual or unexplained death, to establish its cause and to consider whether evidence existed to suggest the commission of a crime. Along with the coroner, there was a jury, made up of between twelve and twenty-four local men. That day Samuel Brighouse, the coroner for south-west Lancashire, swore in fourteen, establishing Mr Fletcher Rogers, a cotton broker and director of the Queen Insurance Company, as their foreman. Michael was the only witness and he was asked simply to identify his brother's body and to confirm James' address, profession and time of death. Despite the fact that it had not been so proved by the post-mortem, Brighouse instructed the jury that enough poison had been found in the body of the dead man to justify a more detailed examination. Then he adjourned proceedings for a fortnight.

Quitting the hotel, Superintendent Isaac Bryning made for Battlecrease House.

Taking the stairs at a measured pace, the police officer reached the first-floor landing. Florence was still confined to her bed. Entering her room without ceremony, Bryning's eyes did not leave her face as he introduced himself and then suggested that she pay attention because *I am about to say something to you and after I have said it, if you reply, be careful how you do reply, because what you say may be given in evidence against you.*

He paused, watching her for a flash of alarm that might give her away. She seemed to have no sense of the portentous hazard of her position.

Then he continued: *Mrs Maybrick, you are in custody on suspicion of having caused the death of your late husband on 11th May.*

The Superintendent retreated, giving orders for a constable to sit in a chair just outside the bedroom and for the door to remain open. Florence was not allowed to leave the room. She was now under arrest.

CHAPTER 14

Locked In

When the first report of James Maybrick's death appeared in the newspapers on Tuesday morning there were already hints that things were not straightforward. *Up to a very recent period,* wrote the *Liverpool Mercury, the deceased had been in the enjoyment of very good health and the fatal result of his short illness has excited universal surprise ... We understand that a coroner's inquest is likely to be held with a view of inquiring more particularly into the matter.*

Michael asked Douglas Steel to represent the interests of the family and Steel advised that Florence needed to be given independent counsel by another firm. Dr Humphreys was therefore asked to call on Messrs Cleaver, Holden, Garnet and Cleaver in Liverpool, which he did at around midday on Tuesday, leaving instructions that someone should go down to Battlecrease House in Aigburth where a lady was being held on a serious charge. The younger of the Cleaver partners, Arnold, duly set off but was utterly baffled to find himself being turned away from the house: without the relevant authority from Superintendent Bryning, Michael would let no one in. Seeking clarification, Arnold Cleaver went on to Dr Humphreys's house where he learned about the suspicious circumstances surrounding James' death, the intercepted letter and the existence of poison in the meat juice. He was also given a draft copy of the post-mortem notes along with the doctors' conclusion that the appearance of the dead man's viscera suggested the possibility of arsenical poisoning.

Realising that a grave investigation was under way, Cleaver set about obtaining the necessary permission to enter Battlecrease. He also met with Douglas Steel, who informed him of the contents of Florence's letter to Brierley.

Matilda Briggs had not left the house since James' death. Once Superintendent Bryning had gone, she went up to visit Florence for the first time. Matter-of-factly, she said that arsenic had been found.

What shall I do? asked Florence.

She had, she explained, already cabled her New York solicitor and her mother in Paris, but as a result, she had no money left.

Have you no one you can turn to? What about Brierley?

Florence caught the older woman's eye but not the edge in her voice or her too-slight smile. Instead, she took Matilda's words at face value, and began:

> *I am writing to you to give me every assistance. I am in custody and without any of my family with me . . . and without money. I have cabled for my solicitor in New York to come to me at once but in the meanwhile send some money for present needs. The truth is known about my visit to London and your last letter is at present in the hands of the police. Appearances are terribly against me but before God I sware [sic] I am innocent.*

Folding the page, placing it in an envelope and turning, she held it out, asking Matilda to post it on her behalf.

Mrs Briggs was staggered. Had this girl no moral compass?

Matilda knew that the note represented a vital connection with the world outside Battlecrease but she could find no compassion for a woman she believed to be a murderess – let alone one stupid enough to allow herself to compound her guilt. Wordlessly she turned away, gliding back out of the room with a whisper of stiff crape, handing the note directly to the policeman at the door. Florence watched. Initially puzzled, it began to dawn on her that her letter would never reach Brierley.

Was she tormented to discover that her trust had been misplaced, that Matilda's concern was a pretence and that there was no tenderness in their friendship? Did her heart miss a beat at the older woman's falsity? Did she now finally realise that she must face what was coming alone?

*

Matilda Briggs left Florence to her fate and packed her bag. In the four days she had been away from Livingston Avenue the trees had almost doubled their lush intensity, the recent rains encouraging everything green into massy luxuriance. After the constricting tension suffusing Battlecrease – where the windows were closed and the curtains were drawn, where the smell of death hung in the air and policemen stood at the gates – to be back on the edge of Sefton Park would be a relief.

In Liverpool, Edward Davies was working through hundreds of bottles and had not yet completed tests on James' viscera or on the water or soil samples taken from the closet and drains. Elsewhere things were moving more quickly.

Recognising the whiff of possible scandal in the suburbs, on Wednesday morning the *Liverpool Courier* announced the ALLEGED POISONING OF A LIVERPOOL MERCHANT. Detailing the *suddenness* of James' death and the *surprise* it caused, it reported that the *grief of the deceased gentleman's friends was intensified by the widely circulated belief that his death was accompanied by suspicious circumstances*.

Tongues had been wagging. The post-mortem results had not been made public yet the *Courier* wrote that the *external symptoms of the presence of poison – either strychnine or arsenic –* had been discovered *and that there is no evidence to show that it was taken accidentally.* The paper tasted drama. *Some extraordinary allegations*, it continued, *are afloat as to the deceased gentleman's death*. It promised to be a story that would cause the kind of commotion for which the public had a ferocious appetite.

While the rest of the world turned about her, Florence remained in the spare room, where solicitor Arnold Cleaver was finally allowed to visit her once he had received the proper authority. She was in bed. The nurse and a policeman hovered, forcing the two to murmur, to keep their voices as low as possible as their heads practically touched and she told her side of the story. Warned that written statements would have to be given up to the police for examination, Arnold chose to take no notes.

*

She must have heard movement in the room next door and knocking as the coffin was closed but, until she was told at eleven-thirty on Thursday morning, Florence had no idea that the family were preparing to leave for James' funeral within half an hour.

When she demanded to see his body, she was told that the oak coffin was already sealed and that she might only kneel beside it momentarily. Back in the bedroom, she stood in the recess of the window and watched the cortège depart: the hearse containing the brass-handled casket now covered in beautiful wreaths; nine carriages, each with its blinds drawn. It would take an hour for the sedate procession to arrive at Anfield cemetery, where acre upon acre of mournful headstones were grouped in lines that stretched to the near horizon. She would not be present at the service conducted by the Maybricks' vicar, the Reverend Fred Barker from St Mary's Cressington, alongside the Reverend Dr Hyde, an old friend of James' from the city.

Nor would she be part of the large group of black-clad relatives, business acquaintances, office staff, neighbours and friends watching James Maybrick's body being interred in the same grave as his parents.

*

By the time Florence's mother received a telegram announcing James' death, the funeral was over. She was told none of the circumstances and so, as she hastened to catch a train that would carry her from Paris to London and thence to Liverpool, she fired off telegrams to Michael and Mrs Briggs, asking them to look after her daughter. Presuming that Florence would be prostrate with grief and in need of a physician, she sent a third cable to Dr Hopper.

The following day – Friday – as reports of the 'mystery' began to seep into the New York press, Michael encountered the florid Baroness von Roques by chance as she arrived at Lime Street terminus. He greeted her gruffly: *Well, this is a nice state of affairs!*

What do you mean?

I mean a question of murder, and there's a man in it.

Tired, now shocked, the Baroness asked Michael to tell her what was going on.

You'd better go up to the house, he said. *She is in a dying condition. Edwin will tell you everything.*

Michael left the Baroness to deal with her own luggage and to make her own way to Battlecrease where Edwin met her in the hall. It took only a short while for him to tell her the worst. It struck her as extraordinary that her daughter was confined without a single friend. Pressing Edwin, discovering that James had been dead for almost a week, she wondered why no one had called on her earlier.

We all lost our heads, Edwin admitted. *Florrie was too ill to know and Mrs Briggs did not know, or had forgotten your address.*

She looked hard at him.

I would never have believed one word against Florrie, he continued, *if it had not been for that letter to Brierley.*

Had they all gone mad, the Baroness wondered. How was it
possible for everyone to have turned so violently against an innocent? Amazed by Edwin's story of flypapers and arsenic, she
demanded whether he thought it plausible for a man addicted to
arsenic to be surreptitiously poisoned by it. Enraged, leaving the
youngest Maybrick brother mute at the foot of the stairs, she
then bustled breathlessly up to find her girl.

Incredulity turned to alarm at the sight of the constable sta-
tioned in the upstairs hallway and the nurse and policeman in the
bedroom as they had been since Florence's arrest. Rushing forward, the Baroness had hardly opened her mouth before these
two each conspicuously snatched up notebooks and pencils.
Speaking in French, the mother asked of her daughter why she
was under suspicion, why so displaced?

The policeman stood. Curtly, he ordered this large woman to
speak in English or not to speak at all.

Von Roques felt she had tumbled into a looking-glass world in
which junior policemen and uppity nurses held sway over their
betters, in which nursemaids turned treacherous informants
on their mistresses, in which brothers turned against wives. She
had never encountered such hostility. Meanwhile, her daughter
seemed unable or unwilling to put up any fight.

To her critics, Florence's lassitude suggested that she simply
knew that the game was up. The sharp-minded Baroness, though,
quickly considered the facts. It seemed obvious to her that her
daughter would have had plenty of time to destroy any evidence
in the form either of poisons or letters that might tell against
her once it became clear that Michael was suspicious and that
James might die. If she had been guilty of planning murder –
the very thought was absurd – then Florence could not have
behaved with more passive stupidity. As she assessed the situation, von Roques began also to believe that it was apparent that

the amount of poison discovered in the house only told in her daughter's favour.

Things were, though, about to get worse. With the arrival of her mother at Battlecrease, the gravity of it all began to sink in and Florence became, for the first time, hysterical. Unhinged by grief and fear, her self-control evaporated. Manners were forgotten. Trying to fight her way into her mother's arms, she was pushed back onto her bed and held there forcibly by the nurse and policeman. Forbidden from approaching her daughter, the Baroness watched, horrified and powerless, before storming out of the room, muttering loudly *better death than such dishonour!*

First thing the next morning, the Baroness hurried into Liverpool to consult with the Cleavers. James had been dead for seven days, during which the air had warmed with the sweet promise of early summer. But if the weather was balmy, judicial minds were sharpening. Her parting words as she left her daughter's room on the previous evening led the police to speculate that the Baroness meant to find a way to help her daughter commit suicide. It was time, they believed, to remove the arrested woman from the house.

As a result Richard Cleaver, the elder of the two solicitor brothers, received a telegram at noon advising him that a magistrate and his clerk intended to meet at Battlecrease at two o'clock, and that his presence was required.

*

The group of black-coated men convened on the cushiony lawn outside the house and were soon involved in urgent negotiations. Heavy drops of rain began to fall. There was a scuttle to the porch, the front door was thrown open, low voices echoed as they filled the hall. Moving almost as one, the small crowd took the stairs and entered the room in which Florence was being held. Among them were the magistrate Colonel Bidwell, his clerk Mr Swift, Superintendent Bryning, both Richard and Arnold Cleaver, and two faces more familiar to Florence: local doctor

Richard Humphreys and her own physician, Dr Richard Hopper. Extraordinarily, Bidwell had agreed to allow a journalist to be present, representing the interests of the city's three main papers. Semi-alert, Florence watched the eight men enter. Shivering despite the closeness of the room, she must have realised that something significant was about to happen.

Minutes earlier Humphreys and Hopper had taken her pulse, noting that she drifted in and out of full consciousness and agreeing that although she was too unwell to attend the inquest she was fit enough to hear the charge against her. In effect, then, the doctors had allowed a police court to be convened in her bedroom. Additionally, during the discussions outside, Richard Cleaver had already consented to the suggestion that Florence should be remanded without any evidence being heard, in order to minimise the strain on her mind.

Without more delay, standing at the foot of her bed where she could look directly into his face, Police Superintendent Isaac Bryning formally charged Florence with murder and asked the magistrate for a remand of eight days. Trained to watch carefully for reactions at such moments, he waited. Her face as white as the bed sheets, her eyes widened fleetingly but she remained impassive.

If Florence was struggling to contain shock, fear or relief then the battle did not play itself out across her features. Asked nothing, she did not speak. If in the speed of his words she was grasping at meaning and failing to understand, she did not ask for clarification. Instead, the men filed out of the room and the nurse ordered her, icily, to rise and dress.

It all happened so fast. There was no chance to take stock of the impending calamity or to collect any of her possessions before she was being carried downstairs in a chair by two burly police officers. Someone wrapped her in a coat that did not belong to her. Then she was installed in a carriage that set off swiftly, turning hard left at the gate and left again where Riversdale met

Aigburth Road. Here the horses were whipped to a canter as they headed towards Kirkdale Gaol, the old county prison.

Baroness von Roques had been with Richard Cleaver in town when the cable came summoning him to Battlecrease. Hurrying back with the solicitor, she made for her daughter's room but was forbidden from entering and so, instead, went up to her top-floor room to rest. Soon after, hearing a commotion, she made to go back down but found that her door would not open. Trying the handle again, she realised with growing astonishment that it had been locked from the outside. Surprise modulated to outrage but, impotent, she could do no more than cross to the window and watch uselessly as, below her, a figure was bundled out of the house and driven away. She dreaded what this might mean. For a few minutes after the carriage had disappeared a straggle of men remained, some deep in conversation, others staring at the ground as they waited for the appropriate moment to take their leave.

Shortly after, the Baroness shook her bedroom door hard. It was soon unlocked by a red-haired policeman she had not seen before – a man who mumbled something incomprehensible in reply to her demand to be told on whose orders her door had been secured. Whether it was the magistrate, Baxendale or Michael, she would never discover.

*

Whirled towards Kirkdale, Florence was confused and uncomfortable. When the carriage stopped, she heard officers explain to her guards that a mistake had been made. The prison contained no accommodation for female prisoners. Instead, they were instructed to take her to Walton, a huge modern gaol on the outskirts of town.

It was therefore almost two long hours after leaving Battlecrease that her strange journey ended. Directed through a wicket gate cut into a gloomy, red brick façade that rose to a pair of

Norman-style turrets, she was met in the yard by the governor, Mr Anderson, before being led away by a female warder. Ahead was the main bulk of the prison with its lines of barred windows. It was cold. A succession of iron gates were unlocked and secured again behind them. A long, dark passage led into a shabby reception room with benches along either side, a bare table in the middle and a weighing machine and height measure beside it. Her watch, two diamond rings and a brooch were removed and handed to a warder, who listed them in a ledger. Accused and degraded, she was weighed and then taken to a cell reserved for sick prisoners. Closing the heavy door and opening the peephole flap, the wardress watched as Florence sank down to the stone floor, the key sounding solidly in the door behind her.

CHAPTER 15

Scandal

As the police continued to look for the truth, Inspector Baxendale collected still more bottles from the house and James' office. He re-interviewed the staff, the family and the doctors and sought out witnesses whose testimonies would be useful for the inquest when it reconvened.

Florence was beginning her second day in prison when, on Monday 20 May, Baxendale called again on the two Aigburth Road chemists, Thomas Wokes at No. 25 and Christopher Hanson further south at No. 4. Having gone back over the facts, he purchased a dozen flypapers from each and, retaining three from each packet, sent the remainder for analysis. Two days later, a small parcel came from Flatman's Hotel in London containing the letters and telegrams they had received from Liverpool earlier in the spring.

Michael gave notice to all the staff to quit Battlecrease and arranged for Florence's things to be removed. Despite the terms of James' will he instructed that the furniture and effects be sold in order to wind up the estate. The bedroom things so lovingly shipped from Virginia, the pictures and vases, the piano, the rugs, chests, silver and dining-room furniture – the props of the Maybricks' married life – would all be taken away and catalogued before going under the hammer.

The story hit the national papers at the start of the new week. Announcing the SUDDEN DEATH OF A LIVERPOOL MERCHANT, the *Daily News* repeated the rumours that had been flying around the city, reporting the dramatic meeting of the magistrate and the police at Battlecrease House. Mrs Maybrick had been arrested and imprisoned: *the unhappy lady*, it wrote, *was extremely pale and haggard, but exhibited no emotion.* Everyone expected that she would attend a magistrates court hearing within the week and, as journalists scrambled to get at the history of the case, she was variously misreported as being *a French Canadian of aristocratic birth … the daughter of a baron … the niece of Mr Jefferson Davis, late President of the Southern Confederacy.* Her nationality and the musical fame of Michael Maybrick made the scrap of a story interesting, but what promised to transform it into something really startling were the mention of poison, the fact of the twenty-four-year age gap between the attractive American and her broker husband and, particularly, the news that *a third party has been frequently mentioned in connection with Mr Maybrick's mysterious death.* Suggestive of a scandal still to be fully revealed, this half-fact pricked at the prurient imaginations of newspaper readers, leaving them eager for more.

Realising that things might start to become really unpleasant, Alfred Brierley kept his head down. He was hardly seen at the Exchange, made no enquiry about Florence's welfare or any effort to communicate with her and began to destroy his copies of their correspondence.

*

As the summary facts of the story filtered from the national to the regional newspapers – making it into every small town's gossip – the telegraph, running hot, channelled the news further afield, to

America and to Europe, promising a mystery sure to boost circulations. Newspaper sales had grown exponentially throughout the mid-nineteenth century, driven by new steam technology, a fall in the price of paper, the abolition of the newspaper tax in the mid-1850s and the railway's ability to distribute further and faster than ever before. During the 'Sensational Sixties' middle-class broadsheet newspaper circulations had risen to a combined total of almost half a million copies a week while the penny press – including weeklies like *Lloyd's* and *Reynolds's* – sold several million between them. By the late 1880s, the *Daily Telegraph*'s circulation had reached three hundred thousand a day and *Lloyd's* would soon be the first to sell a million copies of a single issue. In other words, by 1889 the papers were practised in the truth that real-life drama spelled profit and they were expert at stoking the flames of public outrage by printing the gory details of brutal or salacious crime. Police reports, because they could be so graphic, were located towards the back of each edition and considered by many to be a form of pornography, yet the explicit reports of the Whitechapel murders during 1888 had proved that the public's appetite for scandal, horror and outrage was robust and even rapacious.

The Maybrick story promised to peel back the respectable skin of a typically middle-class family to reveal a thrillingly rotten core. If Michael had worried about publicity, it is unlikely that he anticipated the scope of public reaction to his brother's death. Thick with words like *mysterious*, *deathly* and *fast secrecy*, these early reports threatened the most fearful exposure of the lives of everyone involved, however small their role. Taking a loathsome delight in ignominy, the English newspapers, as Oscar Wilde's Mrs Cheveley knew, would delight in *dragging* [them] *down*. *Think* – Mrs Cheveley said – *of the hypocrite with his greasy smile penning his leading article, and arranging the foulness of the public placard*. Ironically, decency had become the Achilles heel of the middle classes: as she so clearly appreciated, *You have a splendid position, but it is that splendid position that makes you so vulnerable.*

Flinching at moral failure yet titillated by crime, the reactions of the late Victorians to stories like the one emerging from Liverpool was complex. Shuddering with indignation, they were also entertained and delighted, not least because the deviancy of others confirmed their own successful negotiation of the narrow path of virtue. Pretty little Mrs Maybrick, then, might well be offered up as a sacrifice to the gods of domestic conformity and the public would rush to watch.

For a start, there were far fewer female criminals than their male counterparts: excluding prostitutes and vagrants, they made up only around a fifth of the general convict population. Further, female murderers were so unusual that they unleashed an almost obsessive public curiosity and excitement. Added to all of this, middle-class ladies were rarely charged with crime, possibly because when it occurred in the domestic sphere efforts were made to hide or suppress it in order to uphold the myth that women could be relied upon as sources of stability in a fast-changing world.

The Maybrick story hinted uncomfortably at the possibility of subversion lurking beneath the varnished surface of conformity. It insinuated that mute struggle, as much as grand rebellious gesture, could result in violence and death. The truth was that society was likely to do everything possible to protect itself. If it turned out that Florence Maybrick was not naturally passive and innately good – the kind of woman at whom manners books and didactic fiction were aimed – then she would be characterised as degenerate, predatory and vicious. At best, she had offended against her social role. At worst, she was a threat to middle-class complacency, because she proved those ideals to be dangerously fragile.

Florence would be judged, then, not simply under the law but against complex ideals of womanhood, and the fact that poison was involved increased even more the likelihood of an extreme social reaction. Grabbing hold of sketchy suspicions – specifically the coroner's incorrect statement at the opening of the inquest that arsenic had been found in the dead man's body – news reporters knew that this poison was already equated in the public mind with the idea of stealthy female evil. Coming so few years after the Flanagan and Higgins case, Liverpool journalists were especially alive to the fact that these hints would throw the city into a hiatus.

The stance they chose to take was likely to make all the difference to the outcome of the case. Two years earlier, H. R. Fox Bourne ended his *History of English Newspapers* with the observation that journalism had assumed the right and power to control and reform the world. Editorial positions, he argued, were powerfully influential. In effect, Bourne believed that, as opinion-formers, newspapers had taken over from the pulpit.

In this inflamed atmosphere, rumour and speculation blossomed. It was said by some that a Lancashire gentleman had been arrested in Liverpool; others gossiped that a local merchant was involved in the case. The *Daily News* proffered that Mrs Maybrick was perfectly ignorant of the charge against her and that her defence solicitors were *in possession of exceedingly important statements tending to elucidate points which now seem obscure.* Dramatic reports began to make it into the English papers from the American press too. From Galveston to Minneapolis, Denver to Philadelphia, it was being written that Florence's mother was *a Lucretia Borgia* incarnate.

Scandalmongers branded the Baroness von Roques *A Lady of Many Husbands and Some Queer Adventures* and some even began to suggest that her romantic career masked something more sinister. They wrote that Florence's father had fallen ill very suddenly; that his wife had turned friends and relatives away; that when he died there were allegations of foul play but no investigation. They suggested that her second husband's sudden death, in view of this history, appeared suspicious. Further, the papers reported that, having spent some time in Europe, the twice-widowed adventuress *drifted back* to New York where she was involved in *a scandal with some actor* and, shortly after, married the Prussian soldier Baron von Roques, who turned out to be neither faithful nor loving. Indeed, they wrote, he beat her. Separated, she was said to have become *a woman of the world, and when last heard from was filling the equivocal position of 'wife' of an attaché of the British legation in Tehran, Persia.* The *coup de grâce* in all this gossip was that an 'acquaintance' from Mobile, Alabama told local reporters that she believed von Roques to have *a regular mania for collecting all sorts of poisons.*

These stories were libellous, but the Baroness von Roques was in no position to seek immediate retraction or redress. She was a woman with a history, by all accounts portly, loud, a flirt, unreliable and – relatively speaking – poor, and despite her European title, her unconventionality could be counted on to work against her imprisoned daughter. To a middle class worshipping the twin deities of birth and breeding the Baroness was not quite respectable. Florence was said to be lovely, sprightly and in possession of an inheritance of twelve hundred pounds a year from her father. It was, though, easy to assume that she had inherited the sins of her mother – that she came from tainted stock.

The *Liverpool Review*, a middle-class weekly, was almost alone in urging reason, positing that *the case …* [involves] *such a momentous issue for a weak woman, who may be absolutely innocent of her husband's death* [that] *we think it is only honourable, chivalrous and humane that the public mind should not be poisoned by the printing of every piece of unreliable gossip.* Yet the frigid silence maintained by the Maybrick family and their friends created a vacuum in which innuendo and hearsay multiplied. Waiting for the results of the city analyst, the country keenly anticipated the next session of the coroner's inquest.

*

Florence remained broadly oblivious to life outside her cell, so ill for the first four days of her incarceration that the prison's medical officer forbade even her solicitor from visiting her.

In the huge prison, with its four great wings radiating from the centre like the spokes of a wheel, there were about a thousand separate cells. Men and women were segregated and Florence had been put in an 'association cell', designed for prisoners in need of extra care. At the junction of three corridors, it was larger than most, triangular, whitewashed and – because it had no outside walls – its air was close and sour. Her mother had provided a few small items of furniture including a table, armchair and washstand, but she had few fresh clothes and no cosmetics. The local hotel was paid to send in palatable food and, as her strength began slowly to return, she was able to walk for an hour a day in the prison yard, but Florence was isolated and afraid. For a woman so fastidious about her dress and toilette, so used to a house full of staff and the noise of her children, the unbroken boredom and the grimy degradation of Walton Gaol played on her nerves. She longed to touch something soft and, sometimes, she wanted to scream if only to hear her own voice rise above the incessant background murmur of this alien world.

When Arnold Cleaver had met with her in her room at Battlecrease, Florence had been able only to whisper, denied privacy by the presence of the nurse and police officer. When his brother Richard eventually visited her in gaol, on 23 May, she could speak freely. She related her husband's habit of taking unprescribed white powders, and the fact that James insisted that they were the only things that relieved his headaches. She thought they contained bromide and strychnine, and told Cleaver that she had discussed it with Dr Hopper and had written to Michael about it. Then she began to tell a story crucial to her defence.

Florence said that, on the Thursday evening before he died, James had been in so much pain that he had begged her to add some powder to his drink. Nothing the doctors were doing brought him any relief. She had argued determinedly against it, but James had insisted, pleaded and eventually worn her down. A small open packet tied with string at one end was on the wash-stand and contained enough powder to cover a threepence piece. Florence told her solicitor that, against her better judgement, she had added this to the bottle of meat juice, throwing the paper on the floor in the dressing room – where it should still be so long as someone had not cleared it away. By the time she came back into the bedroom James was asleep. This, she insisted, had been a relief and as soon as she was able she therefore moved the bottle away from the medicine table and onto the washstand, thus removing it from her husband's reach. She intended later to throw it all down the sink.

Florence was admitting to tampering with her husband's meat juice and, whatever Richard Cleaver thought of it, there was no doubt that her honesty would work against her if it fell into the hands of the police. Cautioning her to keep this explanation to herself, he advised her to wait for the results of the analyst's tests. If Edward Davies was unable to find poison in weighable quantity in James' body, then he believed that the case against his client would evaporate.

*

It had been so widely speculated that the police planned to take Florence before the county magistrates early the following week that, hours before their regular commencement on Monday morning, the approaches to the Liverpool Sessions House were crowded with people hoping to glimpse the increasingly notorious prisoner. Superintendent Bryning arrived first, followed by the magistrate Mr Barrett, his two clerks and the governor of Walton, who carried a certificate from his medical officer, Dr George Beamish. Once assembled, they consulted in the lofty barristers' library. The doctor had written that Florence was still too ill to attend without serious risk to her health. Richard Cleaver was therefore summoned.

Florence's solicitor saw no option but to agree to the police request to extend her remand at Walton. As the small group of solemn-faced men came back down the front steps of the Sessions House, the disappointed crowd, realising they had wasted their time, groaned and dispersed. Bryning, Barrett, his clerk Mr Swift and Richard Cleaver then headed north-east to Walton. At the prison they waited in the committee room for Florence to be brought before them.

If she was rattled, she did not show it. Coolly, she took her seat before them all.

Mrs Maybrick, your solicitor is present. Any statement you might make in answer to the charge about to be made to you will be taken down in writing and might be used in evidence against you at your trial.

She said nothing. She hardly moved.

Bryning cleared his throat. He stood.

Mrs Maybrick, you are charged with the murder of your husband, Mr James Maybrick, on the 11th inst, at Garston.

Then he asked the magistrate for an extension to her remand and was granted a further week.

The formal business completed, Richard Cleaver and his client were left alone.

It was the second time Florence had been charged and remanded. Meanwhile, Brighouse's inquest was reconvening. Inexorably, the wheels of justice were finding their pace.

CHAPTER 16

Public Testimony

Twenty minutes' walk south along the Aigburth Road from Battle-crease, nearing the Garston Docks, the neighbourhood began to change from one studded with affluent villas to an area in which labourers' terraces were closely packed into narrow streets. Here, in the Garston Reading Room in Wellington Road, and while Florence was being remanded at Walton once more, coroner Brighouse had arranged to continue his inquiry into the death of James Maybrick.

Thin, bearded and very tall, thirty-nine-year-old Brighouse arrived at a quarter past nine, followed in quick succession by witnesses, reporters and illustrators all eager to get inside to escape the blustery rain. Outside, a couple of policemen watched a dozen or so of what the *Liverpool Mercury* termed the *idly curious* while a crowd of well-dressed men and women, some in mourning, took their seats inside – in the gallery at one end or on the platform at the other – talking animatedly as though waiting for the curtain to go up in a theatre.

Brighouse installed himself at the centre of a long table, his clerk to his right, Inspector Baxendale and Superintendent Bryning to his left. Trestles were set at right angles to this to accommodate the solicitors and three barristers: Mr Steel for the Maybrick brothers, Mr Mulholland for Alfred Brierley and William Pickford, QC, appointed by Richard Cleaver to represent Florence. The witnesses, installed on the dais behind the coroner, would each be asked to answer questions from a chair placed directly before him, in the centre of the room.

Chapel-like, with tall windows running along its right flank, the whitewashed room could hold around five hundred people and there were no public spaces left by the time the jury entered. Each juror replied to his name as it was called. At least two of them, including a wealthy Cressington coal merchant, had been among the mourners at James' funeral, but no one thought this strange. Once settled, they were told that Mrs Maybrick had been charged with causing the death of her husband and that she remained in prison, too dangerously unwell to attend. Superintendent Bryning would question each witness, after which the lawyers would be allowed to cross-examine.

Then things got under way.

Michael gave no outward hint of his thoughts or feelings. With a sombre quietness and – the *Liverpool Mercury* reported – *not the slightest sign of animus*, he answered the questions put to him, first identifying Dr Fuller's prescriptions and the letter given by Florence to Yapp. Guided by Bryning, Michael then spoke of his suspicions surrounding his brother's sudden illness, of his concern about the half-full bottle of brandy, his fury when he caught Florence changing the labels on medicine bottles and the moment after midnight on the night of James' death when Alice Yapp brought him the chocolate box with its open packet of arsenic. Confirming that he had been advised to lock this in the cellar, Michael swore the key had been left *on a top shelf in a peculiar manner*: as a result, he was certain that it had not been moved.

It was the first time that the public had heard the nature of the suspicions surrounding James' death, or the involvement of his widow. The painful facts beginning to emerge were simply riveting and the fact that testimony would be sought from the four Battlecrease servants who had been summoned to attend suggested there could be more to come.

When Bryning had finished, Michael's evidence was read over but it turned out that he wanted to make several amendments: he had not, in fact, seen Florence change the labels on the bottles:

I cannot say I saw her doing it. I reprimanded her for doing it, and she gave a reason for doing it, but I did not actually see [her] *change either the medicine or the labels. I certainly ... suspected she was changing the medicine.*

And you accused her? the coroner asked.

Yes; and she admitted it by saying the sediment was so thick.

Then Bryning called Alice Yapp, who was described by the papers as *an intelligent woman apparently about the same age as Mrs Maybrick.* Making it clear that her testimony was particularly important, the policeman asked her to describe the events of April and May at Battlecrease House.

The acoustics of the Reading Room muffled and diffused Yapp's voice; more than once the jury asked her to repeat an answer or to speak up and, when she began to describe the discovery of the soaking flypapers, attention was so keenly fixed on her story that the room fell intensely quiet. With rising agitation, the children's nursemaid went on to relate how she had seen her mistress on the landing, pouring the contents of one medicine bottle into another.

Yapp described the argument on the evening of the Grand National, during which James had struck his wife, and she remembered Florence's refusal to rub his hands during his illness on the pretext that it would do him no good. She had heard that some of the food sent up from the kitchen came back tasting different. She had not believed her mistress when she said the master would refuse to see Dr Hopper. She thought that she had told her mistress that she was wrong.

Then came an exciting episode. Yapp described how Gladys

dropped the letter addressed to Alfred Brierley in a puddle, how she had opened it with the intention of putting it into a fresh envelope, how she had caught sight of the words *My Darling*, which had encouraged her to read the whole thing. *Wondering glances were exchanged in the court*, wrote the *Liverpool Mercury* reporter, *as the coroner read the letter, which is written in pencil on light green notepaper bearing a crest and monogram.* It was heavily underlined:

Dearest – your letter under cover to John K came to hand just after I had written to you on Monday. I did not expect to hear from you so soon and had delayed in giving him the necessary instructions. Since my return I have been nursing all day and night. He is sick unto death! The doctors held a consultation yesterday and now all depends on how long his strength will hold out. Both my brothers-in-law are here, and we are terribly anxious. I cannot answer your letter fully today my darling but relieve your mind of all fear of discovery, now or in the future. M has been delirious since Sunday and I now know that he is perfectly ignorant of everything, even of the name of the street, and also that he has not been making any inquiry whatever. The tale he told me was a pure fabrication and only intended to frighten the truth out of me ... You need not therefore go abroad on this ground, dearest, but in any case please don't leave England until I have seen you once again! ... If you wish to, write now as all the letters pass through my hands. Excuse this scrawl, my own darling, but I dare not leave the room for a moment and I don't know when I shall be able to write to you again. In haste, yours ever, Florrie.

Although it was unclear to most of the spectators exactly what some parts of the letter meant, it certainly implied a shocking affair. It also suggested that – on that Wednesday – Florence already believed that her husband was likely to die. Journalists noted that Alfred Brierley looked badly scared; some wondered whether he was frightened of being suspected of complicity in James' death.

William Pickford, Florence's barrister, asked Yapp *why* she had opened the letter. Did he mean to impute insubordination? Her answer was simply that it had not crossed her mind to put it into a new envelope without taking it out of the original.

Alice Yapp was questioned for over two hours and just one oddity emerged from Pickford's relatively gentle cross-questioning. She swore that she had never known James Maybrick to be ill and had never noticed more than the odd bottle of cod liver oil or glycerine at Battlecrease. Anyone who knew James or the house would have found this strange. Did it suggest that the rest of the nursemaid's evidence was not quite trustworthy?

At a quarter to two Brighouse called for an adjournment. Everyone rose. Jurymen and press reporters both grumbled again that they were finding it hard to hear what passed between the witnesses and Superintendent Bryning. Was it not possible, they asked the coroner, to get everyone to speak up?

When things resumed, it was Bessie Brierley's turn. She, too, was asked specifically to remember James and Florence's very public argument, fixing the perilous state of their marriage to a specific date. Then Mary Cadwallader spoke of the bowl of soaking flypapers. Rising as soon as Inspector Bryning indicated that he had no more questions, Mr Pickford was careful to ask Mary to establish that the bedroom door had been left open, that the bowl stood on the washstand and that, despite seeing the various maids going in and out of the room, her mistress had made no attempt to conceal it.

After that, Thomas Wokes remembered that Mrs Maybrick had complained that the flies were beginning to be troublesome in the kitchen but was unable to say on exactly which date she had come to his shop for flypapers: some time around the end of April, he thought. The other chemist, Christopher Hanson, was more certain: she came on 29 April, she bought two dozen, as well as a face lotion, and she paid cash for the flypapers rather than putting them on account. They were not, Hanson said, the first flypapers he had sold that year.

Elizabeth Humphreys gave her evidence straightforwardly, telling how the staff had wondered about the soaking papers and that at the end of the month – Tuesday 30 April – she had sent up bread and milk for Mr Maybrick's breakfast but it was returned untouched, tasting strangely sweeter. She remembered the chemist's lad delivering medicine to the house the following weekend and her mistress being cross when it was taken straight upstairs, telling her that she had thrown the last lot away because it made her husband so sick. The cook also related how upset Florence had been in the kitchen on the night before James died and how she had then complained bitterly of Michael's spite. In all, cook Humphreys's testimony worked both for and against Florence: it helped that she was adamant that James demanded that his wife make all the decisions about his food and drink, but her recollection that the flies had not yet started to be annoying in April made Florence's purchase of flypapers questionable.

When it was the turn of the nurses, Gore recalled watching Florence take the bottle of Valentine's meat juice into the dressing room and return with it minutes later, and Nurse Wilson's evidence was equally galvanising. On the night before he died, Wilson said, James cried out: *Bunny, oh, how could you do it; I didn't think it of you!* When Pickford asked what she thought he meant, the nurse would say only that it seemed obvious that the patient *had reason to complain of the conduct of his wife.* It was strange: what exactly *had* James meant? Was he referring to Florence's debts? Did he know about Brierley after all? Was he delirious or had his wife, knowing that he was close to death, made some muttered admission as she sat at his bedside? Even

Florence's barrister was, for now, unprepared to probe. As far as the police were concerned, Nurse Wilson's testimony was simply enough to show that James and Florence had been at odds.

Michael was recalled. He accepted that, because the seal on James' new will was unbroken, his sister-in-law was probably ignorant of its contents. He was, though, very reluctant to have it read in court, knowing that it did not – contrary to speculation – make Florence wealthy, thus adding the prospect of financial gain to her motives to kill.

I thought it was suggested that the will was very much in favour of the widow, and that she had an opportunity of knowing it? asked the coroner.

Only two thousand pounds at the outside, I think, Michael replied.

Asked to explain why Florence had complained about his spite Michael answered disingenuously that he had done all he could to assist her and make her happy.

I never, he said, *had a quarrel with her in my life.*

It was already evening when Christina Samuelson took her position in the witness chair to testify that, while staying at the Palace Hotel in Birkdale, Florence had told her that she hated her husband. At the Grand National, she recalled, Florence had been so angry with James that she had muttered that she would make him pay. Were the two women friends? *I suppose so, well ... acquaintances, certainly,* she replied. In fact it was clear that, like Alfred Brierley, Mrs Samuelson was rapidly distancing herself from her erstwhile confidante as the scandal threatened to taint them all.

The public had begun to shift on their hard seats, stifling yawns, wilting with the effort of listening closely for twelve hours. An engrossing picture of marital dysfunction was emerging, of resentment, anger and infatuation with another man. Testimony proved that Florence had bought flypapers and that she had left them to soak: the inference was that her intention had been to extract their arsenic. At almost nine p.m. and much to everyone's relief, Brighouse adjourned proceedings until the following Wednesday.

Spilling out onto the pavements, the well-to-do stepped into waiting carriages as the sun dipped below the horizon. In the deepening dusk, swifts swooped and banked. Pressmen flexed their fingers, stiff from taking the notes that had been sent by relay to their city offices. The following morning, under sub-heads like WHAT THE SERVANTS SAW AND HEARD, their reports would catalogue a real-life story of domestic unhappiness in which medicines were mixed up and incriminating letters fell into the wrong hands. They would record apparently ordinary conversations that took on sinister overtones and angry expostulations uttered in the heat of the moment that may not have been ominous had it not been for James' death. The *New York Times*'s summary would linger on three extraordinary facts: that the prisoner had been changing labels on bottles; that the nurse had handed over medicine supposed to contain arsenic; and that a letter from the wife to a man had been apprehended and was found to contain *very questionable sentences*.

Until the scientific testimony could be presented all this evidence was circumstantial, centring on the way things looked rather than what they absolutely proved. Yet Florence's letter to Brierley, with all that it suggested, was particularly thrilling, not least because the manner in which it had come to light suggested a double disloyalty at the heart of the household. The staff appeared to be model servants – polite, humble and straightforward – but Alice Yapp's actions piqued the curiosity of the staff-employing middle classes while the combination of her youth, apparent intelligence and her confidence in speaking out against her mistress also made them nervous. By opening her mistress's letter and then turning it over to James' family, Yapp had sparked the tragedy, setting a flame to the tinder of concern surrounding James' illness until

suspicion raged. Whether or not she had acted in the best interests of her master, the nursemaid's actions were in direct defiance
of her mistress. Gossamer threads of loyalty and deference, so necessary for the success of the contract that bound employer and
servant, had been broken. Yapp – her very name emphasised it –
had behaved sharply and her motives were unclear. Her apparent
treachery made the broadsheet-reading public shudder.

Everyone knew that servants saved the family from the toil of
cleaning, washing, tidying and ordering. As industrial wealth
fuelled an expansion of the middle classes, achieving the right
level of gentility increasingly meant hiring staff. Their hands
thickened and roughened while their employers' remained soft
and white; they were expected to be respectful, obedient and –
crucially – as invisible and inaudible as possible. Around a third
of all employed women were domestics but the progress of industrialisation was changing the relationship between them and their
employers by creating other work opportunities in factories or
shops. Increasing bourgeois demand and a shrinking pool from
which to choose meant that meek deference was beginning to be
mixed with resistance. The much discussed 'servant problem' had
become the bane of the bourgeois wife's life.

The picture emerging of Battlecrease was one in which Mrs
Maybrick's power was subverted not just by her brother-in-law
but by the children's nurse – a fact that went to the heart of a
deepening middle-class anxiety about progress undermining
the social hierarchy on which they so deeply relied. Yapp was
employed to care for the children but was, it seemed, watchful
and uppity. There was something about her that suggested a sub-
ordinate interfering in matters that were none of her business
and this mattered because, like the female poisoner, the disloyal
servant was a recognisable type to readers of contemporary
fiction. In the early 1860s Elizabeth Gaskell wrote of a young
wife whose aristocratic husband's servants were so frigidly unhelp-
ful that she was driven to despair. Inexperienced, brought up in *a*

household where every individual lived all day in the sight of every other member of the family ... this grand isolation ... was very formidable ... Some were civil, but there was a familiarity in their civility which repelled me; others were rude and treated me as if I were an intruder rather than their master's chosen wife. Surrounded by sinister, surly staff, Gaskell's heroine was afraid of everybody, never daring to issue an order.

Florence had complained to her mother that Yapp had not taken to her little girl: *I am afraid she is getting too old for a young baby and has not the forbearance and patience to look after Gladys ... with her it is a labour of duty only.* Yapp seemed to hold herself apart from both her job and the family. Years later an old lady, who had been a guest at Battlecrease during her girlhood in 1888, described what she had then felt to be a pervading *air of secrecy about the house ... that something was going on that you could not understand.* She remembered that, *in the yard you would see the nurse and lodge keeper conversing in low suppressed tones. If anyone came up they would stop abruptly and disperse. This was the case with the other servants. You would see two talking in low tones and when anyone came up, they would scatter.*

Yapp thus trailed echoes of the eavesdropping, unsafe servants of sensation and detective novels and, like them, her dark discovery both energised and complicated the narrative, crystallising the tension between private and public spheres. *Why is it*, asked Mrs Braddon in *Aurora Floyd*, *that the dependents in a household are so feverishly inquisitive about the doings and sayings, the manners and customs, the joys and sorrows, of those who employ them?* Whether or not the commonly held belief that *servants are only too often terrible liars* was true, Yapp's testimony demonstrated that she had loitered on landings, listened to private conversations and gossiped below stairs, a real-life manifestation of Braddon's warning: *Your servants listen at your doors, and repeat your spiteful speeches in the kitchen, and watch you while they wait at table ... They understand your sulky silence, your studied and over-acted politeness. The most polished form your hate and anger can take is as transparent to those household spies as if you threw knives at each other.*

Like hunchbacked, hysterical Rosanna Spearman in Wilkie Collins's *The Moonstone*, Yapp seemed to be both a manifestation of domestic disorder and an insidious threat, and it was doubly appropriate that her real-life involvement turned on a letter: another well-worn literary convention. In books – everyone knew – letters were always getting lost or misdirected, destroyed, withheld or exploited. Many of Florence's own favourite novels emphasised the potential of letters to be the carriers or interceptors of deception: they had a destiny as well as a destination. If only she had decided to drop her own incriminating letter into the postbox herself.

The startling nature of the evidence at the inquest, wrote the *Liverpool Mercury* on Wednesday 29 May, *was naturally the subject of a good deal of comment in Liverpool yesterday.*

Everyone wanted to see Florence, who remained out of sight in Walton Gaol. On station platforms, at market stalls and on street corners, in the drawing rooms of Regency terraces and in the inns along the docks, her story was rapidly becoming a cause célèbre.

CHAPTER 17

First Verdict

The city analyst had so far failed to establish the cause of James Maybrick's death. Carter and Humphreys believed that the post-mortem appearance of his intestines was consistent with poisoning. Davies's tests had found traces of arsenic, but not the presence of a fatal dose. Despite evidence of arsenic in the meat juice, it made the suspicion of malice irrelevant.

In secret, Inspector Baxendale and the coroner, Brighouse, had therefore applied to the Home Secretary for permission to exhume James' body. Once darkness fell on Tuesday 28 May the large stone was removed from his grave and the soil was cleared away. At eleven o'clock the cemetery superintendent and the clerk of the Burial Board opened the gates. The noise of horses' hooves, the rattle of carriage wheels and the murmur of suppressed voices carried across the vast graveyard in the still night. Hand lamps flared. The police arrived and the coffin was disinterred and placed on two garden seats hauled to the edge of the grave.

It was almost midnight when the doctors began. The press would later report that *the lid was quickly lifted, the linen shroud torn clear from the corpse and in a moment the sharp blade of steel, deftly directed by Dr Barron, had passed down the centre of the body. The lungs, the heart, kidneys, a piece of the lower part of the thigh-bone, were soon removed, and the brain extracted.* Dr Humphreys collected the oesophagus and tongue, a portion of the pelvis on each side, some of the abdominal wall, the liver and a *good piece of the flesh of the thigh.* Each sample was bottled and given to Baxendale. The coffin lid was re-secured, then it was lowered back down and the earth replaced. Solemnly, the party returned to the city.

Once briefed by the police, the newspapers worried over this extraordinary event. Evidence heard at the inquest had established that the dead man's wife had bought flypapers, but the *Mercury* now suggested that *the case against Mrs Maybrick is a weak one.* The exhumation indicated a need, it thought, *to root up in all directions points that might tell against her.* It reminded its readers that she purchased the flypapers openly and paid cash *because* [she] *did not desire that either her husband or acquaintances should know that she used arsenic in her toilet preparations. Arsenic may* – it reported – *disappear in a few days from the stomach and intestines, especially in those cases where violent vomiting and purging have taken place.* In an attempt to under-stand what was going on, the paper also explained that *it is afterwards found in the liver and other organs of the body*, indeed *the poison may be found for years after.*

Speculation flared about what the police might do next. Some hoped for another arrest. Others simply anticipated the public airing of more intensely private letters.

*

On Monday 3 June, after fifteen days in prison, Florence's remand was extended in a repetition of formalities at Walton. She now wore deep mourning and a veil. Her hair, described by the single newspaper reporter present, was done up in curls over her forehead; she bowed and smiled slightly, looking *young, anxious and careworn.* Her composure seemed remarkable in the light of reports that, when Richard Cleaver told her that the police had dug up James' body, she had become hysterical.

Still hoping that she would soon appear at the Liverpool Magistrates Court, crowds refused to be turned away. At Anfield large numbers began to mill around the recently re-opened grave.

At the Royal Institution in Colquitt Street, meanwhile, Edward Davies suggested that it might take days to complete his analyses.

Overwhelming the lives of all involved, the tedious waiting set up a tangible disquiet, fraying the nerves of police and witnesses. Each new rumour hummed through the city, picked up pace, eddied through taverns and swirled through parlours. The Maybrick story held the public in its thrall.

*

When the inquest resumed on Wednesday the 5th the temperature was nudging towards seventy degrees and as the Reading Room doors were opened there was a rush for the gallery by, it was noted, mostly women.

Dr Hopper outlined his attempts to help the Maybricks to reconcile their differences and said that Florence had *felt some repugnance towards her husband.* Mr Pickford raised the fact of James' hypochondria: *he had a very strong habit of taking almost anything that was recommended to him by any of his friends,* agreed Hopper, *I remember* [he] *told me he knew arsenic as an antiperiodic.* The doctor also confirmed that, despite Florence's concerns, he had continued to prescribe nux vomica and strychnine, and acceded that it was likely that traces of arsenic would be found in the body of anyone taking regular doses of Fowler's Solution. *I have never,* he said, *been associated with a case of death from arsenic where no arsenic was found in the body.*

Then young Dr Humphreys reconstructed each of his visits to Battlecrease, James' changing symptoms and the subsequent alteration of his prescriptions. He confirmed that he had initially diagnosed food poisoning and that he had not, of his own accord, considered the possibility of poison. Phrases like *very likely*, *I am almost sure* and *I do not remember* peppered Richard Humphreys's answers, undermining their force. In Florence's favour, he stressed that she had been a tireless nurse, that she was exhausted and that by refusing to allow James to drink the cook's lemonade she was less cruel than obedient to his orders.

Admitting that he was no expert, Humphreys agreed that he knew *The symptoms of arsenical poisoning from reading and not from my own knowledge.*

Pressed to list these symptoms, he thought that

If a large dose is taken you will have all the symptoms of cholera. A moderate dose … a diminished degree of vomiting, diarrhoea and pain in the stomach or perchance none of these symptoms at all. But the patient may be struck down comatosed [sic], or he may have convulsions … If a small dose is taken for a prolonged period then we have pains in the stomach, diarrhoea, pains in the eyes, falling out of the hair and skin eruptions of various kinds.

His belief that James Maybrick's illness was consistent with arsenic poisoning caused an exclamation to ripple through the public seats – yet Dr Humphreys also accepted that his patient had not suffered from sore eyes, intolerance to light, hair loss or boils and he was unsure whether or not numbness in the hands or legs was a general symptom of poisoning.

Pressed under cross-examination Humphreys said that he had only formed an opinion about the cause of James' illness *after a suggestion was made to me.* Why, asked the jury, did he not then give an antidote? Because, he offered lamely, the *deceased never told me he had taken arsenic.* Had the doctor ever seen the post-mortem effects of irritant poisoning before, asked the coroner. He had not. Nor was Humphreys able *to say whether the post-*

mortem appearances of idiopathic gastritis are similar to those produced by an irritant poison. What scientific use, the jury might have wondered, was this doctor who had never witnessed the effects of arsenic poisoning, either in life or in death?

Dr William Carter was more solidly convincing, though he also admitted that it was Michael who had suggested foul play and – even then – he had not considered things sufficiently dangerous to administer an antidote. Carter remembered that on Tuesday 7 May James had complained of vomiting and diarrhoea lasting several days. He also accepted that in the week preceding his death Maybrick had been prescribed over twenty different irritant medicines, including morphia, Fowler's Solution, hydro-cyanic acid, cocaine, nitroglycerine and phosphoric acid.

Following Carter, James' clerk Thomas Lowry spoke about Wednesday 1 May when a new saucepan, basin and spoon were purchased.

These were the only times I had known the deceased take food in the office, he said. *He had a lot of medicine bottles and he took medicine there pretty often.*

The city analyst was not present. The coroner did not explain why.

Instead, it was the turn of two strangers from London.

Arthur Graham Flatman, forty-two, was the rotund, self-important owner of the private hotel just off Cavendish Square and his testimony was brief: between 16 and 19 March he had received three letters and a telegram from someone in Liverpool. The following week a lady calling herself Mrs Maybrick had stayed at the hotel; he had not actually seen her, but his head waiter, Alfred Schweisso, had. Called to give evidence, Schweisso confirmed that on that woman's first evening a gentleman had taken her out. The next morning, 22 March, a different man arrived and had stayed for two nights.

Almost before the assembly could take in the electrifying implication of what the witness was saying, the waiter was invited to step outside. Few realised that Schweisso was being asked formally to identify Florence as the woman at the hotel.

Just before the lunchtime break, accompanied by the prison doctor and a wardress, Florence had been brought to the Reading Room, waiting in a side room where she was offered chicken, lamb and a glass of beer to which, a reporter wrote, she *did full justice*. The colour, he noted, had returned to her cheeks.

In fact, the newspaperman paid minute attention to the way Florence looked. Whereas the voluminous black garments (or weeds) worn by widows were usually considered ugly, he described her as

neatly attired in a mourning Russian cloak, with two broad bands of crape running down the front. A coquettish net veil just reached to the tip of her nose, while the long widow's one hung gracefully behind, falling on what a lady described as a 'nicely tilted up tornure'. Delicate lawn 'weepers' adorned her dark sleeves and her pale but interesting face was set off with a dainty little bonnet. Beneath this headdress and covering the greater part of her brow was a carefully curled fringe, which considerably enhanced her personal charms. Her hair was also worn at the back in the shape of a fringe, and altogether she presented a by no means unattractive appearance. Her figure is petite and seen in the full light her complexion is much fairer than when one observed her in the gloomy precincts of Walton Prison.

She had made a characteristically careful effort and this journalist's appraisal of her was almost reverential. Stressing both her frail delicacy and her attractive physicality, it demonstrated a fascination for the way Florence looked that sat uncomfortably beside the 'appetite' or sexuality for which she was censured.

In the side-room, Schweisso stared at her. Then he turned and walked back into the main hall.

A feverish atmosphere had settled on the room during his

absence. Now, spectators craned to hear what was being asked. Florence Maybrick was positively identified. Was the man who stayed with her at Flatman's Hotel present, asked Superintendent Bryning. Schweisso pointed. All eyes swung towards Alfred Brierley, who was looking extremely hot and confused, striving to maintain his composure as a tumult of groans and hisses erupted. The coroner, battling to restore order, threatened to clear the room.

There was hardly time to assimilate this monstrous proof of Florence's physical adultery before the day's last witness, Mrs Briggs, was called. She recounted Florence coming to her *in great distress* the day after the Grand National, determined to obtain a separation. She identified the small wooden box she had discovered in the dressing room at Battlecrease during the fevered search, along with various bottles of liquids, a tumbler and a rag. As she spoke of opening all the stacked-up bandboxes and hatboxes, of lifting out their contents to see what might be underneath, no one was left in any doubt that this woman had been ferociously assiduous in her quest.

Matilda agreed that there were *a great number of medicine bottles about the house* and that James had been *in the habit of taking things suggested to him by his friends beside what he was ordered by the doctor.* Asked why Florence had written to Brierley to ask for help, she hedged until – pressed firmly by Mr Pickford – she admitted that she *might have said to Mrs Maybrick that if he knew … he might send her money … I made the suggestion and then she wrote.* Did she think the letter would reach Brierley? *I am perfectly persuaded,* Mrs Briggs replied, bristling, *that she knew I should hand the letter to the police before she wrote it.*

That letter, pleading for financial assistance, warning her lover that their liaison had been exposed, was read aloud. *Appearances are terribly against me,* the court heard, *but before God I sware* [sic] *I am innocent!*

Hearing that cry for help for the first time, did Alfred Brierley feel ashamed for failing of his own accord to offer help, for hiding himself away when he became aware of what was going on?

Almost before the assembly could react to Florence's note, Brighouse adjourned the inquest, forcing everyone to filter back outside. Uppermost in most minds was not the quiet cowardice of Florence's lover but the motivations of the older woman, Matilda Briggs. Intimate enough to act as an adviser in a time of distress, it was beginning to look like she had played a cruel trick by encouraging the isolated younger woman to write an incriminating letter. Far from being a friend, Matilda had ensured that Florence's pleas for assistance remained unheard.

Florence did not then return to Walton, but was installed instead in a chilly, domed-ceilinged, flagstoned cell in the local police station at Lark Lane. Its walls were faced with ceramic tiles; the air was sour. Light filtered dimly from four glass bricks set high in the wall; a smoky gaslight glowered. She lay on a wide plank, covered with a grimy blanket while, in an adjoining cell, drunkards cursed. Her adultery was now a public fact. She received no visitors, asked for nothing and displayed no outward sign either of suffering or remorse.

*

The following morning, Thursday 6 June, a strong force of police was evident in the streets around the Garston Reading Room. Edwin Maybrick looked slight as he faced his questions, but was confused only about where he had been when Yapp gave him the letter, thinking at first that it was *in the road* then remembering that it was in the morning room. He said he had purchased a bottle of Valentine's meat juice for his brother. He agreed that all the items passed to the police had been found in unlocked locations, that only the wardrobe had been locked *but we found none of the bottles or things there*. Once the dressing room had been secured he had retained the only key. He refused to accept that James took arsenic – *I knew he used to take certain medicines ... I do not know the kind, but principally medicines for the liver* – but he did agree that the tonic sent from London had made his brother physically sick almost immediately.

Describing where the various bottles and packets had been found, Edwin spoke *with an almost careless sang froid*, wrote one paper. He had *rummaged through drawers and bandboxes and cupboards*. Had he been suspicious of the box of paints he turned up, asked William Pickford coldly. *No*, Edwin replied calmly, looking the barrister straight in the eye. *Mrs Maybrick painted a little.*

Dr Humphreys was recalled and re-examined about the places in and around Battlecrease from which he took soil and water samples for the police. A chemist confirmed that he had made up James' two London prescriptions, but that neither contained arsenic. Both Sergeant Baxendale and Superintendent Bryning clarified the dates on which certain items were found or delivered to Mr Davies. Constance Hughes was treated more gently than her sister: she had only to say that she had found some letters among the effects in Florence's dressing table.

The most crucial witness was Edward Davies, *a business-like little gentleman with steel grey hair and a slight beard ... wearing spectacles*. Finally ready to share the results of his tests, he surrounded himself with a number of blue and white bottles and with cigar boxes containing linen handkerchiefs and other articles: *the phials were so numerous*, wrote one paper, *as to irresistibly suggest the modern 'apothecary'*.

If the public hoped to hear about poisoned handkerchiefs resonant with the significance of a Revenge Tragedy they were given instead what the papers described as a *dull scientific recital* that lulled many into a torpid lethargy. In conclusion, Davies had found arsenic, or traces of it, in the meat juice bottle, the handkerchief, the small bottles discovered inside the wooden box, the glass and rag found in the hatbox, the packet labelled 'Arsenic for Cats', the brown jug used to transport James' lunch and in a bottle of Price's glycerine found on a shelf in the upstairs lavatory.

Arsenic had been found *all over the house*. There were twelve grains in the glass tumbler alone. Yet only unquantifiable, minute crystals had been discovered in James' intestines and there was no poison in his stomach or his spleen. A tiny amount – one-fiftieth of a grain – was present in the liver and probably something less than a hundredth of a grain in the kidney. In sum, the amount of arsenic found in James' body was substantially less than the smallest known fatal dose.

Mr Pickford reminded the jury triumphantly that more than twice this amount was found in one of the victims of those infamous Liverpool poisoners Flanagan and Higgins. *Yes*, countered Davies, but *if a person dies with the symptoms of arsenical poisoning and there is not arsenic sufficient to cause death in the body I should still say the death was due to poison.*

*

Was this stalemate? Superintendent Bryning had no more witnesses and – as was usual – Pickford chose not to call anybody to testify in Florence's defence, hoping that the inquest jury's verdict would absolve her of all suspicion.

At just past four o'clock that afternoon Brighouse began to wrap things up, reprising – as the papers remarked – the *ugly facts* and cautioning the jury to *Put aside any matter you have read in the papers, and give your verdict on the evidence only.*

Then he posed three questions, stressing that it was the jury's duty to reach a conclusion about each one: was James Maybrick's death caused by an irritant poison? If so, who had administered it? If it was Mrs Maybrick, had she intended to kill?

Forty-five minutes after he began, the coroner signalled for the jurymen to retire.

Excitement was replaced by a palpable strain as the assembly waited. Spectators and reporters wondered what would be made of the tiny amounts of poison present in Maybrick's body. They asked themselves whether it was possible to be innocent in the light of proven immorality and they watched Michael and Edwin closely, noting that both managed to remain outwardly impassive.

After thirty-five minutes, at the first sounds of movement from the jury's room, the tension of waiting unlaced propriety. Knowing that the time had come, some of the public surged forward, scrambling over seats and tables to form a solid mass around the counsel table.

Once calm had been restored, the foreman of the jury stated that they were unanimously agreed that James Maybrick's death was caused by an irritant poison.

And do you say by whom that poison was administered? asked Brighouse.

The room strained to hear the answer.

By thirteen to one we decide that the poison was administered by Mrs Maybrick.

A groan. Someone began to clap. Demanding quiet, Brighouse re-posed his third question. Did the jury also believe that Florence Maybrick had given her husband arsenic with intent to kill?

Twelve of the fourteen, said Fletcher Rogers, believed that she had.

That amounts, said Brighouse gravely, *to a verdict of wilful murder.*

The room erupted. Some shouted and stamped their feet, others sat heavily back on their seats. Reporters watched it all and scribbled, knowing it would all make incendiary copy.

Outside, a hoarse roar went up from the crowd as the police cab carrying Florence approached.

CHAPTER 18

Damaged or Deviant?

Calling for calm, Brighouse asked for Florence to be brought in.

Two long minutes passed.

Most of those in the crowded room stared expectantly at the door leading to the side-room, willing it to open, pushing forward eagerly. When it did, Inspector Baxendale led the way, followed by a police sergeant whose height entirely dwarfed the slight woman behind him draped from head to toe in black crape. Her face was covered with a black veil that was not so opaque as to hide what the *Liverpool Weekly Post* would describe as a *square set and determined-looking chin ... a face ghastly pale ... a gleam and an anger in the eyes as there was a stubborn and even daring defiance in the bearing and the demeanour.*

Florence had not been told the verdict. She expected the inquest jury of local tradesmen and businessmen – at least two of whom had, at one time or another, been entertained at Battlecrease – to find in her favour and she looked for reassurance in their expressions. Aware of the dead hush in the room, she noted the stony faces of the lawyers and scanned the crowd of reporters, witnesses and spectators as she stepped forward, her back straight.

Brighouse stood, his voice low but distinct.

Florence Elizabeth Maybrick, the jury have inquired into the circumstances attending the death of your husband and they have come to the conclusion that he was wilfully murdered by you. It is my duty to commit you to the next assizes to be holden at Liverpool, there to take your trial upon that charge.

There was only the slightest inclination of her head. It was a movement so freezingly polite as to suggest, to some, sarcasm, though others believed they saw her tremble, that her behaviour was the outward manifestation of suppressed terror. Turning, Florence then rapidly withdrew.

In the anteroom she was addressed by the coroner's clerk:

Florence Elizabeth Maybrick, having heard the evidence, do you want to say anything in answer to the charge? You are not obliged to say anything unless you desire to do so but whatever you say will be taken down in writing and may be given in evidence against you upon your trial. And you are clearly to understand that you have nothing to hope from any promise of favour, and nothing to fear from any threat, which may have been holden out to you to induce you to make any admission or confession of your guilt, but that whatever you shall now say may be given against you upon your trial, notwithstanding such promise or threat.

She replied quietly as she had been directed: *By the advice of Mr Pickford I reserve my defence.*

Alfred Brierley's counsel, Mr Mulholland, had been present at the inquest only in order to make it clear that Brierley was not involved in any way with James' illness and that his testimony could serve no properly useful purpose. Earlier, Mulholland had attempted to persuade the coroner to prioritise his investigation into the cause of death before proceeding with an examination of possible motive. Florence's barrister, Mr Pickford, had agreed, adding that the exhumation seemed to suggest that the scientific evidence was inconclusive. In the event, Brighouse had demurred and motive had taken priority over scientific proof. Despite the jury's verdict, though, Mulholland and Pickford continued to believe it an unequivocal fact that the cause of James Maybrick's death had not been properly established and, therefore, that the commission of a crime had not been proved. They believed, in consequence, that the question of Florence Maybrick's involvement – let alone Brierley's – was irrelevant.

Despite that conviction, the inquest process had indicted her. Florence would remember feeling overwhelmingly alone as she was hurried away to a police vehicle and returned to the Lark Lane lockup where she would now stay as a result of a complicated legal knot: at Walton Gaol she would be outside the jurisdiction of the coroner and the inquest evidence would become invalid. Under an ancient rule, Brighouse remained responsible for his prisoner until the next assize court sat, and so the cells at the Lark Lane police station provided a compromise.

Pretty, narrow Lark Lane was just a step away from the entrance to Sefton Park and Livingston Avenue where Florence's son James had been born. Re-installed in her cold, dim cell, she fought to still the nausea that rose each time she realised she was now dead to that former world. She would remain in the lockup for a week, suffering alone, prizing the fruit sent to her intermittently by a kindly greengrocer, longing for her mother and her solicitor to visit, poring over the newspaper accounts of the inquest in order to understand the evidence on which the jury had based their condemnation.

The delicate porcelain, bright glass and thick carpets of

Battlecrease, the sound of the piano, the laughter of visitors, the warmth of the kitchen and the squeals of her children – the coordinates on which her former life could be mapped – receded into an unreachable past. Some said that she bore the strain bravely; some that she was prostrate in her grief; others, that Florence was becoming unattractively petulant.

*

Before the jury were allowed to leave Garston, the coroner's clerk made out a certificate recording their decision that *Florence Maybrick did wilfully, feloniously and of her malice aforethought, kill and murder James Maybrick*. Each of the fourteen men signed it. Then the various witnesses were bound over to appear at the next Liverpool assize court and the building emptied.

Rushed out within half an hour of the conclusion of the inquest, the *Liverpool Echo* spread the news of the verdict. Large groups of people began to amass in the busier parts of town to devour the reports. Interest in Florence's fate was fervid. Papers including the *Liverpool Mercury* and *The Times* devoted several columns to *the very extraordinary case whose mysterious circumstances are on everybody's lips throughout the country*, lingering on James' alleged arsenic dependency, on the fact that the poison had no appreciable taste and that it could be taken in fatal quantities *without exciting suspicion*. The symptoms of arsenic poisoning were restated and each of the *remarkable* letters was reprinted.

The *New York Times* printed news of the verdict and over the following weekend the penny press gnawed at the story, listing the *startling* and *dramatic* revelations made by the various witnesses, including the identification of Mr Brierley, Florence's *repugnance* for her husband and a bizarre new suggestion that the second man who came to take her out while staying in London was *a London soap boiler . . .* [in] *a tall bearskin hat and a fur-lined cloak à la Russe*. The doctors' statements that they had not considered poisoning until it was suggested to them were pondered, and it seemed to some rather strange that so much arsenic was found in the meat juice and so little in the dead man's body.

The Maybrick Mystery contained potent ingredients: marital disharmony, a young American wife's misplaced infatuation, disloyal servants, oddly treacherous friends, police rifling through linen cupboards and a flurry of intercepted letters and telegrams. By suggesting that the exquisite multi-layering of middle-class manners might conceal something unattractive and illicit, it hinted at fissures in the bourgeois domestic ideal. Even small details of the post-mortem were scrutinised. One, in particular, presented an unnerving parallel with a description in Flaubert's shocking novel: as Emma Bovary's body was prepared for her funeral, as the wreath was positioned on her head, *a rush of black liquid issued, as if she were vomiting, from her mouth*. In these uncomfortable facts, reality seemed to be mirroring art.

Trumping the horror of James Maybrick's death, though, was the ugly reality of Florence's adulterous intimacy with Brierley. Alfred Schweisso's testimony had turned the hints contained in the letters into something far less palatable. Mrs Maybrick had not simply flirted with another man; she had spent two nights with him. Brierley seemed not to fall under criminal suspicion but he looked – to most – like a contemptible bounder eager to wriggle away from his responsibilities. Slim, elegant, feminine, Florence's story piqued the curiosity of the well-dressed women crushed into the public benches of the Garston Reading Room but it also drew their censure. Her disgrace was likely to sweep aside even the residual sympathy that might have been felt for her as a woman trapped in a miserable marriage. The second and third generation of Victorians excelled at overblown moral outrage: Florence Maybrick's sexuality was likely to unleash a tide of prejudgement in which rationality would, for the most part, be pushed aside.

The suggestion that more than one man might be involved was provocative: in part because the fictional image of the murderess – women like Mrs Braddon's Lady Audley – was often linked with sexual energy. It was bad enough that female poisoners traduced their role as carers. Add sexual appetite, which in women was supposed to be restrained, hidden, even denied, and Florence became something worse than a criminal: a moral menace.

Enlarged portrait photographs of her were soon exhibited in the window of Medrington's Photographic Studio in Bold Street, attracting a good deal of attention from pedestrians as they passed. Lovely in a morning costume or in evening dress, she may or may not have poisoned her husband, but it was proved that she had made the wrong choice between obligation and inclination. She was fallen. She was fascinating. By refusing to adhere to the rules that bound society to its proper course, she was easily turned into a figure of hate and, compounding this, as she began to recover from the shock that had made her so unwell she cleaved to the manners of her class and was said to be (like the best literary poisoners) remarkably 'cool'.

The growing force of public contempt for the accused woman was nourished by two opposing currents of contemporary thought: one, that promiscuity was an indication of criminality, and the other that female expectations were changing so that some women no longer accepted rules that repressed their individuality. Having battled for recognition for two decades or more, the Women's Movement was beginning to gain momentum.

In 1868 the novelist Eliza Lynn Linton, said to be the first female salaried journalist, published a strident essay in the *Saturday Review*, attacking feminist theories. In it, she coined a phrase that would be used both by feminism's advocates and its detractors for generations: 'The Girl of the Period'. This girl was modern, unconventional and bold. She worked outside the home in factories or shops; she broke free of her middle-class restraints, committing small acts of rebellion that illustrated her disinclination to toe the line. Thus, Kate Chopin's Mrs Pontellier, waking up to the reality that her marriage was an *accident*, goes out on 'her' afternoon, caring nothing for the fact that *people don't do such things; we've got to observe 'les convenances' if we ever expect to get on*. Soon after, she leaves her husband and children, hoping *to realize her position in the universe as a human being, and to recognize her relations as an individual to the world within and about her*.

Edna Pontellier, conceived during the decade following the events now unfolding in Liverpool, encapsulated a long-running argument that women needed self-definition beyond the roles of wife, mother and daughter and liberation from the claustrophobia of domesticity. Pontellier, like other Girls of the Period, wanted to stretch her wings, to shuffle off the social constraints described by John Stuart Mill back in 1869: *All the moralities tell them that it is the duty of women ... to live for others; to make complete abnegation of themselves, and to have no life but in their affections. And by their affections are meant the only ones they are allowed to have.*

Mill saw that society was already changing, that *the peculiar character of the modern world ... is, that human beings are no longer born to their place in life, and chained down by an inexorable bond to the place they are born to*, and he argued that women remained nonetheless oppressed. He advocated higher education, professional training and the encouragement of productive work for women: all essential in order to sweep away the *weariness, disappointment and profound dissatisfaction* with life that were so often the female lot and he derided the law of marriage as *the law of despotism*, attacking the mantra of female self-sacrifice. All the while, opponents of such progressive views continued to argue for a preservation of the male fantasy in which the home was the woman's natural domain, a place of peace, shelter and regressive sexuality.

From these opposing points of view, debates about what women needed or deserved had grown: tangling, dividing, angering – and upsetting anyone who brushed up against them by questioning long-accepted norms. From the early days of the Women's Movement in the 1860s, women who lobbied for equal opportunities in education and employment were criticised for threatening the state of motherhood and the institution of the family. To those afraid of change, they were deviant and disordered, adulteresses and whores, promising an immoral future. L. O. Pike voiced a common anxiety in his *History of Crime in England* (1876), when he wrote that female emancipation would lead not simply to corruption but to an increase in crime.

Where before they might have been protected by their class and gender, now middle-class women caught up in murder cases were increasingly pursued by the law – especially if the whiff of sexual scandal was attached to their imputed crime. A very slender boundary existed between what was condoned – because it was smothered, undetected or not quite 'known' – and what was denounced. Convention decreed that openly wayward daughters were heartlessly punished, particularly by their own sex who thereby proved themselves to be above reproach.

Within recent decades, several high-profile trials had centred on the heady mix of bourgeois women, sex and poison. In 1857 Madeleine Smith, an unmarried young Scot, broke with her low-born French paramour in order to make an advantageous marriage. When the lover died, doctors diagnosed a *bilious derangement* as the cause of death until inflammatory letters came to light which appeared to prove a clandestine physical relationship. Charged with murder, Madeleine admitted that she had bought arsenic in order to make a cosmetic face wash. The dead man's friends testified that he took the poison regularly for the health of his teeth and her defence lawyers suggested that the Frenchman had committed suicide. Throughout it all, Madeleine maintained an unflinching pose of innocence and purity; conservative society, preferring to subscribe to the view that she had been seduced rather than face the reality of her sexual appetite, did not condemn her. In the end, she was saved by the Scottish verdict of 'not proven'.

Then, in 1886, Adelaide Bartlett was charged with murder. When her husband, ten years her senior, died suddenly it was discovered that both had been unfaithful. Adelaide claimed that their marriage was platonic but, thrillingly for the public, *French letters* – condoms – were found among the dead man's possessions and a nurse testified that Adelaide and her husband often had sex. Countering the charge that liquid chloroform in Edwin's stomach pointed to murder, Adelaide claimed he was a hypochondriac and had killed himself. Ultimately, and in part because she insisted that she was sexually inert, she was acquitted.

It all suggested that overt libido led to an assumption of guilt while the appearance of physical innocence often swayed juries. The opprobrium attaching itself to Florence Maybrick grew, consciously or not, from this, along with the reality that her story touched on so many of the deep concerns of the period, not least some of these confused and fluctuating attitudes about women. Nowhere was this contradiction between female inertia and vigour more obviously reflected than by many of the artists of the Pre-Raphaelite Brotherhood – Dante Gabriel Rossetti, John Everett Millais, William Holman Hunt and their circle – whose models seemed languid but who were also, often, defiant and strong. Millais's 1879 full-length portrait of the successful artist Louise Jopling presented the Manchester woman – hands behind her back, chin up, frank gaze – as refined, strikingly beautiful and fiercely independent. Frederic Sandys's series of drawings of *Proud Maisie* (1868–1904) – an angry beauty baring her teeth as she bites on a lock of hair – was vividly erotic; in Rossetti's *Day Dream* (1880) the model's apparent passivity barely masked the ferocity of her red lips and nails, the strength of her jaw and her powerful hands.

Florence Maybrick aged nineteen, around the time of her marriage in 1881.

Illustrated London News Ltd/Mary Evans

Richard Whittington-Egan

James Maybrick: Florence's Liverpool cotton broker husband, almost twenty-four years her senior, photographed in 1887.

The Baroness von Roques, Florence's flamboyant mother.

John Harrison

Edwin, youngest of the Maybrick brothers and closest in age to Florence.

Michael Maybrick: also known as 'Blucher', the most dominant of the brothers, a noted composer and singer.

Alfred Brierley, Liverp cotton broker and colleague of James Maybrick.

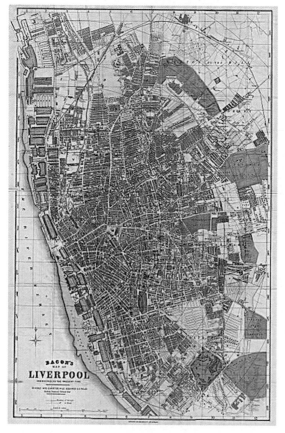

The port city of Liverp 1890. St George's Hall stood proudly at the ci centre and the semi-rur suburb of Aigburth lay just further south.

Battlecrease House, from a sketch published in the *Liverpool Echo*, 5 June 1889.

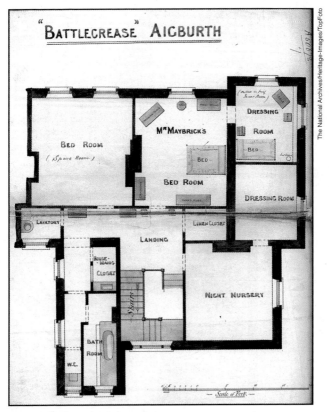

The National Archives/Heritage-Images/TopFoto

Part of the floor plan of Battlecrease House provided for the Liverpool Assizes.

The interior of Wokes's chemist's shop at 25 Aigburth Road.

The Secret of a Good Complexion

TO ALL WOMEN WHO DESIRE BEAUTY.

Until further notice we will send you a 30-day daily treatment of Dr. Campbell's Safe Arsenic Complexion Wafers and a 30-day daily treatment of Fould's Medicated Arsenic Soap FOR ONE DOLLAR.

These world-famous preparations are a never failing remedy for bad blood, pimples, freckles, blackheads, moth patches, liver spots, acne, redness of face or nose, wrinkles, dark rings under the eyes, and all other blemishes, whether on the face, neck, arms or body. They brighten and beautify the complexion as no other remedies on earth can, and they do it in a very short time. They impart to the complexion the most exquisite fairness, make the skin clear, soft and velvety. Until further notice we will send you the wafers and soap as stated above for $1.00. After this offer is withdrawn the price will be $1.00 for the wafers and 60c. for the soap. Address or call on

H. B. FOULD, Dept. A, 214 Sixth Ave., New York.
Sold by Druggists Everywhere.

Arsenical waf[ers,] the benefits of arsenic in the pursuit of bea[uty] were widely discussed dur[ing] the 1880s.

Valentine's Meat-Juice, highly concentrated beef stock whose nutritional qualities were much vaunted.

Valentine's Meat-Juice

In **Diarrhoea, Dysentery** and **Cholera Infantum** where it is **Essential** to **Conserve** the **Weakened Vital Forces** without **Irritating** the **Digestive Organs**, Valentine's Meat-Juice demonstrates its **Ease** of **Assimilation** and **Power** to **Sustain** and **Strengthen**.

Dr. Simonyi Bela, *Physician to the Israelite Hospital, Buda-Pest, Hungary:* "I have tested VALENTINE'S MEAT-JUICE in the case of a child five years old who was much weakened by a severe and obstinate attack of Gastro-Enteritis, during which there was great difficulty in properly feeding him. Two days after he had begun taking VALENTINE'S MEAT-JUICE the extreme weakness began to abate and the patient recovered in a remarkably short time. I find VALENTINE'S MEAT-JUICE an excellent preparation, and in cases where a powerfully stimulating nourishment is needed it answers wonderfully."

For Sale by American and European Chemists and Druggists.

VALENTINE'S MEAT-JUICE CO.,
RICHMOND, VIRGINIA, U. S. A.

P 114

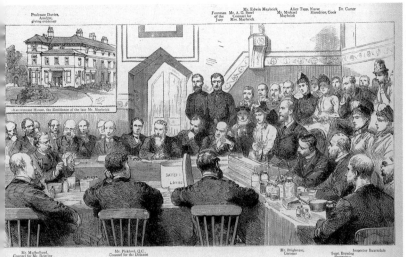

Illustrated London News Ltd/Mary Evans

Professor Davies, Analyst, giving evidence

Foreman of the Jury   Mr. A. G. Steel Counsel for Mrs. Maybrick   Mr. Edwin Maybrick   Mr. Michael Maybrick   Alice Tapp, Nurse Humfries, Cook   Dr. Carter

Battlecrease House, the Residence of the late Mr. Maybrick

GATGO LONGO

Mr. Mulholland, Counsel for Mr. Briering

Mr. Pickford, Q.C., Counsel for the Defence

Mr. Brighouse, Coroner

Supt. Bryning Prosecutor

Inspector Baxendale

THE SCENE AT THE CORONER'S INQUEST ON THE DEATH OF THE LATE MR. MAYBRICK.

Coroner Samuel Brighouse convenes a session of the inquest at the Garston Reading Rooms.

Newspapers nationally and regionally were full of the story; those containing sketches of the witnesses sold fast.

British Library

The trial at St George's Hall, Liverpool: the prisoner in the dock.

Sir Charles Russell, one of the most famous advocates of his day, mounted a bifocal defence.

Judge Sir James Fitzjames Stephen would be bitterly criticised in some quarters for his trial summation.

'The Maybrick Murder Trial' from the *Pall Mall Budget*, 8 August 1889.

Notes prepared by Sir Godfrey Lushington summarising the amounts of arsenic found in various places for the Home Secretary.

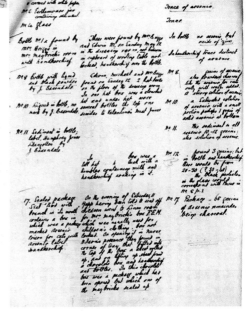

The National Archives

Walton Gaol, Liverpool, where the prisoner was held before trial and before be
transferred to Woking.

WHITECHAPEL AT WHITEHALL.
ATTEMPTED MURDER OF FLORENCE MAYBRICK.—"Only You! Mr. Matthews!"

The difficulty of being Home Secretary. This illustration from *St Stephen's Revie*
August 1889, reflects public disquiet that Henry Matthews was persecuting the
adulteress while failing to bring the Ripper to justice.

The women in these paintings countered the demure ideal of Victorian femininity: with bold mouths and wild, often fiery hair, they broke with convention, pale yet provocative. Simultaneously – look closely – they are not always as free as they might appear: there is an airless quality to the rooms they inhabit, a bored suffocation, as in Rossetti's *Veronica Veronese* (1872). Even the stillness of their honeysuckled bowers is distracting, the clinging tendrils hinting at constraint beyond the appearance of liberty.

The narrative of such paintings reflected a wider battle. Pre-Raphaelite models were liberated, aggressive beauties yet the manuals that aimed to teach women how to construct beautiful homes with Morris & Co. furnishings – the wallpapers, blue and white china, stained glass, gothic-inspired furniture and embroideries contained in the paintings of the period – pressured housewives into submitting to the overwhelming requirement to remain the Angel in the House. In Liverpool, Pre-Raphaelite paintings hung on the walls of the vast mansions of the shipping magnates and were displayed in the Walker Art Gallery yet there were few – if any – families in the mercantile world in which ladies wore corsetless dresses or smocks; there was none of Rossetti's hypnotic indolence and little freedom of form about their daily lives. Liverpool was a city and a society, like most of Britain, curtailed by older conventions and by guarded, circumscribed roles. Hiding the unravelling narrative of a marriage took effort equal to that required to perform in tightly ruched skirts burdened by the weight of projecting bustles, the constraint of rows of tiny silk-covered buttons and tightly banded sleeves. It wasn't always easy to breathe out.

Put simply, the evolving position of women in society played its part in stoking opposing reactions to Florence Maybrick's story until it resonated with silent challenge. Hidden behind the oft-repeated difference in the ages of the married couple was an unarticulated concern about the clash between the old order and the rapidly evolving moral and social code. Enmeshed in the

detailed descriptions of Battlecrease House, stalwart in its bourgeois suburb, was a submerged worry that such bastions of social
stability could also be incubators of surreptitious rebellion.
Importantly, by choosing to stay in a hotel that was the regular
haunt of Liverpool cotton men, by defying her husband at the
Grand National and by writing openly to her lover, some were
beginning to believe that Florence had meant to flaunt her
infidelity. There was a certain shamelessness about her that
directly confronted the forces of conservatism and propriety.

During the previous summer Mona Caird's provocative
Westminster Review essay on marriage had triggered an overwhelming response. Now Florence Maybrick's adultery got under
the skin of those who set their faces against social reform. The
greengrocer's fruit may have arrived at her cell every day *with a
note of sympathy*, but the women attending the coroner's inquest
hissed when the contents of her letter to Brierley became known.
Apart from her mother, few among her own sex were generous
enough to regard her as innocent until proven guilty. Women, it
turned out, would be among her most entrenched and bitter critics. It seemed to be widely accepted that *unnatural* urges and
scandalous sexuality went hand in hand with predatory murder.

In this light it was perhaps unsurprising that the dull horror
of Florence's incarceration was compounded by a new rumour
that she was suffering from some kind of mania. On 8 June the
Liverpool Weekly News reported that an unnamed member of
the jury said to be *intimate with the family* had revealed that
there is 'something wrong' with Mrs Maybrick.

How much easier it might be for society if Michael had had
his way, allowing them all to believe that she was damaged and
deviant – mad – rather than simply foolish or rebelliously immoral.

THREE

CHAPTER 19

Second Verdict

Money was tight. Six days after the close of the inquest, on Wednesday 12 June, one of James Maybrick's two life insurance policies paid out a thousand pounds: less than half the amount due to Florence as his beneficiary. Battlecrease was closed up and empty, and Michael promised to forward a portion of the proceeds once the auction of its contents was complete. Alfred Brierley was in hiding, feeling himself to be *maligned, persecuted and misjudged in every way*. He would tell a journalist that he had sent four thousand pounds as a contribution towards Florence's defence fund, but this seems unlikely: the amount was enormous yet Florence's mother remained desperate, appealing to her friends in America for financial support.

Some time between five and six in the morning on that same Wednesday Florence was taken from Lark Lane in a windowless police van whose hard benches were bruisingly unyielding as it rattled over the deep cobbles of William Brown Street in the heart of the city.

Things were becoming increasingly serious. The County Sessions House was one of a cluster of new civic structures that included the Walker Art Gallery, the Picton Reading Rooms and the city library. In front of it loomed Liverpool's vast monument to industrial wealth, St George's Hall; to its left towered the hundred feet of the Wellington Memorial Column and, beyond that, the imposing façade of Lime Street station.

Florence must have passed here dozens of times, a sprightly, well-dressed young wife enjoying the civic and cultural delights of the seaport city, skirting the great hall as she walked from the shops of Bold Street to the Cotton Exchange district. How alien that world had become. The van now transporting her squeezed up Mill Lane towards the rear of the Sessions House, turning hard to the right and describing a semi-circle before passing through the thick iron-spiked gates of the prisoners' entrance.

Seagulls wheeled overhead, stretching their wings to the wind. Descending a slight incline, the horses drew up short. Bolts were drawn back and Florence got down from the vehicle, passing over rough stone setts whose edges dug into the soft soles of her shoes, then down a flight of broad stone steps into a domed-ceilinged basement. A succession of metal grilles were unlocked, dragged open and re-secured behind her.

The sounds of their feet echoed. Turning to the left, they entered a narrow whitewashed corridor with small cells ranged along its right-hand side, each with a flagstone floor and a murky window set high. More doors, more locks, the echo of steel on steel and the murmur and occasional shout of fellow prisoners waiting for their cases to be heard. Florence may have been relieved to find herself being conducted past these holding cells for she was shown instead into the relative comfort of a separate, small room. Her removal from the police cell so early in the morning was designed to thwart the expected crowds, but it meant that it would be several hours before her case was called.

By around nine o'clock the magistrates' carriages were arriving, the serious-faced men passing swiftly through the paired columns on the grandly carved façade of the Sessions House and through its heavy front door before ascending marble steps under an intricately groined ceiling. Glossy green ceramic tiles faced the lower parts of the walls and a bright, Roman-inspired mosaic decorated the floor. The rooms to the left were sumptuous: elaborate plasterwork transformed ceilings into grottoes; there was precious-wood panelling and pressed-leather wallpapers; the brass door handles took the form of the Lancastrian rose; a marble fireplace was surmounted by a glittering mirror. Everything here was rich and solid, designed to reflect power without stinting on comfort – hot and cold water ran into porcelain hand basins and pairs of small mirrors hung on either side of the walls to facilitate the checking of appearances from all angles.

Across the hallway, the library shelves in the barristers' room were packed with richly bound legal volumes and imposing desks were variously disposed; there was a fireplace and capacious accommodation for robes and case papers. Behind these two large private areas, the internal arrangements of the building were complex: separate entrances for solicitors, witnesses, prisoners and magistrates led to a maze of corridors and staircases all ending in wrought-iron grilles, each designed to keep the various players apart until they confronted one another in court. It was all very new, clever and grand, but the shiny surfaces also made the building noisy, setting nerves on edge.

The charge against Florence was due to be heard in the larger of the two courts, an imposing room with a light-well set in the centre of the plaster-scrolled ceiling. When it rained, it was deafening. At other times the scuttling claws of the pigeons scraped against the glass. Between the raised magistrates' bench and the dock in the centre of the room were benches and desks for the lawyers and spaces for the clerks. Up to the right of the magistrates, behind the witness stand, were gallery seats for privileged members of the public, while down in the body of the courtroom were desks with inkwells for the newspapermen.

The police had instructions to limit the number allowed into the court so that many people still milled around the building once all the public seats were filled, irritated to have missed the arrival of the prisoner, disappointed not to gain entry and determined to wait for news. The empty dock was pitifully exposed, a caged island in a sea of faces.

Under a stained glass, half-moon window set directly in the centre of the front wall of the court, the grandly ornamented wooden doors eventually opened. Two magistrates entered – the local merchant, ship-owner and politician Sir William Forwood, and Mr W. S. Barrett. Taking their seats, they nodded to their officials and to several other magistrates who, one paper wrote, appeared only to have *dropped in to get a good view of the interesting prisoner.*

An order went out:

Put the prisoner in the dock.

There was a lull. Then Florence – flanked by a police sergeant and a wardress – made her way through the hushed room towards the armchair waiting for her in the raised, brass-railed dock. Quietly, she took her bearings, struck by how oddly proximate everything was despite the grandeur of the court. The witness stand in front and to her left, the empty jury box ahead to her right and the public seats were all so close that she could almost have reached out to touch their occupants.

Florence might have been the model for William Frederick Yeames's painting *Defendant and Counsel* (1895), in which a meticulously dressed young woman stares blankly forward, separated from her lawyers not simply by a solid, polished desk but by her gender. The nature of her alleged crime is unknown; her guilt or innocence is unarticulated. What is clear is a mute, vacant despair and the apparently insurmountable divide between her and the male justice system. Trained like all middle-class women to leave business to the men and to concentrate only on looking and acting the part ascribed to her, Yeames makes it clear that, for his subject, the raw difficulty of negotiating the lawyers' conversation while cowering from the glare of public exposure is stupefying.

Beneath a thick black veil, Florence leaned back in her chair, grasping a pencil and blank paper, looking towards her lawyers for anchor. Newspapermen stared hard and then wrote: *she wore a long jacket of black cloth trimmed with crape, a crape bonnet with a crape veil behind and fastened under the chin with a crape bow*, noted one. *Black gloves were on her hands. A strip of white material in the bonnet and the folds of a white handkerchief peeping from the breast slightly relieved the sombreness of Mrs Maybrick's attire... [The] veil, drawn rather tightly across the face, dimly defined the profile but concealed every other feature, excepting the firmly set mouth and the chin, with its strong indication of courage and determination.*

*

In many ways the magisterial proceedings would be a reprisal of the inquest. Mr Pickford again represented Florence, Mr Steel the Maybricks and Mr Mulholland was present for Alfred Brierley. Superintendent Bryning began with a twenty-five-minute summary of the case, detailing the quarrels, Florence's infidelity, her purchase of flypapers and the discovery of arsenic in various places around the house.

Each witness emerged in the stand via stairs that led directly from their waiting rooms. Dr Hopper spoke of marital discord. Matilda Briggs said she had called for a nurse *with Mrs Maybrick's reluctant consent and Mrs Maybrick paid for the telegram.* Her testimony gave the impression of a certain lack of straightforwardness, emphasised by her admission that she had suggested that Florence write to ask Brierley out of *sarcasm.*

Did you tell this to the coroner? Pickford demanded.

I did not.

Alfred Schweisso, hair centre-parted and oiled back over his temples, confirmed that Florence and Brierley had occupied *one bedroom* at Flatman's Hotel. Bessie spoke of the soaking fly-papers, saying that she was sure that her mistress was on the landing when she went into the bedroom where the basin stood; she was equally certain that James' bedroom door had remained open, for the most part, throughout his final illness.

When Florence was led from the court for the half-hour lunch recess her *firmness of bearing* and her *unconstrained* attitude were noted. Everyone wondered at her self-possession.

Though she refused to show it, it was all a kind of torture.

After the break, Alice Yapp took the stand, remaining for what seemed like an age, each of her answers minutely interrogated. Several of the bottles, boxes, handkerchiefs and phials – *links in the chain of evidence*, as the papers called them – were produced. Blandly common, they trailed the whiff of malice so that the public looked on with a concentration of attention, perhaps hoping that any one of them might reveal the whole secret of the case. In Florence's favour, Pickford managed to draw from Yapp that it was her mistress who had insisted on calling for Dr Humphreys when her husband first fell ill. Yapp also conceded that, with regard to the flypapers, *there was no attempt at concealment*.

Mrs Humphreys deposed that her mistress's orders for invalid food had been given as a direct result of the doctor's instructions. Then Edwin was called. Repeating his certainty that his brother had not been addicted to arsenic, he did accept that he might have thought *that if his brother would take less physic he would be better*. Throughout, Florence betrayed no outward emotion other than an occasional *sigh and a movement of the lips*. Inclining her head towards the witness box, determinedly concentrating on the statements as they were given, she regularly handed notes over the front of the dock to be passed forward to Richard Cleaver.

Fourteen long hours after she had left Lark Lane, at seven o'clock, the hearing was adjourned. Clutching her papers, she rose, turned and came face to face with the public seats. Hisses erupted from some of the women, viper sounds that swirled in her face, gathering in intensity as the magistrate shouted for calm. The gleeful self-satisfaction, the expressions of gratified curiosity and censure that shone in these women's faces, wrote one Liverpool paper, were *disgusting*. Braving it all, Florence tried hard not to show her fear.

*

A furnished apartment was provided inside the Sessions House so that she did not have to leave the building, yet Florence hardly slept. In the morning she dressed in the same mourning costume she had worn the previous day, adding a fur boa. Once again, the majority of those in the public seats were ladies or young girls, some raising opera glasses to peer openly at her as she passed. A few thought her step seemed less firm, her resolve less steeled, yet once more she played her part admirably. *On seating herself in the armchair in the dock*, noted one keen-eyed reporter, *she loosened the boa from her neck, and with a graceful movement of the arms threw it back until it hung negligently on her shoulders. Then she resumed the easy reclining attitude which she maintained throughout the first day's hearing.*

Florence's face, veiled, was impenetrable, yet she watched each witness carefully avoid looking in her direction. After James' charlady and his clerk, Michael Maybrick's name was called and he appeared, broad-shouldered, muscular and unusually tanned so that many were surprised to see that he had about him – according to the *Liverpool Mercury* – something of the *appearance of a sea captain*. Michael did not deny that his brother's wife had written to him to express concern about James' liking for unprescribed medicine, also that she had called for him and for Edwin on several occasions during James' previous illnesses.

Boxes, bottles and rags pertinent to his statements were held up by a clerk and on each occasion several members of the public half-stood in their eagerness to see *these leading players in the drama.* Michael also accepted that the bottles he saw Florence 'tampering' with turned out to contain nothing alarming. Countering the suggestion that she had been left penniless and vulnerable immediately following her husband's death, he insisted that he had, at his own expense, sent several telegrams on her behalf both to America and to the Baroness von Roques.

Florence leaned forward with a note. Scanning it quickly, Pickford called for Michael, already half way out of the court-room, to return.

Mr Maybrick, was there not a telegram which Mrs Maybrick wished to send to New York, but which was not sent? Pickford asked.

[After a pause] *There was. I gave it to Inspector Baxendale, and he returned it to me the next day, and said he did not think it was important. I did send it all the same.*

It was delayed one day, however?

Yes, but I sent it off eventually.

Pickford allowed that word 'eventually' to hang.

After Michael, each of the nurses from the Dover Street Institution spoke of the instructions they had received not to allow Florence to be involved in any aspect of her husband's care; consequently she had never been left alone with him and there had been no opportunity for her to give him anything to eat or drink. Specifically, the contents of the tainted bottle of Valentine's meat juice – the one she was seen so oddly to secrete out of the bedroom and to bring back in again – had never been given to James. Gore added something new: that on both the Wednesday and Thursday before he died Mr Maybrick had been strong enough to get in and out of bed without assistance. He had done so, she said, several times.

Asking Dr Humphreys whether it was not possible that James'

infection derived from tainted tinned meat or decomposed food, Pickford wondered why the doctor had not thought of arsenic before Michael voiced his suspicions. Would he confirm that he had prescribed solutions containing arsenic during the final week of the dead man's life? Had Mrs Maybrick not also, several times, told him that she believed her husband took strychnine?

Dr Barron – the third doctor present both at the post-mortem and the exhumation – then made a surprising statement. He agreed that poison had been the cause of the inflammation of James' bowels but, when pressed to answer *what sort of poison*, he replied solemnly that he *could not say*.

Is that the only thing you disagree on? demanded the Clerk of the Court.

Barron's reply – *I am not prepared to go further* – was the first indication that the scientific evidence might not be as clear as everyone had previously thought – that there might be a lurking disagreement among the doctors.

Following a brief break, Florence re-entered the court clutching a bundle of papers – a copy of the list of items sent to the city analyst for testing. During Edward Davies's deposition she made copious notes and appeared not to be in the slightest bit alarmed by his findings. Indeed, it was significantly in her favour that the chemist had found no fibres in the bottle containing a solution of arsenic: if it had been made by soaking flypapers, he told the court, fibres would certainly be present.

Superintendent Bryning's account of her arrest would provide the most titillating fodder for the papers on the following day. Noting that Florence was reputed to be vivacious and talkative, her lack of response to the accusation and the charge seemed to one reporter to mark her out as *possessing in a supreme measure a faculty of silence*. What was one, then, to make of her? She was beginning to elicit a confusing mixture of admiration and distrust. Equally, women able to maintain their self-control in such circumstances (none of the papers pointed out that Florence had been very unwell) were made of sterner stuff than was quite attractive: it may have done Florence more good, in the eyes of the public, to have broken down and wept.

Bryning was done with his witnesses and no one was much surprised to hear Mr Pickford announce that he would once more reserve his defence. Withdrawing, the magistrates and their clerk deliberated for just two minutes before returning to the court. Florence was instructed to stand. Sir William Forwood gravely informed her that they considered enough evidence to exist to send her to trial for wilful murder.

Barely perceptibly, she swayed, clasping the rail before her. Then, refusing the assistance of the policeman or the wardress, Florence turned to her left and waited while the top of the wood panel at the rear of the dock was swung upwards on an intricate, well-oiled mechanism, revealing a steep stairway that descended to the cells. It was like lifting the lid on a coffin to reveal the narrow pathway to hell. Clutching the thin iron rail, ducking instinctively as she went forward, her foot felt for the next stone step and she descended, her skirts snagging against the rough walls that pressed too close on either side.

Seventeen steps. Her breath shallow and rapid. Her concentration centred on the effort not to fall.

She was baffled. She had believed Richard Cleaver when he told her that there was not enough solid scientific evidence to prove that James died of arsenic poisoning. She had heard the doctors disagree in court about causes and symptoms. Edward Davies had admitted that he had failed to discover fibres in either the clear solution or the tainted bottle of meat juice, ruling out the origin of the arsenic being flypapers. Why had these facts been insufficient to set her free? Why had no one asked how the bottles and packets containing arsenic came to be in the house, or who had brought them there?

Sitting, stunned, she was handed a cup of tea. It was six o'clock in the evening. Within the hour she would be hustled out of a side exit and into a police cab waiting in the lane that ran between the Sessions House and the Walker Art Gallery. It would take her once more to Walton Gaol.

Outside, intense excitement combined with mounting indignation. When activity was spotted this mob – remarkable once again for containing a large number of young women – swarmed around the prison vehicle, yelling. Momentarily it seemed that they might overwhelm it. The driver's whip flashed; the horses were urged forward. The carriage pulled away and soon outpaced the horde.

CHAPTER 20

Making it Stick

Superintendent Bryning officially commended Inspector Baxendale for his *able seconding of the case*. Now the police had to concentrate on making it watertight. Items were still being delivered to Edward Davies's laboratory including, at the end of June, Florence's dressing gown and a stained handkerchief found in one of its pockets. The newspapers settled back into conjecture: would she stand trial for her life in London or Liverpool? Was it possible to provide an unbiased jury or was the public mind already prejudiced? All agreed that the Battlecrease servants had turned out to be *rather a good-looking lot dressed out quite stylishly*. All were intrigued by Florence's appearance and bearing. Did her eyes flash fire? What could be read into her cool inscrutability? Was it stoicism or callous indifference? Was it possible that such a physically fragile woman could survive the forceful process of the law?

Papers smart enough to print illustrations of the unhappy couple sold out fast. Among them all, only Liverpool's *Weekly Review* pointed out that, heavily veiled as she was, it had been impossible to see the expression on Florence's face. It wrote that

her carriage in entering the dock and her conduct while there was
graceful and calm being just, in fact, what one would expect
from a woman of first-class social training. It is difficult to see
what else she could do but remain perfectly passive. She could
not have been expected to scream or dance a jig. The same paper
censured what it called the *morbid, shameless* females who had
crammed the public seats, reminding them that even Jesus had
refused to judge an adulteress.

Reaction, then, was tangled. The fact of Florence's adultery
still seemed to outweigh the suspicion that she had poisoned her
husband; yet by expressing their revulsion so forcefully her
female critics were themselves reproved for their unladylike
behaviour. Similarly, Matilda Briggs, Constance Hughes and
Alice Yapp, by their disapproval, put themselves firmly on the
side of morality and public duty; yet their apparent lack of gen-
erosity also appeared spiteful. Sometimes it seemed that it was
not just Florence Maybrick in the dock, but the character and the
role of women as a whole.

By 22 June, a week and a half after Florence's ordeal at the
County Sessions House and a month before the assizes were due
to begin, the prosecution team was established. It would be led
by the Irish Conservative John Addison, QC, MP, assisted by W.
R. M'Connell who, coincidentally, had played a part in prosecut-
ing Flanagan and Higgins five years before. Another Irishman –
Sir Charles Russell, QC, fifty-seven years old, Attorney General
in Gladstone's short-lived 1886 administration and at the peak of
his legal career – was rumoured to be the most likely choice to
head her defence.

Working together to strengthen the case, police and prosecution
recalled all the key witnesses during the first week of July and took
additional statements under oath. Attempting to pinpoint exactly
when the fatal dose or doses had been administered, they questioned the chemists Wokes and Hanson unremittingly about the
dates on which they thought Florence had purchased flypapers.

They went back over the nurses' stories, asking them repeatedly what they thought James Maybrick had meant by his two outbursts *Oh Bunny! I would not have thought it of you* and *Don't give me the wrong medicine again!* They quizzed the office clerk and the bookkeeper about the bottles on the mantelpiece and the dates on which James had brought his own food into work, and they asked Bessie Brierley to be quite certain about the exact days on which her master had been physically sick. Mrs Humphreys, the gardener James Grant (for the first time), chemists from the city firm of Clay & Abraham and the two doctors who had treated James during his final week – Humphreys and Carter – were all re-interrogated. Prosecution juniors pored over a copy of the post-mortem report and Inspector Baxendale took the jars containing Maybrick's viscera to Professor Thomas Stevenson at Guy's Hospital in London. Senior scientific analyst to the Home Office and one of England's leading forensic scientists, Stevenson had been asked by the prosecution to repeat Davies's chemical analyses in order to provide a second expert opinion on the cause of death.

Alfred Brierley was subpoenaed to produce letters or documents in his possession that might relate to the case or to his relationship with Florence. Embarrassed and humiliated, he wanted only to run away and so instructed his solicitors, Banks & Kendall of North John Street, to take a firm stand. In turn they advised the Home Office that their client had no relevant correspondence and that it would not be convenient for him to make any further statements, *as he had made arrangements to go away for his holiday and as you can well understand it is very unpleasant for him to have to attend the court in this case, particularly if his doing so can serve no useful purpose.* Brierley was cutting the ties that bound him to Florence as fast, as effectively and as finally as he could.

If she believed that her lover would remain constant, Florence could not have been more mistaken. Had she been so hot-headed that she had suffered shame and scorn for a handful of days of happiness? Had her dalliance been a fantasy, a vain hope that she could temporarily rewrite the story of her married life, or had she really given no thought to the consequences of her actions, lusting for momentary emotional truth over odious respectability?

Or were Florence's sensibilities so formed by her reading tastes that she had imagined herself stepping out of reality and into the person of a fictional adulteress? Whatever had passed through her mind, however superficially she had considered her actions, she had left a trail of evidence to prove the scandalous truth: telegrams to Brierley when she feared that James was on their trail, further notes to assure him that her fears were mistaken. She had kept the letter from Brierley in which he encouraged her to hold her nerve, comforting her that he would take her away if the true nature of their assignation came to light. She had thought little, if at all, about covering her tracks.

While the bustling Baroness and Florence's lawyers concentrated on formulating her defence, Florence began to dread the exposure of the dock, the fact that she would be forced to suffer the ordeal of it all while maintaining her composure in public view. She shrank from the thought of uncharitable eyes, of a courtroom atmosphere pulsing with scornful judgement. Confined to her cell, she tried to galvanise her courage. Sympathy might have undone her but, receiving none, she managed to maintain a determined façade. She even thought to write a note making suggestions about who might best look after her children if Nurse Yapp was called away from their care in order to testify at the trial.

*

Tirelessly trying to stimulate support while keeping Florence's spirits up, her mother travelled back and forth from London. She rented a room in Great Crosby on the outskirts of Liverpool, living under an alias to avoid the attentions of the press and making the trip between the Cleavers' office in town and Walton Gaol several times a week. Meanwhile, her London lawyers issued a statement deriding as calumnious the tittle-tattle about her past, emphasising that it only prejudiced her daughter's case. *The trouble to her is surely crushing enough*, they wrote to the newspaper editors, *without its being aggravated by slanders, which have no foundation in truth or fact.*

Meanwhile, the Maybrick brothers, eager to draw a line under the whole affair, placed advertisements in the Liverpool press asking for James' creditors to come forward within the week. Trophy hunters had pulled up plants from the Battlecrease gardens and, on 8 and 9 July, the auctioneers sold off the furniture, Japanese wares, Turkey carpets, mantel clocks and curtains, most of it going to *connoisseurs and friends* – according to the local paper – rather than to dealers. While Florence battled with the incessant mental effort of maintaining both hope and self-control, her former life was being comprehensively dismantled.

The beam of newspaper curiosity did, however, begin to swing away from her as reporters looked for fresh facts or worried at details beginning to slip out about James Maybrick's medical appetites. Many commentators believed that the various testimonies already heard materially confirmed his habit of dosing himself with arsenic. The *Daily Post*, setting out to test the theory, had discovered a pharmacist who claimed to have worked for years in several different businesses located near the Exchange, who was ready to swear that he recognised James from illustrations in the papers and that he had supplied him regularly with arsenic. It was said that James had been a frequent though covert customer, that he always asked to be served by the same man, that he never gave his name and that he frequently took away with him as much as forty grains in solution, paying for it in cash. Superintendent Bryning was on holiday, but it was reported by the *Liverpool Mercury* that he had also instructed his team to continue to make detailed enquiries at all the city's chemists in order to draw up a list of anyone who might have sold arsenic to the cotton broker.

The Baroness's American lawyers, Messrs Roe & Macklin of 156 Broadway, were reported by the *New York Times* to be turning up abundant evidence that *Maybrick was habitually addicted to using opium, arsenic, strychnine and other poisons*. One of his former roommates in Norfolk, Virginia – before his marriage to Florence – was said to be ready to swear to James' hunger for poisons and a servant employed by James during the same period was apparently able to corroborate the story. In order to bring potential witnesses back in time for the trial, Arnold Cleaver sailed from Liverpool in mid-July.

The days were slipping away while events in the port city remained the focus of the nation's interest. On 25 July Alice Yapp removed the children from their godmother's house in order to take them to Wales for three weeks' holiday. On the same day, the Criminal Register for the Lancaster summer assizes was produced – a list of every case due to be heard. Heading it was the charge of murder against Florence Maybrick. There was another murder charge, alongside several for wounding, a number of robberies with violence and two charges of attempting to commit buggery. The name of only one other woman appeared on the list: working-class Edith Dunn, charged with wounding with intent to cause grievous bodily harm.

As predicted, Sir Charles Russell had agreed to lead Florence's defence. A Liberal MP, quick-witted Irishman, scholarly and eloquent, Russell had just finished successfully representing Charles Stewart Parnell, the Irish Home Rule leader, before a long-running Special Government Commission. His career was so distinguished that in a handful more years he would be made Lord Chief Justice. Cleaver, in other words, had picked the heaviest of hitters. He had also arranged for Russell to be assisted by William Pickford, at that time the leading junior on the Northern Circuit and already familiar with the case through his involvement at the inquest and magisterial hearing.

Florence had hoped for a London trial, writing to her mother that she believed that *the tittle-tattle of servants, the public friends, and enemies, and a thousand by-currents, besides their personal feelings for Jim, must leave their traces*. In Liverpool, she thought, minds would be prejudiced *no matter what the defence* is. The Cleavers disagreed. They thought it stronger and wiser to remain in the city and so, arriving in Liverpool around the time that Yapp left it with the children, Russell began an intense week of conferences to bring himself up to speed. Although leading barristers usually took their instructions simply from the solicitors involved, he also sought a lengthy interview with Florence at Walton Gaol.

One of the most famous judges in the country, Sir James Fitzjames Stephen, had been appointed to preside over the trial. Physically big, with square shoulders, the jowly face of a statesman, a deep voice and a commanding, not to say intimidating, manner, Stephen was the author of acclaimed works of legal history and had enjoyed a brilliant career. But behind his powerful appearance were concerns that he no longer quite possessed the acute mind on which his reputation was founded: some sort of mental illness back in 1885 had left it – some said – noticeably clouded and there were whispers that his judgement was becoming erratic.

On Friday 26 July, Judge Stephen delivered the charge against Florence to the grand jury in St George's Hall. In effect, his responsibility was to outline the evidence against her in order to consider whether the case was strong enough to proceed. In the event, Stephen expressed more of his personal opinion than some of the lawyers present thought quite appropriate. Touching on the fact that Florence was proved to have stayed at Flatman's Hotel with Alfred Brierley, the judge intimated that he believed her infidelity provided a strong indication of her guilt. *I hardly know how to put it otherwise than this*, he told them, *that if a woman does carry on an adulterous intrigue with another man, it may supply every sort of motive – that of saving her own reputation; that of breaking through the connection, which, under such circumstances, one would think would be dreadfully painful to the party to it. It certainly may quite supply – I wont go further – very strong motive why she should wish to get rid of her husband.*

It was oddly irregular of the judge to hint at his own opinion prior to the trial's commencement, but for now perhaps that was unimportant since a substantial quantity of suspicious evidence already existed. The responsibility of the grand jury was simply to decide whether there was enough of it to bring a 'true bill' against Florence – a necessary part of the process of sending her to trial. By doing so, they ensured that she would be brought into the dock, as scheduled, on the following Wednesday.

On Monday 29 July Judge Stephen heard an application from two lawyers petitioning for their client's trial to be delayed until after Mrs Maybrick's. Agreeing, he was asked whether he thought it likely that the murder trial would last for several days. *You must use your own discretion in the matter*, he replied. *Sir Charles Russell may very likely wish to plead guilty.* There was loud laughter mixed with some astonishment. If Florence Maybrick were so to plead, then the trial would be over in a day. Did the eminent judge really believe this was likely? If so, had he been thus advised, or was he prejudging the outcome of events?

Six weeks after James' death, probate had been granted on his estate. The will, reprinted widely in the Liverpool papers just days before the trial, left everything to Michael and Thomas Maybrick in trust for his children. Contrary to speculation, he had not been poor: in fact, after deductions, James' estate was valued at £3779 or close to a quarter of a million pounds in today's terms. Had she not been written out of the will, his widow would – after all – have been quite comfortably off.

On Wednesday 31 July temperatures in Liverpool, held down
by the fresh sea wind, hardly reached the mid-sixties. One of
the greatest Victorian showpiece trials was scheduled to begin
at ten o'clock and interest in the case, having waned somewhat, was again fevered: *the ins and outs of the strange story
being eagerly discussed by all sorts and conditions of men, to
the exclusion of every other subject of conversation*, according
to one Liverpool paper. The High Sheriff, the under sheriffs,
the police and Mr Jennings – keeper of St George's Hall – had
all been bothered endlessly for tickets of admission; it was
said that five hundred requests were received for each available
space – the great majority from ladies. Special provision had
been made for extra seats in the journalists' gallery in expectation of representatives from the national press and the medical
journalists who were particularly focused on recording the
scientific testimony. Further places for the press were available
on either side of the dock.

The papers fed the morbid appetite of the public for a trial that
promised to provide a spectacle, and rumour had it that new
witnesses for the defence had arrived in Liverpool just in time.
Even those who believed that they already knew all the salient
facts of the case were on edge. It seemed to most that the trial
could go either way. What no one could ignore was the fact that
if Florence Maybrick were found guilty she would hang.

CHAPTER 21

The Trial: Day One

St George's Hall, Liverpool's neo-classical monument to progress, covered three and a half acres, dominating the centre of the city and dwarfing the public buildings ranged behind it. On each of its façades fifty-foot pillars formed colonnades and a line of massive stone lions – front paws crossed, faces passive – guarded the eastern entrance. Outside, the building proclaimed mercantile inviolability and civic pride; inside, its ornate plaster ceilings, gilded doors, vast organ pipes, Minton floor tiles and a great hall capable of seating a thousand, spoke of wealth, craftsmanship and artistry.

The Crown Court used during the quarterly assizes was divided off from the main hall by an intricate brass screen. Spacious by comparison with other law courts, light entered from the glass roof-well and through glazed doors and large windows on its western wall. Despite this, dark oak panelling imbued the space with a dreadful earnestness and its lofty marble pillars reinforced the impression that judgement was wielded here with a stony power. Nine separate entrances led to distinct areas for lawyers, witnesses and the public. The judges' raised bench was wood-canopied, with the county coat of arms suspended at its centre. The wide, square dock sat in the very middle of the room. Between it and the bench were the lawyers' and clerks' desks and space for the press.

For Florence the ordeal so far had been anticipation. Now it was stern reality. Was the previous night sleepless and feverish, followed by a morning in which the indignity of it all – the infidelity, the public scorn, the ugly addiction – seemed over-whelming? Or did she discover – as she hoped she would – that, with the game to play, her anxiety receded, leaving her nerves braced and her mind lucid and calm?

Anyone watching might have said so, for her face gave nothing away. At half-past eight that morning a black van had arrived at St George's Hall from Walton, the male prisoners in a compartment at the front and, separately at the rear, Florence with her two wardresses. Entering the wide, low-ceilinged base-ment corridor along which cells were arranged, her features were composed into a mask of self-possession, but she felt as if she were already buried. Oily hands had marked the walls of her cell. There was a mug, a candle, a bucket. The names of previous occupants were scratched into the walls and the plank bench. Curses, shuffling, howls, coughs and cries rose from the spaces around her: unnerving noises that were not of her world but of the dispossessed. Her breathing was uneven. If she was tempted to cry out, to articulate her own grief, to affirm to herself that she was still alive, then she smothered the impulse. She would not yield to this fear.

The bench was hard. The cold chill of brick seeped into her back. Her hands, gloved in finest black silk, were folded in her lap. She waited.

When it was almost time, Florence was taken from her cell, passing through a substantial gate that echoed metallically as it was re-secured behind her, then mounting a flight of eighteen wide stone steps that curved to the left. The floor of the spacious landing was set with large stone flags. Straight ahead was a single, smaller holding cell with benches on three sides, a narrow barred window, a gaslight mounted high on the wall to the left and – she could not get used to it – no handle on the inside of the door. Nothing was clean. There was time to continue to gain control of her mounting fear, to re-compose herself to face the men on whom her life depended: the judge in his ermine; the black-gowned, wigged lawyers, the suited clerks, uniformed sheriffs and the ordinary men of the jury who would decide her fate.

Above her, the court was packed with Liverpool society: ladies were dressed for a matinée and, once again, there was a striking number of eager young girls. John Addison, QC, MP, and his prosecution team were already in place. To their right sat William Pickford, QC. Directly in front of him was solicitor Richard Cleaver. In the otherwise empty dock, the governor of Walton and his chief warder waited patiently for things to get under way.

At twelve minutes to ten, the jurymen filed in to the left of the judge's seat. Each came from a Lancashire district beyond the city centre of Liverpool. T. Ball (plumber), John Bryers (farmer) and H. Thierens (baker) were from Ormskirk; A. Harrison (wood turner) came from Bootle; W. Walmsley (provision dealer), W. H. Gaskell (plumber-glazier) and H. Sutton (milliner) were all three from North Meols; J. Taylor (farmer) was from Melling; George Welsby (grocer) came from St Helens; James Tyrer (printer) was from Wigan; and John Bryers (farmer) from Bickerstaffe. Their foreman was Thomas Wainwright (another plumber), from Southport. These men, with their rudimentary educations, would be charged with determining one of the most complicated toxicological cases of the day.

On the stroke of ten, Sir Charles Russell *entered the court with an elastic step . . . Every eye was immediately turned towards the clear-cut features of the famous advocate.* A striking, earnest, intellectually masterful man with bright eyes and a grim mouth, Russell had a reputation for success, and it had not escaped the newspapers that this was a case for which he was ably experienced. In 1873 he had successfully prosecuted Mary Ann Cotton for a series of murders using a mixture of soft soap and arsenic. In 1886 he had also prosecuted wide-eyed Adelaide Bartlett for the murder of her husband by chloroform.

Checking the papers handed to him by his clerk, Russell narrowed his eyes and waited.

Florence heard the distant flourish of a trumpet fanfare as the High Sheriff entered the court with his liveried entourage. At three minutes past the hour, the door at the rear of the bench was thrown open and Judge Stephen entered. The court rose to its feet.

Swathed in crimson robes, Stephen bowed gravely to the jury and lawyers before motioning for the court to sit. On the bench to either side of him were the High Sheriff, his chaplain and the Earl of Sefton – coincidentally, the chairman of the Liverpool Cricket Club, which counted the Maybricks among its prominent members and whose grounds were opposite Battlecrease House.

The Clerk of the Crown, addressing the chief warder of Walton Gaol, called loudly for the prisoner to be put up. There were shuffles and creaks as the public leaned forward.

Florence Elizabeth Maybrick, twenty-six years old, looked up as the door of her cell was opened. Leaving it, she turned to her right and climbed a handful of stone stairs to a shallow landing. Ten more steps rose before her, narrowing as they twisted to the left. Emerging into the relative glare of the courtroom, she moved slowly – and with an apparent calm that impressed everybody – through a hip-height swing door and into the iron-railed dock. A cane chair had been placed at the front.

As the charge of murder was read, she clenched her teeth in an attempt to control her agitation. When she was asked for her plea, she took a deep breath and then replied firmly – the reporters called her voice musical – *Not guilty*.

Again, she wore deep mourning. Broad white cuffs relieved the severity of the wide crape sleeves of her jacket and a fine veil, partially covering her face without concealing it, fell from a small bonnet. Her hair was curled in clusters around her forehead and she was considered by all – wrote *Lloyd's Weekly* – to be *a woman of exceedingly attractive appearance – slight, graceful and neat in figure*. Sitting passively, *with downcast eyes and clasped hands*, she was not expected to be heard again for the duration of the trial for, despite urgent lobbying by legal reformers, the law still held the view that defendants in capital cases were 'incompetent' witnesses and that, by allowing them to speak only through legal counsel, they were protected from self-incrimination under cross-examination. It was possible, once the prosecution and the defence had each finished calling witnesses, for a defendant to seek permission from the judge to make a personal statement. No one expected Florence to do so. Instead, she would listen to the testimonies – thirty for the prosecution and twelve for the defence – while remaining silent, barred either from commenting on them or from articulating her own version of events.

Few members of the public would ever have seen a woman of Florence's class and bearing in the dock, and almost certainly not one being tried for a capital offence. In the 1890s women (of all classes) would make up just a sixth of all criminals. Although almost a third of those were convicted of murder, male juries were generally reticent about convicting middle-class women for crimes they found it impossible to believe them morally capable of committing. Thus by maintaining her pose of sexual purity, pretty young Adelaide Bartlett and her brilliant lawyer had manipulated the trial judge's sense of chivalry and she had been acquitted.

For similar reasons, the sentences given to convicted women were often less severe than those apportioned to men. Yet when it came to women accused of violence, both society and the press reacted in contradictory ways. Where there was evidence of promiscuity, an imputation of deviancy was almost inevitable. Then, the more spirited the defendant the more she threatened the social order: back in 1849 the robustly aggressive Marie Manning – murderer of her lover and double-crosser of her husband – had encouraged reactions both of fascination and of revulsion. It was not unusual for journalists to be riveted, as they were with Florence, by the way female defendants accused of murder looked: on their femininity, their waspish waists, petite figures, frail, pale faces and slender hands. Society desired both to protect women and to hold them to stringent moral expectations that were not applied equally to men. Inevitably, an uncomfortable strain resulted from trying to reconcile opposites: the desire to punish aberrance from the social norm and the wish to mitigate the harshness of that sentence because of their sex. The very gender of female defendants was often the defining factor in their trial, getting in the way of judicial clarity.

Women on trial for murder were so much more interesting to watch than their male counterparts. By inverting the stereotype of the Angel in the House they were proof, to some, of the dangers of progressive thinking or of sexual liberty. Reviewing the Maybrick case, the *St James's Gazette* now drew parallels between Florence and the treacherous anti-heroines of 1860s novels, though it might have looked to more recent history for literary echo. Throughout the 1880s and 1890s writers like Henry James were exploring the inner turmoil of women locked into difficult situations, suffering painfully while continuing to behave beautifully. These novelists had become obsessed by the idea that the surface polish of life obscured a maelstrom of domestic difficulties and that the silky folds of suffocating convention housed darker, less palatable realities. Now, the Maybrick story was blasting away the varnish of suburban life, revealing the truth beneath its decorum. As Trollope's Kate Vavasour put it, it showed them something *all clean and polished outside with filth and rottenness within.*

As Florence Maybrick took her place in the dock, spectators wondered whether she was angel or medusa. Was this the human face of female aberration? Was she a vicious whore whose actions flew in the face of patriarchal Victorian ideologies? Had she stealthily plotted her husband's decline or was she a vulnerable fool whose actions had been misunderstood? The difficulty for her defence counsel would be finding a way to untangle proven infidelity from intent to kill.

*

Up in the grand jury box women in bright summer silks were so close to the dock that Florence, if she looked up, would stare directly into their faces. Above them, in a higher gallery, more members of the public craned like so many watchful crows. As if to heighten the drama of the proceedings, Judge Stephen had directed that the witnesses would not use the stand but would be positioned instead between him and the jury, in plainer view of the open court.

The edge of the chair was hard against the back of her knees. Between the dock and the judge's bench the sober lawyers fanned out, a close-knit clique well used to pitting their wits against one another. These men, rearranging their papers and clearing their throats, were about to do battle for Florence's life.

*

John Addison – a broad-shouldered man with a jolly face, a high voice and distinct enunciation – rose at eight minutes past ten to begin the prosecution's case by detailing the suspicious circumstances that had brought Mrs Maybrick to trial: her relationship with Brierley, the argument at Battlecrease on the evening of the Grand National, her desire for a separation and her purchase of flypapers. Russell interrupted, asking for all the witnesses except the scientists to leave the court lest they be prejudiced by what they heard. The judge agreed. Then Addison continued, summarising the discovery of arsenic, the suspicion surrounding various bottles and James' overheard plea, *How could you do it? I didn't think it of you.* Calling on the jury to forget anything they might already have heard or read, the barrister's rhetoric was, on the face of it, designed to persuade them that he would argue the case rationally rather than with passion or prejudice. In fact, Addison was careful quickly to introduce the idea that below the privileged surface of the Maybrick marriage lurked the kind of disharmony that led to malice.

Addison recalled the difference in the couple's ages. He suggested that James' occasional hypochondria was nothing but the mildly irritating neurosis of a generally hale man. Sure that the defence would try to prove that he was an arsenic addict, Addison was also careful to admit that doctors had prescribed nux vomica and even strychnine in small quantities – this, he contended, was not at all unusual. Describing the effects of arsenic on the body, he then told the jury that numbness and pains in the legs would not overly concern a doctor but, combined with vomiting and diarrhoea, they became suspicious. Two grains of arsenic, he said, were enough to kill a man; repeated small doses would have the same effect. *This*, he intoned, *is what renders it such a dangerous poison.*

Over the following two hours Addison speculated that Florence, finding that her husband was recovering from his initial bout of sickness, had bought a second batch of flypapers. Here – he posited – was a mystery: *These flypapers were never seen by any person in the house and the question is, what she wanted with them and what she did with them?* Next, he discussed the invalid porridges taken by James to his office, gently eliding the subjects of food and poison while focusing on the fact that the defendant had openly gone about extracting an arsenical solution from flypapers. It was a masterful speech, leaving the jury and the court in no doubt that he would pick away at the facts of Florence's infidelity while focusing precisely on the dates and times of her husband's fluctuating symptoms. *I have no notion up to the present time what explanation might be given to explain away the facts*, he declared. *The first question ... [is] whether you have any reason to doubt what the doctors will swear to without doubt and that the chemists will swear to without doubt – that he died of arsenic, and arsenic given in repeated doses.* By repeating the phrase *without doubt*, Addison set about erasing any suspicion of uncertainty. His opening salvo linked 'fact' to 'arsenic' with quick precision. Further, he would – he said – marshal the opinions of leading scientists and point to *proof* in the form of bottles taken from Battlecrease and later found to contain poison.

Sir Charles Russell listened closely, taking copious notes, repeatedly interjecting *this is not so!* while refreshing himself with pinches of snuff. He knew that the burden of proof lay with the prosecution and that, in order to convict Mrs Maybrick of a capital crime with its unavoidable penalty of death, the judge would expect the jury to come to a unanimous decision.

Russell's job, therefore, would be to plant and then nurture seeds of doubt and he had one immediate advantage. Addison had assured the jury in his opening address that scientists – both doctors and analytical chemists – would swear to several bottles taken from Battlecrease House provably containing poison. But the sheer volume of packets, tins, vials and bottles that had been collected from so many different places meant that the jurymen would need to keep their wits about them if they were to remember where each was found and what each contained. It was just as likely, Russell believed, that they would be baffled by the sheer variety of evidence and unable to make sense of whether any had played a defining part in the dead man's final illness.

CHAPTER 22

A Strange Fascination

The prosecution required only one thing from its first witness, surveyor William Clemmy: to present plans of the basement, ground and first floors of Battlecrease House. These drawings – indicating the position of beds, side tables, chairs and chests – signalled that the Maybricks' privacy was now open to the most probing curiosity. Family, friends and the police had already rifled through drawers and cupboards; the trial was poised publicly to reveal every one of its intimacies and its potentially sordid secrets.

When Michael was called, Florence flushed noticeably but waved away the wardress's offer of a smelling bottle, whispering *No, thank you*, and when John Addison had no more questions to ask a murmur of excitement went up from the public seats in anticipation of Russell's cross-examination, as if it were felt that the defence stood at the threshold of unforeseen revelations. Quietly, incisively, the defence barrister simply drew from Michael the admissions that Florence's handling of certain medicines was done in plain sight of the nurse, that the labels were accurate and that their contents were later found to be uncontaminated.

Michael agreed that Florence had written to him in March to express concern about James dosing himself with white powders; he conceded that James' health initially improved under the care of the nurses and that the contents of the bottle of Valentine's meat juice were not administered following his sister-in-law's suspicious handling of it. He accepted that the small bottles apparently concealed in the chocolate box turned out to be harmless and that the lesser of the two packets found in the trunk by Alice Yapp contained nothing more dangerous than insect powder.

Chipping away at the illusion of certainty set up by the prosecution, Russell's questions were designed to make Michael appear overbearing and hastily judgemental. Denying that his brother was addicted to arsenic, Michael believed that James had died without having discovered his wife's adultery and accepted that there were *complaints on both sides, the name of a woman being introduced*. This new fact – of James' infidelity – was, despite vague rumours, a surprise. But, before anyone had time to consider the full force of what it might mean, Judge Stephen announced a brief adjournment for lunch.

When things resumed at two o'clock the moment for discussing James' adultery seemed to have passed. Dr Hopper gave evidence much as he had twice before. Then, cross-examined, he added that James had consulted him at least fifteen times between June and December the previous year, that he had complained of numbness in his extremities since 1882 and that he had admitted to double-dosing prescription drugs including strychnine and arsenic. Gently led by Russell, the doctor described James' complexion as smooth and pale – one of the noted effects of arsenic; he also let slip that he thought Mrs Maybrick showed *unreasonable anxiety* about her husband's habits. Russell was building up a picture of Florence's concerns being repeatedly ignored so that both Michael and Dr Hopper might be seen to have facilitated a dangerous addiction. Further, the doctor accepted that James was quick to anger whenever he was confronted, which almost always ensured that the subject was avoided.

Matilda Briggs was called next. When the prosecution's questions were done Russell led her to agree that Florence had already telegraphed for help by the time Matilda insisted on calling for a nurse. Reluctantly, she accepted that her *sarcastic* recommendation that Florence write to Brierley for assistance was done *very bitterly*, and she grudgingly concurred that the only locked article of furniture, Florence's wardrobe, had contained nothing sinister. Bottles, she said, were scattered profusely throughout the house. She admitted she *knew about the deceased's habits of dosing himself. It was well known among his friends.*

When it was Edwin's turn, there was a flutter as a dressing gown *of fashionable type and cut* was brought into court. He identified it as the one worn by his sister-in-law while nursing James but then, rather than its significance in the case being made clear at last, the gown was rapidly removed, leaving everyone rather breathlessly wondering what it actually *meant*. Meanwhile, unlike Matilda Briggs, Edwin flatly denied that James took arsenic and Russell could not get him to shift.

Neither of the two Aigburth chemists changed the statements they had already made twice before, though Christopher Hanson did offer a semi-logical reason why Mrs Maybrick might have paid cash for her flypapers: they had a fixed price that could be paid on the spot, he said, while the cost of the lotion had to be calculated separately according to its ingredients – it all took time and there was no reason for her to wait since it could be added to her account once it had been worked out. Further, Hanson believed that arsenic was a common ingredient in cosmetics and that it would have been *a good combination* with the lotion. Having mentioned neither of these facts at the inquest or magistrates' hearing, his suggestions made Florence's purchase appear a little less suspicious.

James' clerks each answered questions, then proceedings stopped at just before six. The day, full of *dramatic incidents*, had flown. Several small facts had, perhaps, begun to swing things a little to Florence's advantage: Michael had presented as irrationally suspicious and it was clear that the poisoned meat juice had never been administered. Crucially, the dead man had been involved with an unnamed woman whose existence – it was implied – had caused severe marital disharmony, though the defence seemed to have agreed not to probe that fact in depth to avert, at Florence's request, further scandal from settling on the names of her children. Further, both Edwin and Michael had strongly denied that James was addicted to poisons but their evidence was contradicted by Dr Hopper and Mrs Briggs, who each described his hypochondria and his taste for drugs. Some might now have wondered whether James' brothers were lying. If so, was the rest of their evidence believable? Was it, for instance, possible that James really was ignorant of his wife's affair, given her blatant choice of hotel? This was important: if James had been told, then one of the motives imputed to his wife – to keep her secret hidden – became suddenly less plausible.

Intent on seeing the infamous young American, a crowd began to gather around the entrance to the cells from late afternoon. Just before six, the arrival of the horses had caused excitement, but it was more than half an hour before Florence was glimpsed walking *unconcernedly* (according to the reporter from the *Liverpool Mercury*) towards the van. Once she and her two wardresses were installed, it set off at a leisurely pace along Lime Street and up Islington.

The mob eddied. Among its shouts and cries, and only dimly audible, some heard what sounded like an attempted cheer.

*

Because it was unusual for women to attend trials as spectators, the newspapers had already made much of the numbers of well-dressed women and girls taking an active interest in Florence's public ordeal. Their presence in court indicated that proprieties were changing: women were beginning to refuse to be excluded from events that raised issues touching on their own situations or for their appetite for sensation to be suppressed in public. The Baroness von Roques, though – despite being so unconventional in other ways – held to the proprieties of her generation by not appearing at the trial, so Florence had no close female support. Her mother would not even attend as a witness since neither Richard Cleaver nor Sir Charles Russell thought it worth asking her to testify about Florence's beauty regime, believing it would subject her to a trying ordeal for no substantial benefit. Outspoken in so many other ways, the flamboyant Baroness therefore remained both silent and invisible for the duration of the trial.

Her absence detracted little from what the *Liverpool Mercury* called *the strange spell of fascination which this ... case has wrought*. On the following day every seat was again occupied when the trumpets sounded and the judge swept in. Re-entering the dock, Florence noticed that the narrow cane-bottomed chair in which she had suffered the day before had been replaced by something more comfortable, with a padded leather seat and higher back. Taking her place, she resumed – the same paper noted – *the placid attitude with which all who attend the court have become so familiar.*

Dr Fuller told the court that his prescriptions contained no arsenic, though he knew that James was taking Plummer's pills containing antimony. He did not believe arsenic to be addictive, but he had heard of its effectiveness in counteracting skin eruptions. Most importantly, Fuller thought that the symptoms of arsenic poisoning included red eyes, swollen eyelids and intolerance to light. James had suffered from none of these.

When her turn came, Mary Cadwallader spoke for the first time about the medicine that had arrived by post on the day before the Wirral races, and the fact that her master had told her that it had made him ill. She was also sure that the chemist's boy had delivered flypapers and that they had been left on the hall table – she said that she had seen Mr Maybrick pick them up and put them down again when he returned from town. As for the soaking flypapers, she and the cook had assumed that the solution was intended for cleaning the silk dress Mrs Maybrick had picked out for the ball that week. As Addison questioned Mary it emerged for the first time that, following James' death, she and Mrs Humphreys had found some flypapers in the pantry and had decided to burn them *before the police came*. This was extraordinary. Why had she not admitted this before?

I did not think of it, she said. *I did not remember that I had burned a lot of them.*

She did not know how long they had been in the house but she thought *a good bit*. Was it significant? It certainly added to the sources of arsenic in the house, and it also made Florence's purchases from Wokes and Hanson seem less questionable: if there had been no need to buy flypapers then she need not have drawn attention to herself.

The press and public noted again that the Battlecrease servants were admirably well presented. Today, Alice Yapp wore black with a silver brooch and a bunch of pink flowers in her hat, while Mrs Humphreys was in blue with large bronze buttons, a yellow neckerchief, brown kid gloves and a hat with a large feather. Both women were thought to be wonderfully self-possessed yet their attitudes towards the prisoner diverged sharply, for the cook betrayed a deep sympathy for her mistress that Yapp did not. This young woman was more than interesting. When she was called there was a sudden, restless movement in court and Florence raised her eyes, looking at Yapp steadily for some while. As a result, perhaps, Alice began tremulously but then gained in confidence as she repeated the story of the flypapers and the letter addressed to Brierley.

When Addison's questions were over, Sir Charles Russell began suavely, but there was a new steeliness in his tone as he explained that he wanted *to go back a little and understand the position of things.*

Yapp agreed that before the Grand National there had been no obvious division between the Maybricks and none following their later reconciliation.

Russell asked her whether she had ever been a lady's maid.

Yapp: No, sir.

Russell: Was it in the morning that Bessie told you as to having seen the flypapers?

No, sir, it was soon after dinner.

But did she tell you that she had seen them in the morning when she was doing up the room?

Yes, sir.

And you, out of curiosity, went into the room after the dinner was over?

It was about two hours after when I went into the room.

Out of curiosity?

Yes.

You had no business in the room?

No.

In other words, there was nothing clandestine about the soaking papers. Further, Yapp's answers suggested that she had been disrespectfully curious and a bit of a snoop.

There were questions about Mr Maybrick's general health, his illness following the Wirral races and a particularly pointed reference – mostly overlooked by the journalists present – that Edwin had slept at Battlecrease from 25 April to 11 May. Was Russell trying to suggest that Edwin might have tampered with his brother's food? Or that he knew something that he was not letting on? Whatever the learned counsel had in mind, he did not choose this moment to explore the point further.

Instead, focusing on Yapp's statement that she had watched her mistress pouring medicine from one bottle into another, Russell continued quietly:

I wish you to follow this again. Was that on the landing on the first floor?

Yes.

Opposite the bedroom?

Yes.

And is that the landing which all the servants – all the persons in the house, in fact – who desire to go up and down stairs, must pass?

Yes.

At that time you did not attribute any importance to the incident, I presume?

No.

Once again Sir Charles was aiming to impute the ease with which sinister motives could be attached to innocent actions. He appeared not to know that Nurse Callery had already told the Treasury solicitors that *it was at my suggestion that Mrs Maybrick changed the medicine from one bottle to another* later that same week. That significant fact might have reinforced the idea that Florence's actions were sensible rather than sinister.

Changing tack, Russell's tone suddenly became derisory. Why had Yapp opened the letter? She replied that it was because Mrs Maybrick had wished it to go by that post. It didn't make sense. He asked again:

> *Russell: Why did you open that letter?*
> *Yapp: (no reply)*
> *Judge Stephen: Did anything happen to the letter?*
> *Yes, it fell in the dirt, my lord.*
> *Russell: Why did you open that letter?*
> *I have answered you, sir.*
> *Judge Stephen: She said because it fell into the dirt.*
> *Russell: I think, with great deference to your lordship, she did not say so . . .*

Judge Stephen: She has just said so now.

Russell: Well I did not catch it, anyhow, I want to have it out again.

(to witness) Why did you open that letter?

Three times Russell had asked the same question. Twice she had evaded it. Tension crackled. She paused before half-whispering:

I opened the letter to put it in a clean envelope.

Why didn't you put it in a clean envelope without opening it? (no reply)

Was it a wet day? Was she sure of that? Was she certain? Was it really a wet day? Yes or no? Was it a wet or a dry day? Sometimes Yapp tried to answer, but more often she remained mute as Russell spat the same question, seeking not simply to confuse her but to make her story appear untrustworthy. His badgering suggested that there was something fishy about her tale and that he was determined to get to its crux. Holding out the envelope, he asked whether it was dirty enough to warrant being opened. *It was much dirtier at the time*, she replied. But the ink had not run, the address was legible, Russell countered. If the ink was not smudged then why did it need to be redirected?

Alice Yapp faltered. She could not explain.

Russell rounded on her, his black gown billowing as he turned:

On your oath, girl, did you not manufacture that stain as an excuse for opening your mistress's letter?

I did not.

I put it to you again for the last time. Did you not open the letter deliberately because you suspected your mistress?

No sir, I did not.

Yapp's timidity had vanished as she refuted the lawyer's suggestions with growing indignation. *Every ear* – noted the *Liverpool Mercury* – *was strained to catch every word of lawyer and witness* during the exchange. Yapp was clearly rattled as she made her way out of the court, her heels echoing on the boards.

Russell hoped that the picture he had summoned of her apparent disloyalty would feed sympathy for his client, a woman who had not simply been overruled by Michael but who had been faced with Matilda Briggs and Alice Yapp – strong-minded women who appeared to have been set against her from the start.

By providing a foil, the cook's deposition added to this impression. Elizabeth Humphreys told the court that she felt sorry for the way her mistress was treated by Michael. The cook appeared to be kind, perceptive and honest. It had seemed to her that her mistress was downhearted about her husband's illness, that she had nursed him attentively and to the point of her own exhaustion. Although, at the time, Mrs Maybrick's refusal to allow her husband lemonade had seemed harsh, Humphreys understood from the doctor, later, that she was simply doing what she was told. Similarly, when James' food was returned sweeter, darker or with the scent of vanilla, she had not worried because she knew that Mr Maybrick often added sugar to his food and drink. More to the point, in each case the food was barely touched.

Mrs Humphreys deposed that the Du Barry's food given to her by Mrs Maybrick was in a brand new tin. She remembered, too, that when her mistress mixed the mustard and water in order to make her husband sick after the Wirral races, she had stirred it with her finger. It didn't seem like the behaviour of someone who had put poison in the cup. As for the burned flypapers, they had been on the windowsill in the kitchen since the previous October. Russell asked her to repeat this fact, hoping to make the point once again that, had his client's intentions been malevolent, then she would surely have used existing papers covertly rather than openly purchasing a new batch.

The evidence of the servants had taken up the best part of the morning and early afternoon; Dr Humphreys then began his long testimony. He admitted that when Florence had told him back in March that her husband was taking a white powder she thought was strychnine he had not taken her seriously, laughing that if her husband was to die suddenly *you can ask me and I will say you had some conversation with me about it*. An *Oh!* came from the public seats. Judge Stephen turned, incredulously, towards the Garston doctor, shaking his head.

The doctor then described James' symptoms and details of the post-mortem, during which Florence shifted uneasily in her chair, silently declining an offer of water. He accepted that he had pre-scribed Fowler's Solution, which contained arsenic. Under cross-questioning by Sir Charles, who asked him what sort of irritant poison might have killed his patient, though, the doctor seemed confused. It might, he accepted, have come from tainted food. Appearing circumlocutory and sometimes contradictory, it was no real surprise when Russell brought Richard Humphreys to admit that he *had no previous experience of such cases*.

The court adjourned at six o'clock. Florence was taken back to Walton and the jury returned to their rooms in the nearby Victoria Hotel under strict instruction not to read the newspapers or to discuss the trial. Although Florence's impressive defence barrister had not demolished any of the evidence against her, it seemed even less certain at the end of this second day that she was unequivocally guilty. If enough uncertainty could continue to be established, then it seemed to be a real possibility that the tide would turn in her favour.

CHAPTER 23

The Contrariety of Things

Each day, details of 'The Great Trial' electrified the nation. Street-corner newsboys shouted the headlines, their stacks of papers dwindling as fast as they could be restocked. The violent argument between Florence and James had now been related from several different points of view – much to Charles Russell's frustration (*It is useless to go over this ground again!*). Alice Yapp was discussed by strangers and her actions divided opinion. As for the various invalid foods – the Du Barry's Revalenta, the oxtail soup and the bowl of arrowroot – Russell appeared to have established that on the occasions when these had tasted notably strange they had hardly been eaten. Only one lunch – made by Mrs Humphreys, wrapped by Florence and delivered to Tithebarn Street by Edwin – appeared to have been entirely consumed. Was this, then, James' fatal meal?

It seemed that the press was uniformly focused on Sir Charles Russell's cross-examinations rather than the prosecution questions – in all likelihood because most of the witnesses had already been heard twice before, while this was the first time any defence had been mounted – and all the papers gave the impression that the great barrister was making substantial inroads into the case against Florence. Most reporters, though, struggled to keep abreast of the multiplying details of what foods or medicines were prepared, when and whether they were actually swallowed, trying to understand whether there was a clear relationship between these and the onset of the dead man's symptoms. Crucially, while the human intricacies of the household had been laid bare over the previous days, the scientific evidence was yet to be heard. On the third day, this would be redressed: after the attending doctors, the city analyst would be called, followed by professional experts from London.

When the court opened just before ten on Friday morning, 2 August, there was a new air of weariness about the principals. The *Echo* reported that Mrs Maybrick *looked extremely jaded when she entered the dock. Her face is perfectly white and thin and although she still maintained generally her perfect repose there were occasional movements of the head indicating that she was struggling against weakness and illness.* A wardress now sat close up to her on her right-hand side.

Russell's voice was quietly monotonous as he continued his cross-examination of Dr Humphreys, asking whether James had complained of headaches for over a year and whether the stiffness in his limbs was more fanciful than realistic. Humphreys answered yes to both. Countering an earlier suggestion that Florence had disposed of the 'slops' from his chamber pot before the doctors could examine them, he confirmed that he *could have seen them on any occasion I desired.* Turning then to the tests the doctor performed on James' urine and faeces, Russell asked whether any deposit had been found on the copper foil, indicating arsenic:

No.

So that would be a negative test?

No, not of necessity.

Why?

Because the quantity I used was so small and the time I boiled it such a short period ... I am not skilled in the details of testing and my test might have been inefficient.

With a half-smile and a tip of his head, Russell knew that the hook was in. He pulled a little at the line:

That is candid, doctor. Then you mean to say that your test might not have been conducted successfully?

I cannot say. I do not pretend to have any skill in these matters.

It is not a difficult test?

No.

Russell did not want to undermine the fact that Humphreys's tests for arsenic were negative, a fact clearly advantageous to his defence. His questions were designed rather to prove that (despite the doctor's lack of confidence) they had been performed accurately. Yet he also wanted twenty-eight-year-old Richard Humphreys's inexperience to lodge itself in the mind of the jury, so that his certainty about the cause of death would carry less force.

Playing his line with careful skill, the barrister appeared then to change direction, eliciting two astounding admissions. Dr Humphreys was asked whether, but for the suggestion of arsenic, he would have been prepared to give a certificate of the cause of death and he replied that on the Wednesday prior to death – before Michael Maybrick arrived – he would have done so.

And in your judgement, what was then the cause of death?

Acute congestion of the stomach.

Russell allowed a moment for this to sink in.

Now, Dr Humphreys, I wish to ask you this question, and just consider, please, before you answer it. Mention any post-mortem symptom – never mind the analysis for the present – but mention any post-mortem symptom which is distinctive of arsenic poison and which is not also distinctive of gastritis or gastro-enteritis.

I can't.

There is none?

I can't give you it.

That is because you believe there is none?

I should not like to swear to distinguish between them.

It comes to this, you are not able to point it out?

I am not able to point it out.

Casting a triumphant glance at his junior, Mr Pickford, Russell once more allowed the silence to linger while those who had closely followed the medical evidence so far cast meaningful looks at one another. The doctor appeared to be swearing to the fact that nothing about James' illness pointed, uniquely, to poisoning.

Addison stepped up, looking for a chance to steal back the advantage. Stressing the need for absolute clarity, he asked Dr Humphreys again whether he had any doubt about the cause of death. Humphreys said he had none whatsoever.

The judge interjected. Did the doctor base his opinion on the scientific analysis of the viscera alone or did he include the poisoned meat juice in his conclusion?

No, my lord. I do not include that.

Addison had thus succeeded in re-establishing the fact that the physician was convinced James Maybrick had died of an irritant poison, probably arsenic. But how much weight Humphreys's judgement carried in the minds of the jury, it was now impossible to guess.

*

There was a general whispering as the public tried to understand the significance of what had just passed. In the dock, Florence began to show signs of exhaustion. Dr Carter entered the court.

Knowing that it would be difficult to fault this more senior doctor, Sir Charles Russell took a decidedly courteous approach. His goals were threefold: to show that it was practically impossible to differentiate between the effects of food poisoning and of malicious poisoning; secondly, that it could not be established exactly when the fatal dose was taken – if it was taken; finally, that the prosecution's catalogue of suspicious events bore no relation to the onset of James Maybrick's symptoms.

While Carter insisted that the acuteness of Maybrick's illness pointed towards a metallic rather than a natural poison, he also admitted – significantly – that, like Dr Humphreys, he did not have any actual experience of the symptoms of arsenic poisoning in the living or the dead. He believed that it took anything from *a short while* to ten hours for arsenic to begin to work on the body. *What?* asked Russell. He knew – and told the court so – that it was far more ordinarily within half an hour; ten hours would be exceptional. When Carter then said that he had *read up* on the indications of arsenical poisoning, the barrister shook his head. The doctor was presenting an alarmingly partisan figure; he even refused – until very firmly pushed on the point – to accept that redness and irritation of the eyes (a symptom from which Maybrick had not suffered) was very common in arsenic cases.

> Russell: *You were asked to give your opinion as to when the*
> *fatal dose was administered and you fixed Friday 3 May.*
> *I want to know why you fixed that date.*
> Carter: *I had that date in my mind.*

Carter's unsatisfactory response was based on the fact that when he saw James on the following Tuesday he had been vomiting for several days. Russell reminded the jury of Dr Humphreys's belief that James' sudden illness on the Friday afternoon was derived from nothing more sinister than a visit to an overly vigorous Turkish bath.

Carter then deposed that Maybrick's diarrhoea *was just appearing* on Tuesday the 7th, contradicting his own already slightly varying evidence at both the inquest and the magistrates' hearing, as well as the memory of Dr Humphreys, who thought it began two days later. No one could agree on the exact date, nor whether morphia suppositories might have retarded its onset, and as a result it was proving very difficult to pinpoint a specific date on which poison might have been ingested.

Before letting Carter go, Russell had one more point to establish. John Addison had made much of the fact that Dr Humphreys denied telling Florence that her husband was seriously ill. The prosecution's imputation was that when she wrote the phrase *He is sick unto death!* it was because she knew that she had poisoned him. Now Russell returned to Carter's diagnosis. When James' bowels became inflamed:

You mentioned it to Mrs Maybrick?

No, not to her.

Well, to Dr Humphreys in her presence?

It might be.

At all events, on the day when you came to the conclusion that there was inflammation of the bowels, Mrs Maybrick told cook Humphreys that there was inflammation?

I believe so.

The suggestion, then, was that Florence had innocently repeated what she had heard the doctors discuss.

Russell was focused on destabilising the prosecution's case so as to render a conviction impossible. Before the trial, public opinion had run against his client, but that half-heard cheer as she was removed the previous evening might have suggested a change of heart. Feelings were certainly running high: during the lunch-time adjournment, several of the witnesses were pursued by a crowd that included, according to the press, a number of scruffy, loudly vocal women – or *tatterdemalion viragoes*, as the *Echo* called them. Brierley came in for some hooting and poor, good-natured Mrs Humphreys, mistaken for Alice Yapp, was howled at and called filthy names.

Russell took it all as an indication that the mob was gradually shedding its derision for Florence and beginning to take her part. Newspaper sympathy was also growing for her, though the words used to describe the women in the crowd outside St George's Hall – suggesting beggarly, impudent scolds – nevertheless reflected a prevailing disgust at women who disregarded forms and norms and thus made themselves both ugly and ridiculous.

Coincidentally, the *Pall Mall Gazette*, a penny London newspaper, would print on its front page that evening an interview with 'the first lady barrister', Mrs Belva Lockwood – an American whose career *throws strong light upon the eventualities and possibilities of the woman movement.* Aged fifty-nine, full of energy, Lockwood had practised law in America for fifteen years and had, according to the *Gazette*, twice contested the American Presidency, but, while she was a beacon for the 'equal rights' party across the Atlantic, English women would not be admitted to the Bar for thirty more years.

Lockwood was not asked by the *Gazette* to express her views on the Maybrick case, yet the trial was providing a stage on which the vacillations of a changing world were being played out. Women – it turned out – were both the most interesting objects and spectators, and the story inevitably provided a focus for feminist views: the strength of the initial reaction against Florence, some argued, was an indication of gender inequality and the power of patriarchal society. That women enjoyed more freedoms than they had done for generations – such as the ability to partake in university education, to have control of their own money and property within marriage, even to attend sensational capital trials – was not at issue. The effects of these first stirrings of feminism on the nation as a whole, though, were.

That very year, Emmeline Pankhurst and her daughters would found the Women's Franchise League in order to lobby for votes for women in local elections. Beyond the issue of suffrage, however, feminists were more generally focused on debunking the myth of the Angel in the House and exposing the moral inequality of the sexes. Hankering after a new set of values, they argued against listlessly unrewarding domesticity and the cramping conventions that prevented women from seeking independence. Those who set themselves against a fairer deal for women, meanwhile, argued that increased liberties would turn women into loathsome, self-assertive creatures who would refuse to get married or to bear children. Civilisation would crumble, the family would decline and female criminality would increase. Worse, liberated women threatened to subvert or even erase the established power of men.

Developing from the 'Girl of the Period' and in parallel with the ideas of the Women's Movement, by the late 1880s a new genre of literature – termed, by Ouida, 'New Woman Fiction' – had emerged. Largely forgotten writers such as Olive Schreiner became enormously successful, and in 1893 Sarah Grand's *The Heavenly Twins* would sell forty thousand copies within weeks of its publication. Written by women, about women and for women, these novels concentrated on explicitly sexual and marital themes, on the troubling questions *what is a woman?* and *what does a woman want?*, on ardent girls with radically progressive views. They glorified the spinster, applauded the daughter who revolted and women who chose openly to break from convention. Like the similarly provocative dandyism and decadence typified by Oscar Wilde, New Woman Fiction propounded views that challenged the prevailing sexual code, reflecting the sense of imminent warfare within gender relations that would characterise the 1890s.

Two of the most psychologically complex novelists of the age – Thomas Hardy and Henry James – were preoccupied by the stresses inherent in marriage and wrote, in their own ways, New Woman novels, creating heroines who were undone by their innate sexuality or their inability to manage submerged sexual disloyalties. By pretending not to notice the fact of her husband's infidelity while trying invisibly to wrest back the advantage from her competitor Maggie Verver, the heroine of James' *The Golden Bowl*, might have showed Florence the way to behave. Instead, Florence's carelessness allowed the public and the court to poke at her failings with salacious fervour while hints about James Maybrick's infidelities were left unexplored.

Sir Charles Russell's defence partly relied on his establishment of the fact that, by sinning against her sex, Florence had fallen victim to the sinister censure of females who made it their business to oppose her. Like the women who hissed their opprobrium when the story first broke, Yapp and Briggs – he suggested – had judged her quickly and spitefully while fawning over Michael in his assumed position as master of Battlecrease. Florence's case thus exemplified the entrenchment of double standards; as Trollope's Lady Monk admits: *There is nobody alive who has a greater horror of anything improper in married women ... When Lady Madeline Madtop left her husband, I would never allow her to come inside my doors again – though I have no doubt he ill-used her dreadfully, and there was nothing ever proved between her and Colonel Graham*. Like so many of the heroines of New Woman Fiction, Florence was being demonised for an act that passed almost without censure in a man.

The irony was that Florence – despite her reckless behaviour – was a traditionalist at heart, interested not in the fiction of female liberation but that of courtship and betrothal. Far from embracing the women's cause, she repeated endlessly her need for and lack of male protection. None of this, though, prevented her from becoming a cipher both for those grappling towards a different way of being and for conservatives who believed that her alleged crime struck not simply at a single man but at the prevailing hierarchies that kept men on top.

Her story thus pricked at the fears and obsessions of disparate ideologies. To some, she was proof of the link between female sexuality and crime; to others she represented oppression within marriage, tied inescapably to an unfaithful husband whom she had come to find physically repulsive. Reaction to the events that took place in Battlecrease House had flowed out from the city of Liverpool, heading south to become involved with the salons and politics of the capital before rippling back in subtly changed form. Florence Maybrick was no longer simply the living embodiment of literary demons like Lady Audley or Lydia Gwilt, she was also a disenchanted and undefended victim. Further, partly because of the gender politics that characterised her age, she was pursued as a murderess when a decade or so earlier she might have been considered above suspicion by virtue simply of her class.

For all these reasons, the trial of Florence Maybrick was becoming a national morality fable, the inevitable result of too much spirit or too little independence, depending on your point of view.

CHAPTER 24

Scientific Truth

A number of facts combined suspiciously against Florence, but no evidence had yet been advanced to prove that there was enough arsenic in James' body to kill him, let alone that she had given it to him with murderous intent. Scientific evidence would form much of the remainder of the prosecution's case and though Sir Charles Russell was noted for his remarkable grasp of these *recondite technicalities*, the same could not quite be said for the judge, the jury or the public.

When the court reconvened after lunch on the third day, Dr Alexander Barron was questioned belligerently by Thomas Swift, the prosecution junior. Unlike the other two doctors Barron, as Professor of Pathology, had extensive experience of the effects of poison on the human body and he was unwilling to swear that arsenic was the cause either of James Maybrick's illness or his death. Russell, delighted, wanted Barron to confirm that it was usual for diarrhoea to begin within a number of hours of the administration of arsenic and certainly within twenty-four. Since James' diarrhoea had not begun immediately, Barron stated that the *gastro-enteritis* had been caused by something other than an irritant poison – some sort of impure food, perhaps: *sausages from Germany*, or mutton or grouse.

Is it possible to differentiate the symptoms from arsenical poisoning? asked Russell.

I should not be able to do so, Barron replied.

The doctor told the court that the poison had been discovered in bodies seven months after its administration and that it could remain in the stomach as long as six weeks after ingestion. Russell reminded him that his colleagues had spoken about the petechious condition of Maybrick's stomach – in other words, that it contained some livid red spots similar to fleabites, indicating arsenical poisoning. Barron disagreed. He had, he said, made no note of it: *there may have been one or two but they must have been doubtful or we should have made some mention of them*. All these contentions were direct blows at the prosecution's case.

Addison knew it. Rising, he asked whether the doctor knew of patients poisoned by meat. Did they get better? Had any of them died? Barron conceded that all had recovered. He admitted, too, that the presence of arsenic in the stomach of a poisoned man would depend on the amount he vomited and agreed that traces were likely also to be found in the liver. Addison was, of course, alive to the fact that the city analyst had indeed discovered small amounts of arsenic in Maybrick's liver.

The opposite of the sharp pitch of his opposing counsel, William Pickford was praised for the *warm tones* of his address when he rose for the first time in the trial in order to cross-question solemn Inspector Baxendale. Inspector Bryning and Sergeant James Davenport had already described the arrest of Florence and the discovery of several bottles and pillboxes. Now Baxendale described the letters he received from Mr Flatman, the dressing gown identified by Edwin Maybrick and the many bottles and packets he had collected from Battlecrease for analysis.

May I take it that of all these things none were locked or sealed?

No, none were locked or sealed.

*

Edward Davies was sworn. Spare of form, shrewd-faced, there was an overwhelming expectation that this scientist would finally produce the proofs needed to unlock the mysteries surrounding the case.

While Davies deposed to the finding of arsenic and traces of arsenic in some of the many vessels handed to him by the police, he also explained the methods used to test for poisons. Florence watched him closely. Like Carter, he had found arsenic in the meat juice bottle – about a grain of it, and he considered it to have been added in solution since the specific gravity of the remaining fluid differed from a sample taken from a new bottle. There was also detectable arsenic (around one-eighth of a grain) in Maybrick's liver and amounts so small as to be unquantifiable in his intestines. Davies then repeated what he had said twice before – that the spleen, stomach, pelvic bone, lungs and heart had all tested negative to the presence of arsenic.

Delicately holding up a handkerchief between his forefinger and thumb to show a hole cut in its middle where a sample had been taken for analysis, the chemist said that he had found evidence of the poison here, but not in the bottle of unidentified black powder around which it was wrapped.

It went on and on. There was a distinct trace of arsenic in a medicine bottle from Clay & Abraham chemists, though subsequent tests on samples of all the ingredients used by that shop had been clear. A blue bottle containing nitroglycerine must have contained up to two-thirds of a grain. Bottles, boxes and packets were referred to by their police numbers rather than their labels, so that – because there were so many – they were hard to fix in the mind, as were the details of where each had been found and what each contained. In a growing mountain of detail, the significance of it all was sometimes opaque but for the fact that, since poison had been found in cloths, tumblers, chemists' bottles and packets, large quantities of it had evidently been present in solid and solution form all over Battlecrease House. There were seventy-one grains in the packet labelled 'Arsenic for Cats' and a total of between thirty and forty grains in various other exhibits. In the pan and basin recovered from James' office, *two little drops of dried skim, rather less than quarter of an inch long, such as might have come from gruel* contained arsenic; by testing a new pan of the same kind Davies believed that he had ruled out the possibility that the poison had leached from its glaze. As to the flypapers, Davies said that a single hour's soaking would extract three-quarters of a grain of arsenic from each one.

Just as it was all beginning to become baffling, Davies turned to a tin box and removed from it the fashionable dressing gown identified by Edwin, a garment of such thrilling intimacy that it turned the atmosphere in the court from one approaching torpor to something more like excitement. So meticulous had the analyst been in his examination of it that he could describe the little bit of label found in a pocket and even the fluff caught in the internal corner seam. Traces of arsenic had been found on it, he said; also on a household apron, and two hundredths of a grain came from a handkerchief embroidered with Florence's name that was bunched up in one of the gown's pockets.

For the defence, Russell wanted to focus on the actual amounts found. A 'minute' trace, said Davies, might be as small as a thousandth of a grain but the smallest weighable amount was one hundredth. Asking for one of the tubes containing coppers apparently 'filmed' with arsenic crystals, Russell then made a play of examining it closely, holding it up at different angles and remarking that *it requires a strong glass* – or magnifier – *to see.*

In a marvellous bit of theatre, he then asked for the little glass tubes to be passed to Judge Stephen and the jurymen. The phials were held up against the black cloth of other men's coats and the court watched as the men narrowed their eyes, hunched their shoulders and peered, twisting the tubes and grimacing in an attempt to see the evidence they were told was there. Magnifying glasses were passed around. It was a clever illustration of Russell's point: so little arsenic had in fact been found in the body of James Maybrick that it was almost impossible to see, let alone to prove that it had caused his death.

Russell asked Davies: wasn't arsenic often used as a cosmetic? Was it not possible that the glaze on the pan used to reheat the food at James' office had contained arsenic (*not possible*, the analyst replied, according to his tests). Could the reddish stain on Mrs Maybrick's handkerchief not be rouge? Or toothpowder? Could Davies confirm that there was practically no arsenic found on the wrapper and nothing in the scent bottle?

Exhorting the analyst to answer clearly – *I wish you would listen to me, Mr Davies* – Russell focused again on the discovery of arsenic in the pans found in the Tithebarn Street office, aiming to show that the chemist's tests were ineffective since he had not tested the glaze, did not know how old the pan was or when it had last been used, and that, anyway, the amount of arsenic discovered – as with the Clay & Abraham bottles – was *minute*.

> Russell: *I would like to ask you one question more. You have candidly told us what would be the entire quantity [of arsenic] of the entire liver from the fractional portion you dealt with?*
>
> Davies: *What I found would amount to one eighth of a grain.*
>
> *But you did not find one eighth of a grain; you found two hundredths of a grain ... in the six ounces.*
>
> Yes.

Russell contended that the chemist's conclusions were based on incorrect estimations, that he had made mistakes in his trials and that – Davies agreed to this – he had performed one Marsh test erroneously and had in the process lost an important sample. He continued:

In this case you found half the arsenic you have found in any other case which ended fatally.

Yes; it was one half of what I found in the case of Margaret Jennings and that was half of the smallest amount I have ever known.

Who was Margaret Jennings?

One of the women poisoned by Mrs Flanagan.

This was important. In order to ensure that it stuck in the minds of the men who counted, Russell had purposely introduced the spectre of the notorious Liverpool poisoners, Flanagan and Higgins. By so doing he not only reinforced the point that the amount of arsenic found in the dead man was – very probably – not enough to have killed him, but he made an implicit comparison between those hardened, working-class murderers and the refined, delicate creature in the dock. He was playing on subconscious but entrenched notions of chivalry, class and deference, on the belief that gently educated ladies did not descend to murder.

Florence began to flag, asking for water and appearing to be close to collapse before falling into a *semi-comatose condition*. It was unclear whether she was unwell or simply exhausted. As Davies's long hours of evidence finally concluded, the widespread hope among the assembly was that the judge would adjourn early. Russell, though, feeling that his argument was gathering strength, was keen to press ahead and was therefore pleased when Addison called for Nurse Gore. She stepped up in the blue cape of the Dover Street Institution with its dramatic red-lined hood.

Explaining that Mr Maybrick was conscious and alert on her arrival, that she had administered medicines given to her by

Florence from bottles openly arranged, Gore confirmed that her patient's tenesmus had begun on Wednesday night. Just before midnight on Thursday she had given him some Valentine's meat juice from a brand new bottle provided by Edwin; at intervals throughout the night she had administered small amounts of champagne from an open bottle.

Some time between midnight on Thursday and dawn on Friday, said Gore, she had watched Florence take the bottle of meat juice from the chest into the dressing room, where she remained for a couple of minutes, pulling the door behind her. On her return, while asking the nurse to fetch some ice the defendant had returned the bottle to the side table. Questioned by Addison, Gore agreed that it seemed shifty:

She had her hand by her side, and while speaking to me raised it and put the bottle on the table.

So that you could see?

I did see.

Gore remembered that Mrs Maybrick had returned to the dressing room to lie down. Later, she was seen moving the suspect bottle again, this time from the table to the washstand.

If not new, the nurse's evidence was potently dangerous to Florence. It was approaching six o'clock and there was no time for cross-examination. Russell could only hope that the jurymen had noticed in Gore's evidence a curious fact: although she had gone off duty at eleven on Friday morning, although she had told Nurse Callery about the suspect bottle, she had not talked to Michael Maybrick about what she had seen until later that day. The bottle had therefore remained on the washstand until after lunch.

As Florence left the dock she was momentarily brought face to face with the public benches. Their occupants stood as one in order to see her face, a wall of humanity rising as if to demand an encore. This time, not one hiss was heard.

*

On Saturday morning the Cleaver brothers posted small notices in the city newspapers, thanking the public for their many letters containing suggestions to bolster the defence. As they prepared to embark on the fourth day of her trial, both press and public felt that things were going in Florence's favour.

Addison's first move was to reconstruct that crucial scene described by Nurse Gore on the previous evening. Carefully he asked her again whether the little bottle of Valentine's meat juice was new. Had she removed the seal covering the cork? Had she tasted it after she had mixed it for her patient? Where exactly had she then placed the bottle? Was this the position from which she had watched Mrs Maybrick scoop it up and take it out of the room?

Charles Russell did not want to antagonise Gore. He was deferential. Asking her repeatedly about her vigilance, questioning her about the precise times she had begun and ended her shifts, wondering whether she remembered exactly when she had administered certain medicines and from where they had come, he mused about whether she might – just once – have left the room unattended or fallen asleep. *Let me see if I have rightly followed you*, he crooned as he quizzed her on the details of her watch. Gore answered quickly and firmly, building up a picture of dutiful professionalism that played right into his hands.

On the subject of the meat juice, he wanted to be explicit:

Your suspicions being aroused, you took care not to give it to the patient?

Yes.

You are clear on that point?

Yes, not by me.

Nor by anyone else so far as you remember?

No.

On that you are clear?

Yes.

So that it stands thus. You are positive that during your watch nothing was given from that bottle?

No.

By establishing the nurse's rigour, Florence's impressive counsel had drawn from Gore an oath that none of the tainted meat juice had been given to the dead man, either by her or by any of the other nurses. However suspicious it was that the bottle contained poison, it could not thus have been the cause of James Maybrick's death.

The judge was becoming muddled. He asked to be reminded who had tasted the beef juice that was offered to James and seemed to think that this had been a poisonous solution. Russell reminded him that it was tasted before Mrs Maybrick apparently tampered with the bottle. So who tasted it? the judge asked again. It gave Russell the opportunity to cover the ground one more time, pressing home his point.

Let's go back on that, he said, *because I want to make it quite clear.*

Turning to the witness, he recapped:

You recollect telling us that you got a fresh bottle, apparently untouched; you took the capsule off; then you took the cork out; then you took some food out, and reduced it to the proper strength in water? Then you gave it to your patient? Then I suppose you corked the bottle ... and again placed the bottle on the table?

Nurse Gore answered *Yes* to all his questions. She also repeated both that she had thrown away the only glass of medicine handed to her by Mrs Maybrick because she wanted to use the glass for preparing food and that she had warned her replacement, Nurse Callery, not to use the contents of the suspect meat juice bottle.

The jury must now have been convinced that, whether or not

Florence had poisoned the meat juice, her husband had swallowed none of it. Russell might also have made the point that there was plenty of time for the bottle to be interfered with by someone else or for Mrs Maybrick to destroy it if she feared detection. He did not. Content that he had done enough, he nodded at the witness, grasped his arms behind his back and returned to his seat with the sort of quiet assurance that made people think he was winning.

Addison had noticed something that might undermine all that apparent surety elicited by Russell: that on Wednesday Gore had given James some medicine handed to her by the sick man's wife.

He sprang up.

So far as you know, you gave him nothing with anything wrong in it?

Not that I know of.

Will you speak up, please. You told us at half-past two that you did give him some medicine?

Yes.

Do you know what that was?

I do not know but I was under the impression that it was from a medicine bottle.

Despite this, no matter how hard Addison plugged away at the nurse about bottles, prescriptions, food, milk and salves – no matter how many times he asked her to be sure about the origin of everything she had given to her patient – she remained adamant that all of it had been prepared by herself or one of the other nurses or had been given to her by Michael. Apart from that one glass on the afternoon of her arrival, she was determined that no food, drink or drug intended for the patient had been touched by his wife.

Addison then asked Nurse Gore again – despite the constant, loud objections of Russell – about the underhand way the prisoner had behaved with the bottle. He asked her to repeat the manner in which Mrs Maybrick had picked it up and covered it with her other hand, how she had dropped her arm to her side before transferring it out of sight, how all her actions were designed to obfuscate and to deceive.

The prosecution thus reminded the jury of Florence Maybrick's questionable actions. Determinedly, Russell returned to the imputation of wrongdoing in the administration of the early afternoon dose on the day Gore first arrived. By establishing that James had not been sick until a quarter past eight the following morning, he fulminated that there could therefore have been nothing wrong with the dose in question. Only then did he let Gore stand down.

The battle over the nurse's testimony had been tightly fought. Neither the prosecution nor the defence had emerged with a clear advantage.

CHAPTER 25

Dark Clouds Gathering

Only a handful of prosecution witnesses remained to be called, and then the worst of the accusations against Florence would be over. Anticipation grew about whether Sir Charles would then attempt actively to prove her innocence or whether his defence would rely on reinforcing the existence of significant doubt.

Nurse Margaret Callery had a relatively easy time of it, confirming that the defendant was never alone in the sickroom and that she gave nothing but ice to her husband. Once, when Florence was trying to persuade her husband to take his medicine, he had complained that she had *given him the wrong medicine again.*

To whom did he say that? asked Addison.

To Mrs Maybrick.

What did she say to that?

She said, 'What are you talking about? You never had wrong medicine.'

The overheard comment set up the unfortunate impression that James distrusted his wife. Did the jury also note Nurse Callery's crucial testimony that her patient had not suffered from diarrhoea on either the Thursday or Friday? Or were they, like the judge – who asked increasingly for clarification on simple points – beginning to get muddled about the various days, times, doses and symptoms? Cross-examining, Russell focused simply on establishing Margaret Callery's vigilance and Florence's gentle anxiety about the comfort of her husband.

Nurse Wilson's brief testimony followed. Addison asked her to concentrate on hearing her patient say three times to his wife on the night before he died: *Oh Bunny, Bunny, how could you do it? I did not think it of you!*, to which she had replied, *You silly old darling, don't trouble your head about things*. What did it mean? Did James suspect his wife was trying to kill him or, despite Michael's belief that his brother was ignorant of it, had she confessed her adultery? The plaintive cry of a dying man echoed in the courtroom, unexplained. In the dock, Florence looked at her hands. There was little Russell could do to reduce the damage. He merely asked Wilson to confirm that from then until his death the following day Maybrick had been in a state of delirium.

Next, Alfred Schweisso, the waiter at Flatman's Hotel, told the court that he had seen Florence on her first evening at the hotel with one gentleman, on the following morning with a different man and then, from Friday 22 March, with Alfred Brierley, who *occupied the same bedroom ... up to Sunday when they left ... Mrs Maybrick paid the bill*. Russell and his team remained resolutely in their seats. There was nothing to contest.

Addison had kept Professor Thomas Stevenson until last. A thin, slightly stooping, full-bearded man in his early fifties, Stevenson was one of several senior scientific analysts to the Home Office and the editor of a standard work on medical jurisprudence. In addition to having studied Davies's results and the post-mortem report, he had also conducted his own tests on Maybrick's viscera. His conclusion was that death was caused by arsenic.

An expert witness in several trials, Stevenson spoke with calm deliberation, confirming that he had isolated amounts of the poison as minuscule as thousandths of a grain. He said that there was around one eleventh of a grain in James' intestines, an unquantifiable trace in his kidney and about a third of a grain in the liver. Parts of his evidence were disturbing: by the time the jars reached him, the liver and kidney were putrid and the spleen was so decomposed as to have liquefied *and I could not find it.* Yet from these samples he estimated that there had been around two grains in the body at death and, emphatically, *That the body at the time of death probably contained a fatal dose of arsenic. I have found a little more or a little less than the quantity I did find here in undoubtedly fatal cases of arsenical poisoning ... I have no doubt that this man died from the effects of arsenic.*

Charles Russell might have pointed out that the presence of arsenic in the intestines was known generally to retard decomposition and that, therefore, the rotten state of the samples ran contrary to the suggestion that there was much of it present. He did not. Instead, he allowed Professor Stevenson to continue unchecked.

Stevenson believed that in cases of poisoning the liver was a more important indicator than the stomach and therefore discounted the lack of arsenic in James' stomach as insignificant. He was sure that the symptoms described by the doctors – the dry throat, the foul mouth which did not smell and the vomiting – together indicated arsenical poisoning and that the post-mortem appearances supported this. There were no 'usual' symptoms of arsenic poisoning, he told Addison, since they varied according to the patient and the dose. What was certain was that two grains or even *a smaller dose than that may kill*, and that death in such a case would usually follow within twelve to twenty-four hours, though repeated smaller doses would cause the illness to be *more spread out*. A whole ounce of the poison could be added to a pint of rice pudding, said Stevenson, *and yet not be detected* by taste. If it had been administered in solution form, it would be absorbed more readily and the effect on the body would be correspondingly more severe.

Stevenson specifically ruled out the notion that James' illness was due to food poisoning, saying that in such cases it was the lower bowel, rather than the stomach, that showed post-mortem signs of inflammation or ulceration. He also refuted that arsenic was common in cosmetics – *it irritates the skin* – and suggested that Fowler's Solution was only dangerous in vast quantities. In his opinion, the amount of arsenic in James' liver suggested that he had taken the poison three or four days before he died – on the Tuesday or Wednesday, before the arrival of the nurses from Dover Street, but well after the period during which he took food to the office.

The scientist appeared unassailably confident as the prosecution left its witness to the defence. Within minutes, by vigorously questioning the reliability of all these judgements, Sir Charles would begin to fragment the expert's self-satisfaction.

Asked to describe the last time he had examined a living person suffering from arsenical poisoning, Stevenson was stumped. Nor could he recall the name or the date of a case in which he had been involved in a post-mortem following arsenic poisoning. Attempting to dodge questions with generalities (*Oh, frequently; I have seen many; I have several*), Russell exhorted him to recall specifics: *Have you a definite case in your recollection? Will you fix one and tell me the circumstances of it? Will you kindly fix your mind upon one case of a post-mortem in which you yourself took part?*

Uncomfortable, Stevenson dredged up a case from 1858. Russell wanted something more recent.

After some prevarication, Stevenson professed perfectly to remember a case from *a few years ago*. Russell asked:

What was the dose taken?

Unknown.

What?

It was unknown.

But you found out afterwards, later?

No.

What was the quantity found?

I don't know.

But I thought you assisted at the post-mortem, and had the circumstances in mind?

Yes, but when death occurs from suicide ... we don't analyse the amounts.

Expressing surprise with every gesture, Russell was indignant:

Have you any case in your mind where you know the time of administration, the time of death, and the quantity found at the post-mortem at which you have assisted?

I think so.

Well, will you please keep your mind on that case. When did it occur?

Some years ago.

When?

About a dozen years ago.

Not nearer than that?

With a comic gesture of despair, Russell signalled that the expert witness was a great deal more fallible than he claimed.

Russell next asked Stevenson whether the symptoms of arsenical poisoning and gastroenteritis differed substantially. The professor said there were both similarities and differences. What were these? He could not say. What did he mean by this answer? The professor explained that in the case of arsenic poisoning, symptoms were likely to appear more quickly: nausea within half an hour, followed by vomiting and then diarrhoea by an hour or two. Wanting him to be quite clear, Russell asked whether diarrhoea was likely to be persistent and excessive, and were abdominal pain, inflammation of the eyelids and bloodshot eyes usual symptoms? Stevenson thought so. Since it had already been comprehensively established that the exact onset of Maybrick's diarrhoea was disputed and that he had suffered from neither abdominal pain nor ocular irritation, the court might have been forgiven for wondering why arsenic had been suspected at all.

Had Stevenson found – asked Russell – a weighable quantity of the poison in the kidneys?

I had not enough to act upon and—

I really think you ought to answer me. As a matter of fact, did you find any weighable quantity?

No.

Russell's contention was that, since Stevenson and Davies differed in their estimations of the total amount of arsenic in Maybrick's body, both were inaccurate. Both had taken small portions of the viscera and extrapolated from their findings what might have been present in the whole. They should, Russell suggested, have macerated the whole organ in order to obviate false results given by small pockets of poison. Arguments about thousandths of grains and the different types of arsenic were, he contested, beside the point. The reality was that the maximum actual amount of arsenic found, however it was computed, was ninety-one thousandths of a grain and this tiny amount was not, under any circumstances, enough to kill. When Stevenson grudgingly accepted, it seemed that Russell had succeeded in reducing the prosecution's case to tatters.

*

An air of expectancy hung over the public benches when the court resumed at two o'clock. Grasping the lapels of his robe, Russell began speaking in such subdued tones that heads inclined towards him. A new order of concentration was manifest. It took several minutes for some to realise that the barrister's long-awaited, gravely measured argument for the defence was already under way.

Addressing the jury, Sir Charles's voice began to tremble dramatically as he characterised the lady in the dock as *friendless*, the charge as cruel and their duty as serious. His defence would be, he explained, 'double barrelled', founded on proving two crucial truths: that James Maybrick's death was not provably due to arsenic, and that there was no evidence that his wife had administered poison. Their judgement – his voice began to swell – must not be founded upon probabilities *even if supported by an apparently ample motive*, unless the cogency of the evidence was such that it expelled all doubt. Whatever their suspicions, they were required simply to weigh up the facts and, unless the prosecution's case was proved with absolute certainty, their duty was to acquit. Not to do so – he turned, throwing out a hand towards Florence Maybrick – would be *to snap the thread of this woman's life*.

A collective shudder rippled through the room. Usually so admirably composed, Florence was weeping silently and *the effect upon everybody in the court was strongly visible, the magnetic personality of the advocate influencing all around him as he pursued his merciful task*.

It was common in murder trials for the defence to remind the jury of the effect of returning a guilty verdict: that it meant sending the prisoner to their death. Emphasising her isolation, referring to the dark clouds gathering over her, Russell characterised Florence as helpless and vulnerable rather than brutally scheming – a woman who had frequently expressed concern about her husband's medicinal habits only to be ignored. He promised that he would prove that James was an habitual arsenic-eater and that this fact accounted for the presence of poison in his body. *In view of the warning to Dr Hopper in 1888*, said Russell, *in view of the warning to Dr Humphreys in the beginning of March 1889; in view of the letter to Mr Michael Maybrick in March 1889*, Mrs Maybrick had, in fact, been the only person to try to save her husband from himself.

Russell argued that there was too little arsenic in James' body to have caused death and that Maybrick's symptoms were any-way inconsistent with arsenic poisoning. Recalling that Florence had been deposed in her own house from Tuesday 7 May, he stressed that it had been impossible for her to harm her husband from that date. Why, he asked, had suspicion never been thrown elsewhere? Why, when she had been disempowered by her brothers-in-law, was there no one *manly enough … friendly enough … honest enough to go to her and make the charge to her … to see whether she had any explanation to offer?* If she was so wicked, why had she purchased the flypapers so openly and, given that so much arsenic had been discovered in the house, how was it that the prosecution were unable to prove her purchase of anything other than the flypapers? The family had rushed to judgement. Mrs Maybrick was a woman wronged; a victim and not a murderess.

Then came a surprise. His client, said Russell, would seek per-mission from Judge Stephen to speak. Before anyone could wonder what she wanted to say, the judge began to explain to the jury that, since defendants could not be sworn and therefore were not under oath, Florence could not be cross-examined; as a result, her statement should not be afforded the same weight as evidence given by sworn witnesses and could only be heard when they had all been called. He would allow Russell's request but he would also insist that between the rising of the court that day and the recommencement of the trial on Monday Florence should receive no visitors and that she could not take legal advice on what she might say.

Assenting, Russell continued, describing Florence's mental agony. In the dock, she raised her black-bordered handkerchief to cover her trembling lips and bowed her head, tears falling. The court was agog as the lawyer focused on the jury, entreat-ing them not to allow their repugnance of what he called her *abhorrent faithlessness* to influence their decision. They must remember, he warned, that transgression did not lead inexorably to the conclusion that she deliberately and wickedly sought to destroy her husband's life. Looking directly at each of the twelve men, Sir Charles held their attention silently before returning to his seat. The pace of events was about to change.

First, witnesses were called to swear to James' arsenic addiction. Nicholas Bateson, a Liverpool man living in Memphis, said he had shared rooms with Maybrick in Norfolk, Virginia between 1877 and 1881 during which period James took arsenic and strychnine against malarial fever while complaining constantly of numbness in his hands and limbs. A former sea captain, R. Thompson, had been with James in 1880 at Santo's drugstore on Main Street in Norfolk where he procured a white powder. The druggist said that it was arsenic, but when Thompson later raised it James got angry and the subject was dropped.

Thomas Stansell, a man conspicuous by his *ebony skin and woolly* head, according to the Liverpool papers, and by his 'Iss, Sar' accent that brought the whiff of the cotton plantations to the court, was next. Formerly employed by Bateson and Maybrick as a servant, Stansell said that he regularly went to the druggist for arsenic for James: it came in small packets and he used to stir it into warm beef tea. The man remembered that James was constantly rubbing his hands together against numbness and that he surrounded himself with copious medicines in the form of liquids, powders and pills.

Cumulatively, these three witnesses painted a picture of a man in the grip of a ferocious dependence. Then came Edwin Heaton, a retired chemist who had formerly run a shop at Exchange Street East, close to James' office. Heaton had recognised an illustration of Maybrick in the *Liverpool Echo* and had come forward of his own accord to say that the dead man had been a regular customer, frequently demanding a 'nostrum' or 'pick-me-up' laced with up to seven drops of *liquor arsenicalis* – sometimes as often as five times a day.

Seven drops taken five times a day would, mused Russell, amount to close to a third of a grain of white arsenic.

He gave you a reason why he wished it? asked the barrister.

Yes.

Do you know that liquor arsenicalis has aphrodisiacal qualities? Do you know that word?

I do not.

Did it excite passion? the judge queried.

Yes sir, it had that effect.

Russell did not pursue the subject of sexual appetite: the fact that James kept a mistress had already been aired and Florence had asked him for the sake of the family's reputation not to pursue this thread. Instead, the lawyer concentrated on drawing from Heaton the fact that when James planned to be out of town he asked for a bottle containing up to sixteen doses.

A Liverpool homeopath, Dr Drysdale, then swore that James had consulted him several times before 7 March that year and that he had admitted to dosing himself with nitro-hydrochloric acid, strychnine and other preparations. Then William Thomson, a business friend, said that James told him that he had taken a double dose on the morning of the Wirral races in April. Next a wholesale druggist, John Thompson, deposed that James used to visit a cousin employed at his warehouse: that cousin was dead, but the imputation was that he had been the source of a regular supply of arsenic.

So much for James' past. It was time for Sir Charles Russell to examine his own expert witness. Three years earlier, during the sensational trial of Adelaide Bartlett, Professor Charles Meymott Tidy – Examiner of Forensic Medicine at the London Hospital, one of several official analysts to the Home Office and widely considered to be England's leading forensic physician – had been employed by the prosecution. Then, disagreement between the eminent scientists had led to her acquittal. Now Russell called Professor Tidy to give evidence for the defence.

In short, while Tidy agreed that symptoms of arsenic poisoning differed widely, he believed that there were four prominent indicators and that it was impossible for all four to be absent. In James Maybrick's case the vomiting was neither excessive nor persistent; chronic diarrhoea seemed not to occur and loose bowel movements came on too long after the vomiting began; there was no irritation to his eyes; and no severe abdominal pain. These facts, Tidy believed, utterly countered the argument that the man had been poisoned.

Unlike Stevenson, Tidy had attended hundreds of post-mortems relating to the discovery of arsenic and he argued forcibly that in the case of James Maybrick three post-mortem indications also disproved the charge: no poison was found in his stomach; there was an absence of petechiae; and there was no evidence of fatty changes in the viscera. Having seen a great many cases of inflammatory conditions caused by tainted food, Professor Tidy asserted that the cause of James Maybrick's death was food poisoning or gastroenteritis.

Lastly, Tidy directly challenged Edward Davies's and Thomas Stevenson's estimations of the total amount of poison that *might* be in the body. Multiplying the sample size by a factor consistent with the weight of the entire organ was, he believed, absurd. The only way of arriving at proper fact rather than assumption was to mash up the whole organ and then analyse a small sample. Countering his learned colleagues, Tidy was certain that there was far too little arsenic in Maybrick's body to have caused his death.

Unlike the prosecution's scientific expert, Tidy's evidence was based on recent, well-documented cases and it withstood cross-examination well. Try as John Addison might to make him waver, the scientist held firm, his refutations peppered with amiable exclamations – *Oh dear, no* and *Quite so* – as he returned again and again to the pernicious possibilities of bad sausages, cheese or lobster. Re-examined by Charles Russell, Tidy added that he considered the tests done by Dr Humphreys on May-brick's urine and faeces to be perfectly adequate: since the test itself was so sensitive, Humphreys's lack of rigour would make no difference to the result.

The experts had reached stalemate.

It was late. Judge Stephen wrapped things up until Monday.

CHAPTER 26

A Hundredfold Curiosity

The weekend newspapers called it an *absorbing drama of life or death being unfolded daily*, focusing on the *well-dressed* ladies in the public seats and on Florence in the dock, her features hardly moving even while she wept. *Reynolds's* was struck by her cut-glass manners: at the close of each day, she rose and bowed to the judge before quitting the dock.

Lloyd's Weekly reported that a man had been arrested in Lowestoft on suspicion of the latest murder of a prostitute in Whitechapel. The discovery of Alice McKenzie's body on 17 July had reignited fears that Jack the Ripper, whose first five victims were killed between August and November 1888, had struck again. News was also filtering into the papers of the shocking murder of a young London clerk while on holiday in Arran. Though no one yet knew it, his assailant – Glasgow pattern-maker John Watson – had fled to Liverpool, from where he taunted the police in gloating letters sent to the press.

Yet if the Ripper's ghastly spree sent shivers down the spines of newspaper readers, then the dark alleys of London's East End and the working-class poverty of his victims were a world away from the majority of the readers' bourgeois lives, with their smart dining-room tables and reserved church pews. The physical brutality of these killings could be held at arm's length, while Florence's trial touched the British public more nearly, so that focus on her remained undimmed. Her case hinted that even the loveliest female, casting off her prescribed role and taking poison as her weapon against suppressed but febrile disharmony, could succeed in silent-footed violence.

Opinion divided. Across the country men and women took up their pens, addressing letters to newspaper editors that expressed outrage at, or support for, the young widow. The Cleavers were swamped.

Clearly Florence could not play the same game as Lizzie Borden, Madeleine Smith or Adelaide Bartlett, whose barristers manipulated the prejudices of male juries with professions of their moral purity. Because her sojourn with Brierley at Flatman's Hotel had been proven, she could not claim to be sexually apathetic. So far, she had been the model of composed self-control. By electing to make a statement would she now put herself in danger of seeming a little too spirited, lacking in the proper female virtue of docility? Two decades earlier, in his *History of Crime in England*, L. O. Pike had suggested that women who chose to be independent of men would forfeit their protection, that *every step made by woman towards her independence is a step towards that precipice at the bottom of which lies a prison*. It was still the case that outspokenness in women attracted censure. Florence's determination to be heard might turn out to be too much of a risk.

Throughout Sunday 4 August, alone in Walton Gaol, she considered what she wanted to say, knowing that the battle was drawing inexorably to its end.

*

It was cold on Monday, hardly even sixty degrees, and rain threatened the enjoyment of the public holiday. The shutters of the shops were drawn but theatres and music halls anticipated full houses and a stream of people began to flow into the city from the country – some heading out to the landing stages, carrying picnic baskets. Speculation about Florence's statement had *increased the public curiosity a hundredfold*, so that in the square outside St George's Hall an eager crowd of people fought for a place at the front of the queue for the court. A few of the Liverpool elite, their number swelled by interested lawyers, arrived early. Then, just before ten o'clock, an impetuous rush of the general public in their holiday finery rushed forward. Those fortunate enough to gain a place in the courtroom passed the time by openly gawping at Michael and Edwin Maybrick, who had already taken their seats at the front.

At ten-thirty, preceded by the usual flourish of trumpets, Judge Stephen entered. Then Florence appeared in the dock, clutching a piece of blue foolscap. Though white-faced, her step was firm.

Sir Charles Russell intended to question two more experts before calling his final witnesses. First was Dr Rawdon MacNamara, past President of the Royal College of Surgeons of Ireland and author of a standard work on the action of medicines on the body. He would support Dr Tidy, particularly in his belief that arsenic poisoning was habitually marked by redness of the eyelids and pain in the pit of the stomach. MacNamara believed that Dr Humphreys's descriptions of Maybrick's hawking and the efficacy of his blister also pointed to gastroenteritis. Under cross-questioning from Addison he even added his conviction that someone already troubled by a weak stomach and then exposed to wetness and chill became susceptible to harm from even a *trifling error of diet*. Yet, as Addison pointed out, the problem with the theory of food poisoning and gastroenteritis was that Maybrick had not suffered from fever. To this, MacNamara had no effective reply.

Frank Paul came next, a young but distinguished Professor of Medical Jurisprudence at University College Liverpool who also believed that everything pointed to gastroenteritis. In direct contradiction to the results offered by Edward Davies, his own experiments on pans identical to those used by James to warm up his food in the office had detected arsenic in the glaze on four separate occasions. Professor Paul also contended that even minute amounts of arsenic would be discernible in urine boiled for as little as a minute using the Reinsch test if any had been administered within the previous fortnight. His testimony thus undercut not just the city analyst but the contention that Dr Humphreys's negative tests had been improperly done.

Like Tidy, Dr Paul considered that the absence of petechiae in the dead man's stomach counter-indicated arsenical poisoning and, further, that it would take at least three grains to kill a man of Maybrick's height, weight and age. His evidence weighed compellingly in Florence's favour. In the course of his deceptively gentle cross-examination, though, John Addison discovered – to his apparent incredulity – that Paul's experience of arsenic in the body was not practical but derived from *reading up* on cases: in a swoop, he had diminished the force of the defence expert's testimony.

Russell next called Hugh Lloyd Jones, the owner of a chemist shop in Wales who believed that, from the number of ladies purchasing flypapers when no flies were about, the domestic preparation of arsenical face washes was widespread. James Bioletti, a Liverpool hairdresser and perfumer, agreed: arsenic in solution, he said, was *good for the complexion*, as well as for removing hair.

As Bioletti walked from the court, Charles Russell produced a pillbox from his pocket. Loudly, slowly, he said: *I should like to call someone to speak of a box I have here, which is labelled 'Taylor Brothers, pharmaceutical chemists, Norfolk, Virginia' and the description of the contents of which says 'Iron, quinine, and arsenic, one capsule every three or four hours, to be taken with food'.*

After some muttering between Addison and the Maybrick brothers, Edwin agreed to be re-sworn.

Waiting for him to make his way up to the front, Russell mused disingenuously: *I do not wish to make any complaint about this not being produced by any one.*

The imputation was clear. Russell was suggesting that the pill-box and its contents had been suppressed.

It is in the printed list, returned Addison.

It is not, Russell barked, knowing that he was correct.

To the question of how this box had escaped being recorded by the police, Edwin thought that it had simply been *overlooked*. He admitted that it had turned up in a drawer of the bedroom washstand a week or two after his brother's death, during the removal of furniture from the house.

> Russell: *You knew that Mr Cleaver ... was acting for this lady?*
> Edwin: *I did.*
> *Did you communicate it to him?*
> *No.*

Trying to diminish the impression of evidence being withheld, Addison sprang up and asked Edwin to confirm that he had eventually passed the box to the police. When had he found it? countered Russell. Despite his earlier explanation, Edwin stuttered that he could not say. Rising again, Addison suggested that it was during the removals. Edwin agreed.

In other words, potentially vital evidence discovered weeks earlier had not been communicated to the police until 1 August, just days before the trial began. It was dramatic and puzzling news. Did these pills ratify the testimony of the men who deposed to

James' arsenic-eating while in America? Why had Edwin not told anyone about them before the start of the trial? Vehemently denying that James was addicted to poisons, had one or both of James' brothers knowingly concealed this box? The impression lingered that, at the very least, Edwin had tried to cover it up.

Russell had just one remaining witness, Sir James Poole, a former mayor of Liverpool, whose statement would bring the defence argument full circle – back to James' addictions. Poole said that he had run into Maybrick at their club – the Palatine – back in April. James had talked about taking poisonous medicines. *How horrid*, Poole had exclaimed. *Don't you know my dear friend that the more you take of these things, the more you require, and you will go on till they carry you off?* Maybrick had shrugged and changed the subject, expert at bringing critical conversations to an abrupt end.

*

The moment had come. Russell looked enquiringly at Florence. She nodded.

Do you wish to make a statement? he asked.

Yes.

Her voice was soft. Following a brief, whispered conversation between barrister and defendant, Russell told the judge that she had made some notes simply to help her remember what she wanted to say.

Pale, tearful, Florence rose from her chair and took a faltering step forward. The courtroom stilled. Accepting a small glass of water, she paused, sipped, nervously drew herself up and, holding the cold rail with one gloved hand and her paper in the other, she quietly began.

The charge against her, said Florence Maybrick, was crushing. At the mention of her children her voice broke, she faltered and tears began to fall. Her hand tightened around the rail. Taking in a deep breath, she let it slowly out and then resumed:

*For many years before my marriage I have been in the habit
of using a face wash prescribed for me by Dr Griggs of
Brooklyn. It consisted, I believe, principally of arsenic,
tincture of benzoin, elderflower water and some other ingredients, applied in a handkerchief well soaked in the solution
beforehand.*

She explained that, having lost the doctor's prescription, she
had continued over the years to make the preparation herself and
it was for this reason that she had soaked flypapers in a basin in
her room.

My Lord, I now wish to refer to the bottle of meat essence.

Necks craned. Every eye in the court was fixed on the face of
the woman in the dock. Everyone knew that the discovery of
arsenic in the meat juice, coupled with the nurse's deposition that
Florence was seen to tamper with the bottle, was the most dangerous – if circumstantial – evidence against her. Was it possible
that she would have a rational, believable explanation?

In *piteous* tones, Florence murmured that she had

*Not one true or honest friend in that house. I had no one to
consult and no one to advise me. I was deposed from my
position as mistress in my own house and from the position
of attending upon my husband, notwithstanding that he
was so ill.*

She was, she told them, exhausted, overwrought, miserable and
terribly alone. On Thursday evening James had been *very sick and
very depressed* and had implored her to give him some powder.
She refused but, *unnerved* by his distress, comforted by his assurance that it would not hurt him, she had finally assented. Taking
it and the meat juice into the dressing room she had introduced
the powder into the bottle. In the course of doing so, some of the
juice had spilled and she had made up the amount with water.

By the time she returned to the bedroom James had fallen asleep and so she placed the bottle on the table by the window. Later, when he woke choking and vomiting, he did not ask for it, *So I removed the bottle from the small table, where it would attract his attention, to the top of the washstand, where he could not see it.*

She paused; then, falteringly, continued. Days after James' death – on Tuesday – when Matilda Briggs mentioned that arsenic had been found in the meat juice, Florence said that she realised for the first time what the powder had been. Knowing that James had taken none of it but that she could explain how it got there, she had tried to tell, but the policeman had silenced her. When Arnold Cleaver arrived, she told him instead. There was, then, a perfectly innocent explanation for the arsenic being in the bottle of Valentine's meat juice: she had put it there herself, in perfect ignorance but in deference to the wishes of her sick husband. It was foolish, but it was not malicious.

In conclusion, my Lord, I wish to add that for the sake of the life of our children and for their future a perfect reconciliation had taken place between us and that on the day before my husband's death I made him a full and free confession and received his entire forgiveness for the fearful wrong I had done him.

After a brief pause, moving uncertainly, Florence resumed her seat.

The usual groans and murmurs that chased around the room following sensational statements did not erupt. So absorbed by Florence was everyone that the silence when she sat down was oppressive. Her voice, reported the papers, had been *low, her accents ... most musical; culture was apparent in the language ... and the vein of pleading and repentance which ran through it was impressively touching.* Admitting to adding something to the meat essence because she believed it might help, admitting to her adultery, she seemed contrite. Was this very un-English candour born of an admirable determination to clear her name, or was it proof of her shocking and unnatural intemperance?

It was uncertain whether, by choosing to speak rather than remain silent, she would be applauded for her pluck or would forfeit the emotional sympathy of the jury. Standing, Charles Russell broke the silence, asking Judge Stephen for permission to call two further witnesses who could ratify Mrs Maybrick's contention that she had explained about the powder in the days immediately following James' death. It was a reasonable request, replied the judge, but since the prisoner's statement was not given under oath, there was no provision under the law to allow him to grant it.

*

The atmosphere in the court was still highly charged when Russell began his closing speech at a quarter past twelve. Glancing at Florence, whose hands were clasped tightly together, he then faced the jury, reminding them that his client had chosen to take her trial in Liverpool where her husband had been well liked, where there would probably be prejudice against her, rather than request for it to be heard elsewhere. Deeply solemn, he asked for their attention and sympathy. Was there unequivocal proof that James Maybrick's death was caused by arsenic, or proof that she had given it to him, he asked.

Recapping the evidence concerning James' pharmaceutical habits, Russell then scornfully derided the man who had lured Florence from fidelity. So much contempt did he have for Brierley that he refused even to utter his name yet, he insisted, Florence's grave moral guilt did not prove a deliberation to murder. With a rising inflection, tinged with sadness, he lamented that

For faults like hers the judgements of the world are indeed unequal. In a man such faults are too often regarded with

toleration ... But in the case of ... a woman, it is ... the
unforgiveable sin ... She is regarded as a leper, deprived of
sympathy and encouragement and affection, of advice and
consideration.

Pointing out that James might have offered sympathy but
delivered blows, Russell stressed that Florence had nevertheless
manifested a profound anxiety for her husband during his illness
that was simply irreconcilable with a desire to destroy his life. He
asked whether her prostration after his death was the behaviour
of a guilty or a heartbroken woman. But for the intercepted letter,
he reminded the jury, there would have been no suspicion.
Maybrick's *Bunny, Bunny, I did not think it of you* – far from
being an accusation that she was harming him – was his response
to her admission of infidelity.

Russell contested that Florence had bought and soaked the
flypapers openly and that the police had made no attempt to
link any of the other arsenic found in the house to her. He
focused on the irreconcilability of the expert testimonies and the
failure of the prosecution to prove the cause of death. Reprising
every point in her favour, he reminded the jury that doubts, con-
jectures, suspicions and ambiguities could not be allowed to
triumph over direct, unequivocal proof. *And now* – his voice
swelled and he looked each juror, one by one, in the eye –

I end as I began, by asking each one of you, in the per-
plexities, in the doubts, in the mysteries, in the difficulties
which surround this case, in view of the contrariety of
things presented to you ... whether you, any one of you,
can with satisfied judgement and safe conscience say that
this woman is guilty? ... You cannot, you will not, you
must not unless the whole purpose and facts and weight of
the case, fairly, honestly considered with honest and impar-
tial minds, drives you irresistibly to that conclusion.

It was a master-class in legal oratory, tunnelling effectively under the prosecution's case, reminding them repeatedly of the uncertainty that existed and the moral importance of deciding fairly. At twenty-five minutes past three, Russell stopped. Something like a ripple of applause went up.

Addison stood.

By calling his witnesses in an order that tended to befuddle the chronology of events, there were a great many followers of the trial who did not believe that Addison and his prosecution team had proved its case beyond all doubt. Over the next two hours he would attempt to erase that impression. First he exhorted the jury, since Mrs Maybrick had received the best defence possible, to set pity aside.

> To have to urge against a woman – attractive to you by her cleverness, by her appearance, by her social position which puts you more or less into sympathy with her – to have to urge that she had been guilty of a deliberate and cruel murder was not an enviable task.

The best legal minds, he continued, had offered only empty theories in her defence and the jury must steel themselves to consider the case as they would for any poor or ill-favoured woman. He submitted that the intercepted letters between the lovers were not consistent with her story and the police investigation had *brought to light a very terrible deed of darkness and proof of murder founded upon profligacy and adultery and carried out with a consummate cunning which has rarely been equalled in the annals of crime.*

Carefully refuting each of Russell's arguments, Addison restated the prosecution's case, stressing the defendant's admission with regard to the meat juice and the white powder, leading many in court to consider that her statement had been a terrible miscalculation.

At five o'clock the judge adjourned proceedings and retired. Tomorrow he would begin his summation. Papers were collected, shuffled and stuffed into cases as the barristers prepared to leave. Florence passed out of the dock, down the narrow stone stairs to the basement corridor and into a waiting police van.

The crowded courtroom dispersed more slowly than on any previous day. It was as if, after the dramatic intensity of the preceding hours, the spectators could not tear themselves away, reluctant to return to the squabbles and petty triumphs of their own homes.

CHAPTER 27

The Last Act

It escaped few waking up in England on Tuesday 6 August 1889 that the last act in Florence Maybrick's trial was about to begin. Gusting winds and showers dispelled the crowds outside St George's Hall, save for a few who huddled under the gloomy colonnade. Inside the court, inexplicably, the trumpeters did not sound the appearance of the judge, a change of procedure that set the players unconsciously on edge.

Russell's characterisation of his client as a *friendless lady* had touched the public: in the dock, sheathed in black, she appeared increasingly frail, weary and sad. As everyone prepared for the sixth day of her trial it was, wrote one reporter, like the opening scene in *Hamlet*: *there was a shiver in the air*.

The courtroom was filled with the same uniforms, the same faces, the same wigs, books and piles of papers, the same well-dressed ladies and grey granite columns. The same gas jets flickered and dust continued to spin in the dim daylight that fell from the roof lights. There was the High Sheriff in his red coat reading the day's newspaper. The judge's clerk sat pasting clippings into a scrapbook. Judge Stephen began his summation in a dull monotone, checking his voluminous notes from time to time. The bony-fingered, tousled-haired reporters strained to catch each almost-inaudible word.

There was something indefinably different about the tension in the court – a feeling of melancholy, perhaps – as events approached their crisis. Judge Stephen was a little confused about exactly when the flypapers had been purchased – was it March or April? – but he appeared generally to give weight to most of the arguments put forward in the prisoner's favour. Inclining her head, Florence was not the only one finding it hard to hear all he said, but her watchful eyes left his face only to scan those of the jury from time to time. As the lunchtime adjournment approached, Addison withdrew the suggestion he had made in his own speech the previous afternoon that the handkerchief on which arsenic was found had been used to slake James' thirst. There was, he now agreed, no evidence whatsoever to support such a contention. Meanwhile, Stephen lugubriously pointed out that Mrs Maybrick had been deposed in her own house, that she appeared to have told an untruth about the flies being troublesome in March, that arsenic had found its way into bottles provably free from it at the outset and that the Grand National argument *went to the extreme limit of such quarrels*. His direction to the jury was clear: if there was any doubt, then they must acquit.

By lunchtime the rain had stopped and a crowd of two thousand or so forced the nurses, whose presence was no longer needed, to fight their way from St George's Hall towards a waiting cab. As it pulled away, they were cheered. *There was no particular reason for this*, wrote the *Echo*, *except that the crowd wanted someone to cheer, and it didn't much matter who it was.*

Someone must have said something, because when they all returned the judge spoke more loudly, though no less tediously, reprising testimony after testimony and admitting that he found the evidence of the doctors rather confusing. Deciding that it was not necessary to go over the depositions of the scientists, he

explained that his own notes were rather patchy and so –
extraordinarily – he called for the scrapbook of newspaper clippings, trusting that they agreed with him in his recollection of the
examinations. Accepting that the experts were at loggerheads, he
considered that the length of time that arsenic can remain in the
human body had been imperfectly ascertained. Had these senior
men, he pondered, proved that James had the right kind of sickness and what exactly did the absence of diarrhoea suggest?
Charles Russell may have been right to suggest that the Maybrick
brothers were unduly suspicious; yet he also wondered how they
were supposed to behave once their misgivings were aroused.

The judge's summation was so involved that the day drew to
a close before it was complete. Leaving the hall, other witnesses
needed police assistance to push through the mass of people.
Those who had longed for an end to the gruelling trial were disappointed. It was by no means clear that the judge would even
conclude the following day.

*

Nothing could have been as *dreary, dull or depressing* as that day,
thought the papers, and when he began again on Wednesday
morning it seemed that Judge Stephen would continue in the
same vein. Beginning with the irreconcilability of the scientific
opinions, he pointed out that if the authorities could not agree
then untrained men (including himself) could not be asked to
form an opinion on the subject. Turning to James' symptoms, he
reminded the jury that there had been severe vomiting and restlessness – both indications of arsenical poisoning – but that the
fact that diarrhoea was mainly absent was at least unusual. In
this regard, he thought Russell's reliance on the absence of certain key symptoms inherently weak and that it would have been
more satisfactory if he had posited an alternative theory.

*You are there – and you alone are the persons – to find a ver-
dict in this case*, he told the jury.

Insofar as the jurymen were not scientists, he advised them to put aside the medical questions:

> *You cannot decide on medical refinements. I must point out to you again and again that I think that Mr Addison was perfectly justified in what he said, that you are not to decide this case as if it consisted of some one argument. It might do so ... but I do not think it does so. It depends upon a combination – a great number of different things.*

Was he instructing the jury to ignore scientific uncertainty and decide on the balance of probability, on the accumulation of general circumstantial evidence? Was he really advising them to set Russell's defence – built on the existence of considerable medical doubt – aside?

The judge pondered whether it was meaningful that the fly-papers had been paid for with cash and whether it was indicative of a desire to escape detection. The jury, he said, should guard against attaching too much importance to trifles like these for the trial was not a novel in which clues were carefully, consciously arranged. Life, he argued, was less orderly. He was referring to the fact that the events that took place at Battlecrease House during April and May, the police investigation and the trial did seem to many to have followed the conventions of fiction, so that Mrs Maybrick had been repeatedly compared to Wilkie Collins's malevolent Lydia Gwilt. Others thought her a different kind of heroine, immoral but honest, pitted against the suffocating impositions of society as a whole.

Stephen's turgid summation sent many imaginations wandering, but as he approached the issue of motive his formerly impartial tone altered noticeably, demanding attention. After a short break, without warning, the judge began to work himself up into a state of vituperative fury against what he called Florence's *disgrace*. It was not a question of determining morality, he said, since her adultery was proven and Brierley was – outrageously, to his mind – one of several men to have been seen with her at the London hotel. Reading each one of the letters between her and Alfred Brierley aloud again, Stephen put particular emphasis on her phrase *He is sick unto death!* Surely this proved her calumny, he suggested, since it was written when the doctors still expected their patient to recover.

As for the argument on the evening of the Grand National:

A blow, a black eye, a half-leaving the house ... and then is it a complete reconciliation for the sake of the children? Do you believe that people change in that kind of way? Do you think that a quarrel of the sort can be made up by the family doctor, who is not very intimate with them?

Surrounded by so many bottles of poison, Stephen posited that Florence may have surrendered to the temptation to do away with a husband she could not love in favour of a man with whom she was infatuated. Suffused with moral disgust, he appeared to be instructing the jury to consider the fact of her infidelity as evidence that she was not simply capable of murder but guilty of it. In his outraged view, if she was able so to deceive, then she was inherently evil. Implying that there were spaces in the defence, Stephen questioned why no witnesses had been called to corroborate Florence's use of arsenic as a cosmetic. Why had neither Dr Gregg of Brooklyn nor her mother given evidence on her behalf? Why had she not explained her actions with the meat juice earlier? Who on earth was the John whose letters she had kept, or the second man seen with her at Flatman's Hotel?

Judge Stephen clearly believed that, beyond all the complicated and contradictory scientific elements of the case, Florence Maybrick's relationship with Brierley *may supply every sort of motive ... why she would wish to get rid of her husband.* His previous day's instruction that the jury must take care to arrive at a decision by judging the evidence rather than probability seemed to have been cast to the wind.

> *You must decide it as a great and highly important case,*
> *involving in itself not only medical and chemical questions*
> *but involving in itself a most highly important moral ques-*
> *tion ... Your own hearts must tell you what it is. For a*
> *person to go on deliberately administering poison to a poor,*
> *helpless, sick man upon whom she has already inflicted a*
> *dreadful injury – an injury fatal to married life – the person*
> *who could do such a thing as that must indeed be destitute*
> *of the least trace of human feeling. You must consider ... a*
> *horrible and incredible thought that a woman should be*
> *plotting the death of her husband in order that she might be*
> *left at liberty to follow her own degrading vices.*

While her husband's life trembled in the balance, said Stephen, Florence Maybrick had written in terms of endearment to another man with whom she had behaved disgracefully. It was an awful thing to think of, and one that they must consider when judging whether she was guilty or innocent.

It seemed almost as an afterthought that he added – unconvincingly, some thought – *You ought not to convict a woman of such a crime as this unless you are sure in your own mind that she really committed it.*

Then, after twelve long hours of summation, Judge Stephen ended abruptly, sending the jury to consider their verdict. It was a handful of minutes after three o'clock. He withdrew. Florence was led out of the dock.

Turning to one another to compare opinions, stretching stiff limbs, rolling shoulders, the press and public openly relaxed, anticipating a lengthy wait. Victorian juries were encouraged to deliberate swiftly, but it was generally felt that the intricacies of the expert testimonies in this case would make the process

intense and prolonged. Most believed the evidence to be so contradictory that Mrs Maybrick would be released. All longed for the
end of an unhappy and wearying trial. In the well of the court, the
lawyers and solicitors talked. Reporters began to organise
elaborate signalling systems in order to convey the verdict to
their offices as quickly as possible in the race to have the first
printed sheets available for sale.

Some of the women in the public seats carried congratulatory
bunches of flowers in the expectation that they would be able to
pass them forward on Florence's acquittal. She was, to all who
had watched her so closely, a conundrum. Terribly feminine in
her frailty, her waxy pallor contrasting with the black of her
mourning dress, she appeared exhausted and although there was
an impressive firmness about her demeanour, her helplessness
elicited growing sympathy. Yet her admission that she had slept
with a man other than her husband and the possibility that she
had calculated James Maybrick's death while pretending to nurse
him also made her frightening. For the umpteenth time people
wondered whether she was a grieving widow, pining mother, ter-
rified girl or calculating murderess.

In the dingy light of the holding cell beneath the court, Florence strove to remain calm. She had slept little during the past
eight days, confounded by the fearful gravity of it all. Events
seemed to have spun out of control, to have caught her up in a
vortex from which there was no clear escape. She could not
imagine the relief of release but knew that she must try to quieten
the insistent hammering of her pulse. Expecting to be acquitted,
she also knew that in these precious minutes her life hung in the
balance. Beyond that heavy, breathless reality nothing mattered.

There were men, though – among them Thomas Sherman, the US
Consul in Liverpool, and William Potter, her American solicitor –
who demanded to see her. Despite Florence's insistence that she be
left alone to master this appalling suspense, to labour at detachment,
they entered her cell and urged her, in the company of a male and

female warder, to sign some papers allowing the sale of some inherited lands in Kentucky. The proceeds, they explained, would pay the debts accumulated by her defence and her signature must be made before the verdict was delivered. Convicts, they warned, forfeited all rights, including those over the disposal of their own property.

In a daze, Florence signed. Minutes later, she was recalled to the dock.

It was time.

When Judge Stephen reappeared in court at around ten minutes to four, dead silence fell, his early return taken by many as a sign that the jury's decision would be favourable. The dark curtain that opened onto their box shivered and a red-coated officer entered, followed by the twelve men. Some of the public rose, briefly, to their feet. After deliberating for just forty-three minutes would any of them look towards the dock? Could their verdict be intuited from the way they took their seats?

> *The Clerk of the Arraigns: Have you agreed upon the verdict, gentlemen?*
> *The Foreman: We have.*
> *Clerk of the Arraigns: And do you find the prisoner Guilty of the murder of James Maybrick, or Not Guilty?*

In the painful soundlessness of the court, a pause of mere seconds seemed to hold eternity.

Then:

Guilty.

The leaden quiet indicated that the verdict had come as a surprise until it was broken by a prolonged *Oh*, a murmur or astonished groan that reminded Florence of the sighing of wind through a forest.

She began to rise to her feet before dropping her head down

onto one quivering hand. For about fifteen seconds she sat, the focus of the entire room's attention.

She was asked to stand. A wardress stepped forward, halting immediately behind her, ready for her to swoon.

Clerk of the Arraigns: Florence Maybrick, you have been found guilty of wilful murder; have you anything to say why the court should not pronounce sentence upon you?

Something altered in Florence. She was overwhelmed and she almost faltered but she nerved herself, stepping forward with what some thought was a proud and defiant air. Then she said in a low voice, but emphatically, *I am not guilty. With the exception of my intimacy with Mr Brierley, I am innocent of this crime.*

Some thought her too bold.

Others found her attitude heart-breaking.

Judge Stephen reached for the black square of fabric. *Prisoner at the bar*, he began, effectively stripping Florence of her self-determination as he began the ceremony of sentence, the theatrical fulfilment of the public role of the court,

I am no longer able to treat you as being innocent of the dreadful crime laid to your charge ... The jury have convicted you and I must pass on you the sentence of the law; and this sentence of the law is – This court doth ordain you to be taken from hence to the place from whence you came, and from thence to the place of execution, and that you be hanged by the neck until you are dead; and that your body be afterwards buried within the precincts of the prison in which you shall have been confined after your conviction, and may the Lord have mercy on your soul.

She winced, trembled and clung to the rail. The wardress stepped forward but, by the turn of her head, Florence indicated that she did not want support. There were murmured 'Amens'. Many eyes filled with tears as she quit the dock, bending her shoulders forward and drawing up her skirts in order to begin her descent.

Behind her, the air began to throb. Hisses writhed, gathering in force. Some female spectators reeled. A bouquet was dropped. As news of the verdict made its whispered way through St George's Hall to the crowds outside, a great angry howl went up. Waves of human sound rose, augmented, waned and then swelled again as the judgment gave rise to convulsions of public feeling.

The basement below the court was colourless: white walls, grey passageways, metal grilles, the dark uniforms of her keepers. It was chill. Florence, dazed, tried to bring her breathing under control as she heard, as if in the distance, the sound of feet on stone and a succession of locks being opened and closed.

CHAPTER 28

Public Recoil

The hundred policemen deployed during the first six days of the trial were bolstered by fifty more, including thirty in plain clothes. Ropes were fastened between lamp-posts in an effort to keep sensation-mongers back from the approaches to St George's Hall. Yet by the time the jury had been discharged, a crowd of thousands surrounded the building.

One keen-eyed reporter noted that, throughout the trial, Alfred Brierley had seemed very agitated and that he tried to leave the courtroom at every opportunity. As soon as the judge finished his summation, declining the offer of police protection, he slipped out of a private door at the rear of the hall that opened on to William Brown Street. From there, Florence's erstwhile lover ran across the street to a cab stand before many in the crowd realised who he was. He had thus escaped some time before the verdict was even announced: if Florence sought out the comfort of his face as she stood to hear the jury's decision, she would have discovered an empty place.

By comparison, when Alice Yapp left the building at the end of proceedings she was jostled and forced to take refuge in a private room at Lime Street station while the mob pummelled at the doors. Mrs Briggs – so powerful at Battlecrease, so upright as a witness – had to be unceremoniously bundled into the safety of the North Western Hotel, her feet hardly touching the ground, her bonnet dented. A little later, when Judge Stephen's carriage drove up there was a rush while hundreds shouted *Shame!* and threatened to overturn it. It was, reported the evening paper, *an incident unparalleled in modern times*.

In expectation that the crowds would thin, Florence was held for two hours until, at six o'clock, the black van carrying her back to Walton emerged from the gates at a rapid trot, pushing through the tumultuous hordes that surged around and after it, slapping its sides with the flats of their hands.

James Berry, ex-policeman, pious Yorkshireman, England's Executioner, marked Mrs Maybrick's name down in his log. That morning he had hanged Lawrence Hickey at Ireland's Tralee Gaol.

Sir Charles Russell, shocked by the odd logic of a verdict that took Florence's proven infidelity as a sign of her murderous guilt, dashed off a letter to Home Secretary Henry Matthews, deploring the befuddlement of Judge Stephen's mind – his conversion of possibility into probability and then certainty. *I am sorry to say*, Russell wrote, *it will be necessary for you fully to consider this case*. There was much evidence against Mrs Maybrick – indeed, motive had been established – but Russell argued that *there was no direct evidence of administration* [of arsenic] *by her* and only a very small amount had been found in the dead man's body. More importantly, *the woman had been unfaithful to her husband and I am afraid this fact and her subsequent improper letter to her paramour unsettled Stephen's ordinarily fair judgement. In a long experience I have never heard any summing-up which gave a jury less chance of differing from his clearly conveyed adverse view*.

Writing fast and forcefully, sticking to the concision for which he was renowned, Russell complained that the judge *appears to* *have suggested that even if the <u>cause</u> of death was doubtful they might look to the other facts*. This, he wrote, was a legal impropriety; the judge should have made it clear to the jury that if they felt any doubt about the cause of death, then they must acquit. Consequently Russell believed that there were significant grounds for demanding a reprieve.

*

As news of the verdict reached London, talk in theatres and clubs touched on a general horror at the *impending murder of an innocent and beautiful woman*. Most anticipated that her execution would take place after the usual interval of three Sundays: that would mean 26 or 27 August.

During the trial the *Liverpool Echo* had sold over a million copies, printing close to a quarter of that total on Tuesday evening alone. Now headlines trumpeted MAYBRICK MYSTERY UNRAVELLED, THE SHOCK OF SURPRISE, CLOSING OF A SENSATIONAL TRIAL and even NOT PROVEN but the country was split – the *Standard*, *Morning Post* and *Daily Chronicle* supported the verdict; the *Daily Telegraph* and *Daily News* were undecided; the *Evening Post* and others came out on Florence's side.

The Times was concerned not to retry the case in its pages but believed that it was *useless to disguise the fact that the public are not thoroughly convinced of the prisoner's guilt* and that it therefore constituted a proper case for reconsideration by the Home Secretary. There was, it wrote, strong suspicion of Florence's guilt, but most people believed the medical evidence too unclear to convict. Several other newspaper editors cautioned that, since no Court of Appeal existed, public opinion must not be ignored; there were renewed demands for a change in the law to allow prisoners to take the stand, to be examined and cross-questioned. Elsewhere, papers like the *Liverpool Echo* censured the apparent existence of what they called *depraved* businessmen who *needed to screw up their nerves* once or twice a day with chemical tonics.

They also pondered the Maybricks' mismatched alliance – the differences in their nationalities, their education and their ages – such that they found that *they* [had] *little or nothing in common and that they must look elsewhere for the satisfaction which marriage has failed to give to them.*

There were plenty of protests that Florence had been convicted for adultery and not murder. The *St Stephen's Review* – a weekly magazine of political comment – believed that *some men look upon Mrs Maybrick's admitted offence as something it is their duty to society to stamp out ...* [she] *has been sacrificed to the prejudices of hypocritical morality and to the apprehension that husband poisoning would be extensively practised if not at once nipped in the bud.* Partly inspired by the story, Thomas Hardy's *Tess of the d'Urbervilles*, the bestselling novel of 1892, would argue that even illicit love was powerful and right so long as it was honest. But where did this leave things in reality? The difficulty (as even Hardy accepted) was that it was practically unheard of for a sexually independent woman to survive public derision.*

The *Spectator* used the verdict to attack women's emancipation, suggesting that Florence's position was the inevitable consequence of rebellion. Criticising the element of female *partisanship which we can hardly be mistaken in referring to something like a claim for women of the right to observe or disregard the obligations of marriage at their own pleasure,* it censured women tempted to forfeit their responsibilities. The *Liverpool Courier* agreed. Elsewhere, it was suggested that the great middle class, half-suspecting its own young wives of dreams of infidelity, was threatened; when these fears were compounded by an irrational dread of domestic poisoning it resulted in a *ferocity of panic.*

---

* There were, of course, exceptions. George Eliot famously and openly lived with a married man during the 1860s. In part, her position was accepted because of her commercial success (which gave her independence) and because the arrangement was rarely discussed, always discreet.

Sir Henry James, former Solicitor General and Attorney General, gave public voice to a swelling antipathy to the verdict. The leading medical journals promised to review the scientific evidence. The postbags of the national and regional papers began to bulge with letters ranging from the sentimental to the logical, both in support of a reprieve and advocating unbending adherence to the sentence. Alfred Stokes, Public Analyst in the Paddington District of London, sent a report to *The Times* listing numerous *muslins, cretonnes, mats, paints, wallpapers, cards, stew-pans etc ... found to contain arsenic.* A man was arrested for brawling in an argument over the verdict.

In Liverpool, the Cleaver brothers issued standard petition forms and within days over half a million signatures had been sent to the Home Office in hundreds of separate documents. One contained seventy thousand Liverpudlian signatures, another listed a thousand members of the Liverpool Cotton Exchange, while a *gigantic parcel* contained the support of thirty thousand Mancunians, including ministers, clergymen, magistrates, surgeons, solicitors, merchants and manufacturers. The Home Office received multiple statements from the Bar and the medical professions, each claiming that the verdict went against the weight of evidence, that the proof was unreliable and inconclusive, that it was easily possible to be addicted to arsenic, that there had been grave judicial errors, that too much stress was laid on her statement that he was *sick unto death*, which was simply a common expression from the Southern states, and that – as one put it – there *was no primary proof ... that a murder has been committed.*

It was said that the depth of public recoil from the verdict was unprecedented and that overwhelming dissatisfaction was sweeping the country. Yet, on Sunday, *Lloyd's Weekly* devoted several pages to what it called the resolution of a mystery, pointing out that all three verdicts agreed and that clear motive had been established. Almost lost in the columns of speculation was a short paragraph in the *Pall Mall Gazette* stating that James

Maybrick's friends wanted it to be known that he *was not a person of gay and frivolous and sensual life, that he scarcely ever participated in sports and gaieties of the kind so prominently made mention of in the recent trial, that he was a particularly domestic man, spending a remarkable proportion of time at home, that he was a great reader and extremely fond of music.* One of his former business partners, G. D. Witt, also wrote privately to the Home Office denying James' arsenic-dependency and stating that, on the contrary, Maybrick was *always trying to take a generous view of his wife's shortcomings.* Witt believed that Florence had begun to poison her husband the previous summer, during which James began to be troubled by watery eyes. The murder had been hastened, Witt suggested, when she discovered that James was altering his will.

Had Florence been tried for adultery and not murder? It troubled many that so much circumstantial evidence had been stacked against her while hints about James' own adulteries remained unexplored. Most confusingly, her admission of infidelity appeared to be something both brave and vulgar. Josephine Butler, famous advocate of the welfare of prostitutes, was concerned that – *sin* aside – Judge Stephen had *exhausted the English vocabulary for terms of horror, reprobation and shame ... I must express my surprise that such strong expressions should be reiterated ad nauseam when dealing with a woman, while they are not made use of at all in the case of men of high rank who have been notoriously unfaithful to their wives. We have not yet passed out of the old world of 'such should be stoned' into the new world of equal morals and just judgements as between the sexes.* Mrs Cunninghame-Graham, wife of the suffragist Liberal politician, agreed: to have a jury made up uniquely of husbands who *must be protected from adulterous and murderous wives* was, she said, absurd.

The Maybrick story continued, simply, to insinuate itself into many hotly debated issues: the conflict between male and female spheres, between public and private, between honesty and deception, estrangement and infatuation, dependence and emancipation. A stream of morbidly curious sightseers traipsed past the life-sized model of Florence displayed in Madame Tussaud's waxwork gallery in Baker Street: there was said to be *a 'beauty in distress' look about the face which makes irresistible appeals to the popular mind*. A Liverpool paper thought the story would *supply the material for innumerable novels ...* [for] *nothing could be more thrilling and dramatic.*

*

Florence's composure in court had exemplified an extraordinary effort of will. Away from the public eye, as wild rumours of her pregnancy and of multiple offers of marriage flared and were crushed, she was reported to be prostrate with shock. *She seems to me*, the Baroness von Roques told a reporter waiting at the wicket gate of Walton Gaol, *like a poor little rabbit who has been chased by dogs until it has neither sense nor spirit left. I was not allowed to approach* [her]. *I could not kiss her or touch her hand. I asked her to try and control herself ... She only shook her head and all she said was 'my strength is all gone'.*

In the musty, grey-walled, brick-floored condemned cell close to the entrance of the gaol Florence could no longer receive food from the local hotel. The prison doctors put her on 'hospital allowance'. Her clothes were replaced by a dress of washed-out, coarse blue homespun with a stiff brown cape printed with black arrows, and a small white cap. On her mother's visit she could hardly stop weeping and *seemed dazed ... crushed ... miserable*. Asking after the children, Florence was distraught when told that Edwin had arranged for their care but would not reveal their address.

Oh mama, she replied on being pressed about the letter to Brierley, *I don't know why I wrote it. I was half distracted with all that had taken place and I had no sleep for four days and four nights. He had been kind to me and I was very miserable.*

*

Two wardresses took turns to watch her, though she hardly moved from the straw mattress of her narrow wooden bed. For security the door to the lavatory, several feet away from the cell, had been taken away so that any passing prison official could see directly into it: it was the most shocking and humiliating element of this new phase of incarceration.

Removed from proximity to any other inmates, the cell occupied by those sentenced to death embodied the most deadening isolation. The wardresses were the same two who had guarded Mrs Berry – the only woman ever to be executed at Walton – two years before. These two knew that the scaffold would be erected some sixty yards from where Florence now lay: a dark shed set over a deep hole cut into the earth, its trapdoors level with the floor. Their duty would be to walk with her across the yard. She would step directly on to the trapdoors. The noose would be put around her neck and a tight hood drawn over her face. James Berry would pull a lever. Florence's body would fall into oblivion. Later, it would be buried within the prison grounds. A black flag would be raised to signal that the sentence had been carried out.

Reduced, degraded, voiceless, panic sometimes caught in Florence's throat and her skin prickled with cold dread. There was nothing but waiting, while outside the prison a war of words was unleashed.

Newspapers fought for the chance to publish the views of anyone involved in the case. First, the *Daily Post* caused a flurry by reporting that Thomas Wainwright, the jury foreman, let slip that they had made up their minds before they retired. Wainwright subsequently complained that a private conversation had been misinterpreted, but two other jurors admitted that he was correct. Then, on Monday 12 August, Florence's mother tried to fuel public sympathy by telling reporters that her daughter was prostrate, that she hardly ate, that she fretted constantly about the children and that she prayed with the prison chaplain. Printed in the form of an open letter addressed to a 'friend', the Baroness conveyed her *sincere appreciation of the efforts being made by the generous and just English people to save my unhappy daughter*. Wishing, she wrote, to refrain from the appearance of making a personal appeal, she hoped only for *kindness* for an *innocent* girl who mourned for her *helpless little children*.

Attempting to restore something of her daughter's character, the Baroness revealed that the 'John' referred to in court – a man imputed to be a second lover – was an *old family friend*. Furthermore, she pointed out that Florence had ample proof of James' infidelity and thus significant grounds for separation so there had been no reason to poison him: *Sir Charles Russell merely mentioned that there was a 'lady' in the case and why the matter was not pursued I cannot for the life of me understand*.

The following day, able publicly to vent her anguish at last, the Baroness gave an exclusive interview to the *Liverpool Mercury*. Emphasising her isolation – *I am not an Englishwoman* – she goaded with the suggestion that Americans had more influence with their politicians than the British. She wheedled – Florence would be killed by stress before the hangman constructed his scaffold – and she was provocative, suggesting that the children were now with Mrs Briggs and Nurse Yapp. Expressing her faith in English justice, robustly earnest, Carrie von Roques impressed the newspaper so forcefully it asserted that, had she given evidence in court, the jury would have reached a different conclusion.

Alfred Brierley had not been seen at his office for weeks, but he too was tracked down and encouraged to talk. The scoop was claimed by the London correspondent of the *New York Herald*. Described as tall and slender with a fine business reputation, Florence's lover was very agitated. *I wish you would make a note*, he said, *that I was going away. The last interview I had with Mrs Maybrick was on April 6th. Between our meeting in London on March 21 and this ... I had seen her only once, and that was at the Grand National Meeting*. He wanted to make it clear that, despite what the judge had repeatedly suggested in court, they had not continued to be intimate. In fact they had agreed while in London never again to meet in private. When he heard that she was in trouble he had cancelled a planned trip around the Mediterranean (forfeiting, he gracelessly added, half the cost of his fifty-pound ticket). He complained that *most inju-rious misconstruction and misinterpretation has been put on my relations with Mrs Maybrick, as unjust to her as ... to myself. Our meeting in London was a grave wrong: but in this trial it has been magnified greatly to her injury and mine, and assumptions have been based upon it which are entirely unwarranted by the actual facts.* Brierley appeared, wrote the journalist, to be under great mental strain. Feeling himself to be disgraced, he could hardly bear to be seen and, as a result, his business was failing. In order to leave the city – to escape – he was making plans to dissolve the partnership and close the business down. Telling the reporter that his future was unclear, Brierley said he just wanted to be left alone. Almost as an afterthought he added, simply, that 'John' was *a perfectly innocent party.*

The public lapped it all up. The *New York Herald* had also got to the Baroness, who was becoming intemperate. *I am a woman, and perhaps I take a woman's view of things,* she said, *but I don't know that a woman's view is necessarily a wrong view. I am going to speak only of women.* Florence had, following James' death, been *helpless, without a friend ... surrounded by enemies whose bitterness I need not call your attention to, for it is in evidence. A nurse, the woman Yapp, whom my daughter had some months before reprimanded ... communicated her suspicions to Mrs Briggs ... [who] was the moving agent in all that ensued. My daughter was satisfactorily convicted of murder before Mr Maybrick died by Miss Yapp, Mrs Briggs and Michael Maybrick.* James was an arsenic addict, said the Baroness, and Mrs Briggs' suspicions had been misjudged, leading to a grievous miscarriage of justice. *My daughter is not a woman of very much penetration.*

If you could see her you would not wonder at the ease with which she has been deceived.

When a reporter from the *Daily Post* arrived on Matilda Briggs's doorstep on Wednesday 14 August, she could not forbear from replying to the Baroness's accusations. Alice Yapp, she said, had called to her and her sister across the lawn when they arrived at Battlecrease during James' final illness. Accusing Mrs Maybrick of poisoning the master, Yapp had handed over the letter meant for Brierley. As to the imputation of treachery, it was *monstrous! I am sure there was not the slightest ill feeling on my part. We were in a delicate position, being told not to speak to her about the suspicions which pointed to her... We did what we conceived to be our duty under painful circumstances.* Yet since everyone knew how she had behaved towards Florence following her arrest, Matilda's pleading words – to most who read them – sounded unbelievably hollow.

The Baroness issued an immediate, passionate response, speaking again of the *mystery surrounding this case ... created by ... women.* Mrs Briggs had met Michael secretly in town; she claimed only to have searched the bedroom but had combed through all the main rooms in the house; she had initially maintained that she did not know about the telegraph Florence sent asking for a nurse but then admitted to writing it herself. Amidst all these inconsistencies Florence's mother contended that there was a central truth: Matilda Briggs – in what the judge had called a *grim joke* – had spitefully encouraged Florence to compromise herself.

Thus the Baroness stoked public uncertainty. Days passed, bringing the execution closer. Suspense tightened, snagging in the bellies of Florence's defenders, undermining the composure of the men in black suits. Ignorant of the efforts being made, Florence felt herself to be *held fast on the wheels of a slow-moving machine, hypnotised by the striking hours and the flight of my numbered minutes.*

CHAPTER 29

The Benefit of Doubt

The Capital Punishment Amendment Act of 1868 had brought to an end the ghastly spectacle of public execution in England, though it did little to stem growing distaste for the death penalty itself. Conservatives believed that hanging signified the re-imposition of the moral order, demonstrating the state's power to root out and triumph over murderous crime. To others, it was no more than judicial killing. Advocates for the abolition of capital punishment variously argued that it was ungodly, inconsistent with the precepts of civilisation and – crucially – that it was irreversible despite the fallibility of the law.

Cases where the verdict was not clear-cut, where opinion was ambivalent, fuelled the debate and threatened to undermine the legal process by encouraging a horror of putting an innocent to death. Without a Court of Criminal Appeal, the only way to side-step execution was to appeal to the Queen's mercy through the Home Secretary in a 'Memorial' that argued judicial irregularity, attempted to present new evidence or tried to introduce new witnesses. Memorials almost always relied on the existence of public concern and, sometimes, sentences were commuted to life imprisonment. Most Home Secretaries, though, were reticent about overturning verdicts, wary of appearing to interfere with the impartiality of the legal system.

Sir Charles Russell had already indicated by his letter to Home Secretary Henry Matthews that he believed there were grounds to seek Mrs Maybrick's reprieve. The reality was that in the previous decade, only eight female convicts had been hanged. Nonetheless, Richard Cleaver knew that he had just two weeks to assemble a dossier persuasive enough to save Florence's life. He needed to find new ways to destabilise the prosecution's argument, bolster perceived weaknesses in her defence and effectively counter the judge's summation. Particularly important, Cleaver must argue his case analytically rather than relying on the prevailing distaste for executing middle-class women for, while it was true that the commotion surrounding Florence would have been less vociferous if she had been a laundry-maid, Henry Matthews was not the kind of man to be swayed by assumptions based on class.

In the press, lawyers protested that the trial was a travesty, while chemists argued that James Maybrick suffered from none of the well-known signs of arsenic poisoning such as hair loss, flaking or mottled pigmentation, thickening of the skin on the palms or soles, nail weakness or swelling of the eyelids. It was also said that considerable efforts were being made in America to uncover new evidence. Public memorials were sent directly to the Queen as well as to the Prince and Princess of Wales, and more petitions were signed in major towns and cities including Newcastle, Dover, Eastbourne, Windsor, Newry and Norwich. The *Lancet*, having considered the scientific evidence, solemnly asserted that *the verdict arrived at in Mrs Maybrick's trial was warranted by the evidence*. Its rival, the *British Medical Journal*, remained undecided.

In the House of Commons, a movement was afoot on the Liberal benches to lobby for a reprieve. Separately, three thousand people gathered on Monday 12 August in front of St George's Hall to protest against the verdict. Then a *boisterous* public meeting was held in the great hall of London's Cannon Street Hotel on Tuesday afternoon, at which a retired Scottish barrister, Alexander MacDougall, urged the assembly to make a formal protest against the judge's summing-up. To resounding cheers he asserted that even Thomas Maybrick said he would sign their petition, and he proposed the formation of a Maybrick Committee to present arguments in the poor woman's defence.

Swamped, Henry Matthews announced that he would not, under any circumstances, receive deputations and the *Pall Mall Gazette* reported that he had privately sworn that he would rather resign his ministry than be coerced by popular clamour. Sixty-three years old, his receding hair carefully combed back from a clear, broad brow, Matthews had held the position of Home Secretary within the Conservative government for three years. Roman Catholic, clever, elegantly dressed and beautifully mannered, his firm mouth and steely eye made him seem coldly authoritarian, even obdurate, and as a result he was generally unpopular. *The Home Secretary is*, wrote the *Liverpool Review*, *a stubborn man entirely out of touch with the opinions of the country and with public feeling generally. He is constitutionally incapable of realising the bearing of an event until long after it has happened. In the face of this fact, some people will say 'be quiet, don't annoy him; if he is vexed he is sure not to act as he ought to act'.*

Matthews's decisions had caused outrage on several occasions and he had been loudly criticised for the failure of the detective police to solve the serial murders of female prostitutes in Whitechapel during the previous year. The murder of Alice McKenzie in July refocused public ire: on the one hand the Ripper, a multiple murderer who eviscerated his victims, remained free; on the other, a young widow surrounding whose guilt there was palpable disquiet was about to be hanged. In this atmosphere,

Matthews's ability to maintain the finest of judicial balances was questioned, particularly by the sensationalising penny papers whose readers were more likely to use the warren of dark alleys that made up London's East End than live in the broadsheet-reading, middle-class suburbs.

Despite such criticisms Matthews was determined to give Florence's case his impartial and forensic attention. The Clerk of the Liverpool Assizes had already forwarded to him copies of all the depositions in the case, including duplicates of the results of the chemical analyses of both Professor Stevenson at Guy's Hospital and Edward Davies in Liverpool. Judge Stephen had also delivered a copy of his trial notes along with a letter advising – in a spiky, rushed hand – that he believed the verdict of the jury was right, *though it may be necessary to ascertain the views of the highest medical authorities*. On Monday evening, 12 August, Matthews and the judge met. The Home Secretary's reliance on the opinion of the trial judges in these instances was well known: in view of this, reported the *Daily News, it is believed in official circles that a decision has now been practically arrived at*.

Two days later Richard Cleaver submitted his preliminary arguments, which included countering several of the adverse points made by the judge. With regard to Florence's statement that she had added powder to James' meat juice, Cleaver wrote that she had told this to his brother Arnold on 15 May while at Battlecrease and had repeated it on 23 May at Walton Gaol. He admitted that he had *perhaps wrongly, never attached great importance to the evidence as to the flypapers* since he considered the circumstances of their purchase and soaking so open as to admit of no suspicion. He hoped soon to be able to send an affidavit from Dr Griggs in New York confirming the truth of Florence's assertion about the arsenical face wash and he asked why James Maybrick's pockets had not been analysed, given the evidence of his secret addiction to the poison.

Regarding the judge's criticism that the Baroness von Roques had not been called to confirm her daughter's use of arsenical cosmetics, Cleaver wrote that he had simply considered that *the value of her evidence did not appear to warrant the infliction of the pain of such an appearance.* He also suggested that the reason no evidence was found for James Maybrick's powders was *the confusion of the drawers, cupboards and other receptacles when on 22nd May I was permitted to make a cursory inspection.* Despite being told there were no flypapers in the house, several later turned up and it took until 1 August for Edwin to admit to the box of pills that had *escaped all the searches made through the house.* The explorations had been, suggested the solicitor, chaotic: Battlecrease was ransacked but much had been overlooked.

As for the judge's critical comments about 'John', the Treasury Solicitor had since *examined this Gentleman and ascertained that he was a friend of Mrs Maybrick's childhood, that this meeting with her was perfectly innocent and that the phrases and allusions in his letter are susceptible of explanation in such a way as at all events not to increase the presumptions against her.* Promising that 'proofs' would follow shortly, Cleaver exhorted Henry Matthews to postpone making a final decision.

What Richard Cleaver did not know – because it remained private – was that Judge Stephen had recently written to the Home Secretary to convey the details of a statement made to him by Dr Humphreys at the close of the trial. The young Garston doctor said that Florence had suffered a miscarriage earlier in the spring, that James Maybrick had asked *how old is this thing?* and, discovering that it was four or five months old, had exclaimed that he could not possibly be the father. If Maybrick's words were to be trusted, the doctor's statement suggested that Florence's infidelity began far earlier than she had admitted. Had this suspicion fuelled the judge's sudden vituperative outburst during his summation to the jury?

Closeted with the Permanent Under-Secretary to the Home Office, Sir Godfrey Lushington, Henry Matthews considered which medical experts he could most profitably consult. The Presidents of the Medical Council and the College of Physicians were both abroad, Stevenson and Tidy were already involved in the case. Dr Poore, Professor of Forensic Medicine at University College, London – a man said to be remarkably shrewd and able – was mooted. Separately, Matthews was also focusing on the contents of the bottle of Price's glycerine which had tested positive for arsenic: he wanted to establish who had prescribed it and when, and he wished to know whether Nurse Gore used this bottle when applying salve to James' mouth.

On Thursday 15 August a second, clamorous meeting at the Cannon Street Hotel was convened by Alexander MacDougall, at which five hundred telegrams were read out in the prisoner's favour and the celebrated 'alienist' Dr Forbes Winslow pointed out that twenty-one irritant poisons had been given to James during the last week of his life.

The following day, a small group of men began to arrive at the Home Office. During the six hours of conference that followed, Henry Matthews listened avidly to the opinions of Judge Stephen, the Lord Chancellor Lord Halsbury, doctors Tidy and Stevenson and the third scientific expert, Dr Poore. The sensitivity of the Reinsch and Marsh tests were explained, the question of Maybrick's addiction to arsenic was debated and the potential difference to test results if flesh samples were macerated or not was vigorously argued.

Negotiating a delicate course between competing opinions, Matthews had prepared carefully. Moving things on when they threatened to get bogged down, asking pertinent questions about addiction, infection, analysis and symptoms, the Home Secretary insisted on returning to the witness depositions in an attempt absolutely to ascertain the amounts of medicine administered on each date. He asked whether the illness on the day of the

Wirral races was caused by the tonic contained in that unidentified bottle of medicine delivered by post or by a double dose of one of Dr Fuller's prescriptions. He wondered whether Dr Humphreys's evidence was reliable. To his insistent questions – *What I want to know is ... How do you account for? ... Is this an indication that?* – the group considered the importance of the flypapers, decided that the tumbler with the milky residue corroborated the cosmetics theory and speculated as to whether Mrs Maybrick administered arsenic as an aphrodisiac rather than with intent to kill.

As time passed, Matthews became frustrated. Every surety from one scientist was countered by doubt from the other. Trying to get at the truth, he found only contradiction. Dr Tidy was vehemently against the verdict for all the reasons he had articulated in court, including the absence of petechiae in the viscera, the late onset of diarrhoea, the non-arsenical nature of the vomiting and the absence of stomach pain, calf pain or eye irritation. Stevenson shook his head. Tidy was wrong: *I cannot reconcile to my mind the amount of arsenic in the viscera with any theory that I have heard.*

The meeting thus proved the contention that it was absurd to rely on carpenters, plumbers, grocers and milliners to determine one of the most difficult legal conundrums of the decade. If professors of chemistry and forensic toxicology failed to arrive at consensus, how could the jury of tradesmen possibly arrive at a proper decision? *The thing's a farce!* trumpeted the *Liverpool Citizen*.

*

Rushing between magistrates in London and Liverpool, Richard Cleaver procured sworn depositions from John Knight, the Baroness von Roques, his brother Arnold and Alfred Brierley, each substantiating points made in his earlier letter to the Home Office. The week was drawing to a close. Nine days had passed since Florence's conviction and his formal plea for a reprieve was ready.

The solicitor's memorandum took the form of a printed document seven and a half pages long. It began with the two questions that had formed the basis of Russell's trial defence: had it been proved beyond reasonable doubt that Maybrick died from arsenical poisoning? If so, was it equally proved that the prisoner criminally administered that poison? It asked why neither of the attending doctors had initially considered poisoning as the cause of illness and pointed to symptoms in life and death that disproved the theory. It agreed that the circumstantial evidence and motive were strong, yet posited that there was no direct evidence of administration by the prisoner, reminding Matthews that Mrs Maybrick had been absolved of responsibility for the apparently tainted food. James Maybrick was addicted to arsenic and his wife had warned repeatedly about the dangers of his habit. Cleaver contended that the expressions in her letters were misunderstood and that the judge had wrongly directed the jury by passionately inviting them to find her guilty. *The verdict came as a surprise upon the trained minds of the Bar of the Northern Circuit*, he wrote. Under such circumstances, the irrevocable penalty should be set aside.

Henry Matthews knew that even those who believed in the guilt of the woman sometimes dubbed *horribly wicked* were troubled. As one who wrote to the editor of the *Liverpool Weekly News* put it: *I believe* [her] *... to be guilty of the crime ... but ... the links in the chain of evidence have fitted better together than in this case and yet the accused person has ultimately had his or her innocence established beyond a cavil; and I think the convict should have the benefit of the doubt.* Along with his closest advisers, the Home Secretary therefore read Cleaver's formal plea for a reprieve carefully. Point by point he accepted or denied its contentions, scribbling his thoughts in the margins, cross-referencing the solicitor's arguments against trial transcripts, depositions and the separate opinions of the experts.

Matthews read extra notes sent by Dr Tidy, asked Dr Poore to give his opinion on the presence of bismuth (an arsenic-like metallic poison) in Maybrick's body and heard from the Treasury Secretary that Inspector Baxendale and a Liverpool solicitor had taken further statements from Mary Cadwallader and Bessie Brierley, who each swore that the bottle of Price's glycerine discovered by the police had been in the house during the whole period of their service. Nurse Gore was summoned to Whitehall. Wokes the chemist and nursemaid Alice Yapp were both re-questioned in Liverpool and the Treasury Solicitor noted that there were inconsistencies, including the fact that *Yapp's present statement shows that she was talking about poison and suspicious medicines on the morning of the 8th at which time in her evidence she declared she had no suspicion of the prisoner.* Wokes had deposed about his refusal to make up a prescription brought to him by Cadwallader on 7 May, since it contained *a deadly poison*. Although Dr Humphreys was at fault, the circumstance had been wondered at between the servants and Yapp now admitted that she passed on the information to Mrs Briggs and Hughes *some hours before I opened the letter addressed to Mr Brierley*. In this light, her story about Gladys dropping the letter into a puddle seemed less and less believable.

Tirelessly wading through the case documents over the weekend, Matthews received Dr Poore's vast report on Monday 19 August. Assessing the medical aspects of the case, investigating Dr Tidy's evidence and countering it with extracts from textbooks, Poore wondered at the absence of arsenic in Maybrick's faeces or urine but concluded that Dr Humphreys's tests had been incompetent. The post-mortem findings he thought *suggestive of arsenic, but I do not think it is possible even in the most marked cases for anyone, even the most skilled pathologist, to say from the post mortem appearances alone that arsenic was the poison.* Despite this, he found it impossible *to avoid the conclusion that arsenic was the cause of death*, though he accepted that it was difficult to establish when the fatal dose was ingested: because poisoning was not suspected, the doctors' treatments (particularly the morphia suppository) had both masked the symptoms and made things worse by retarding the body's *own efforts to throw off the poison.*

Matthews wrestled with it all, distilling – with Lushington's help – the key facts into a minutely handwritten table that listed every item in which any trace of arsenic had been found: what it was, where it was found and how much of the poison it contained. It seemed to show that there was a gravitation of arsenic *from all quarters of the earth at the same time to Mr Maybrick's house, his food, his medicine, his body, and yet we are asked to believe that none of this came from the prisoner.* Did Maybrick's habits account for the quantities of the poison in the house, the traces on the food jug or in the glycerine or the Clay & Abraham medicine bottle? Did his addiction tally with the medical evidence? Could he have taken these large doses without the results being obvious either to the doctors who he consulted or to his friends? Did glycerine ever contain arsenic? How much of the poison was required for cosmetic use? Was it credible that Mrs Maybrick should give in to her husband's demands for arsenic when there were doctors and nurses present?

Lushington wrote further summaries for Matthews's consideration, carefully balancing arguments for and against the prisoner in parallel columns. He toyed with the significance of Edwin's visit to Battlecrease and the fact that he had slept there during James' illness, noting that Edwin had free access to the dead man and that Mrs Maybrick had, creditably, taken initial charge of calling for doctors. He did not pursue the fact that Edwin had delivered food to his brother's office, though he did wonder why Florence had bought two lots of flypapers. He saw that on 30 April and the first two days of May James' food was made by the cook, that on the 30th very little was eaten, that it was after dinner on 1 May that Maybrick complained of being unwell and that *none of the food except that of the 30th is traced to have passed through her* hands. He wondered about the absence of fever in the sick man, the non-appearance of arsenic in the stomach tissues, faeces and urine and the administration of Fowler's Solution, bismuth, antimony and other similar poisons by the attending doctors. He was perfectly aware that the amount of arsenic found in the kidney and liver were half the amount generally accepted to cause death.

On Tuesday 20 August Lushington advised Matthews of his view that *this is a case in which there should be no interference with the sentence unless the verdict of the jury is the subject of reasonable doubt ... Having read the papers with careful attention I have no doubt whatsoever that the verdict was right. I am completely satisfied that Mr Maybrick died of arsenic and that the prisoner administered arsenic.*

The several conferences with 'experts' had failed to arrive at agreement; Lushington's conclusion suggested that he was swayed by a balance of probabilities and that he believed in an unprovable truth. Was it the case that, in his mind as in that of the judge, moral evidence held sway over its legal equivalent?

Judge Stephen was recalled to Whitehall. It was widely reported that the Home Office's various experts had reached deadlock.

CHAPTER 30

The Inexorable Passing of the Hours

Judge Stephen's overwrought prejudice turned Florence Maybrick, for some, into a victim in need of a male champion. A
growing number of women were developing a strong sympathy
with her and feminists had begun to use her case to attack male
laws and moral hypocrisies. Yet women had also given crushing
evidence against her. As if to emphasise the divide between tradition and emancipation, it was endlessly repeated in the popular
press that *if Mrs Maybrick is executed she will have been done
to death by women.*

A mere three hundred pounds of the proceeds from the
Battlecrease sale had been sent to Richard Cleaver to go towards
her legal costs. Her fashionable silks and personal effects were in
storage at Woolright's warehouse in Bold Street. The curious still
went to stand and stare in Riversdale Road. Strangely, Mr
Fletcher Rogers, foreman of the inquest jury, had taken on the
lease of Battlecrease and had already given orders for it to be
thoroughly redecorated.

While Florence's fate hung in the balance the Master of the
Rolls – the second most senior judge in England – called again for

the establishment of a proper Court of Criminal Appeal. *What the public feel*, he wrote, *is that they would rather have the fallibility of trained judges than the fallibility of an individual.*

Distancing themselves from it all, Michael and Edwin Maybrick had retreated to *a pretty little cottage on the outskirts of the village of St Helens, Isle of Wight.* Arrangements had been made for the children, James and Gladys, to live with Michael's London physician Dr Fuller and his much younger wife Gertrude: the childless couple would receive a hundred pounds a year to bring them up as their own. Then, as the nation waited for the decision of the Home Office, Michael finally spoke to the press. Piqued by the comments made by the Baroness, he said that the police had been in possession of James' clothes for weeks and that there had been no concealment. *The truth is*, he told a reporter from the *New York Herald, I thought that no one connected with the case tried very hard to have Mrs Maybrick convicted. I know I tried my best to have the physician give a death certificate that would have prevented the trial entirely but he refused to do so.* Did Michael expect anyone to believe him when he added *I do not think that the prosecution even desired Mrs Maybrick to be found guilty or expected that she would be. No one seemed to desire it.* Nothing would have pleased him more, he said, but to hear that she had been acquitted. He did, though, repudiate most of the Baroness's statements, denying that he had conspired against his sister-in-law or that he had been involved in the searching of Battlecrease after his brother's death.

The hotel waiter Alfred Schweisso told the *Liverpool Weekly Post* that he had *been very badly paid, did not get sufficient to eat and the crowd in the street knocked two of his teeth out*, but it was the *New York Herald*'s correspondent who was most dogged in his pursuit of interviews. Judge Stephen refused, as did the governor of Walton Gaol, but on Tuesday 20 August Alice Yapp was also induced to talk, perhaps in an attempt to restore her reputation. She claimed that she thought her mistress *an exceedingly nice woman*; she believed there had been no quarrel between her employers before the Grand National; she said that the servants all knew about Mrs Maybrick's debts since a money lender had called at Battlecrease weeks earlier. Yapp spoke, too, of the staff's concern when food came back to the kitchen tasting odd. She vehemently denied being in league with Mrs Briggs but did admit that *things have quite jumbled together in my mind since that awful trial*.

Chemist Wokes and Mary Cadwallader also spoke to the *Herald*. Breaking ranks, Cadwallader expressed surprise that Yapp was telling stories about poisonous prescriptions: *she knew that the police knew all about the prescription, and Mr Cleaver as well, and the police had done nothing further because they said there was nothing in it*. Yapp, she seemed to be suggesting, was a troublemaker.

On Wednesday 21 August Judge Stephen and the medical experts came and went from the Home Office, locked in their ongoing discussions with Henry Matthews. Two days remained before the time set for Florence's execution. Westerly winds threatened storms. Intermittent bursts of rain spattered hard against windows and turned the skies over Liverpool to lead. In the yard of Walton Gaol, the dull thud of hammers, the rasp of saws and the voices of the joiners all invaded Florence's cell in waves as workers began to construct the gallows meant for her. It was said that she received many hundreds of letters a day yet looked at only a few, lying on her bed, unmoving, counting the inexorable passing of the hours.

Waiting for a decision, innervation rose to a peak. A flood of public letters dominated the press. As she left Walton following one of her regular, brief visits, the Baroness told reporters that her daughter was changed beyond recognition, *in the most agonising distress* and unlikely to *sustain the awful anxieties of the past month or two*. Separate reports suggested the opposite – that Florence had rallied and was gaining in strength.

The analyst Edward Davies returned to Liverpool from a short holiday and, on Thursday the 22nd, was reported as saying that he believed that Mrs Maybrick would not be reprieved because *I don't think there is logically any middle course between confirmation of the condemnation and an acquittal*. Reminded that many had their sentences commuted to penal servitude, his riposte was sharp: *If that is so, I think Mrs Flanagan must have been hardly dealt with for there was really no conclusive proof that she used the poison from flypapers at all.* That same day, the letter written by James Maybrick to his brother Michael in which he complained of fears of death and suggested that doctors might wish to cut him open to determine the cause of his illness was leaked to the press, igniting misgivings that he knew that he was being poisoned, confusing public opinion still further. During the afternoon, the governor of Walton spoke to Florence as she was exercising in the prison yard. Her sentence had not been commuted, he said; she should abandon hope and prepare for her death.

Two days later the *British Medical Journal* would publish its own opinion that the scientific evidence was irreconcilable. Unlike the *Lancet*, it considered it to be *a positive duty in this important case to point out the striking anomalies which remove it from the category of cases in which there is no room for doubt.* In such circumstances, would the government really send Mrs Maybrick to her death?

On that Thursday evening, Alfred Brierley, accompanied by his brother, boarded the SS *Scythia* at the Liverpool docks. The ship was scheduled to sail for Boston with the tide. After fourteen years of cotton trading, he had wound up his partnership and dissolved his ruined business. Letting his beard grow long, wearing shabby clothes, he hoped to escape recognition – indeed, he would remain taciturn for most of the voyage, keeping to his cabin, nursing his relief to be gone from Liverpool along with his lingering shame.

Night fell. The officials at Walton Gaol were on alert for news from London but nothing came. Visiting the condemned cell, the governor gravely told Florence that she must expect to be executed early the following morning. After he withdrew, the chaplain sat with her, noting the growing strain, the nervousness in her features. The countdown to her punishment had begun.

Earlier in the day James Berry had checked the mechanism and the rope, prepared the straps for binding her arms and laid out the white hood that would cover her eyes. No one now believed that Henry Matthews would interfere with the process of the law. At daybreak, Florence would be roused. She would be allowed to dress once more in her own clothes – those she had worn at her trial. She would take breakfast. She would pray. Then, at the appointed hour and while the chaplain read aloud the service for the dead, Berry would ask her to follow him the short distance across the prison yard.

*

When the bell of the wicket gate sounded thinly at half-past one on the morning of Friday 23 August, the gaol was still. Only the turnkey had not gone to bed. A huddle of reporters loitering on Hornby Road, roused by the arrival of a messenger from London, shuffled their feet and pulled their coats close against the chill, pushing hands deep into pockets, wondering what it meant. The man had not left London until after eight and had arrived so late in Liverpool that it was rumoured that he had been forced to walk the six miles out to the gaol. Now he disappeared through the door into the prison yard and was led to an office where he waited for the arrival of Governor Anderson and the prison chaplain David Morris. Ten minutes later, these two were making their way along the flagstones of dimmed corridors towards the condemned cell, in which a single gas jet burned.

Dozing, Florence heard the heavy sound of the key turning and turned her eyes towards the scuffle of their footsteps. She was dazed. Understanding that a message had arrived, she struggled to comprehend whether it was one of life or death. The governor stood by her bedside, reading from a paper. Then he stopped, his hand dropping to his side. Momentarily stunned, she stretched out her hand towards him and then burst into tears.

Thank you, she whispered. *It is hard to bear.*

Late the previous evening, Henry Matthews had humbly advised the Queen that he recommended that *the capital sentence on Mrs Maybrick should be commuted to a sentence of penal servitude for life.* He had, he told Her Majesty, sought the advice of the Lord Chancellor, had repeated discussions with Judge Stephen and had consulted *medical men of experience.* They had all decided that *the evidence clearly establishes that Mrs Maybrick administered poison to her husband with intent to murder; but that there is grounds for reasonable doubt whether the arsenic so administered was in fact the cause of his death.* Believing her guilty, he accepted that Florence was entitled to the benefit of that doubt to the extent of escaping the extreme penalty of death but he considered that it was proper that she should remain in prison for life, *which is the legal punishment for attempts to murder.*

An official statement along the same lines was released to the press. *This decision*, it added, *is understood not to imply the slightest reflection on the able and experienced practitioners who gave evidence, nor on the tribunal before which the prisoner was tried ... The course adopted has the concurrence of the learned judge.*

*

Henry Matthews had fought to reconcile two bodies of opinion that would not agree. Surviving notes show that he tried to re-compute the amount of arsenic found in James' body from the various sources, struggling with the science and with generalisations about what constituted a fatal dose. In the end, he believed Florence Maybrick had attempted to murder her husband, though he understood that the cause of death remained unproved. His decision was extraordinary: it ensured that she would remain in prison for a crime – attempted murder – for which she had not been tried, while admitting that enough doubt existed for her conviction for murder to be set aside.

Relieved but confused, Florence remained prostrate, calculating the significance of her new fate.

At their Friday breakfast tables, as they boarded their trains, as they passed newsstands on their way to work, the population learned that Florence Maybrick would not hang as the news rippled out through the streets of every city and village in the country. Via telegraph and sub-oceanic cable, the details of the Home Secretary's deliberations and of Queen Victoria's Prerogative of Mercy were also communicated to news agencies on the continent and in the United States.

The *Daily News* found the decision *singular*, even illogical, though its editor confessed that he failed to see what else the Home Secretary could have done, torn between allowing an innocent woman to hang or a cold-blooded killer to walk free. It was a compromise and it was, the editor thought, justified, based on *a moral if not mathematical certainty of a convict's guilt*. Against this, the *Daily Telegraph* criticised Matthews's lack of decisiveness in either condoning the jury's verdict or admitting that enough doubt existed to free the prisoner. *The Times* anticipated a reaction of widespread relief while accepting that *the case against Mrs Maybrick was and remains a case of terribly strong suspicion, but suspicion which, after all is said, just misses moral certainty.* It praised Henry Matthews for not allowing himself to be swayed by public clamour, for keeping his head, maintaining his independence and arriving at a conclusion that was rational and just. On the whole, the Home Secretary appeared to get away with a decision based on somewhat fudged logic, though a vocal minority censured him for a *parody on legal procedure and ... burlesque on the administration of the law*.

In Kensington, Alexander MacDougall proposed to a disorderly public meeting of around two thousand people, including many hundreds of women, that the Maybrick Committee should begin to agitate for a free pardon.

The Baroness von Roques was advised that, as Florence was now beginning her sentence for life, she was allowed only one more visit. Von Roques should consider carefully all that she wanted to say. Downcast but practical, she turned away from Walton Gaol, postponing her call until the following week.

Reports multiplied that Florence was now so weak that she was unlikely to survive incarceration for more than six months.

Hoping to cauterise the excitement by removing her from the scene of her crime, the Home Office directed that she should be taken south as soon as possible, to Woking Prison. They wanted things wrapped up: payments of thirty guineas each to doctors Tidy and Stevenson were authorised for their post-trial advice; Dr Poore was due seventy guineas and Stevenson would be paid an estimated 160 to 180 guineas more for his work on behalf of the prosecution prior to and during the trial. The voluminous papers over which Matthews and Godfrey Lushington had squinted for ten days were bound into folders, packed into sturdy boxes and hefted into storage as the two men turned their official attention towards other ministerial responsibilities.

*

Shortly before noon on Tuesday 27 August the Baroness von Roques travelled to Walton for the last time. Now that the process was complete, regulations dictated that Florence be treated as an ordinary prisoner; their meeting took place in a room divided by two lines of vertical iron bars set about five inches apart, reaching from the floor to the ceiling. Sitting in a chair on one side of this barrier she waited for her daughter to appear in her rough, shapeless prison uniform. The two women were not allowed to touch. Fighting down their emotions and their shock they each sat in silence for some time. Raising her blue-violet eyes to hold her mother's gaze, Florence then asked unhappily after her children.

The Baroness, who had vainly hoped to be allowed guardianship of little James and Gladys, could do little but shake her head. Beseechingly, Florence repeatedly stuttered her innocence of the crime and pleaded with her mother to *Save me ... if only for the children's sake.*

After a pause, she added, *Cannot the generous public influence my liberty?*

Beyond that dull expression of hope, knowing that she would soon be taken elsewhere, Florence remained mute as her mother exhorted her to look to the future and not to give in to despair.

CHAPTER 31

A Colony of Dead Hopes

However shocking the many events of the previous four months had been, Florence had managed to keep about her a handful of comforts and there had always been something in which to have faith.

Now, hope fell away.

On Thursday 29 August, a week after the reprieve, Henry Matthews received a note from Queen Victoria's secretary, Sir Henry Ponsonby, thanking him for his consideration of Mrs Maybrick's case and letting him know that the Queen, believing Florence guilty, regretted that *so wicked a woman should escape by a mere legal quibble!* The monarch wished to express her belief that *the law is not a moral profession* and to make clear her wishes that the *sentence must never be further commuted.*

On the same day, the Baroness returned to Paris and, at half-past eight in the morning, Florence was removed from Walton Gaol. Quietly, in the greatest secrecy, she was taken in a closed cab to Lime Street station where she boarded a special third-class compartment of the London express accompanied by two female warders and a male guard. Wearing an ordinary brown dress and

a grey hooded travelling cloak branded with broad arrows, she
went unveiled. Members of the public came to a halt on the platform as she appeared, and stared. Distressed, humiliated,
Florence trembled as she stepped quickly over the fifteen yards
between the station building and the train. Onlookers thought
she seemed half her original size.

How different this basic compartment, its blinds drawn, to
the plush first-class seats on which she was accustomed to travel.
How powerless she was, hustled to a connecting train at
Willesden Junction, then through the crowded station at Woking
into the prison van that would bear her towards what she called
a living tomb. Trying both to conceal her emotion and to prevent people from seeing her, she held her handkerchief to her
face.

The prison, around three miles from Woking – twenty-odd
miles from London – was perched high on Knapp Hill, surrounded by quiet fields and orchards and bounded by an
eighteen-foot-high wall. The gaunt buildings were all relatively
new: the male wing was opened in 1859 and the female one in
1867, but the former was about to close and therefore almost
empty while the women's prison had just 409 prisoners for its
seven hundred cells. Half-deserted, the frowning structure
housed, according to one contemporary writer, *a colony of
wasted lives and dead hopes*.

Stunned, Florence was conducted through the outer gates and
across the yard. In an open washroom she was told to bathe and
to dress in a brown serge uniform. She was weighed and measured, and then sat passively while her hair was cut to the nape
of her neck, the sound of the scissors near to her ear, the touch
of the chill steel blade close to her skin, clumps of her damp
auburn curls dropping almost silently around her feet. Then
she was taken to an infirmary cell. Breathless with the throat-
constricting terror of this cold, hard place, the multiple locks,
the blood pounded in her ears as she stepped inside. When her

pulse began to calm she heard only retreating steps and the rants of a patient in the cell next door.

Florence faced a bleak and unforgiving future. Embroidered in white thread on her dress was LP29: L for life, P for the year of her conviction, 29 to denote that she was the twenty-ninth convict to arrive that year. A crimson star on her shoulder marked her as a first-time offender.

Her cell was eight feet by five feet and contained a hammock, shelves for books and blankets and a flap of wood to serve as a table. It had a window at one end and a small pane of thick glass at the other, through which the light from the gas jet in the corridor filtered weakly. The floor was unforgiving slate. On the other side of the door matrons in brown dresses patrolled, heavy bunches of keys suspended by chains from their waists.

In a handful of days Florence would turn twenty-seven and her former lover would land in Boston to face the American press, his face flushed and his nerves fortified by brandy and Scotch. Trying to dodge anyone holding a notebook, Alfred Brierley would repeat endlessly *I have nothing to say. I have nothing to say.* He stressed that he had come away in order to escape notoriety; he wanted to see Montreal, Niagara Falls, New York and New Orleans. He wanted to rest. Like Thomas Hardy's Angel Clare, reports suggest that Brierley was lured by the promise of profit in South America and that he headed there both to test its agricultural bounty and *to escape from his past existence.*

By comparison, Florence's days were drained of colour, comfort or even conversation, for Woking was run on the silent system. The first stage was the worst: nine months of solitary confinement during which she was forbidden to speak, dressing in the dark, eating 'skilly' or gruel for breakfast, cleaning her cell, marching to and from chapel twice a day and around the exercise yard once. She was expected to work, teasing fibres from tarred rope in order to make twine for the Post Office, making uniforms for the sailor boys at Greenwich or knitting stockings. Surrounded by former charwomen, machinists, servants, factory workers and laundresses – tradespeople among whom her manners and bearing were conspicuously different – she suffered mutely while being assailed by the noises of feet on stone, metal on metal, the shrieks, laughter and moans of prisoners in cells that ranged in long lines and rose over tiers connected by iron staircases.

Advocates of the silent system believed that it encouraged self-control and unquestioning obedience. Critics called it unnatural, dehumanising, oppressive and petty, and believed it cruelly compounded the isolation of new prisoners when they were at their most raw and sensitive. Florence felt that she was dead to the world. Far from the din of traffic, the vivid, ceaseless energy of the city, this silent world in which the threat of violence was implicit, sent – as a prison visitor at the time put it – *memories and thoughts curdling round the heart.*

*

Nine months after her arrival, in May 1890, Florence entered the second stage of imprisonment, becoming a probationer. The size of her cell doubled, her bed was now camp-style, the inner door of her cell was left open during the day, gruel could be substituted with tea and, during one precious hour, she was allowed to speak. Good behaviour was rewarded with more frequent letters and visits. Another nine months and she attained the third level, exchanging her brown uniform for green. Nine months more and she reached the level of greatest prisoner freedom: wearing navy blue, she was allowed to work in the kitchens or laundry, could talk to other prisoners for two hours a day and was given more, better, food. While she struggled to scrub the kitchens or to heft heavy baskets of bread, her mother made the journey from Paris every six weeks for a half-hour visit in a room divided into three compartments by grilled screens, with a matron present in the centre section. How Florence both longed for and dreaded these meetings. Each one reignited her passionate longing for freedom and partially unravelled the façade she fought so hard to maintain. Finding the conflict between the outside and inside worlds unbearable, she chose to try to shut out the past, finding safety *in compressing* [her] *thoughts to the smallest compass of mental existence.*

Outside the prison her case was kept alive by the increasingly desperate energy of her mother, who sent a stream of letters to the Home Secretary that claimed to have discovered new evidence or begged for clemency on the grounds of her daughter's tenuous health. Almost single-handedly the Baroness kept 'Maybrickmania' alive, ensuring that there was always something for the press to report, whether it was the effect on Florence's mind of menial drudgery, or that she was so precariously ill that she had received the last sacraments. Von Roques even sent a lengthy petition directly to the Queen; it was returned to Whitehall without comment.

Separately, Richard Cleaver's efforts were focused less on lobbying for Florence's release than on a suit against the Mutual Reserve Fund of America which, he hoped, would lead to a retrial. The fund had paid half of the amount due on James' life insurance policy but refused the remainder on the grounds that a convict should not benefit from the death. In order to expedite his suit, Cleaver hoped that the Queen's Bench would order a new trial on the charge of attempted murder, but it was a fruitless dream. After years of litigation he succeeded in forcing payment but the triumph was empty: under English law prisoners were officially dead, so Michael Maybrick claimed the money on behalf of the children. Cleaver did receive a few thousand dollars raised by the *New York World* for this *cruelly wronged woman*, and five thousand from a mortgage arranged on a New York warehouse that Florence had inherited. He also had the foresight to register copyright in a number of photographs of Florence taken in the early years of her marriage and these provided a small income. Yet, as he wrote to the Home Secretary in

1894, *funds ... have so far been insufficient to meet the heavy costs of the original trial and the expense involved was in itself a serious deterrent from* [taking] *further active steps.*

And so Florence languished, less flesh-and-blood convict than symbol of rebellion or injustice, depending on your point of view. As the years passed, some claimed that they had further proof of James' arsenic addiction and of his brothers' knowledge of it. Most were ignored. Charles Tidy, who had during the trial so energetically believed that the scientific evidence disproved the theory of poisoning, added his own thought-provoking pamphlet to the many that appeared in Florence's defence in the months immediately following the trial. MacDougall remained tireless in his petitions and, in 1891, published a six-hundred-page tome that earnestly if intemperately scrutinised the minutiae of the case. Among its many questions, it asked sharply how it was that, of all Battlecrease's inhabitants, Mrs Maybrick was selected as the only suspect, why she was arrested before any evidence of poison had been discovered in her husband's body and why Richard Cleaver had first agreed to her remand without demanding any evidence of her guilt.

In the same year, Judge Stephen resigned from the bench. Two years later, in 1893, he was installed in an asylum for the mentally ill, his degenerating condition adding tinder to continued speculation about the probity of his summation at the Maybrick trial.

Plagued on all sides by calls to reconsider the case, the Home Office stood its ground in the years immediately following the commutation of Florence's sentence. In 1892, in expectation of a change of government, the Baroness engaged prestigious London solicitors Lumley & Lumley to draw up a new brief. Reminding the Home Secretary that there was no conclusive evidence of the cause of James Maybrick's death, nor that Florence had attempted to administer poison to him, the solicitors also alleged that certain facts cast new light on the case. First, the jury had been so poorly supervised that they were seen gossiping in various Liverpool hotels and openly reading the newspapers. Next, the original prescription issued to Mrs Maybrick by Dr Griggs for an arsenical face wash had been discovered lodged between the pages of her Bible. Additionally, several new witnesses offered proof of James Maybrick's addictions. The Lumley & Lumley document cited Dr Tidy's new toxicological studies, the results of which pointed unequivocally away from poison as the cause of death. Most importantly, the solicitors appended a letter signed by Sir Charles Russell and three other senior legal men, all of whom considered the trial so flawed that these new facts *would be matters proper for the grave consideration of a Court of Appeal if such a tribunal existed in this country*.

That this very public document had the backing of one of the most respected legal minds of the age – Russell would shortly be appointed Lord Chief Justice – made no difference. Despite these and a multitude of other, less forceful, efforts the Home Office, convinced of Florence's guilt, refused to be moved. The years passed while, in Woking Prison, Florence felt both her youth and the world recede. She began to change. She learned that outwardly docile prisoners concealed weapons; she curried favour and she practised forbidden communication with her fellow prisoners through looks and gestures. At every opportunity she petitioned the governor for a reconsideration of her case and she began to test the rules, wheedling for extra visits or letters in order to be allowed to *settle her business affairs*. For a few years she received photos of her children, until Michael Maybrick informed her that they would be discontinued.

While the Baroness continued to present a picture of Florence as obedient, frail and unable to survive the harshness of her treatment, others watched her nascent pride modulate into intractability and her middle-class delicacy develop into malingering. Reports sent to the Home Office by the governor of Woking Prison suggest that her constant complaints of ill-health were *fictitious*, that she could be *difficult to manage* and *wilful*. When depressed she could be *morose and bad-tempered*; she had been discovered rubbing black lead from the grate into her face and lips in an attempt to make herself look ill. On one occasion, *she spit up a small quantity of blood-tinged fluid*, following which she claimed to have consumption, *but this was counterfeit. The night officer believes she obtained it by sucking her gum.* On another, she was foiled in an attempt to persuade a prisoner employed as a cleaner in the hospital to procure a needle for her. Constant requests by the Baroness for special treatment for her daughter were refused on the grounds that there was already *some discontent among the other prisoners ... that she is favoured ... by the special considerations accorded to her.*

The press repeated false rumours that Florence swallowed pins in an attempt to commit suicide, while prison officials reported that she refused on occasion to eat or to sleep in her bed. By the end of 1892, with the obvious failure of the Lumley brief, she was at her lowest ebb. In early December she attempted to draw blood in order to fool the doctors into believing that she really had developed consumption and, in the process, severed her vaginal artery with a kitchen knife. For several days she was as close to death as she had always wanted them to believe and, as a result of the injury, remained in the prison infirmary for almost two months.

Behind the scenes, the American government intermittently raised questions about her release and then, in May 1894, the Home Office received a formal petition signed by the Vice-President, the Speaker of the House of Representatives, members of the President's Cabinet, the General-in-Chief of the American army, the chiefs of all divisions at the War Department and the Cardinal Archbishop of Baltimore, among others. Requesting clemency, their memorial cited a *profound impression of miscarriage of justice*, the fact that no Court of Criminal Appeal existed, Mrs Maybrick's frail health and the mental state of the trial judge. Godfrey Lushington, still Permanent Under-Secretary at the Home Office, annotated it with his impression that it was *a truly astonishing document for if ever there was a criminal not entitled to mercy it is Mrs Maybrick*. She was anyway – by virtue of her marriage – a British and not an American citizen. The fact that the minister could discover no grounds for clemency was related to the American government via the Foreign Office.

The Baroness refused to give up. By 1894 Alice Yapp had become Mrs Murrin and her husband Edward complained to the police and the Home Office that private detectives were harassing his wife. He had had enough and feared that he and Alice would have *to leave* [our] *present abode* ... [she] *is continually weeping and thoroughly depressed*. That same year a Mr Valentine Blake volunteered that he had provided both white and black arsenic to James Maybrick following a meeting in January 1889 during which James had agreed to promote a cotton substitute – ramie – on the Liverpool market. Blake's sworn statement was forwarded to the Home Office but, despite the fact that it might have explained the amount of arsenic found in Battlecrease House, it was ignored.

Florence was thirty-four years old when in November 1896, as part of the preparations for the closure of Woking Prison, she was moved to Aylesbury, chained in a line of ten other women of the star class, each wrapped in long, dark cloaks imprinted with arrows. In the grey dawn, needled by lashing rain, the women were transported by prison van to a special train then hurried through crowds at connecting stations until they arrived five hours later before a sternly unyielding red brick structure that seemed to float in the fog. Crossing its broad yard, traversing gloomy passageways and climbing two flights of iron stairs, the women were once again locked into separate cells, their wrists bruised and sore from the pressure of the metal cuffs.

To the east, invisible in the fog, the tree-covered Chiltern Hills formed Florence's new horizon. She would need to start all over again. She could barely remember the days during which she had made decisions for herself, could no longer imagine pushing open the doors of her own parlour to gaze at the trappings of mercantile success. The longest-serving of any prisoner now at Aylesbury, her former world of glass, of mirrors, of light and laughter seemed to her nothing but a dream.

*

Florence would soon discover that the regime at Aylesbury was far more enlightened than at Woking. Wardresses in fresh Holland uniforms and white caps could have passed for hospital nurses but for the keys at their waists and the whistles suspended on gleaming steel chains. Good behaviour was rewarded with small mirrors or strips of bedside carpet – echoes of a more comfortable world. It helped, but there was still an air of apathy about the hundred-and-fifty-odd prisoners who had little to do but routine piecework. Women's demands for greater involvement in the business of politics and governance were leading to calls for a reformed approach to female convict rehabilitation and the banishment of the stolid despair and broken nerve of the silent system, but these calls came broadly too late to affect the experience of the little American woman whose story had once galvanised feminist views.

Yet Florence was not forgotten. Back in April 1891 James Blaine, American Secretary of State, had instructed his Ambassador in London, Robert Lincoln, to lobby for her pardon and that August the President's wife ill-advisedly petitioned Queen Victoria for mercy. In 1896, the question of the US government's official involvement was raised briefly in the Senate and a succession of unofficial meetings aimed at putting pressure on the British government to release her took place throughout the rest of the decade. American public interest was enlivened by a fiery journalist writing under the name of Gail Hamilton, who formed the

Women's International Maybrick Committee with the First Lady, Caroline Harrison, as its chair. Hamilton portrayed Florence as a *mater dolorosa*, improperly imprisoned, tortured into a state of mental agony and heartbreak, *dying by inches*. Believing her case to be one of *blundering stupidity and criminal neglect and indifference*, Hamilton railed at British politicians who refused to consider either inquiry or pardon.

None of it made any difference. At the Home Office in Whitehall, successive ministers remained implacable.

CHAPTER 32

Changed Utterly

When in 1895 the possibility of a public inquiry into the Florence Maybrick case was raised, six years into her imprisonment, by the incoming Conservative government, the new Home Office minister was Sir Matthew White Ridley and Kenelm Digby had replaced Godfrey Lushington as Permanent Under-Secretary. Taking confidential legal advice, these two men considered asking three eminent judges to re-read the voluminous case papers in order to rule on whether Florence should be respited in view of existing doubt, believing that *One great advantage of this reference would be that it would end the case for ever ... even better, the position would be logical and impregnable and* [the Home Office] *would avoid taking up the hereditary sword of Damocles of Mr Matthews' decision which is the most awkward feature in the case now*. Yet there was a problem: if the judges ruled that she should be released, Florence would undoubtedly demand compensation, opening a Pandora's Box of resentments and accusations. Consequently, the idea of an inquiry was shelved. The following year Lord Halsbury, the Lord Chancellor, wrote to Sir Charles Russell that he believed no suspicion attached itself to anyone but *the adulteress and angry wife*.

Whitehall was wary. When the analytical chemist Edward Davies decided to move house that year he applied for permission to destroy what remained of James Maybrick's bottled viscera. *I do not think it would be wise*, countered Digby, *while there is so much agitation*. Concerned lest the samples fall into the hands of scientists who might use them to try to re-prove Mrs Maybrick's innocence, they were sent instead for safekeeping to the prosecution's expert scientist, Professor Thomas Stevenson.

Months turned to years and the years dragged, yet clamour for Florence's release continued, particularly on the occasion of the Queen's Diamond Jubilee in 1897. In the modernising world, official documents relating to her case began to be produced on new-fangled typewriters while, left behind, Florence was still completing the blue prison forms that requested reconsideration of her case in inky copperplate. Year after successive year her applications were returned, stamped with the intransigent, unchanging response *Insufficient Grounds*. In 1898 Charles – now Lord – Russell wrote to the Home Office pointing out that Mrs Maybrick had now served four times the minimum sentence for the crime of attempted murder for which she was apparently imprisoned, though not convicted.

It was murmured that her position was similar to that of the notorious French army officer Captain Alfred Dreyfus. Made out by his accusers to be a two-faced monster living a double life, Dreyfus's infidelities were used to 'prove' that he was a spy. It seemed to some that both he and Florence Maybrick had fallen foul of an ideological struggle and, in both cases, that there was plenty of doubt, though it refused to work in their favour. Their fates – it could be argued – were each determined by a twisted logic. After five years in the Devil's Island penal colony in French Guiana, Dreyfus was released. Within a decade of his conviction he was pardoned. Florence knew nothing of his trials. Denied a proper legal appeals process her supporters lamented that, if she were innocent, then she had suffered ten times more than Dreyfus.

In 1899, a decade after her conviction, J. H. Levy famously used the Maybrick case as the basis for an impressive but unsuccessful demand for the establishment of a proper system of criminal appeal. It was countered by those who believed that such a process would result in the abolition of trial by jury and thus blunt the edge of the law.

On the cusp of the changing century, now nearly forty, Florence was visited in Aylesbury Prison by an old cotton colleague of James' from America. He wrote later that *she advanced to meet him in her prison garb, her grey hair straight back from her forehead, eyes sunken, complexion pale and sallow*. Watching her, he remembered *the beautiful woman so handsomely dressed, standing in her palatial home, greeting her guests*. Now her hands were callused, her fingers pricked by sewing needles and cut from peeling potatoes. Her decayed teeth had been removed. Her blue eyes had faded. Unable to imagine how she had managed to survive without becoming hopelessly insane, his tears began to flow. *I do not wonder at them*, she told him, *but mine have ceased*.

During her trial and throughout the next few years it had been difficult for society to discuss female sexuality without attaching opprobrium. Since then, far wilder men than Florence Maybrick had ever met – including Edward, Prince of Wales and Oscar Wilde – had openly challenged the repressed moral climate in England: what had provoked outrage only a decade before became, as the world sped up, less potent. Partly as a result of this, when the old Queen, moral guardian of her age, died in 1901 petitions for Florence's release were renewed and the Home Office began to consider when they might legitimately set her free. Given that she had served almost twelve years, they decided to wait a further three, after which they would insist that she leave the country and not return. Meanwhile, all those who continued to press for her pardon were informed that Florence would be kept in gaol unless their agitation stopped.

In 1903 the Home Secretary, Aretas Akers-Douglas, announced publicly that Mrs Maybrick would be freed in the summer of the following year, having served a full fifteen years. For a generation that hardly recognised her name, the mass-market newspapers began to reprise her story in serial form, repeating the most salacious details, reprinting her letters to Brierley, delving into the intricacies of the evidence about arsenic addiction, publishing photos of a sprightly young woman utterly unrecognisable from the middle-aged prisoner counting off the days in a Buckinghamshire gaol. For a while, the Maybrick case was again the subject of dinner-party conversation and backyard gossip.

A regular visitor to Aylesbury Prison, Adeline, Duchess of Bedford – founder of the influential National Association of Lady Visitors, an organisation that lobbied forcibly for penal reform – now offered to effect for Florence a transition between prison and freedom. She would stay for six months preceding her release at the peaceful rural convent of the Sisters of the Epiphany in Truro, Cornwall. Consequently, in January 1904 Florence left Aylesbury Prison, requesting – and being granted – the right to sidestep the usual practice of being photographed holding a convict board imprinted with her name and prisoner number. Granted a conditional licence she remained, in effect, a prisoner, without being subject to police supervision. In retreat under an assumed name – Mrs Graham – only the Mother Superior and the Head Constable of the City police force were told the secret of her true identity.

*

In Cornwall Florence Maybrick finally began to practise what it meant to be free. She wore an ordinary black dress with a white frill at the throat, rose at six each morning, took her meals in silence and conversed only on religious topics, except at teatime when, for an interval, the sisters were permitted to talk of *mundane things*. She was prohibited from seeing newspapers, but she read books supplied by the nuns, walked and sewed in silence for several hours each day. Each night she was in bed by nine.

After six months, shortly after nine o'clock on the morning of Wednesday 20 July 1904, Florence emerged from the front door and stepped down onto the driveway, wearing a neat, dove grey dress sent by her mother from Paris. A white fur curled around her shoulders. Aged forty-one, her hair was threaded with grey beneath her wide-brimmed hat and the lines of middle age drew at the corners of dulled blue eyes. Her skin was papery. Her mouth thin. Her youth was scattered.

Behind her, the century-old high-ceilinged house was still. Fields of ripening corn stretched gently away beyond the shady lane. Morning sunlight dappled the soft lawns and shrubberies so that she and the Mother Superior, from whom she took her leave, were both dimly aware of the promise of a warming day behind the pearly chill. Her pulse quickening, her mouth dry, Florence turned towards the gate, determined not to look back.

Walking briskly away from the slow accumulation of days, weeks and months that had made up the last fifteen years, she made her way to a nearby house in order to meet the wardress who had arrived from London two days earlier. Straightening her back a little and lifting her chin, she steeled herself for the journey. Hoping to dodge reporters camped around Truro station, they took a closed carriage to St Austell, making for the express train due to depart at fourteen minutes past midday for the roaring, bewildering capital where there were papers to sign before Florence could begin to reclaim her life.

Assisted by the Baroness's lawyer, she went to Rouen, to her ageing mother who, in order to hide her identity and attract no attention, was now styling herself Madame de Moremont or Mrs Morehouse. Somehow getting wind of the story, a pack of journalists swarmed outside the walls of the house and one – a reporter from the *Daily Chronicle* – was granted an exclusive interview. He thought Florence *a pleasing-looking little lady* who was *clear witted and outspoken, mildly robust, perfectly calm*. At first she seemed to him the very antithesis of the *mental and bodily wreck she has been painted*, though he began to notice that her eyes were listless and by the end of their long interview she had become tearful. *I shall feel safer when I get to America*, she faltered. Asked whether she hoped to be reconciled with her children she replied that it was *too early to say*.

While tabloid headlines asked again whether Florence May-brick was guilty or not of the crime of which she was accused, the model of the once-famous murderess was removed from Madame Tussaud's.

On 13 August 1904, accompanied by solicitor Samuel Hayden and his wife, Florence embarked on the SS *Vaderland* in Antwerp under the assumed name of Rose Ingraham. Nine days later she arrived in New York where she was, for a while, hailed as a wronged and prodigal daughter of the New World. Her American citizenship was restored and she wrote an emotionally charged memoir maintaining – among much else – that the full and free confession she told the court she had made to James concerned not an admission of infidelity after all but the fact that she had attempted to secure a divorce. Such statements enabled her to maintain a public profile, talking about her case while lobbying more generally for prison reform, so that for a short while she was able to earn a living on the lecture circuit.

*

The world into which Florence re-emerged was one almost unrecognisable to that from which she was removed in 1889. She had never seen a motor car, had not heard of New York's Wal-dorf Astoria Hotel or the Flatiron building. Women's demands for equality were now strident, forcefully political. Edwardian ladies wore physically freer clothing while her preference for the constricting bustles, pads and frills of her youth remained unchanged. In the shops the *little woman in white* was perplexed to find that she no longer knew the right words for the items she desired. In the American streets, electricity was everywhere and machines had replaced horsepower. Everything looked, sounded and smelled bewilderingly different. Crowded spaces confused her.

People noted that her expression was haunted, that there was a small scar under her left eye and that the mouth that had been full and slack in those early photographs had become a thinner, compressed line. Soon after her return to New York Florence told the *Tribune* that she felt *pushed into a world which had outrun me for fifteen years ... the mad rush ... the decline of manners ... Or was it always so, and is the difference in myself?*

During the year following her release Alfred Brierley, now fifty-three, married Flora Hemphill – eighteen years his junior – in a private ceremony in the south of France, possibly designed to evade press interest. On the marriage certificate Brierley described himself as a widower: had he, as was rumoured years earlier, married first in South America? Whatever the case, he and Flora settled in Blindley Heath, a remote village south of Godstone in Surrey. In September 1906 they had a son and called him Patrick.

In May 1927 – thirty-eight years after her last meeting with Brierley – Florence was reported to have made a secret visit to England. *Sad-faced, gentle-voiced, with hair turned to silver*, she told the *Sunday News* that I *was foolish enough to think that I could find happiness with the man who offered me the love my husband denied me.* She said that she had believed that he would wait for her and was *bitterly disappointed* to discover, on her release from prison, *that the man for whom I had sacrificed everything had forgotten me.* Did she write to Brierley, either before or after her trial, asking him to wait? Certainly she did not describe such hopes or disappointments in her post-release memoir. Hardened by prison life, when Florence walked away from Aylesbury Prison she was no longer the wistful girl who had once sought comfort outside her marriage. Were these, then, the manipulative words of a woman practised in working on the sympathies of the public, adept at casting herself as a victim?

Florence was never pardoned. A Home Office note from 1905 shows that the department believed that *we should* [then] *lose all hold over Mrs Maybrick if she chose to come back to England and make a scandal by showing herself in some sort of public performance ... I think it would be better not to raise this but to refuse the free pardon on the grounds* [that] *... The Secretary of State has carefully considered ...* [but] *cannot advise a free pardon in such a case where it could only be regarded as an admission that Mrs Maybrick had been wrongly convicted.*

Nor did she ever see her children again. Her mother had promised at the time of Florence's respite to play an active role in the care of little James and Gladys, but was never able to find them. The Baroness died penniless in a convent in Paris in 1910 and was buried beside her son in the Passy cemetery. The following year Florence's twenty-nine-year-old son, now a mining engineer known as James Fuller, died after drinking potassium cyanide at the Le Roi goldmine in British Columbia. It was said that he reached for a cup of water while taking a hasty lunch and mistook the beaker: the colourless poison, accidentally swallowed, killed him within minutes. His sister married, moved to Wales and died, childless, aged eighty-five.

'The Holy City', a song Michael Maybrick composed in 1892 under the name Stephen Adams, turned out to be one of the most popular ballads of the century and made him very wealthy. Despite having been so critical of his brother's choice of wife, he married his long-term mistress Laura Withers – a butcher's daughter – in 1893. Living on the Isle of Wight, he served five terms as the Mayor of Ryde, stalwart of the community, icon of responsibility, respectability and civic control. He died in 1913.

Three years after the trial Edwin, aged forty-two, married Amy Tyrer. It is impossible to know whether she was related to one of the jurymen, printer James Tyrer from Wigan. Years later their only daughter – also called Amy – would describe Edwin as *absolutely a bachelor at heart*, so remote that he made her feel unwanted and, like *all the Maybricks, cold, very formal*.

Alice Yapp and her printing compositor husband Edward set up house in Holborn, London. In 1892, three years after the events at Battlecrease House, aged thirty, she had a daughter – Marjorie. By 1901 the three had moved to a small terrace in the northern suburb of Hackney. Alice died in 1953, aged ninety-two.

Matilda Briggs moved south when her daughter Constance married. She died in Kensington, London, in 1915, aged sixty-five.

Elizabeth Humphreys, Bessie Brierley and Mary Cadwallader all disappear from the public record after Florence's trial.

In 1911 the Maybrick case was cited as a precedent in a hearing to consider whether Mrs Crippen's life insurance should be paid out to her murderous husband but, by then, few remembered either Florence's name or the scandalous reaction her case had generated twenty-two years earlier. Her own claims for ownership of lands in Richmond, Virginia left to her by her grandfather rumbled on for years: there were rulings in her favour but she never benefited financially. She drifted, unanchored, until money became scarce. Then, in 1919, she used the last of it to build herself a small three-room cottage on the outskirts of South Kent, an uneventful hamlet in Connecticut's Berkshire Hills.

There she survived on hand-outs, a cultured woman who called herself Mrs Chandler and who told anyone who asked that her husband and children had been killed in an accident in Paris. Seeking obscurity, living on the edge of the community, she became increasingly furtive and eccentric, gradually losing interest in the trappings about which she had once been so fastidious. By the early 1930s the few who saw her noticed that her clothes were held together with safety pins; wrapped in blankets, she often pulled a wool cap low down over her brows. Yet, despite casting off every vestige of her younger self, the letters Florence wrote during this period were styled in the same bold, neat hand with which she had written to her lover and her doctor from the morning room of Battlecrease House. However odd her behaviour seemed to her neighbours, however tattered her person had become, these notes alone suggest that her mind remained clear enough to ensure that she never lost the ability to express herself according to the expectations of her education and class.

On Thursday 23 October 1941 Florence Elizabeth Maybrick's fully dressed, lifeless body was discovered half-slumped on an old sofa in her decaying cottage by a neighbour delivering milk. Destitute, in her eightieth year, she was surrounded not by souvenirs of the brightness of her early life but by a tribe of scruffy cats.

Just one South Kent resident had figured out her true identity, but *swore to keep it a secret*. A couple of years after arriving in the hamlet, Florence had given Mrs Thomas Austin an exquisite black Spanish lace dress with a flowered silk bodice. Still in the cleaning wrapper from the last hotel in which she had stayed, Florence had overlooked the fact that it was labelled with her former name. It was one of the last possessions linking her to a world of dressy parties, cosmetic washes, dinner menus and competitive socialising, the kind of life she took for granted before the turbulent spring of 1889.

A time will come, she wrote soon after her release from prison, *when the world will acknowledge that the verdict that was passed upon me is absolutely untenable.*

What then? Who shall give back the years I have spent within prison walls; the friends by whom I am forgotten, the children to whom I am dead; the sunshine ... my woman's life and all I have lost by this terrible injustice?

An old scrapbook found in the squalid poverty of her rooms after her death was filled with clippings relating to her past. It was the last, slender thread linking her to Liverpool and its cotton-broking society, to an older husband, a smart home, giggling children, a young lover and watchful staff. Its fading entries charted in part the disintegration of a privileged life. Once she was gone, it confirmed to a world that no longer really cared *who* – if not *what* – Florence Maybrick really was.

Afterword

During 1889 and for some years after Florence Maybrick's story got under people's skin because it plaited together some of the great themes of the age: the 'invasion' of spirited American girls, a growing appreciation of women's stultifying isolation within marriage, society's hypocritical attitudes to sex and the emergence of a new generation of women eager to play a useful and fulfilling role in a modernising world. The adulterous husband and the scheming, libidinous wife reflected the battle between the sexes that characterised the last years of Victoria's reign and traditionalists held up the Maybrick marriage as an example of everything that could go wrong when unequal unions were forged, or when men and women failed to stick to the rules. Beyond all that, the story titillated, proving that even ostensibly respectable families incubated feuds, addictions and immorality.

Did Florence have the strength and the courage (as Oscar Wilde might have put it) to risk everything on one throw? Was she, as some papers wrote after her trial, a woman of extraordinary nerve and determination who, marrying for reasons other than love, revolted against her situation with a great intensity of feeling? Was she embittered by life's failure to live up to the romance of her fictions, her girlish dreams? Did she want simply to be herself, to be free? Or was she a weak, inconsequent

American cuckoo in a Liverpool nest, lacking the vaunted Victorian virtue of self-mastery, easily manipulated by the Maybrick family, a victim of her husband's shocking lifestyle?

Was her sentence a proper victory of substantive justice in the face of shaky scientific evidence? Despite the rise of the chemical analyst as 'poisons detective' and the development of toxicology in jurisprudence, the experts, it turned out, lacked certainty. In this light, her courtroom admission may have been a terrible miscalculation, ensuring that the scientific issue was sidelined while public morality became the central issue. Certainly Sir Charles Russell repeatedly argued that it was never proven that James died from arsenic – that, in fact, there was no murder since the amount of arsenic found in his body, totalling less than two grains, was considered by most to be insufficient to cause death.

If James was poisoned, was the arsenic self-administered? The example of the Styrian peasants suggested that *when a man has begun to indulge in it he must continue to indulge, for if he ceases the arsenic in his system poisons him*: so did James die for the lack of his regular dose? In the days before his death he was prescribed almost two dozen different irritant poisons including nux vomica, henbane, jaborandi, codeine and morphia. Did the poison found in his body derive from the doctors' treatments, or did the fact that it was also found in the meat juice and the jug in his office prove foul play? Dr Carter's private notes written at the conclusion of the trial emphasise his absolute belief that if solid arsenic had been added to the bottle of Valentine's meat juice, as Florence Maybrick claimed, there would have been discernible residues: *It is not merely that Mrs Maybrick could not do what she said she had done*, he wrote; *it is that no one could do it*. Yet although it was accepted at the time, Carter's belief that solid arsenic was not completely soluble has since been contested. Then again, testimony proved that James had not swallowed the contents of the poisoned bottle of meat juice, so perhaps that argument is irrelevant after all.

Some time after the trial, a private investigator claimed to have found a Liverpool chemist who said he had provided Florence with quantities of arsenic on two separate occasions. Considered unreliable, the details were never made public. Others argued that she had no more access to the arsenic found all over Battlecrease House than anybody else – that if she had murdered, she would not have left so much lying around. When Michael told her that he was not satisfied with his brother's care, or later when it became clear that James would die, would she not – were she guilty – have destroyed any evidence that might be used to convict her? Only trace arsenical deposits were found in the lavatory and the drain running from the upstairs basin and the bottle of meat juice to which she admitted adding a white powder remained in its place on the washstand. Was Florence blind, then, to her brother-in-law's suspicions? Did she assume that he condemned her as useless rather than malevolent?

The case was sensational partly because it raised as many questions as it answered. Was it true that Florence had discovered the fact of James' adultery when she saw the woman's name on an accounts ledger in his study? Was this the defining breach in their marriage and a motive to kill? A chain of circumstantial evidence certainly pointed to the fact that Florence had poisoned James, but testimony also suggested that Michael and Edwin lied about their brother's arsenic addiction and concealed the pillbox that later appeared in court. Other questions were hardly addressed, or were ignored, such as who sent the bottle of medicine that arrived on the day before the Wirral races and what did it contain? How was the coroner able to say that there was arsenic in James' body – leading to Florence's arrest – before any tests had been completed; what were James' brothers asking his clerks to get him to do when he was heard to lament *let me die in peace*?

There were procedural oversights, too. Did Florence's defence team overlook a crucial piece of evidence that might have corroborated the chemist Edwin Heaton's deposition that he regularly supplied James with arsenical tonics? In the list of bottles taken from the Tithebarn Street office by the police, one was noted as bearing the label 'Edwin G Easton, Exchange Street East ... contents – light-coloured liquid', a fact that suggests what Heaton contended in court was true. Other oddities also went unnoticed: three separate bottles of meat juice were mentioned, yet only two were sent for analysis. What happened to the third? Could this have been the bottle that Bessie saw Michael slip into his pocket when she took up a cup of tea for her mistress and, if so, what did it contain? Then, if the nurse had opened a new bottle of Valentine's meat juice and given only one dose to James, if Florence had then added poison to this bottle (either in solution or as a powder plus water) and if everyone was right in their conviction that nothing further was taken from it then why was the bottle only *half full* when Edward Davies received it? Given that so little arsenic was found in James' dead body, perhaps it is unimportant. Is it not strange, though, that the police, prosecution and defence all failed to notice the anomaly? Was this detail simply lost in the welter of evidential and scientific detail?

At the time, the choice of Flatman's Hotel convinced many that Florence and Brierley flirted with the danger of being discovered. Is it really possible that James did not know? Or did he find out, and did his shock and humiliation lead to a fatally misjudged increase in his self-medication on the day of the Wirral races? Florence told her friend John Baillie Knight that James kept a mistress, that he was cruel, that he struck her. Did he hit her often, or just once when, at the Grand National, her defiance of him was so openly flaunted as to be undeniable?

Was she habitually rebellious? Or was her behaviour during spring 1889 a momentary inability to maintain the enamel front concealing her unhappiness? Was it that she tired, like Henry James' Maggie Verver, of the false position in which she found herself and which required such an effort of social performance? After the trial, the letter she wrote to her husband on 14 April when he was in London consulting Dr Fuller and arranging to liquidate her debts came to light. Weeks after staying at Flatman's Hotel, this note was cajoling and apologetic; she professed to despair of her reputation and to feel such guilt that she could not sleep: *I have deceived and nearly ruined you*, she wrote in an unusually incoherent script.

Was Florence only referring to her financial stupidity? Was she reacting to the realisation that Brierley was unreliable? Or was it an indication – countering Michael's testimony at trial – that she had frankly confessed her affair and was waiting to learn whether James would cast her off? She was clearly distraught. It is possible – perhaps even probable – that she believed that she was pregnant by Brierley and therefore needed to do everything in her power to avert a separation from James in order both to avoid her own humiliation and to ensure that the child had a legitimate father. Was her contrition genuine? Over a century later the whiff of fear still clings to that letter and it conjures a picture of a young woman so neurotically anxious about her position and her future that she is prepared to *live a life of atonement for yours and the children's sakes.*

When Dr Hopper visited Florence at Battlecrease days after James' death, she was bleeding and told him that she had not menstruated since 7 March. If she conceived when she and Brierley were together at Flatman's Hotel, she was two months pregnant when James died. She had told Hopper that she felt strange on 1 April when he came to smooth things over following the Grand National argument, but he refused then to examine her. Pregnancy might explain her exhaustion, her lack of caution in giving the letter to Alice Yapp and her prostration following James' death.

If Florence was expecting Brierley's child, then her infidelity really was her undoing and divorce would not have represented the obvious alternative to murder argued by her defenders. On the last day of the trial Dr Humphreys privately told Judge

Stephen his suspicion that she may have been with child earlier in the year, and the judge later repeated this to Henry Matthews at the Home Office. Did Stephen then believe, despite the fact not coming out during the trial, that Florence's motive for murder was clear? Was the old man's furious denunciation of her towards the end of his summation born of this specific understanding rather than – as his detractors insisted – of a more general moral horror of infidelity?

Or were Stephen's critics right? So many similar cases in the recent past linked pretty young girls to sexual intrigue, arsenic and death: Madeleine Smith in 1857, Florence Bravo in 1876, Adelaide Bartlett in 1886. Did these murders of middle-class men by women seem to Stephen to strike at the roots of established society, threatening the family and the home from within? Did this bastion of the old guard presume that, ancient as the story of Eve, female sexuality went hand in hand with criminality?

Male reporters and commentators were fascinated by Florence's physicality. Women asked whether her husband treated her as a man should treat his wife, why women were not called to the jury, if it was fair that laws were uniquely enacted by men. She became a cipher for her gender and her generation: apparent proof both that pretty, cultured women could be self-seeking and violent, and that they could be ground down by unequal conventions.

Recently, there have been attempts to prove that James Maybrick was the serial murderer known as Jack the Ripper, a contention based on the discovery of a much-challenged 'pseudo-diary'. Separately, some have argued either that Florence clearly did kill James or that she had every intention of doing so, and that the fatal dose was hidden in the food taken to Tithebarn Street on Wednesday 8 May. Simultaneously, those believing in her innocence have characterised her as too childlike, too stupid to have effectively concealed a stealthy intent to kill.

It is almost certain that, when things went wrong, she dreamed of being liberated from her much older husband. But did she hasten his death? Was James redrafting his will on the day Edwin came to his office because he was now intent on pursuing a divorce, having discovered her guilty secret? Were his hands shaking because, knowing this, his wife had begun to poison him? Was the disagreeable woman she became in prison – by turns fretful and sullen, increasingly devious and mendacious – a result of the desolation of her imprisonment or the emergence of her true character? Was Henry Matthews right to stick to the spirit of the law rather than its letter, or were the fifteen years of her incarceration one of the greatest miscarriages of justice in English legal history?

*

Whatever actually happened in Battlecrease House, the nation's response to it speaks volumes for the spirit of an age characterised by George Gissing as one of *sexual anarchy*. In 1891 Thomas Hardy's *Tess of the d'Urbervilles* so challenged the sexual mores of its time that it was heavily censored. During Florence's trial, Hardy wrote that the story he was working on would be that of a young country girl; *I should say that her position is based on fact.* Immediately after Florence's conviction, he observed that *when a married woman who has a lover kills her husband she does not really want to kill the husband; she wishes to kill the situation.*

With *Tess*, Hardy explicitly pitted convention against nature; *but for the world's opinion*, he wrote, Tess's experiences *would have been simply a liberal education*; her humiliation would neither have crushed hope nor made it impossible to survive. Tess – *a vessel of emotion rather than reason* – pays the ultimate price for being 'impure' in deference to the prevailing bourgeois definitions of right and wrong, yet Hardy's novel argues fundamentally for the opposite – that the *arbitrary law of society* ...

had no foundation in nature. Believing that prevailing definitions of morality were both ensnaring and destructive, the novelist directly confronted the contradictions in society's treatment of women, laying bare contemporary anxieties about sex and gender.

Tess put a woman's sexuality – her thoughts as well as her feelings – at the heart of the story and, in consequence, is often claimed for New Woman Fiction, a literary genre that mirrored and fed contemporary debates about femininity: what it meant to be a woman, to desire, to be married. Similarly, Florence's behaviour both sprang from and reflected the profound sexual and gender anxieties of an age in which progressive social ideas, including feminism, began to flourish and rub uncomfortably against each other. It seemed not to matter how loudly her defenders clamoured for her release because she epitomised a threat to moral certainties. Caught up in these complex cultural and political agendas, it was inevitable that she remain imprisoned.

Even if she did strike out at an abusive man, Florence was not Tess: she was less generous, less clever, more conventional and she courted her own tragedy. In the end, unlike Tess and partly because of her class, she escaped the hangman's noose. Nor was Florence quite like Henry James' Maggie Verver or Isabel Archer, though at times her effort to maintain her composure with as much throat-constricting effort as either of these two was positively Jamesian. She was not, either, Kate Chopin's Madame Pontellier, radically, openly, rejecting constriction. Florence did, though, fit the contemporary novelistic pattern of the nightmare of unhappily married life and the isolation of the stranger: part Emma Bovary, married to a bore, and part Isabel Archer, repressed by a dominant husband and his over-mastering friend Madame Merle, a vulnerable American girl suffocated by the *rigid conditions* of European life. US Secretary of State James Blaine expressed to the British government his belief that she had simply made a youthful mistake, *influenced by the foolish ambition of many American girls for a foreign marriage, and to have descended from her own rank to that of her husband's family, which seems to have been somewhat vulgar.*

For her, as for so many of Henry James' heroines, the Old World had turned out to be a snare.

Some thought that she lacked self-will, that she was – as her mother characterised her – a *woman of little penetration.* For others, Florence's glacial self-control during the trial perfectly fitted the ideal of Victorian middle-class womanhood. In so many ways, her story momentarily embodied 'the woman question' that obsessed so many of the era's novelists: just as it did in many of their works, it was almost inevitable that violence should erupt. Florence might, then, have been a model for Alexandre Dumas (*fils*) whose pamphlet, published nine years before James' death – *Les Femmes qui Tuent et les Femmes qui Votent* – argued that if women were continually denied the rights for which they lobbied, they would inevitably be driven to violence. It is true that none of the infamous middle-class Victorian female killers enjoyed a happy marriage. Indeed, schooled to repress their personal desires and to conceal their feelings, it was perhaps unsurprising that they made such good criminals.

As the nineteenth century wore on there was no doubt, as Edith Wharton put it, that *society was getting tired of pretences and compliances, of conformity and uniformity.* Before they were cast off, though, literary interest fixed on the tensions playing out beneath the surface of well-to-do families. For Henry James, the home was less idealistic sanctuary than battleground in which alienation and resentments went to war, where emotional pain was suppressed behind a lovely smile. Thus Maggie Verver admits that she goes *about on tiptoe. I watch for every sound. I feel every breath, and yet I try all the while to seem as smooth as old satin dyed rose colour.* Florence's married life, too, was underpinned by deep-rooted, late-Victorian hypocrisies. Once the nineteenth century was over Virginia Woolf – Judge Stephen's niece – would argue that family life during this period was nothing short of damaged, distorting and dangerous.

*

The Baroness von Roques believed her daughter to be *a victim of intrigue and deceit. A stranger ... isolated by her husband, from all her own people, and left to die a victim of ... jealousy and lies.* She would claim that Florence had been drugged on the forenoon of James' death, accounting for her lasting swoon, that all James' clothing was unaccountably destroyed following his death along with compromising letters from his mistress, that the suspicious activities of others were never properly investigated and that Mrs Briggs and Mrs Hughes acted *inhumanly* towards Florence.

W. M. Stead, the infamously unconventional editor of the *Review of Reviews*, believed the case to be *a generally botched business with wrong headedness on one side and semi-dotage on the other that sent a woman to a living tomb.*

Because Florence's incarceration rested on the belief that she was guilty of attempted murder, a crime for which she was not tried, her conviction has been characterised as a judicial travesty. Even Judge Stephen admitted that out of 979 cases tried before him it was *the only case in which there would be any doubts about the facts.* Some thought the situation so illogical and the Home Office's refusal to reconsider the case so stubborn that it could only be explained by their possession of a secret dossier that proved Florence's guilt or contained a confession. Surviving records indicate simply that Henry Matthews and Godfrey Lushington, after painstaking consideration, made up their minds that she was guilty. Because the Home Office maintained a tradition of not overruling previous ministers, it found itself in a position from which it could not retreat.

The majority of Florence's most vocal defenders marshalled emotional arguments rather than attacking the legal illogicality of the respite ruling, though Sir Charles Russell never wavered in his opinion that, whether she was innocent or not, *Florence Maybrick ought never to have been convicted and ... her imprisonment* [was] *an injustice*. He believed that Henry Matthews had made an assumption that she had committed the crime in the absence of solid proof, that *the Brierley episode had alienated the sympathies of many and predisposed to a conclusion of guilt.* Russell died in 1900, four years before Florence was released.

Florence was allowed to make her trial statement thanks to the Criminal Procedure Act of 1865, but it was not until 1898 that the Criminal Evidence Act gave defendants the right to testify under oath. Had she been put on the stand it is possible that the truth about so many stubbornly lingering questions might have been established. Then, once convicted, there was no legal mechanism for her defenders to question the decision of the jury or the running of the trial. Demands for the establishment of a proper Court of Appeals continued for years. In 1907, after prolonged condemnation of an unjust system, the Criminal Appeal Act finally established a process within which to challenge capital convictions.

Innocent or guilty of murdering her husband by slipping him arsenic, Florence Maybrick embodied the numerous paradoxes that typified late-Victorian conceptions of the feminine, polarising opinion to such an extent that everything about her story excited either sympathy or ire and it became the very stuff of contemporary melodrama, New Woman novels and even literary fiction. The complex, convulsive reactions to her case were born of the fact that she typified numberless women trapped by the demands of traditional authorities, negotiating the disorienting realities of a middle-class world in rapid flux. The domestic tensions and unhappiness that she experienced were common to a large number of similar households but her involvement with the law unlocked the closed doors of Battlecrease House to shocking revelations about sexual appetite.

Whether Florence was scheming and guilty or innocent and wronged, her history is a barometer of the shifting pressures faced by women at the end of the nineteenth century. Her fate was to suffer almost wordlessly the conflict and violence of her life, concealing it behind a highly mannered façade. Victim of the age in which she lived, her story is, above all, an example of the slipperiness of truth in an era overwhelmingly puzzled by the mutations and evolutions in so many things it had, for centuries, taken for granted.

People

Addison, John, QC	Barrister. Leads the prosecution at the Maybrick trial
Barron, Dr Alexander	Present at James Maybrick's post-mortem. Witness for the defence
Baxendale, Richard	Inspector of Police, Garston Police Station
Brierley, Alfred	Cotton broker, Liverpool
Brierley, Bessie	Maid, Battlecrease House
Briggs, Matilda	Family friend of James Maybrick
Brighouse, Samuel	Lancashire County Coroner
Bryning, Isaac	Superintendent of the Police for the County of West Derby
Cadwallader, Mary	Maid, Battlecrease House
Callery, Nurse Margaret	From Dover Street Nurses Institution, Liverpool
Carter, Dr William	Liverpool physician, Rodney Street, Liverpool
Cleaver, Arnold	Younger of two Liverpool solicitors representing Florence Maybrick
Cleaver, Richard	Elder of two Liverpool solicitors representing Florence Maybrick
Davies, Edward	Analytical chemist
Fuller, Dr Charles	Michael Maybrick's London physician

Gore, Nurse Ellen	From Dover Street Nurses Institution, Liverpool
Hanson, Christopher	Chemist, 4 Aigburth Road
Hopper, Dr Arthur Richard	Former Maybrick family physician, Rodney Street, Liverpool
Hughes, Constance	Matilda Briggs's sister, family friend of James Maybrick
Humphreys, Elizabeth	Cook, Battlecrease House
Humphreys, Dr Richard	Garston doctor
Knight, John Baillie	Childhood friend of Florence Maybrick
Lushington, Sir Godfrey	Permanent Under-Secretary to the Home Office
MacDougall, Alexander	Scottish barrister convinced of Florence Maybrick's innocence
Matthews, Henry	Home Secretary
Maybrick, James	Married to Florence
Maybrick, James (also known as Sonny or Bobo)	Son of James and Florence Maybrick
Maybrick, Gladys Evelyn	Daughter of James and Florence Maybrick
Maybrick, Edwin	Youngest of the Maybrick brothers
Maybrick, Michael	Third Maybrick brother, two years younger than James
Pickford, William	Barrister. Represents Florence Maybrick at the inquest; trial junior
Russell, Sir Charles, QC	Barrister. Leads Florence Maybrick's defence
Samuelson, Christina	Acquaintance of Florence Maybrick
Schweisso, Alfred	Head waiter, Flatman's Hotel, London
Stephen, James Fitzjames	Leading judge on the Northern Circuit. Presides over the Maybrick trial

Stevenson, Thomas   Professor of Chemistry, Guy's
Hospital. Home Office expert

Tidy, Dr Charles Meymott   Professor at the London Hospital.
Home Office expert

von Roques, Baroness   American, née Carrie Holbrook.
Mother of Florence Maybrick

Wilson, Nurse Susan   From Dover Street Nurses
Institution, Liverpool

Wokes, Thomas   Chemist, 25 Aigburth Road

Yapp, Alice   Nursemaid to the Maybrick children

Select Bibliography

ARCHIVES

The National Archives, Kew
HO 144.539.A50678
HO 144.1638.A50678 (which includes inquest statements)
HO 144.1639.A50678 (which includes various assizes statements)
HO 144.1640.A50678
HO 144.1641.A50678

Centre for Buckinghamshire Studies
HMP A/9/1 – Register of Descriptions of Inmates 1891–1909
HMP A1/2 – Governor's Journal December 1897–November 1903
HMP A/2/2 – Board of Visitors Minute Book 1899–1910

Lancaster Records Office
The Lancashire Constabulary Examination Books: PLA 11/10; 11/16; 11/20

American Heritage Center, University of Wyoming
Trevor Christie Papers

WEBSITES

www.archive.org/stream/verdictindispute00lustuoft
www.findarticles.com/p/articles/mi_qu4113/is_200401/ai_n9351005
www.historicaldirectories.org/hd/

NEWSPAPERS, MAGAZINES AND JOURNALS

British Medical Journal
Chambers' Journal of Popular Literature, Science, and Art
The English Review of Reviews
The Fortnightly Review
The Lancet
Medical History Journal
The Pharmaceutical Journal and Transactions
The Pall Mall Gazette
The Practitioner

NEWSPAPER DATABASES

British Library Nineteenth Century Newspapers
Nineteenth Century US Newspapers, published by Gale, part of
        Cengage Learning
The Times Digital Archive
The Daily Express Digital Archive
Chronicling America
Gale Newsvault

MAPS

OS map of Central Liverpool, 1890
OS map of Aigburth, 1904

PUBLISHED BOOKS AND ARTICLES

Altick, Richard D., *Victorian Studies in Scarlet* (London: Dent, 1972)

Amos, Sarah M., 'The Prison Treatment of Women', *Contemporary Review*, 73, June 1898, 803–13

Anon, *The Maybrick Poisoning Case: An Extraordinary Letter. A Comic Song on Naughty Mrs Maybrick*

Armstrong, Richard A., *The Deadly Shame of Liverpool: An Appeal to the Municipal Voters* (London: George Philip, 1890)

Atherton, Gertrude, *American Wives and English Husbands* (London: n.p., 1898)

Aughton, Peter, *Liverpool: A People's History* (Preston: Carnegie Press, 1990)

Ballin, Ada S., *Personal Hygiene* (London: Rebman, 1894)

Bartrip, Peter, 'A "Pennurth of Arsenic for Rat Poison": The Arsenic Act, 1851 and the Prevention of Secret Poisoning', *Medical History*, 36, 1992, 53–69

Belchem, John (ed.), *Liverpool 800: Culture, Character & History* (Liverpool: Liverpool University Press, 2006)

Bell, Jacob, 'Poisoning with Arsenic', *Pharmaceutical Journal*, vol. 1, 1841–2, 277–82

Blake, Victoria, *Mrs Maybrick* (Kew: National Archives, 2008)

Blyth, Alexander Wynter, *Poisons: Their Effects and Detection* (London: n.p., 1884)

Boswell, Charles and Lewis Thompson, *The Girl with the Scarlet Brand* (New York: Fawcett Gold Medal, 1954)

Boumelha, Penny, *Thomas Hardy and Women: Sexual Ideology and Narrative Form* (Brighton: Harvester Press, 1982)

Boyle, Thomas, *Black Swine in the Sewers of Hampstead: Beneath the Surface of Victorian Sensationalism* (New York: Viking, 1988)

Brodie, Allan, Jane Croom and James O. Davies, *English Prisons: An Architectural History* (Swindon: English Heritage, 2002)

Brooklyn Daily Eagle, *A Visitor's Guide to the City of New York* (Brooklyn: Brooklyn Daily Eagle, 1899)

Brooks, Peter, *The Melodramatic Imagination: Balzac, Henry James, Melodrama and the Mode of Excess* (1976; New Haven: Yale University Press, 1995)

Brownstein, Rachel M., *Becoming a Heroine: Reading about Women in Novels* (New York: Viking, 1982)

Buckle, George Earle (ed.), *The Letters of Queen Victoria. Third Series: A Selection from Her Majesty's Correspondence and Journal between the Years 1886 and 1901*, vol. 1 (London: John Murray, 1930)

Burke, Vincent, *Merseyside Murders & Trials* (Stroud: History Press, 2008)

Burney, Ian A., 'A Poisoning of No Substance: The Trials of Medico-Legal Proof in Mid-Victorian England', *Journal of British Studies*, vol. 38, no. 1, 1999, 59–92

Burney, Ian A., *Poison, Detection, and the Victorian Imagination* (Manchester: Manchester University Press, 2006)

Butler, J. E. (ed.), *Woman's Work and Woman's Culture: A Series of Essays* (London: n.p., 1869)

Caird, Mona, 'Marriage', *Westminster Review*, July 1888, vol. 130, no. 2, 186–201

Carter, William, 'Notes on the Maybrick Trial', *Liverpool Medico-Chirurgical Journal*, 18, 1890, 117–145

Christie, Trevor L., *Etched in Arsenic: A New Study of the Maybrick Case* (Philadelphia: Lippincott, 1968)

Clark, Michael and Catherine Crawford, *Legal Medicine in History* (Cambridge: Cambridge University Press, 1994)

Coley, Noel G., 'Alfred Swaine Taylor, MD, FRS (1806–1880): Forensic Toxicologist', *Medical History*, 35, October 1991, 409–27

Collins, Wilkie, 'The Poisoned Meal' in *My Miscellanies* (1863)
————, *The Law and the Lady* (1857)

Cunnington, C. Willet and Phillis, *Handbook of English Costume in the Nineteenth Century* (London: Faber & Faber, third edition, 1970)

Daisy Bank Print and Publishing Co., *Full Account of the Life & Trial of Mrs Maybrick: Interesting Details of Her Earlier Life* (Manchester: Daisy Bank, 1901)

Davidoff, Leonore, 'Mastered for Life: Servant and Wife in Victorian and Edwardian England', *Journal of Social History*, vol. 7, no. 4, 1974, 406–28

Densmore, Helen, *The Maybrick Case: English Criminal Law* (London: n.p., 1892)

Dyhouse, Carol, *Girls Growing Up in Late Victorian & Edwardian England* (Boston: Routledge & Kegan Paul, 1981)

Elshtain, Jean Bethke, *Public Man, Private Woman: Women in Social and Political Thought* (Princeton: Princeton University Press, 1981)

Emmerichs, Mary Beth Wasserlein, 'Trials of Women for Homicide in Nineteenth-Century England', *Women & Criminal Justice*, vol.5, no. 1, 1993, 99–109

Emsley, Clive, *Crime and Society in England, 1750–1900* (London: Longman, 1987)

Emsley, John, *The Elements of Murder* (Oxford: Oxford University Press, 2006)

Evans, Stewart P., *Executioner: The Chronicles of James Berry, Victorian Hangman* (Stroud: Sutton, 2004)

Farrie, H., *Toiling Liverpool: A Series of Articles Reprinted from the Liverpool Daily Post* (1886)

Flanders, Judith, *Consuming Passions: Leisure and Pleasure in Victorian Britain* (London: HarperPress, 2006)

Flanders, Judith, *The Victorian House: Domestic Life from Childbirth to Deathbed* (London: HarperCollins, 2003)

Flanders, Judith, *The Invention of Murder: How the Victorians Revelled in Death and Detection and Created Modern Crime* (London: HarperPress, 2011)

Fletcher, J. A., *Travelling Places* (1913)

Foster, John Watson, *Diplomatic Memoirs* (Boston: Houghton Mifflin, 1909)

Foucault, Michel, *Discipline and Punish: The Birth of the Prison* (London: Allen Lane, 1977)

Foxcroft, Louise, *The Making of Addiction: The 'Use and Abuse' of Opium in Nineteenth-Century Britain* (Aldershot: Ashgate, 2007)

Gaskell, Elizabeth, 'The Gray Woman' in *Cousin Phyllis and Other Tales* (1861)

Graham, Anne E. and Carol Emmas, *The Last Victim: The Extraordinary Life of Florence Maybrick, The Wife of Jack the Ripper* (London: Headline, 1999)

Grand, Sarah, 'The New Aspect of the Woman Question', *North American Review*, vol. 158, no. 448, March 1894, 270–6

Griffith, Arthur, *Secrets of the Prison House: or, Gaol Studies and Sketches*, 2 vols (London: Chapman and Hall, 1894)

Grisewood, W., *The Poor of Liverpool and What is Done for Them* (Liverpool: n.p., 1899)

Hardy, Thomas, *Tess of the d'Urbervilles* (1891)

Harris, Michael, 'Social Disease?: Crime and Medicine in the Victorian Press', in W. F. Bynum, Stephen Lock and Roy Porter, *Medical Journals & Medical Knowledge: Historical Essays* (London: Routledge, 1992), pp. 108–25

Harrison, Constance Cary, *The Anglomaniacs* (London: n.p., 1890)

Hartman, Mary S., 'Crime and the Respectable Woman: Toward a Pattern of Middle-Class Female Criminality in Nineteenth-Century France and England', *Feminist Studies*, vol. 2, no. 1, 1974, 38–56

Hartman, Mary S., *Victorian Murderesses: A True History of Thirteen Respectable French & English Women Accused of Unspeakable Crimes* (London: Robson Books, 1977)

Heidensohn, Frances, *Women and Crime* (Basingstoke: Macmillan, 1985)

Hume, Abraham, *Condition of Liverpool, Religious and Social* (London: n.p., 1858, second edition)

Irving, H. B., *The Trial of Mrs Maybrick* (Edinburgh: Hodge, 1912)

James, Henry, *The Golden Bowl* (1904)

J.L.F., *The Maybrick Case: A Treatise Showing Reasons for Dissent from the Verdict* (London: n.p., 1890)

Johnston, M. F., 'The Life of a Woman Convict', *Fortnightly Review*, vol. 69, March 1901, 559–67

Jones, Christopher, *The Maybrick A to Z* (Birkenhead: Countyvise, 2008)

Jordan, Ellen, *The Women's Movement and Women's Employment in Nineteenth-Century Britain* (London: Routledge, 1999)

Kaye, Brian H., *Science and the Detective: Selected Reading in Forensic Science* (Weinheim: Wiley VCH, 1995)

Kelly, F., *Kelly's Directory of Liverpool and Birkenhead, 1894*

Knelman, Judith, *Twisting in the Wind: The Murderess and the English Press* (Toronto: University of Toronto Press, 1998)

Ledger, Sally, *The New Woman: Fiction and Feminism at the Fin de Siècle* (Manchester: Manchester University Press, 1997)

Levine, Philippa, *Victorian Feminism, 1850–1900* (London: Hutchinson Education, 1987)

Levy, J. H., *The Necessity for Criminal Appeal: As Illustrated by the Maybrick Case and the Jurisprudence of Various Countries* (London: P. S. King, 1899)

L.E.X., *The Maybrick and Madeline Smith Cases Contrasted. Is Mrs Maybrick Guilty? A Defence* (Manchester: n.p., 1889)

Lombroso, Cesare, *The Female Offender* (London: T. F. Unwin, 1895)

MacDougall, Alexander William, *The Maybrick Case: A Treatise ... On the Facts of the Case, and of the Proceedings in Connection with the Charge, Trial, Conviction and Present Imprisonment of Florence Elizabeth Maybrick* (London: Baillière, Tindall and Cox, 1891)

MacDougall, Alexander William, *The Maybrick Case: A Statement of the Case as a Whole: Being Three Letters Addressed to Sir Matthew White Ridley, Bart., M.P., H.M. Secretary of State for the Home Department, etc.* (London: Baillière, Tindall and Cox, 1896)

Mant, A. Keith, 'Science in the Detection of Crime', *Journal of the Royal Society of Arts*, vol. 131, no. 5325, August 1983, 548–58

Matarosso, Pauline Maud, *A Voyage Closed and Done* (Norwich: Michael Russell, 2005)

Maybrick, Florence Elizabeth, *Mrs Maybrick's Own Story: My Fifteen Lost Years* (London: Funk & Wagnalls, 1904)

Mayhew, Henry and John Binny, *The Criminal Prisons of London, and Scenes of Prison Life* (London: Griffin, Bohm, 1862)

Mcilwee, Michael, *Tearaways: More Gangs of Liverpool 1890–1970* (Wrea Green: Milo, 2008)

Midwinter, Eric C., *Old Liverpool* (Newton Abbot: David & Charles, 1971)

Mill, John Stuart, 'The Subjection of Women' (1869)

Morland, Nigel, *This Friendless Lady* (London: F. Muller, 1957)

Morris, Allison, *Women, Crime, and Criminal Justice* (Oxford: Blackwell, 1987)

Morris, Virginia, *Double Jeopardy: Women who Kill in Victorian Fiction* (Lexington: University Press of Kentucky, 1990)

Murphy, Sir Shirley Forster, *Our Homes, and How to Make Them Healthy* (London: Cassell, 1883)

Nightingale, Florence, *The Organisation of Nursing in a Large Town* (Liverpool and London: A. Holden and Longman, Green, Reader and Dyer, 1865)

Nott-Bower, Sir John William, *Fifty-Two Years a Policeman* (London: E. Arnold, 1926)

Orme, Eliza, 'Our Female Criminals', *Fortnightly Review*, vol. 63, May 1898, 790–6

Ouida, 'The New Woman', *North American Review*, vol. 158, no. 450, May 1894, 610–19

Przygoda, Gudrun, Jörg Feldmann and William R. Cullen, 'The Arsenic Eaters of Styria: A Different Picture of People who were Chronically Exposed to Arsenic', *Applied Organometallic Chemistry*, vol. 15, no. 6, June 2001, 457–62

Purdy, Richard Little and Michael Millgate, *The Collected Letters of Thomas Hardy, Volume I: 1840–1892* (Oxford: Clarendon Press, 1978)

Pykett, Lyn, *The 'Improper Feminine': The Women's Sensation Novel and the New Woman Writing* (London: Routledge, 1992)

Rich, C. E. F., *Recollections of a Prison Governor* (London: Hurst and Blackett, 1932)

Robb, George, 'Circe in Crinoline: Domestic Poisonings in Victorian England', *Journal of Family History*, vol. 2, no. 2, April 1997, 176–90

Rowland, John, *Poisoner in the Dock: Twelve Studies in Poisoning* (London: Arco Publications, 1960)

Ryan, Jr., Bernard with Sir Michael Havers, *The Poisoned Life of Mrs Maybrick* (London: Kimber, 1977)

Scougal, Francis, *Scenes from a Silent World: or, Prisons and their Inmates* (London: W. Blackwood and Sons, 1889)

Shanley, Mary Lyndon, *Feminism, Marriage, and the Law in Victorian England, 1850–1895* (London: Tauris, 1989)

Shimmin, Hugh, *Liverpool Life: Its Pleasures, Practices and Pastimes* (1856)

Smith, John, *The Register of Death: A History of Executions at Walton Prison, Liverpool* (Birkenhead: Countyvise, 1989)

Spencer, S., 'A Minister in Prison', in *Penal Reform and Prevention of Crime*

Stephen, Sir Leslie, *The Life of Sir James Fitzjames Stephen* (London: n.p., 1895)

Strachey, Ray, *The Cause: A Short History of the Women's Movement in Great Britain* (London: G. Bell and Sons, 1928)

Thompson, C. J. S., *Poisons and Poisoners, with Historical Accounts of Some Mysteries in Ancient and Modern Times* (London: Harold Shaylor, 1931)

Thompson, Charles John S., *The Cult of Beauty: Handbook of Personal Hygiene* (London: n.p., 1894)

Tidy, Charles Meymott and Rawdon MacNamara, *The Maybrick Trial: A Toxicological Study* (London: n.p., 1890)

Trodd, Anthea, *Domestic Crime in the Victorian Novel* (Basingstoke: Macmillan, 1989)

Trollope, Anthony, *Can You Forgive Her?* (1864–5)

Verne, Jules, *A Floating City* (1874)

Vicinus, Martha, '"Helpless and Unfriended": Nineteenth-Century Domestic Melodrama', *New Literary History*, vol. 13, no. 1, autumn 1981, 127–43

Vicinus, Martha (ed.), *Suffer and be Still: Women in the Victorian Age* (Bloomington: Indiana University Press, 1972)

Wagner, Charles L., *Seeing Stars* (New York: G. P. Putnam's Sons, 1940)

Walton, John K. and Alastair Wilcox (ed.), *Low Life and Moral Improvement in mid-Victorian England: Liverpool through the Journalism of Hugh Shimmin* (Leicester: Leicester University Press, 1991)

Wharton, Edith, *The Buccaneers* (1938)

Whorton, James C., *The Arsenic Century: How Victorian Britain was Poisoned at Home, Work, and Play* (Oxford: Oxford University Press, 2010)

Wiener, Martin J., 'Alice Arden to Bill Sikes: Changing Nightmares of Intimate Violence in England, 1558–1869', *Journal of British Studies*, vol. 40, no. 2, April 2001, 184–212

Wiener, Martin J., 'Judges v. Jurors: Courtroom Tensions in Murder Trials and the Law of Criminal Responsibility in Nineteenth-Century England', *Law and History Review*, vol. 17, no. 3, fall 1999, 467–506

Winslow, Lytton Forbes, *Recollections of Forty Years: Being an Account at First Hand of Some Famous Criminal Lunacy Cases, English and American, Together with Facsimile Letters, Notes and Other Data Concerning Them* (London: J. Ouseley, 1910)

X.Y.Z., 'England's Convict Prison for Women', *Englishwoman Magazine*, vol. 14, no. 42, 266–76

Yonge, Charlotte M., *Womankind* (London: Walter Smith, 1877)

Zedner, Lucia, *Women, Crime and Custody in Victorian England* (Oxford: Clarendon Press, 1991)

Acknowledgements

Librarians and archivists are unfailingly helpful, particularly those at the British Library St Pancras and Colindale and the National Archives in Kew. I would also like to thank Rachel A. Drayer at the University of Wyoming American Heritage Center; Christopher Low and Ian Jones at the Centre for Buckinghamshire Studies; Roger Hull at the Liverpool Record Office; Ann Bukantas and Steve Ferguson at the Walker Art Gallery in Liverpool; Joan Self at the National Meteorological Archive; Laura Walker at the Surrey History Centre; Robert Noel, Lancaster Herald at the College of Arms; and David Blake at the Lancashire Records Office.

For their particular help with other aspects of research I am grateful to Stewart Evans, Richard Whittington-Egan, Christopher Jones, Susan McDonald, Anne Graham, Shirley Harrison, Paul Bickley at New Scotland Yard, Keith Skinner, and Alfred Brierley's great-great nephew Gerard Brierley. At HMP Aylesbury, Craig Chinn. For advice on the Victorian medicine cabinet, Dr Stuart Anderson, Associate Dean at the London School of Hygiene and Tropical Medicine. For access to the 19th Century US Newspapers digital database, Nicholas Berg at Gale/Cengage.

Laura Cumming, Frank Wynn and Joanna Sharland read all or parts of the manuscript in its various forms and were incisively helpful. Colin Mansell held me to accuracy and gave generously of his genealogical know-how. The Royal Literary Fund's Writer in Residence scheme has, throughout the process of researching and writing this book, helped to keep me afloat.

Thank you Christine Smith, Epoh Beech, Max and Noland Carter, Laura Cumming (again), Jo Korn, Geraldine and Jonathan Mendelow, Shaheen Sayed, Tiggy Sharland, Jonathan Payne and Alison Roberts, Venetia Forbes, Elspeth Scott, Julie Lynn Evans, Jem Lineham and Kate Cook, Nell Lindsell, Kate Mayfield, Lisa Highton, Annabel Rosenhead, Anthony and Didi Given, and my parents, Iain and Sally Colquhoun.

Lastly, my thanks for the support and energy of my agent, Caroline Dawnay at United Agents, and, at Little, Brown, David Shelley, Claudia Dyer, Zoe Gullen, proof-reader Daniel Balado and the rest of the superlative publishing team.

Notes

CHAPTER 1: MARCH 1889

7 **When Jim comes**: The original of this letter of October 1887 is lost but is quoted in full in Christie, *Etched in Arsenic*, p. 36.

7 **Description of Battlecrease**: Taken from Aunspaugh letters in the Christie Papers; from description of the sale of the contents, *Garston and Woolton Reporter*, 13 July 1889, p. 4; from my visit, 2012.

8 **Description of Florence Maybrick**: Aunspaugh letters, Christie Papers.

8 **protective instincts**: Ibid. See also Graham and Emmas, *The Last Victim*, p. xvii.

9 **assertion of their conformity**: Flanders, *The Victorian House*, p. xxxivff.

9 **Madame Merle**: Henry James, *Portrait of a Lady* (1881), Chapter 19.

10 **businesses on Aigburth Road**: Kelly, *Kelly's Directory of Liverpool and Birkenhead*, 1894.

10 **a fine view**: Now Otterspool Park.

10 **penny seat**: Jones, *The Maybrick A to Z*, p. 59.

10 **two hundred horse-drawn trams**: Flanders, *Consuming Passions*, p. 99.

10 **five railway termini**: Kelly, op. cit.

11 *great caravansaray*: *Liverpool Review*, 26 January 1889.

11 **a third of all the country's business**: Christie, op. cit., p. 4.

11 **collieries**: Kelly, op. cit.

12 **Cotton was the king**: See, e.g., 'Latest American Cotton Advices', *Liverpool Mercury*, 11 June 1889, for total bales imported.

12 **Lancashire cotton mills**: Morland, *This Friendless Lady*, p. 7.

12 *I had seen wealth*: Armstrong, *The Deadly Shame of Liverpool*. In 1889 a series of articles entitled 'Liverpool Slum Life' appeared weekly in the *Liverpool Review*, the first running on 1 July (p. 11).

13 **poked fun:** From the sale catalogue for the contents of Battlecrease, a pair of engravings entitled 'When a man's single he lives at his ease' and 'When a man's married, his trouble begins'. There is no proof to substantiate my decision to furnish James Maybrick's study with these pictures.

14 *a man's life*: Oscar Wilde, *An Ideal Husband* (1895), Act 4.

CHAPTER 2: EXPECTATIONS

15 *a monstrous leap*: Anthony Trollope, *Phineas Redux* (1873), quoted in Glendinning, *Trollope*, p. 140.

16 **coats were admirably fitted:** Aunspaugh letters, Christie Papers.

17 **sudden friendships:** Anthony Trollope, *Can You Forgive Her?* (1864–5), chapter 73.

17 **partying and flirtation:** For a description of journeys on board ships of the White Star Line (which James Maybrick generally favoured), see Frances Wilson, *How to Survive the Titanic: or, The Sinking of J. Bruce Ismay* (London: Bloomsbury, 2011), p. 66ff.

17 *Time Reveals All*: Documents in the archives of the Royal College of Arms, London.

17 **fast-talking:** Hartman, *Victorian Murderesses*, p. 51.

17 **Was she coaxed:** Suggested by Whorton, *The Arsenic Century*, p. 278ff.

18 **blond and distinguished:** *Kansas Newspaper*, 31 July 1889.

18 **organist:** Shirley Harrison, *The Diary of Jack the Ripper: The Chilling Confession of James Maybrick* (London: John Blake, 2010).

18 **arrogant:** Aunspaugh letters, Christie Papers: *he was a snob ... my father used to scoff that he'd already booked himself a tomb in Westminster Abbey.*

18 **best looking:** Ibid.

19 **dropped his knife:** Ibid.

19 **Sefton Park:** James Maybrick junior's birth certificate shows he was born here. The Briggs children are listed as living at that address in the 1881 census; Matilda was visiting her parents.

20 **building its post-Civil War recovery:** Christie, *Etched in Arsenic*, p. 23.

20 **Renting:** Flanders, *The Victorian House*, p. xxxix.

20 **phaeton, groom and riding:** Aunspaugh letters, Christie Papers.

21 **financial prop:** The litigation records are in a *tin box* in the Virginia Archives, USA, according to Trevor Christie's notes (op. cit.). The Baroness's financial past is evoked in his handwritten notes: *she was, I am sorry to say, a ruthless, grasping old harridan who violated her pledged word time and again.* See also *New York Times* reports, e.g. 12 March 1897.

21 **exasperated:** Christie Papers, typed notes of relationship between James Maybrick and the Baroness, including a letter to William Potter, 6 December 1887: *experience has taught me that I cannot rely on the verbal promises of the B.*

21 **taken without authorisation:** Christie Papers. The amount is equivalent to around eighty thousand dollars today.

21 *bully:* Christie, *Etched in Arsenic*, p. 39.

22 *utterly worn* out: Ibid., p. 36.

22 **spoiled child:** Aunspaugh letters, Christie Papers.

22 **Betting shops:** Flanders, *Consuming Passions*, p. 432.

23 **success depended:** Belchem (ed.), *Liverpool 800*, p. 290.

23 **contemporary household manual:** George Somes Layard, 'How to Live on £700 a Year', *Nineteenth Century*, vol. 23, January–June 1888, 239–44. A range of family budgets from contemporary household manuals is available at <http://www.victorianlondon.org/finance/money.htm>.

23 *wealth:* Oscar Wilde, *An Ideal Husband* (1895), Act 2.

24 **scarlet fever:** Interview with Baroness von Roques, *Liverpool Weekly Post*, 17 August 1889.

24 **James' mistress:** It has been variously suggested that Florence did not know of James' mistress, but a deposition dated 18 July 1889 in archive material at the National Archives (HO 144.1638.A50678) shows that she discussed it with her friend John Baillie Knight: *he kept a woman – I don't remember whether she told me so verbally or by letter.* Both Emsley (*The Elements of Murder*) and Christie (*Etched in Arsenic*) suggest that James paid his mistress a hundred pounds a year, without attributing a source. Michael Maybrick would later be coy about the woman and her name was never published, though MacDougall published her address as 265 Queen's Road, New Cross, London SE (*The Maybrick Case*, pp. 20–1). Further research in the census by both Keith Skinner at the Metropolitan Police History Society and by Colin Mansell reveals that Sarah Ann Robertson, born *c.* 1837, called herself Sarah Maybrick for a time in 1871. Skinner has traced this woman to living friends who swear that she was James' mistress. The connections are convincing. But no marriage certificate, nor any birth or death records for any of her children, have ever been found. See the Afterword notes (p. 404) for an unauthenticated supposition printed later by the *Atlanta Constitution*.

CHAPTER 3: ONE MAN'S POISON

25 **beneficiary:** *Liverpool Daily Post*, 31 July 1889.

26 **Small diamonds:** Aunspaugh letters, Christie Papers.

26 **Social obligations:** Belchem, *Liverpool 800*, p. 297.

26 **patting them:** Aunspaugh letters, Christie Papers.

26 *American savage:* Jehanne Wake, *Sisters of Fortune: The First American Heiresses to Take England by Storm* (London: Chatto & Windus, 2010), p. 339.

27 **took for granted:** Wharton, *The Buccaneers*.

27 **New York women:** For example, Anthony Trollope. See Glendinning, *Trollope, p.* 320.

27 **the *Titanic*:** Frances Wilson, *How to Survive the Titanic: or, The Sinking of J. Bruce Ismay* (London: Bloomsbury, 2011), p. 89.

28 **old-fashioned deference:** For more on this see Davidoff, 'Mastered for Life'.

28 **'Gentle Mary':** Jones, *The Maybrick A to Z*.

29 **soles and chickens:** E. Humphreys, assizes statement.

29 **a year or so earlier:** Inquest deposition, 28 May 1889, HO 144.1638.A50678. Alice Yapp had been employed by the Maybricks for a year and eight months.

29 **largish nose:** Images of Alice Yapp in *Liverpool Echo*, 1 August 1889, and *Liverpool Weekly Post*, 15 June 1889.

29 **prepossessing:** Interview with Alice Yapp, *New York Herald*, 21 August 1889.

29 **wealthy suburban families:** In the 1881 census Alice Yapp is nurse servant to the Smith family in Toxteth Park. Mr Smith was a shipbuilder employing 120 men and thirty boys.

30 *it matters little:* Christie, *Etched in Arsenic*, p. 40.

31 **£125 a year:** Ibid., p. 29.

32 **'Not to be Taken':** On James Maybrick's melancholia, see Aunspaugh letters, Christie Papers. List of bottles and pills collected during May 1889 supplied by the analyst Edward Davies, HO 144.1368.A50678.

32 **Irish-born Hopper:** *Liverpool Review*, 8 June 1889, p. 13.

32 **strychnine:** Hopper's court evidence, reported in *Lloyd's Weekly Newspaper*, 4 August 1889, p. 3. See also assizes statements.

32 **nux vomica:** R. Hopper, inquest statement.

32 *he takes some poison:* R. Hopper assizes statement.

33 **decided not to:** Hopper's statement, Treasury notes post-trial, HO 144.1639.A50678.

33 **raise the subject:** R. Hopper inquest statement.

33 **James' appetites:** Aunspaugh letters, Christie Papers: *always having the druggist prepare some kind of tonic*.

33 **whooping cough:** E. Humphreys deposition, in folder 'Additional statements taken at Liverpool Summer Assizes on 3, 4, 5 July 1889', HO 144.1639.A50678.

33 *You can always say:* Ibid.

CHAPTER 4: THE MARRIAGE QUESTION

35 **Her wire enquired:** Trial exhibit K, HO 144.1638.A50678.

35 **at greater length:** Trial exhibit N, HO 144.1638.A50678.

35 *Mrs Maybrick hopes*: Trial exhibit L, HO 144.1638.A50678.

36 *Dinner about 7.15*: Ibid.

36 **Another wire arrived:** This change is unexplained, since the cable or letter communicating it has not been preserved. We know of Florence Maybrick's arrival, though, from Alfred Schweisso's inquest deposition.

37 **entire block:** Ironically, this block would, from 1910, form part of the large site housing the buildings of the Royal Society of Medicine and the Royal College of Nursing.

37 **Café Royal:** Emsley, *The Elements of Murder*, p. 171ff.

38 **Knight's advice:** John Baillie Knight deposition, 18 July 1889, HO 1638.A50678.

38 **Acts of Parliament:** For more on these see Shanley, *Feminism, Marriage, and the Law in Victorian England*.

38 **right to their wives' bodies:** This Act (sometimes known as the Weldon Act) would be passed in 1891.

38 **cruelty, desertion or worse:** Morris, *Double Jeopardy*, p. 48.

38 **submission and self-effacement:** Zedner, *Women, Crime and Custody in Victorian England*, p. 15ff.

39 *full of lead*: Letter from Charles Ratcliff to John Aunspaugh, 22 November 1888, Brierley Folder, Box 1, Christie Papers.

40 **She should ask him:** According to John Baillie Knight deposition, op. cit.

40 **made Caird the most infamous feminist:** For this and a wider discussion of Caird's essay, see Ledger, *The New Woman*, p. 21ff. Also Pykett, *The 'Improper Feminine'*, p. 144ff, and Judith Knelman, 'She Loves Me, She Loves Me Not: Trends in the Victorian Marriage Market 1', *Journal of Communication Inquiry*, vol. 18, no. 1, winter 1994, 80–94.

40 *an aroma of love*: Anthony Trollope, *Framley Parsonage* (1860), chapter 27.

40 *so far advanced*: Anthony Trollope, *Can You Forgive Her?* (1864–5), chapter 11.

41 **some wondered:** Ledger, op. cit., p. 20.

42 *The Buccaneers*: Though published in 1938 in unfinished form, the novel looks back to the late 1870s and 1880s.

42 *the long and short of it*: Atherton, *American Wives and English Husbands*, p. 320.

43 **restrictive standards:** Boumelha, *Thomas Hardy and Women*, p. 73.

43 *too indecently moaning*: Henry James, *The Golden Bowl* (1904), chapter 30.

CHAPTER 5: RACING

44 *it didn't matter*: G. Smith, assizes statement. Several accounts of the
    Maybrick case have suggested that Gertrude Janion was at the races,
    hoping to flirt with Brierley, but Mrs Briggs made it clear in an interview
    in the *Liverpool Weekly Post* (17 August 1889, p. 5) that Gertrude was
    not present. Elizabeth Humphreys deposed at Liverpool assizes in
    July 1889 that she heard that Brierley *was paying attention to Miss
    Gertrude ... who used to stay with Mrs Maybrick*.

45 Florence's mother would later say: *Norfolk Virginian*, 20 August 1889,
    p. 1.

45 excitement thickened: See 'The Aintree Meeting' in Walton and Wilcox
    (ed.), *Low Life and Moral Improvement in mid-Victorian England*,
    p. 78ff.

45 lived for a season in Savannah: *Norfolk Virginian*, op. cit.

46 Description of Brierley: from Trevor Christie's handwritten notes,
    Christie Papers; also from illustration in *Lloyd's Weekly Newspaper*, 4
    August 1889, p. 3. See also *New York Herald*, London edition, 13
    August 1889.

46 paying more attention to Florence: The Baroness's suggestion, reported
    in *Norfolk Virginian*, op. cit.

46 *hot and heavy*: C. Samuelson, inquest statement.

47 Not a word had been spoken: A. Yapp, inquest statement.

47 heard the commotion: B. Brierley, inquest statement.

47 *all over the town tomorrow*: A. Yapp, inquest statement.

48 watching from the foot of the main stairs: Trial evidence. Irving, *The
    Trials of Mrs Maybrick*, p. 80.

48 torn: This detail about torn clothing is not in the existing inquest dep-
    ositions but is quoted as Elizabeth Humphreys's statement by Christie,
    Etched in Arsenic, p. 45. The following day at the doctor, Florence
    Maybrick had a black eye.

48 *by heaven, Florrie*: A. Yapp and E. Humphreys, inquest statements.

48 *like a madman*: Not in the Home Office files. Quoted by Christie,
    Etched in Arsenic, p. 45.

48 *Don't send the mistress away*: Christie, *Etched in Arsenic*.

48 to see the baby: A. Yapp, inquest statement.

49 *quite stiff*: Elizabeth Humphreys's evidence, not in the Home Office
    files. Quoted by Christie, op. cit., p. 45.

49 to be forgotten: A. Yapp, inquest statement.

49 bruised eye was painful: Dr R. Hopper, inquest statement.

49 didn't go too far: Emsley, *Crime and Society in England*, p. 159.

49 Matilda had managed: Matilda was married, aged twenty, in 1871 to
    Thomas Charles Briggs. Their children were twelve, eleven and nine

years at this time and the address is listed as her brother's from 1881. Baroness von Roques, in an interview with the press on 16 August 1889, mentions that Matilda was divorced on account of her ex-husband's conduct.

50 **receive her mother's letters:** M. Briggs, inquest statement.

50 **then to consult:** Matilda Briggs trial evidence. Irving, op. cit., p. 39.

50 *they had ceased:* Dr R. Hopper, assizes statement. Additionally, a note from Judge Stevenson to the Home Office dated 14 August 1889 records that Dr Humphreys made a statement to him on the last day of the trial that James Maybrick had told him that he had not slept with his wife for months when she miscarried earlier in the year. This suggests that James was aware of his wife's adulteries, whether she knew it or not (HO 144.1638.A50678).

51 *half undressed:* Much quoted; taken here from Emsley, op. cit., p. 46.

52 *I cannot understand:* This and following account of Hopper's involvement at this time are from his inquest statement. See also 'Additional statements taken at Liverpool Summer Assizes on 3, 4, 5 July 1889', HO 144.1639.A50678.

52 **None of it was entirely clear:** Dr R. Hopper, statement, Treasury notes post-trial, HO 144.1639.A50678.

52 *not quite right internally:* Dr R. Hopper, additional statement at Liverpool assizes, July 1889, HO 144.1639.A50678.

53 **she scribbled several long letters:** Trial exhibit I, HO 144.1638.A50678.

53 **agree to a separation:** John Baillie Knight deposition, 18 July 1889, HO 144.1638.A50678.

CHAPTER 6: DANGEROUS POTIONS

54 *only the pleasure of the association:* Aunspaugh letters, Christie Papers.

54 *I was willing to meet you:* Trial exhibit H, HO 144.1638.A50678.

55 *beating her:* Liverpool Weekly Post, 17 August 1889, p. 5.

55 **neither meet nor correspond:** Post-trial affidavit for Cleaver, HO 144.1638.A50678.

55 **ever meet alone:** Ibid.

55 **Three days later:** According to Michael Maybrick's inquest statement, though Thomas Lowry suggested it was later, around the 12th (HO 144.1639.A50678).

55 **Regent's Park rooms:** The term Michael Maybrick used to describe his accommodation, inquest statement.

55 **a rickety table:** For example, Anthony Trollope, *The Three Clerks* (1858), chapter 18.

56 **60 per cent:** Letter from William Swift to the Home Office, 19 August 1889, enclosing letters written by James and Florence, HO 144.1639.A50678.

56 **he also made sure:** T. Lowry, inquest statement.

56 **repeated his usual complaints:** Dr C. Fuller, trial testimony, Irving, *The Trials of Mrs Maybrick*, p. 58.

56 **three prescriptions:** Dr Stuart Anderson, Associate Dean at the London School of Hygiene and Tropical Medicine, has been of inestimable help with his explanations about the nineteenth-century medicine cabinet. See also William Martindale, *The Extra Pharmacopoeia* (London: Pharmaceutical Press, 1967, twenty-fifth edition), or James Grier, *A History of Pharmacy* (London: Pharmaceutical Press, 1937).

56 **potential to do more harm:** Whorton, *The Arsenic Century*, p. 229.

56 **somewhat confused:** See George K. Behlmer, 'Grave Doubts: Victorian Medicine, Moral Panic, and the Signs of Death', *Journal of British Studies*, vol. 42, no. 2, April 2003, 206–35.

57 **prophylactic against infectious disease:** *British Medical Journal*, 1892, (ii), 1247.

57 ***if a law were passed:*** Whorton, op. cit., pp. 239–40.

57 **noxious compounds:** Such as Pearson's solution (potassium arsenate), Donovan's solution (arsenic iodide), Bieto's solution (ammonium arsenate), de Valagin's solution (arsenious acid), etc.: see Whorton, op. cit.

57 **dangerously toxic reaction:** Flanders, *The Victorian House*, p. 323.

58 ***doubtful of the truth:*** Trial exhibit F, HO 144.1638.A50678.

58 ***My own darling Hubby!:*** Letter from Florence Maybrick to James Maybrick, 14 April 1889, HO 144.1639.A50678.

59 **Others heard:** T. Lowry, inquest statement.

59 **altered his prescriptions:** Dr C. Fuller, trial testimony, Irving, op. cit., p. 58; also HO 144.1638.A50678 for the statement of Frederick Tozer – chemist at Clay & Abraham chemists – about making up these prescriptions.

60 ***to economise:*** Morland, *This Friendless Lady*, p. 36, quotes a letter without giving the source.

60 ***we are requested:*** Ibid., p. 42.

61 **Exchange Flags:** Description from Kelly, *Kelly's Directory of Liverpool and Birkenhead*.

61 **white snow of threads:** Belchem (ed.), *Liverpool 800*, p. 293ff.

62 **the Albany:** Belchem (ed.), op. cit., p. 295.

62 **Exchange station:** Kelly, op. cit.

62 **Edwin arrived:** E. Maybrick, inquest statement.

62 ***The furniture I desire:*** *Liverpool Daily Post*, 31 July 1889.

CHAPTER 7: MORE LIKE DYING THAN LIVING

64 *an overdose of medicine*: A. Yapp, inquest statement.

65 threw the remains ... down the sink: E. Humphreys, assizes statement.

65 looking pale: T. Lowry, inquest statement. Also T. Lowry and G. Smith, assizes statements.

65 *on the WC for an hour*: G. Smith, assizes statement.

65 resembled a chemist's shop: Captain Irvine interviewed by *Liverpool Daily Post*, 9 September 1889.

66 go and stay with master: Dr R. Humphreys, A. Yapp and E. Humphreys, inquest and assizes statements.

66 *Humphrey*, she said: E. Humphreys, inquest statement.

66 a slight nose injury: Irving, *The Trial of Mrs Maybrick*, p. 87.

66 Description of the bedroom: From Clemmie's floor plans, HO 144.1639.A50678, with the exception of the low chair by the window, which is from Dr Carter's account of his first visit to Battlecrease.

67 *looked a long way off*: Dr R. Humphreys, assizes statement.

67 lying on the sofa: E. Maybrick, inquest statement.

68 pains in his legs: E. Humphreys, assizes statement.

68 *dizzy and fainty*: M. Cadwallader, inquest statement.

69 self-indulgent letter: Letter dated 29 April 1889, HO 144.1639.A50678.

70 severe and bloody diarrhoea: William Martindale, *The Extra Pharmacopoeia* (London: Pharmaceutical Press, 1967, twenty-fifth edition), describes papain as being derived from pawpaw juice, to help digestion of protein. Iridin was derived from iris species root and was a purgative and liver stimulant; in large doses it could cause these symptoms. Humphreys's diagnosis from his inquest statement.

71 insipidity of the gruel: Dr R. Humphreys, inquest statement.

71 Edwin ... agreed to deliver it: E. Humphreys, inquest statement.

71 The charwoman: E. Blucher, inquest statement.

71 his tongue had cleared: Dr R. Humphreys, assizes statement.

CHAPTER 8: THE SLAVERY OF THE SICKROOM

72 always popping in and out: B. Brierley, inquest statement.

72 *makes that complaint about everyone's medicine*: Dr R. Humphreys, assizes statement.

73 to some warmed stock: E. Humphreys, inquest statement.

73 the children to say good night: A. Yapp and B. Brierley, inquest statements.

73 *all doctors are fools*: A. Yapp, inquest statement.

74 **ate her dinner alone**: E. Humphreys, inquest statement.

74 *Cheap sherry*: Dr R. Humphreys, inquest statement.

74 **morphia suppositories**: Dr R. Humphreys, assizes statement.

74 **small pieces of ice**: Ibid.

75 **vapour was highly poisonous**: Information from Dr Stuart Anderson of the London School of Hygiene and Tropical Medicine.

75 **build up his declining strength**: T. Wokes, post-trial statement to Treasury Solicitor, 23 August 1889, HO 144.1639.A50678.

76 *The doctor says*: E. Humphreys, inquest statement.

76 **a small cup of the broth**: E. Humphreys, assizes statement. On taking medicine upstairs, see her inquest statement.

76 **Various mouthwashes**: On several occasions, Dr Humphreys's statements at the inquest and at the assizes show he gave medicines that had been prescribed on earlier occasions and which were still rattling around the house – c.f. the morphia suppository.

76 **More bottles and packets**: A. Yapp, inquest statement.

76 **temperature was normal**: E. Maybrick, inquest statement. Dr R. Humphreys, inquest statement, re. events of Sunday evening.

76 **the doctor changed his mind**: Dr R. Humphreys, inquest statement.

76 **chemically treated plaster**: Flanders, *The Victorian House*, p. 316.

77 **insolently obvious surprise**: Alice Yapp admits that she questioned Florence Maybrick about going out in her inquest statement.

77 *Why wont you call for Dr Hopper?*: Ibid.

77 **The following day**: Dr R. Humphreys, inquest statement.

77 **Maddened**: Ibid. She said words to the effect *as many medical men have seen him and he has derived so little benefit from their treatment*. The cook said that she had suggested to Florence Maybrick that she make some more nourishing food but Florence said that the doctors would not allow it. Florence thought that *inflammation has set in* and agreed that he needed strength to battle the sickness (E. Humphreys, inquest statement).

77 **changing his bed sheets**: A. Yapp, inquest statement.

78 **Carter learned**: Carter, 'Notes on the Maybrick Trial', 118.

78 *foul as a midden*: Ibid., 120.

79 *His breath is sweet*: Dr W. Carter and Dr R. Humphreys, inquest statements.

79 *much in the habit*: Dr W. Carter, inquest statement, and 'Notes on the Maybrick Trial', op. cit.

79 **New medicines were directed**: Taken from Dr Humphreys's separate statements, particularly at the inquest. Also Carter, 'Notes on the Maybrick Trial' and his manuscript notes made post-trial, held in the New Scotland Yard Crime Museum.

79 **she told Bessie**: B. Brierley, inquest statement.

80 **Somewhere close**: A. Yapp, inquest statement.

80 *he is quite delirious*: E. Humphreys, inquest statement.

80 *Jim worse again*: Christie, *Etched in Arsenic*, p. 79.

80 **made** *a mess of it*: Trial exhibit G, HO 144.1638.A50678.

81 **upbraiding him**: This is inferred from the contents of exhibit B, which refers to previous correspondence no longer available.

81 **to read Brierley's note later**: Brierley's note has not survived but is referred to in John Baillie Knight's letter to Florence Maybrick.

81 *you can't have it dear*: E. Humphreys, inquest statement.

CHAPTER 9: THE LETTER

82 **proceeded directly upstairs**: By Matilda's own admission, under cross-examination by the inquest jury.

82 *come downstairs*: M. Briggs, inquest statement.

83 **The Nurses Institution**: Nightingale, *The Organisation of Nursing in a Large Town*.

83 **their weekly rate**: Ibid. One pound a week plus travelling and washing in 1864. No details available for 1889.

83 **Rules for nurses**: Ibid.

84 *far more patients die*: Ibid.

84 **Ellen Gore, arrived**: 'The Grassendale Mystery', *Liverpool Mercury*, 29 May 1889, and Ellen Gore, inquest statement.

84 **stick-thin**: And insolent, according to the Baroness von Roques.

84 **James, who replied**: E. Gore, additional statement at Liverpool assizes.

84 *The doctors don't know*: Ibid.

84 **painful side effects**: Belchem (ed.), *Liverpool 800*, p. 230.

85 **Making the sickroom ready**: Flanders, *The Victorian House*, p. 316.

85 **just the photographs and books**: Florence Maybrick's statement to Cleaver, sent as part of a memorial. Letter from Richard Cleaver to the Home Office, 17 August 1889, HO 144.1638.A50678.

85 **Florence handed her some medicine**: This was at about 2.30 p.m. on Wednesday 8 May, according to Ellen Gore's inquest statement.

85 **Then she showed Gore the lavatory**: Ibid.

85 **champagne had a reputation**: Dr Tran Ky and Dr F. Drouard (trans. Reginald Duquesnoy), *The Healing Power of Champagne: History, Traditions, Biology and Diet* (Bristol: Savoir Boire, 2006) p. 15.

85 **the nurse went downstairs**: E. Humphreys, assizes statement.

85 *Come quick*: *Liverpool Weekly Post*, 17 August 1889, p. 5.

86 **something was awry**: A. Yapp, post-trial statement to Treasury Solicitor, 23 August 1889, HO 144.1639.A50678. Reported too in *Liverpool Weekly Post*, 17 August 1889.

86 *never does you any good*: A. Yapp, inquest statement.

86 **trying to keep the staff away**: Interview with Alice Yapp, *New York Herald*, 21 August 1889.

87 **There were several of them**: A. Yapp, inquest statement.

87 **Mrs Maybrick saw her**: B. Brierley, inquest statement.

88 *until I have seen you once again*: Trial exhibit B, HO 144.1638.A50678.

88 **After a spattering of rain**: Weather observations supplied by the National Meteorological Archive

88 **Handing Yapp a small, crisp envelope**: Alice Yapp, inquest statement. The chemists Wokes and Hanson, at No. 25 and No. 4 Aigburth Road, both served as post offices. Yet Yapp talks about standing on the steps of the post office and this suggests a main office rather than a satellite, possibly that at 48 Aigburth Road: Kelly, *Kelly's Directory of Liverpool and Birkenhead, 1889*.

89 *Dearest!*: A. Yapp, inquest statement.

89 **Edwin in the parlour**: E. Maybrick, inquest statement. He originally said that Yapp met him in the road, but amended his statement to say that she came to him in the morning room. It seems odd, in retrospect, to have misremembered so fundamental a fact.

90 **Edwin remembered**: Ibid.

90 **he instructed the nurse to make absolutely sure**: Gore throws away medicine that Florence makes for her at 6.30, before Michael arrives; Edwin speaks generally of 'instructions' given to the nurse: inquest statements.

CHAPTER 10: STRONG SUSPICIONS

93 **to taste it**: E. Gore, assizes statement.

93 **thrown it down the sink**: E. Gore, inquest statement.

93 **sore throat**: E. Gore, assizes statement.

94 *I have strong suspicions*: This and the rest of the conversation, M. Maybrick, inquest statement.

94 **Without asking her**: Ibid.

94 **lost his self-control**: Michael Maybrick's admission that he was excited and harsh from interview printed in the *New York Herald*, 20 August 1889.

94 **a piece of ice**: According to the Baroness von Roques; interview in *Liverpool Weekly Post*, 17 August 1889, p. 5.

95 **she must get some rest**: Interview with Michael Maybrick, *New York Herald*, 17 August 1889.

95 **to return the following morning**: Dr R. Humphreys, assizes statement.

96 **opium suppository**: Dr R. Humphreys, inquest statement.

96 *They are blaming me*: A. Yapp, inquest statement.

97 *I am blamed for all this*: E. Humphreys, inquest statement.

98 *What is the matter with my brother*: Dr W. Carter, post-trial manuscript notes, New Scotland Yard Crime Museum. Also his assizes statement. These both inform the entire conversation that follows.

98 **Wondering what was coming next**: Carter, 'Notes on the Maybrick Trial'.

99 **they had conceded**: This entire conversation from Carter, post-trial manuscript notes, op. cit.

99 **Returning to the bedroom**: Ibid.

100 **They did agree ... to perform**: Dr R. Humphreys, assizes statement.

100 **To help James rest**: Dr W. Carter, assizes statement.

100 *Never*: E. Humphreys, inquest statement.

100 **Bessie saw him**: B. Brierley, inquest statement.

101 *He's had it before*: Quotation, and the rest of this scene, from Ellen Gore's inquest statement.

CHAPTER 11: TESTS

103 **Marsh's test**: Whorton, *The Arsenic Century*, p. 86.

103 **The results of a Reinsch test**: For more on the tests see ibid., p. 82ff. Arsenic was used in its generic sense to include arsenical compounds rather than simply elemental arsenic which was gritty, hard to dissolve and, since it is silvery black, also difficult to conceal.

104 **Dr Smethurst**: Whorton, op. cit., p. 103ff.

104 **ascendancy of chemistry**: Marsh first described his test in 'Account of a method of separating small quantities of arsenic from substances with which it may be mixed', *Edinburgh New Philosophical Journal*, 21, 1836, 229–36.

104 **impure copper foil**: For more on Swaine Taylor and his embarrassment, see Whorton, op. cit., pp. 102–11.

105 **expelled from the body**: Whorton, op. cit., p. 190ff.

105 **The Reinsch test used by Dr Humphreys**: The doctor used copper. Irving, *The Trial of Mrs Maybrick*, p. 93.

105 **a ruse**: E. Gore, inquest statement.

106 **He resolved to give this**: M. Maybrick, inquest statement.

106 **on the mend**: Dr W. Carter, inquest statement.

107 *How dare you change that medicine?!*: M. Maybrick, inquest statement.

107 **circulatory failure**: Dr W. Carter, inquest statement. Also his 'Notes on the Maybrick Trial'.

107 **to halt his obvious decline**: S. Wilson, inquest statement.

107 *Don't give me the wrong medicine*: Ibid.

108 *silly old darling*: Ibid.

108 *Oh Lord*: Morland, *This Friendless Lady*, p. 56. Substantiated in Thomas Lowry's inquest statement: *I did not go to the house until the 11th*.

108 *Will you cut me a sandwich*: E. Humphreys, inquest statement

109 *Tell her*: Ibid.

109 Reinsch test: Irving, op. cit., p. 115.

109 foil in a test tube: Dr W. Carter, assizes statement.

110 *I am extremely sorry*: Dr W. Carter, post-trial manuscript notes, New Scotland Yard Crime Museum.

110 re-testing James' excreta: Morland, *This Friendless Lady*, p. 57.

110 Agreeing to the plan: Dr R. Humphreys, assizes statement.

110 The nurse rubbed his hands: Ibid., and Dr William Carter assizes statement.

111 *I am sure you must have heard*: Source unclear. Quoted Graham and Emmas, *The Last Victim*, p. 4, and Christie, *Etched in Arsenic*, p. 55.

111 *apparent unconsciousness*: Carter, post-trial manuscript notes, op. cit.

CHAPTER 12: WHIPPED INTO A FRENZY

112 *specific gravity*: Dr W. Carter, assizes statement. Also his post-trial manuscript notes at New Scotland Yard Crime Museum.

112 A handful of years earlier: *Liverpool Echo*, 22 August 1889, p. 3.

113 Blyth's magisterial compendium: Blyth, *Poisons*, p. 508ff.

114 *curious remission*: Ibid., pp. 509–10.

114 peasants from Styria: Emsley, *The Elements of Murder*, p. 93ff. Also Whorton, *The Arsenic Century*, p. 270ff.

114 improved the coats of horses: Blyth, op. cit., p. 508.

114 *Chambers' Journal*: *Chambers' Journal of Popular Literature, Science, and Art*, 3:79 (1885).

115 'milk and roses': Whorton, op. cit., pp. 237–8.

115 arsenical toilet soaps: Flanders, *The Invention of Murder*, p. 233. Also Whorton, op. cit., p. 274.

115 Toxic to most plants: Whorton, op. cit., p. 9.

115 Arsenic in household goods: Blyth, op. cit., p. 499ff. Flanders, *The Victorian House*, p. 153.

116 *Lancet*: R. H. Brett, 'Arsenical Fly-Papers', *Lancet*, vol. 75, no. 1902, February 1860, 149–50.

116 *slow poisoning of our little ones*: *The Times*, 12 September 1884, p. 6.

116 *mere folly*: Whorton, op. cit., p. 219ff.

117 **schedule of poisons**: The Sale of Poisons and Pharmacy Act. Ibid., p. 139ff.

117 **peppermint drops**: Whorton, op. cit.

117 **babies dying**: *Lancet*, 1879 (2), 96.

117 **Easily suspended**: Dr Donkin's paper in *Pharmaceutical Journal and Transactions*, 3, third series, 1872–3, 472.

117 *Minsterborough*: By Humphrey Sandwith (1876); *The Green of the Period*, Anon (1869). See also *Chambers' Journal of Popular Literature, Science, and Art*, 18, (1862), 165–72.

117 **Lucretia**: By E. Bulwer Lytton (1866), vol. 6, chapter 21.

118 *she had hardly time*: Flaubert, *Madame Bovary*, part III, chapter 8.

118 **educated ... in fear**: Whorton, op. cit., p. 107.

118 **upwards of a third**: Ibid., p. viii.

118 **subversion of the role of the caregiver**: Robb, 'Circe in Crinoline'.

118 *If you feel a deadly sensation*: *The Times*, 15 December 1855.

119 **Horrified and excited**: *Liverpool Weekly Post*, 17 August 1889, p. 5.

120 **In the corner was**: S. Wilson, A. Yapp and M. Maybrick, inquest statements.

121 **present them to Michael**: E. Maybrick, inquest statement.

121 **forbidden them from saying goodbye**: Ibid.

121 **only the wardrobe was locked**: Ibid. Also interview with the Baroness von Roques, *Liverpool Weekly Post*, 17 August 1889, p. 5.

121 **Constance found**: C. Hughes, inquest statement. Also M. Maybrick, inquest statement.

121 **not yet ten o'clock**: M. Maybrick, inquest statement. Also *Liverpool Courier*, 29 May 1889.

122 **dropped the key into his pocket**: E. Maybrick, inquest statement.

122 **back into a stupor**: Maybrick, *Mrs Maybrick's Own Story*, p. 24.

CHAPTER 13: SCRUTINY

123 *if I would call her mad*: Letter from Baroness von Roques to the Secretary of State, 4 August 1892, HO 144.1639.A50678.

124 **Thomas at his side**: Dr W. Carter, post-trial manuscript notes, New Scotland Yard Crime Museum. Thomas is an inference; Carter called him 'Michael's married brother'.

124 *the unhappy woman*: Ibid.

125 *no longer mistress of this house*: Morland, *This Friendless Lady*, p. 62.

125 *sanguineous discharge*: Dr R. Hopper, assizes statement.

125 **corrupt and subversive**: Boyle, *Black Swine in the Sewers of Hampstead*, p. 171.

125 **Later that afternoon**: Dr R. Humphreys, assizes statement, op. cit. He says

he informed the police at about 9 a.m. but this does not elide with Carter's notes that Michael visited him during the morning, before the results were known. Since the police did not arrive until evening it seems likely that they were told later in the day than Humphreys remembered. Richard Baxendale deposed (inquest statement) that he was informed at 8 p.m.

126 **now half-empty:** E. Davies, inquest statement. Dr W. Carter, post-trial manuscript notes, op. cit.

126 **two and three grains:** E. Davies, inquest statement.

126 **nine o'clock on Sunday evening:** R. Baxendale, inquest statement.

126 **unlocked the door to the dressing room:** Ibid.

126 **Gathering them all up:** Ibid.

126 **Description of Bryning:** Image in *Liverpool Echo*, 2 August 1889. Also *Liverpool Review*, 8 June 1889, p. 13, and Lancashire Police Records, PLA 11/10/315.

127 **Once a factory weaver:** Lancashire Police Records, op. cit. Also 1871 census.

128 **At half-past four:** The post-mortem notes list death +44 hours. The following description of the post-mortem is taken from the various doctors' inquest statements, from the statements at the July assizes, from Dr Carter's published medical notes, op. cit., and from Trial exhibit J, HO 144.1638.A50678.

129 **most damage in his digestive tract:** Whorton, *The Arsenic Century*, p. 66ff.

130 **several other symptoms ... were not present:** Pathological symptoms of arsenical poisoning post-mortem, from ibid., p. 66ff.

130 **purging action:** Blyth, *Poisons*, p. 521.

131 **Dozens of products:** The list of the bottles analysed by the Royal Institution Library is dated between 14 May and 1 June 1889 and is exhaustive. HO 144.1638.A50678.

131 **striking, red-faced figure:** *Liverpool Review*, 8 June 1889.

131 **In the linen closet:** J. Davenport, inquest statement.

132 **twelve and twenty-four local men:** Ian A. Burney, *Bodies of Evidence: Medicine and the Politics of the English Inquest, 1830–1926* (Baltimore: Johns Hopkins University Press, 2000), p. 5ff.

132 *I am about to say something to you*: I. Bryning, inquest statement.

CHAPTER 14: LOCKED IN

133 *Up to a very recent period*: *Liverpool Mercury*, 14 May 1889.

133 **independent advice:** R. Cleaver, statement to Home Office, 17 August 1889, HO 144.1638.A50678.

133 **a lady ... held on a serious charge:** Ibid.

133 **without the relevant authority:** A. Cleaver, statement to Home Office, 17 August 1889, HO 144.1638.A50678.

134 **met with Douglas Steel:** R. Cleaver, statement to Home Office, op. cit.

134 *What shall I do?*: This and following conversation, Irving, *The Trial of Mrs Maybrick*, p. 41.

134 *I am writing to you:* Trial exhibit A, HO 144.1638.A50678.

135 ALLEGED POISONING OF A LIVERPOOL MERCHANT: *Liverpool Courier*, 15 May 1889.

136 **nurse and a policeman hovered:** A. Cleaver, statement to Home Office, op. cit.

136 **James' funeral:** Details of the cortège and names of mourners from *Liverpool Echo*, 16 May 1889 and *Liverpool Mercury*, 17 May 1889. Also *Liverpool Weekly Post*, 17 August 1889 (interview with Baroness von Roques) and Maybrick, *Mrs Maybrick's Own Story*.

137 **fired off telegrams:** *Liverpool Weekly Post*, 17 August 1889, p. 5.

137 **seep into the New York press:** 'An English Poisoning Case', *New York Times*, 19 May 1889.

137 *nice state of affairs!*: *Liverpool Weekly Post*, 17 August 1889. This is the source for the rest of the Baroness's experience of arriving at Battlecrease.

138 **looking-glass world:** Ibid. *Through the Looking Glass, and What Alice Found There* by Lewis Carroll was published in 1871. That the Baroness was astonished is made clear in the interview she gave later.

139 **held there forcibly:** Maybrick, *Mrs Maybrick's Own Story*, p. 30.

139 **Among them were the magistrate:** Various reports, including 'The Mysterious Death at Grassendale', *Liverpool Mercury*, 20 May 1889, from which most of the detail of this scene is taken.

140 **Her face as white as the bed sheets:** Ibid.

141 **demand to be told:** MacDougall, *The Maybrick Case*, p. 12.

141 **two long hours:** Ibid., and Maybrick, op. cit., p. 33.

142 **entry to Walton Gaol:** From Maybrick, op. cit., p. 33. Also, generally, from Rich, *Recollections of a Prison Governor*.

CHAPTER 15: SCANDAL

143 **sent the remainder:** R. Baxendale, inquest statement.

144 SUDDEN DEATH: *Daily News*, 20 May 1889. See also, on the same date, *London Standard*, p. 5, and *London Morning Post*, p. 9.

144 *a third party*: *Daily News*, 20 May 1889.

144 **began to destroy his copies:** Alfred Brierley, in his post-trial affidavit for Richard Cleaver, swears that he no longer has copies of the correspondence. HO.1638.A50678.

145 **robust and even rapacious:** Glendinning, *Trollope*, p. 397.

145 *dragging* [them] *down*: Oscar Wilde, *An Ideal Husband* (1895), Act 1.

146 **entertained and delighted**: As Richard D. Altick maintains generally in *Victorian Studies in Scarlet*.

146 **Deviant women sacrificed to gods of domestic conformity**: These statistics and arguments are taken in the main from Zedner, *Women, Crime and Custody in Victorian England*, p. 27ff.

146 **curiosity and excitement**: Morris, *Double Jeopardy*, chapter 2.

146 **stability in a fast-changing world**: Zedner, op. cit., p.13

146 **complex ideals of womanhood**: Ibid, p. 11; also Morris, op. cit., p. 44.

147 **newspapers had taken over from the pulpit**: H. R. Fox Bourne, *English Newspapers: Chapters in the History of Journalism*, vol. 2 (1887), p. 390, quoted in Knelman, *Twisting in the Wind*, p. 42.

147 *exceedingly important statements*: 'The Suspected Murder at Liverpool', *Daily News*, 23 May 1889.

147 *Lucretia Borgia* incarnate: For example, *Milwaukee Sentinel*, 24 May 1889, p. 5; also *Chicago Inter Ocean*, 24 May 1889, p. 5.

147 *A Lady of Many Husbands*: *Atlanta Constitution*, 1 June 1889.

148 **twelve hundred pounds a year from her father**: 'Death of Mr Maybricks' Brother', *Lloyd's Weekly Newspaper*, 26 May 1889.

148 **[involves] *such a momentous issue***: 'Battlecrease House', *Liverpool Review*, 25 May 1889.

149 **forbade even her solicitor**: R. Cleaver, statement to Home Office, 17 August 1889, HO 144.1638.A50678.

149 **the huge prison**: Description from Rich, *Recollections of a Prison Governor*. Also Midwinter, *Old Liverpool*, chapter 3.

149 **a few small items**: From *Liverpool Echo*, 22 August 1889, p. 3. There is confusion about what type of cell Florence Maybrick occupied. In her memoir she writes of being moved from a dirty cell to a larger one costing five shillings a week.

149 **she wanted to scream**: Maybrick, *Mrs Maybrick's Own Story*, p. 36.

150 **crowded with people**: This and following details of the morning taken from 'The Mysterious Death at Grassendale', *Liverpool Mercury*, 28 May 1889.

151 *your solicitor is present*: Ibid.

CHAPTER 16: PUBLIC TESTIMONY

152 **the *idly curious***: 'The Grassendale Mystery', *Liverpool Mercury*, 29 May 1889. Most of the following chapter is taken from this two-page feature, as well as from the *Liverpool Courier* of the same date. The

arrangement of the room is from illustration in the *Graphic*, 15 June 1889.

152 **around five hundred people**: *The Times*, 6 June 1889.

153 **mourners at James' funeral**: *Liverpool Mercury*, 20 May 1889.

153 *sign of animus*: 'The Grassendale Mystery', op. cit.

154 *I cannot say I saw her doing it*: *Liverpool Courier*, 29 May 1889.

155 *light green notepaper*: 'The Grassendale Mystery', op. cit.

155 *Dearest*: Trial exhibit B, HO 144.1638.A50678, and ibid.

156 **badly scared**: 'The Grassendale Mystery', op. cit.

157 *complain of the conduct of his wife*: S. Wilson, inquest statement, and 'The Charge of Poisoning at Aigburth', *The Times*, 29 May 1889.

158 *I thought it was suggested*: This and following quotations from 'The Charge of Poisoning at Aigburth', op. cit.

158 *acquaintances, certainly*: C. Samuelson, inquest statement.

159 **relay to their city offices**: *Liverpool Review*, 8 June 1889, p. 13.

159 WHAT THE SERVANTS SAW: 'The Aigburth Mystery', *Liverpool Courier*, 29 May 1889.

159 *very questionable sentences*: 'Current Foreign Topics', *New York Times*, 29 May 1889.

160 **achieving the right level of gentility**: See Davidoff, 'Mastered for Life', for discussion about hierarchy and deference in late-nineteenth-century households

160 **Around a third**: Ibid.

160 **the disloyal servant**: For more see Trodd, *Domestic Crime in the Victorian Novel*, pp. 49–61.

161 *this grand isolation*: 'The Grey Woman', in Elizabeth Gaskell, *Cousin Phillis and Other Tales* (1861).

161 *too old for a young baby*: Christie, *Etched in Arsenic*, p. 37.

161 *the nurse and lodge keeper conversing*: Aunspaugh letters, Christie Papers.

161 **private and public spheres**: Robb, 'Circe in Crinoline'.

161 *Why is it*: Braddon, *Aurora Floyd*, vol. 1, chapter 16; Trodd, op. cit., p. 65.

161 *servants are ... terrible liars*: *Liverpool Citizen*, 21 August 1889, in defence of Alice Yapp.

161 *Your servants listen*: Braddon, op. cit.; Trodd, op. cit., p. 45ff.

162 **manifestation of domestic disorder**: See Trodd, op. cit., p. 5.

162 **destiny as well as a destination**: Glendinning, *Trollope*, p. 194; and for Trollope on letters, see p. 368ff.

162 *startling nature of the evidence*: 'The Grassendale Mystery', *Liverpool Mercury*, 30 May 1889.

CHAPTER 17: FIRST VERDICT

163 **The police arrived:** Exhumation reports from *Liverpool Mercury* and *Garston and Woolton Reporter*, both 1 June 1889. Dr Humphreys and Inspector Baxendale confirm the date of the exhumation in their inquest statements.

164 *the case ... is a weak one:* 'The Grassendale Mystery', *Liverpool Mercury*, 1 June 1889.

164 *young, anxious and careworn:* Ibid.

165 **large numbers began to mill:** Ibid.

165 **mostly women:** 'The Maybrick Mystery', *Liverpool Mercury*, 6 June 1889.

165 *felt some repugnance:* Dr R. Hopper, inquest statement.

166 *symptoms of arsenical poisoning:* Ibid.

167 **twenty different irritant medicines:** Winslow, *Recollections of Forty Years*, p. 156, and Dr W. Carter, inquest statement.

167 *These were the only times:* T. Lowry, inquest statement.

167 *self-important:* *Liverpool Review*, 13 June 1889, p. 13.

168 *neatly attired:* *Liverpool Weekly News*, 8 June 1889.

169 *great number of medicine bottles about the house:* M. Briggs, inquest statement.

170 **strong force of police:** 'The Aigburth Poisoning Case', *The Times*, 6 June 1889. Also *Liverpool Review*, 8 June 1889, p. 13.

170 **thinking at first:** E. Maybrick, inquest statement.

170 *I knew he used to take certain medicines:* Ibid.

171 *sang froid:* *Liverpool Weekly Post*, 8 June 1889.

171 *business-like little gentleman:* Ibid., and 'The Maybrick Mystery', op. cit.

171 *dull scientific recital:* *Liverpool Weekly Post*, 8 June 1889.

172 **twelve grains in the glass tumbler:** *Liverpool Mercury*, 7 June 1889.

172 **a hundredth of a grain in the kidney:** E. Davies, inquest statement.

172 *if a person dies:* Ibid.

172 *Put aside any matter:* 'The Aigburth Case', *The Times*, 7 June 1889.

173 **some of the public surged:** *Liverpool Review*, 8 June 1889, p. 13.

173 **police cab ... approached:** 'Verdict of Willful Murder!', *Liverpool Mercury*, 7 June 1889.

CHAPTER 18: DAMAGED OR DEVIANT?

174 *square set and determined:* *Liverpool Weekly Post*, 8 June 1889.

174 **She expected:** Maybrick, *Mrs Maybrick's Own Story*, p. 36ff.

175 *there to take your trial:* *Liverpool Mercury*, 7 June 1889.

175 **freezingly polite**: *Liverpool Weekly Post*, 8 June 1889.

175 **suppressed terror**: *Liverpool Mercury*, 7 June 1889.

175 *By the advice of Mr Pickford*: Closing statements attached to inquest depositions, 6 June 1889.

175 **Mr Mulholland, had been present**: Letter from Brierley's solicitors Banks and Kendall to the Home Office, 6 July 1889, HO 144.1639.A50678.

176 **the exhumation seemed to suggest**: 'The Maybrick Mystery', *Liverpool Mercury*, 6 June 1889.

176 **She would remain ... for a week**: The grocer was Mrs Pretty and she sent fruit (Maybrick, op. cit., p. 38). Florence Maybrick, in her memoir, wrote that she returned to Walton after a night but contemporary newspapers disagree (ibid., p. 41).

176 **poring over the newspaper accounts**: 'The Maybrick Mystery', *Liverpool Mercury*, 6 June 1889.

177 **petulant**: Ibid.

177 **witnesses were bound over**: *Liverpool Mercury*, 7 June 1889.

177 **Large groups of people**: *Liverpool Weekly Post*, 8 June 1889.

177 *very extraordinary case*: 'The Maybrick Mystery', *Liverpool Mercury*, 6 June 1889.

177 *without exciting suspicion*: 'The Aigburth Poisoning Case', *The Times*, 6 June 1889.

177 *startling and dramatic*: *Liverpool Weekly Post*, 8 June 1889.

177 *a London soap boiler*: Ibid.

178 *a rush of black liquid*: Gustave Flaubert, *Madame Bovary* (1856), part III, chapter 9.

178 **contemptible bounder**: *I have been maligned, persecuted and misjudged*: Liverpool newspapers of 16 August 1889 report a statement made through his solicitors and an interview with the London edition of the *New York Herald* on the 14th.

179 **often linked with sexual energy**: Knelman, *Twisting in the Wind*, p. 262.

179 **traduced their role**: Zedner, op. cit., p. 40.

179 **Medrington's**: 'The Maybrick Mystery', *Liverpool Mercury*, 11 June 1889. National Archives photographs Ref 1/396 (291-296) and 1/397 (247ff).

179 **the wrong choice**: Described by Knelman, op. cit., p. 15, as the 'embodiment of the classic Victorian conflict'.

179 **remarkably 'cool'**: 'The Maybrick Mystery', *Liverpool Mercury*, 10 June 1889.

179 **promiscuity ... an indication of criminality**: Knelman, op. cit., p. 232.

179 **'The Girl of the Period'**: For much more on the effect of the rise of the New Woman on attitudes to female crime, see Zedner, op. cit. and Hartman, *Victorian Murderesses*.

180 *people don't do such things*: Kate Chopin, *The Awakening* (1899), chapter 17.

180 *her position in the universe*: Ibid., chapter 6.

180 *All the moralities tell them*: John Stuart Mill, *The Subjection of Women* (1869), chapter 1.

180 *weariness, disappointment*: Ibid., chapter 4.

180 the male fantasy: For a summary of the argument between Ruskin and Mill, see Kate Millett, 'Ruskin vs Mill', chapter 7 of Vicinus (ed.), *Suffer and Be Still*.

181 an increase in crime: L. O. Pike, *History of Crime in England*, vol. 2 (London: Smith, Elder & Co., 1876), p. 529. See also Zedner, *Women, Crime and Custody in Victorian England*, p. 70ff.

181 increasingly pursued by the law: Hartman, op. cit., p. 132.

181 Madeleine admitted: Whorton, *The Arsenic Century*, p. 262ff.

183 how to construct beautiful homes: For example, Clarence Cook, *The House Beautiful* (1881).

183 paintings hung on the walls: Frances Wilson, *How to Survive the Titanic: or, The Sinking of J. Bruce Ismay* (London: Bloomsbury, 2011), p. 82. The Walker Art Gallery bought *Dante's Dream* by Rossetti in 1881, *Isabella* by Millais in 1884 and much other Pre-Raphaelite art during the 1880s and 1890s.

184 *note of sympathy*: Maybrick, op. cit., p. 38ff.

184 Apart from her mother: Ibid.

184 most entrenched and bitter critics: Trollope also knew this. See, e.g., *An Eye for an Eye*, chapters 7 and 9. The issue is noted by Trollope's biographer T. H. S. Escott and quoted in Glendinning, *Trollope*, p. 399.

184 *'something wrong'*: *Liverpool Weekly News*, 8 June 1889, quoted in Jones, *The Maybrick A to Z*, p. 176.

CHAPTER 19: SECOND VERDICT

187 less than half the amount due: Christie, *Etched in Arsenic*, p. 66.

187 *maligned, persecuted*: Interview with the London edition of the *New York Herald*, 14 August 1889.

187 He would tell a journalist: *Boston Herald*, 13 September 1889, p. 3.

187 appealing ... for financial support: The Baroness also tried to remortgage a New York property at 27 East 14th Street in which her daughter had an interest in order to secure Richard Cleaver's fee; see *Atlanta Constitution*, 25 October 1889, and Christie, op. cit., p. 66.

187 taken from Lark Lane: *The Times*, 13 June 1889, p. 10.

188 passing over rough stone setts: Description is taken from my own visit

and from an article on the new building published in the *Builder*, 7 August 1884.

190 **Two magistrates:** *The Times*, 13 June 1889, p. 10.

190 *dropped in to get a good view:* *Liverpool Review*, 15 June 1889, p. 3.

190 **Put the prisoner in the dock:** *Liverpool Mercury*, 13 June 1889.

190 **Defendant and Counsel:** Morris, *Double Jeopardy*, p. 32.

191 *she wore a long jacket:* *Liverpool Mercury*, 13 June 1889.

191 **a reprisal of the inquest:** *The Times*, 13 June 1889, p. 10. The bulk of the details of the County Sessions House events are taken from this source, as are all the following quotations from witnesses, unless otherwise noted.

192 **hair centre-parted:** Illustration in *Liverpool Review*, 15 June 1889, p. 4.

192 **reveal the whole secret of the case:** *Liverpool Mercury*, 13 June 1889.

192 *take less physic:* Ibid.

193 *disgusting:* *Liverpool Review*, 15 June 1889, p. 3.

193 **On seating herself:** *Liverpool Mercury*, 14 June 1889.

193 **Florence's face … was impenetrable:** *Liverpool Review*, 15 June 1889, p. 4.

193 *sea captain:* Ibid., and *Liverpool Mercury*, 14 June 1889.

194 *was there not a telegram:* *The Times*, 14 June 1889, p. 7.

195 *what sort of poison:* Ibid.

195 *faculty of silence:* *Liverpool Mercury*, 14 June 1889.

196 **Clutching the thin iron rail:** We do not absolutely know that Florence Maybrick descended these stairs from the dock to the cells though we know that she was conveyed from the cell corridor to an exit – reportedly Mill Lane – in order to be returned to Walton Gaol so she must at some stage have descended to it. She could not have come via any other staircase without being taken into parts of the County Sessions House reserved for witnesses, lawyers or judges. Nevertheless, although likely, it is not proven that her egress from court was via these steps and the fear and concentration described in the paragraph are conjecture inferred but not explicitly stated in her memoir.

196 **Why had no one asked:** Maybrick, *Mrs Maybrick's Own Story*, Part II: Analysis of the Maybrick Case restates all these points (and more).

197 **the horses were urged forward:** 'The Maybrick Case', *Liverpool Mercury*, 15 June 1889.

CHAPTER 20: MAKING IT STICK

198 **Items … being delivered:** Lancashire Records, PLA 11/13/62; list of items delivered for analysis, with dates of delivery, HO 144.1639

198   conjecture: *Liverpool Weekly Review*, 15 June 1889, p. 3.

198   *rather a good-looking lot*: Ibid., p. 4.

198   illustrations of the unhappy couple: *The Porcupine*, 15 June 1889, p. 11.

199   *woman of first-class social training*: *Liverpool Weekly Review*, 15 June 1889, p. 3.

199   the prosecution team: 'The Maybrick Case', *Liverpool Mercury*, 22 June 1889; Christie, *Etched in Arsenic*, p. 71.

199   took additional statements: 'Additional Statements taken at Liverpool Summer Assizes on July 3rd, 4th and 5th 1889', HO 144.1639.A50678.

200   Thomas Stevenson: Obituary, *The Times*, 27 July 1908, p. 3; his record of this delivery and his report in HO 144.1638.A50678.

200   *he had made arrangements*: 'Additional statements taken at Liverpool Summer Assizes on 3, 4, 5 July 1889', HO 144.1639.A50678.

200   fictional adulteress: For example, Emma Bovary after sleeping with Rodolphe.

201   She had kept the letter: Trial exhibit H, HO 144.1638.A50678.

201   Sympathy might have undone: Maybrick, *Mrs Maybrick's Own Story*, p. 38.

201   thought to write a note: Letter from Florence Maybrick to her mother, sent from Walton Gaol, 21 July 1889, reprinted in Morland, *This Friendless Lady*, facing p. 142.

201   living under an alias: *Evening Express*, 14 August 1889.

202   several times a week: Ibid.

202   *The trouble to her*: 'To the Editors of the Liverpool Mercury', *Liverpool Mercury*, 19 June 1889.

202   placed advertisements: 'Re James Maybrick, Deceased', *Liverpool Mercury*, 19 June 1889.

202   *connoisseurs and friends*: *Garston and Woolton Reporter*, 13 July 1889, p. 4.

202   incessant mental effort: Maybrick, op. cit., p. 46.

202   to test the theory: Reported in *Liverpool Echo*, 15 June 1889, p. 3.

202   instructed his team: 'The Maybrick Case', *Liverpool Mercury*, 17 June 1889.

203   abundant evidence: 'Mrs Maybrick Trial', *New York Times*, 26 July 1889.

203   hunger for poisons: *New Orleans Times Democrat*, reprinted *Liverpool Mercury*, 29 June 1889.

203   Arnold Cleaver sailed: 'Mrs Maybrick Trial', *New York Times*, 26 July 1889. It was reported only that one of the Cleavers sailed and that it was Arnold is an assumption since Richard, the senior partner, was crucial in the briefing of Florence Maybrick's defence team.

203   take them to Wales: Interview with Alice Yapp, *New York Herald*, 21 August 1889.

203 **one other woman:** Returns of County of Lancaster, Criminal Registers, 25 July 1889, HO 27 piece 213, p. 72.

203 **Sir Charles Russell:** *Daily Mirror*, 15 July 1904, p. 4.

204 *tittle-tattle of servants:* This letter is lost. It was dated 28 June and is quoted in Irving, *The Trial of Mrs Maybrick*, p. xxiii.

204 **arriving in Liverpool:** Accounts differ about when he arrived; some suggest it was as late as 30 July (*Liverpool Mercury*, 30 July 1889, p. 5).

204 **Physically big:** Charles Kingston, *Famous Judges and Famous Trials* (London: S. Paul, 1923), p. 33.

204 **noticeably clouded:** Emsley, *The Elements of Murder*, pp. 171–93. Stephen's brother Leslie married William Makepeace Thackeray's daughter Minnie. His daughters by his second marriage were Virginia Woolf and Vanessa Bell. He wrote the biography of his brother after his death.

204 *I hardly know how:* Irving, op. cit., p. 360ff.

205 *You must use your own discretion:* **Liverpool Mercury*, 30 July 1889, p. 5.

206 *the strange story:* *Liverpool Mercury*, 1 August 1889, p. 6.

206 **Special provision:** *Liverpool Mercury*, 30 July 1889, p. 5; also 'The Maybrick Trial', *Liverpool Mercury*, 31 July 1889.

206 **on edge:** 'The Maybrick Trial', *Liverpool Mercury*, 31 July 1889.

CHAPTER 21: THE TRIAL: DAY ONE

207 **St George's Hall description:** Kelly, *Kelly's Post Office Directory 1894*.

208 **as she hoped she would:** Letter from Florence Maybrick, quoted in Christie, *Etched in Arsenic*, p. 69.

208 **two wardresses:** *Liverpool Mercury*, 1 August 1889, p. 7.

208 **already buried:** Maybrick, *Mrs Maybrick's Own Story*, p. 52.

209 **jurymen:** Irving, *The Trial of Mrs Maybrick*, p. 3.

209 *with an elastic step:* *Liverpool Mercury*, 1 August 1889, p. 6.

210 **trumpet fanfare:** Ibid.

211 *exceedingly attractive appearance:* *Lloyd's Weekly Newspaper*, 4 August 1889, p. 3.

211 *downcast eyes:* *Liverpool Mercury*, 1 August 1889, p. 6.

211 **Few members of the public:** By the late nineteenth century, women made up less than a quarter of those tried for murder. Zedner, *Women, Crime and Custody in Victorian England*, p. 38.

211 **almost a third of those:** Knelman, *Twisting in the Wind*, p. 15ff.

211 **sense of chivalry:** Ibid., p. 236. See also Heidensohn, *Women and Crime*, p. 88; also Hartman, *Victorian Murderesses* for similar arguments.

212 **fascination and of revulsion**: See Knelman, op. cit., p. 15ff.

212 **proof, to some**: Ibid.; also Heidensohn, op. cit.

212 *clean and polished outside*: Trollope, *Can you Forgive Her?* (1864–5), chapter 6.

213 **angel or medusa**: Trodd, *Domestic Crime in the Victorian Novel*, p. 134.

213 **John Addison**: *Liverpool Mercury*, 1 August 1889, p. 6.

214 **not at all unusual**: Details of Addison's opening speech in *The Times*, 1 August 1889, p. 12, from which all the following quotes are taken unless otherwise detailed. See also Irving, op. cit., p. 3ff.

215 *The first question*: *Liverpool Mercury*, 1 August 1889, p. 7.

215 **pinches of snuff**: Ibid.

CHAPTER 22: A STRANGE FASCINATION

216 *No, thank you*: *Liverpool Mercury*, 1 August 1889.

216 **unforeseen revelations**: Ibid.

217 *complaints on both sides*: Ibid.

218 *very bitterly*: *The Times*, 1 August 1889.

218 *deceased's habits*: Ibid.

218 *fashionable type and cut*: *Lloyd's Weekly Newspaper*, 4 August 1889, p. 3.

219 *dramatic incidents*: *Liverpool Mercury*, 2 August 1889, p. 6.

219 **to avert ... further scandal**: See, e.g., 'Is She a Poisoner?', *Chicago Daily Inter Ocean*, 1 August 1889, and 'Mrs Maybrick on Trial', *New York Times*, 1 August 1889.

219 **walking *unconcernedly***: *Liverpool Mercury*, 1 August 1889, p. 7.

220 **the proprieties of her generation**: Her interests had been watched during the inquest and magisterial hearing by London lawyer J. Treeve Edgecombe but he was absent too, bedridden after an accident. *Liverpool Mercury*, 1 August 1889, p. 7.

220 *strange spell of fascination*: *Liverpool Mercury*, 2 August 1889, p. 6.

221 **cleaning the silk dress**: *The Times*, 2 August 1889, p. 10.

221 *I did not think of it*: Irving, *The Trial of Mrs Maybrick*, p. 78.

222 *understand the position of things*: Ibid., p. 67ff for the rest of her testimony under cross-examination as it follows here.

223 *follow this again*: Ibid., p. 70ff for the rest of this testimony.

223 *it was at my suggestion*: M. Callery, additional statement at Liverpool assizes, July 1889, HO 144.1639.A50678.

224 *On your oath, girl*: Irving, op. cit., p. 72.

224 *Every ear ... was strained*: 'Aigburth Poisoning Case', *Liverpool Mercury*, 2 August 1889.

225 since the previous October: Irving, op. cit., p. 80.

226 declining ... water: *Liverpool Mercury*, 2 August 1889, p. 6.

226 tainted food: Ibid.

CHAPTER 23: THE CONTRARIETY OF THINGS

227 *It is useless to go over this ground*: *Liverpool Mercury*, 2 August 1889, p. 7.

227 Was this ... fatal meal?: Emsley, in *Elements of Murder*, thinks that it was. For his argument, see pp. 178–81.

228 *jaded*: *Liverpool Echo*, 2 August 1889, p. 4.

228 quietly monotonous: Ibid.

228 *seen them on any occasion*: Irving, *The Trial of Mrs Maybrick*, p. 104.

228 *not of necessity*: Ibid., p. 107.

229 *congestion of the stomach*: This and following testimony, ibid., p. 107.

230 meaningful looks: *Liverpool Echo*, 2 August 1889, p. 4.

230 signs of exhaustion: Ibid.

231 Carter's testimony: This and Russell's cross-examination, Irving, op. cit., p. 118ff.

231 *You were asked*: Ibid., p. 124ff.

232 *tatterdemalion viragoes*: *Liverpool Echo*, 2 August 1889, p. 4.

233 ugly and ridiculous: See, e.g., Trollope, *Barchester Towers*, quoted in Glendinning, *Trollope*, p. 229.

233 *throws strong light*: *Pall Mall Gazette*, 2 August 1889.

233 women would not be admitted to the Bar: Morris, *Women, Crime, and Criminal Justice*, p. 42.

233 women enjoyed more freedoms: The Married Women's Property Act 1882 (45 & 46 Vict c.75) significantly altered the law regarding married women's property rights.

234 Hankering after a new set of values: Strachey, *The Cause*, chapter 12.

234 loathsome, self-assertive: Ibid., chapter 4.

234 family would decline: Zedner, Women, *Crime and Custody in Victorian England*, p. 69ff.

234 established power of men: Knelman, *Twisting in the Wind*, p. 233.

234 Ouida: Ouida, 'The New Woman', taking the term from Sarah Grand's essay, 'The New Aspect of the Woman Question'. Both were published in issue 158 of the *North American Review* in 1894.

234 by women, about women: See Boumelha, *Thomas Hardy and Women*, pp. 63–4.

234   **sexual and marital themes:** Ibid., p. 7.

234   *what is a woman?*: Pykett, *The 'Improper Feminine'*, p. 137.

234   **prevailing sexual code:** Ledger, *The New Woman*, introduction. The rest of this argument is strongly reliant on the case Ledger makes in her book.

234   **warfare within gender relations:** Ibid., quoting Elaine Showalter.

235   **Lady Monk:** Trollope, *Can You Forgive Her?* (1864–5), chapter 48.

236   **pursued as a murderess:** Hartman, *Victorian Murderesses*, p. 132.

CHAPTER 24: SCIENTIFIC TRUTH

237   *recondite technicalities*: *Liverpool Mercury*, 3 August 1889, p. 6.

238   *I should not be able to do so*: This and Barron's testimony following, Irving, *The Trial of Mrs Maybrick*, p. 125ff.

238   *warm tones*: *Liverpool Mercury*, 3 August 1889, p. 6.

239   *none were locked*: Irving, op. cit., p. 129.

239   **Spare of form:** *Liverpool Mercury*, 3 August 1889, p. 6.

239   **Florence watched ... closely:** Ibid.

240   *little drops of dried skim*: Edward Davies's testimony, Irving, op. cit., p. 129ff.

240   **As to the flypapers:** In 1890 Davies's analysis of the flypapers was repeated by a Dr Coates who reduced this quantity by half. See Irving, op. cit., p. xv.

240   **something more like excitement:** *Lloyd's Weekly Newspaper*, 4 August 1889, p. 3.

240   *it requires a strong glass*: This and Davies's following testimony, Irving, op. cit., p. 135ff.

241   **Magnifying glasses were passed around:** *Liverpool Mercury*, 3 August 1889, p. 6.

242   *semi-comatose*: *Lloyd's Weekly Newspaper*, 4 August 1889, p. 3.

243   **Gore confirmed:** This and Gore's following testimony, Irving, op. cit., p. 143ff.

243   **as if to demand an encore:** *Liverpool Mercury*, 3 August 1889, p. 6.

244   **Gore's continuing testimony:** Irving, op. cit., p. 148ff.

CHAPTER 25: DARK CLOUDS GATHERING

248   **Callery's testimony:** Irving, *The Trial of Mrs Maybrick*, p. 152ff.

249   **beginning to get muddled:** For example, ibid., pp. 152, 153, 155.

249   *silly old darling*: Ibid., p. 155.

249   **Alfred Schweisso:** Ibid., p. 156.

249 **Description of Stevenson:** *Liverpool Mercury*, 5 August 1889, p. 6.

250 *could not find it*: Irving, op. cit., p. 158. See also Stevenson's deposition, 10 August 1889, forwarded to the Home Office by assize clerk, HO 144.1638.A50678.

250 *fatal dose*: Irving, op. cit., p. 159.

250 **retard decomposition:** Whorton, *The Arsenic Century*, p. 68.

250 *smaller dose than that may kill*: This and rest of cross-examination, Irving, p. 161ff.

251 **Tuesday or Wednesday:** *Liverpool Mercury*, 5 August 1889, p. 7.

251 *Have you a definite case*: Irving, op. cit., p. 167ff.

252 **gesture of despair:** *Liverpool Mercury*, 5 August 1889, p. 6.

253 **tremble dramatically:** 'The Maybrick Murder Trial', *Liverpool Courier*, 5 August 1889.

254 **'double barrelled':** 'The Maybrick Murder Trial', *Liverpool Courier*, 6 August 1889.

254 *snap the thread*: *Liverpool Mercury*, 5 August 1889, p. 7. For Sir Charles Russell's opening speech see also the same newspaper, and also *Lloyd's Weekly Newspaper*, 4 August 1889, p. 1.

254 *effect upon everybody*: *Liverpool Mercury*, 5 August 1889.

254 *In view of the warning*: Ibid.

255 *manly enough*: Ibid.

255 **He would allow Russell's request:** Ibid.

255 **tears falling:** Ibid. For Sir Charles Russell's opening speech, see also Irving, op. cit., p. 176ff.

256 **Bateson:** The afternoon's defence testimony from Irving, op. cit., p. 185ff.

256 **Stansell:** *Liverpool Review*, 10 August 1889, p. 11.

257 **Adelaide Bartlett:** Tidy's Treasury deposition in the case of Adelaide Bartlett, 1886. Copy in Stewart Evans's private collection.

257 **England's leading forensic physician:** George K. Behlmer, 'Grave Doubts: Victorian Medicine, Moral Panic, and the Signs of Death', *Journal of British Studies*, vol. 42, no. 2, April 2003, 206–35.

CHAPTER 26: A HUNDREDFOLD CURIOSITY

260 *absorbing drama*: *Lloyd's Weekly Newspaper*, 4 August 1889, pp. 1 and 4.

260 **bowed to the judge:** *Reynolds's Weekly Newspaper*, 4 August 1889, p. 8.

260 **taunted the police:** J. H. H. Gaute and Robin Odell, *The New Murderer's Who's Who* (London: Headline, 1989), pp. 188–9.

261 **moral purity:** Knelman, *Twisting in the Wind*, p. 236.

261 *every step*: L. O. Pike, *History of Crime in England*, vol. 2 (London: Smith, Elder & Co., 1876), p. 527.

262 *shutters of the shops*: *Liverpool Review*, 10 August 1889, p. 11.

262 *increased the public curiosity*: *Pall Mall Gazette*, 'extra special edition', 5 August 1889. The following description of the rush to obtain public seats for Florence Maybrick's statement is taken from the same source.

262 *trifling error of diet*: Irving, *The Trial of Mrs Maybrick*, p. 213.

263 *good for the complexion*: Ibid., p. 224.

263 *I should like to call someone*: This and Edwin's following testimony, Irving, op. cit., p. 226ff.

265 **tried to cover it up:** It has been suggested that among the letters found in Florence's dressing table after James' death were notes to and from Edwin and from another man – a lawyer in London called Williams – that indicated that these two had been Florence's lovers. No proof of this has ever been found.

265 *How horrid*: Irving, op. cit., p. 227.

265 **Her voice was soft:** *Liverpool Mercury*, 6 August 1889, p. 6.

265 **The courtroom stilled:** See Irving, op. cit., p. 227ff; also *Pall Mall Gazette*, 'extra special edition', 5 August 1889.

267 **So absorbed by Florence:** *Liverpool Mercury*, 6 August 1889, p. 6.

268 **forfeit the emotional sympathy:** See Trodd, *Domestic Crime in the Victorian Novel*, p. 146.

268 **Closing speeches:** Taken mostly from Irving, op. cit., p. 229ff, and from *Liverpool Mercury*, 6 August 1889, p. 6.

270 **Illogical order of witnesses:** See Emsley, *The Elements of Murder*, p. 190ff.

270 **To have to urge against:** Irving, op. cit., p. 256ff.

CHAPTER 27: THE LAST ACT

272 **change of procedure:** *Liverpool Daily Post*, 7 August 1889, p. 7. This piece is the source of most of the description of Stephen's summation and all quotations unless otherwise specified.

273 **His direction to the jury:** *The Times*, 7 August 1889, p. 11.

274 *dreary, dull or depressing*: 'The Liverpool Cause Célèbre', *Liverpool Echo*, 6 August 1889.

274 *you alone are the persons*: Irving, *The Trial of Mrs Maybrick*, p. 323. All other details of his summation unless noted are taken from this source. *Liverpool Mercury*, 8 August 1889, p. 7, also contains a full report.

275 **a different kind of heroine:** The fact was picked up by the papers, including the *St James's Gazette*. See Knelman, *Twisting in the Wind*, p. 30.

275 **Florence's *disgrace*:** Irving, op. cit., p. 327.

276 **in favour of a man:** Ibid., p. 333. For consideration of Stephen's hostility, see also Carol Smart, *Women, Crime, and Criminology: A Feminist Critique* (London: Routledge & Kegan Paul, 1977), p. 45, and Morris, *Double Jeopardy*, p. 44ff.

277 *You must decide it*: Irving, op. cit., p. 351ff.

278 **nothing mattered:** Details of being asked to sign papers etc. are taken from Florence Maybrick's deposition in Washington in 1905, Prison Folder, Christie Papers.

279 **Convicts, they warned:** Christie, *Etched in Arsenic*, p. 145.

279 **ten minutes to four:** The following description of the verdict and sentence are taken from *Liverpool Echo*, 7 August 1889, p. 4; Irving, op. cit., p. 355ff; Maybrick, *Mrs Maybrick's Own Story*, p. 55ff.

279 **followed by the twelve men:** *Lloyd's Weekly Newspaper*, 11 August 1889, p. 3.

279 **sighing of wind:** Maybrick, op. cit., p. 55.

279 **She began to rise:** *London Star*, 8 August 1889, p. 2.

CHAPTER 28: PUBLIC RECOIL

282 **bolstered by fifty more:** *Pall Mall Gazette*, 8 August 1889, p. 4.

282 **Ropes:** *Lloyd's Weekly Newspaper*, 11 August 1889, p. 3; *Liverpool Echo*, 7 August 1889, p. 4.

282 **Brierley had seemed very agitated:** An unidentified post-trial newspaper clipping in the Home Office scrapbook.

282 **slipped out of a private door:** *London Star*, 8 August 1889, p. 2.

283 **bundled into the safety:** Ibid.

283 *an incident unparalleled*: *Liverpool Echo*, 7 August 1889, p. 4.

283 **James Berry:** Stewart P. Evans, *Executioner: The Chronicles of a Victorian Hangman* (Stroud: Sutton, 2004), p. 311ff.

283 **odd logic:** Obituary of Russell, *The Times*, 11 August 1900.

283 *I am sorry to say*: Letter from Sir Charles Russell to Henry Matthews, dated 7 August 1889, received at the Home Office 9 August, HO 144.1638.A50678.

284 **a general horror:** The Argus London Correspondent, syndicated and reported in e.g. the New Zealand *Wanganui Herald*, 2 October 1889.

284 **three Sundays:** *Liverpool Mercury*, 8 August 1889, p. 7.

284 **a quarter of that total:** *Pall Mall Gazette*, 8 August 1889.

284 *not thoroughly convinced*: Leader, *The Times*, 8 August 1889, p. 7.

284 **renewed demands:** Ibid.

284 *depraved* businessmen: *Liverpool Echo*, 8 August 1889, p. 3.

285 *hypocritical morality*: Hartman, *Victorian Murderesses*, p. 304; Knelman, *Twisting in the Wind*, p. 244.

285   *Liverpool Courier* agreed: Knelman, op. cit., p. 244.

285   *ferocity of panic*: The Argus London Correspondent reported in New Zealand newspapers, e.g. *West Coast Times*, Putanga, 1 October 1889.

286   *muslins, cretonnes*: *The Times*, 12 August 1889, p. 4.

286   **arrested for brawling**: Law reports, *The Times*, 12 August 1889, p. 3.

286   **Petitions**: The Home Office files still contain lists of the petitions received, though most of the original documents have not survived. HO 144.1638.A50678. Bundles arrived at Westminster daily.

286   **Mancunians**: Ibid. See letter from Ruggles Brise, 17 August 1889.

286   *no primary proof*: Ibid. See also HO 144.539.A50678 for general letters received at the Home Office during August 1889.

286   **public recoil**: *Liverpool Mercury*, 10 August 1889, p. 5.

286   **resolution of a mystery**: *Lloyd's Weekly Newspaper*, 11 August 1889, p. 1.

287   *gay and frivolous and sensual life*: *Pall Mall Gazette*, 9 August 1889.

287   **G. D. Witt**: Letter dated 24 August 1889, HO 144.1638.A50678.

287   **Josephine Butler**: 'A Plea for Women as Jurors', *Pall Mall Gazette*, 10 August 1889.

287   **Cunninghame-Graham**: 'A Woman's Verdict' in ibid.

288   *'beauty in distress'*: *Lloyd's Weekly Newspaper*, 11 August 1889, p. 5; 'Mobbing Mrs Maybrick – in wax', *Pall Mall Gazette*, 13 August 1889.

288   *innumerable novels*: *Liverpool Review*, 10 August 1889, p. 10.

288   **wild rumours**: 'The Maybrick Mystery: A Startling Rumour', *Pall Mall Gazette*, 9 August 1889; *Lloyd's Weekly Newspaper*, 11 August 1889, p. 7.

288   *poor little rabbit*: 'Another Interview with the Baroness von Roque [*sic*]', *Liverpool Echo*, 22 August 1889.

288   **condemned cell**: *Liverpool Echo*, 22 August 1889, p. 3; 'Important Statements', *Evening Express*, 22 August 1889.

288   **Her clothes were replaced**: *Evening Express*, 22 August 1889.

288   *Oh mama*: Ibid.

289   **shocking and humiliating**: *Liverpool Citizen*, 21 August 1889.

289   **body would fall**: Smith, *The Register of Death*, Part I.

289   **subsequently complained**: *St James's Gazette*, 9 August 1889; *Liverpool Daily Post*, 10 August 1889.

289   **two other jurors**: *Pall Mall Gazette*, fourth edition, 12 August 1889.

289   **the Baroness conveyed**: Letter from the Baroness's solicitor J. Treeve Edgecombe, *Pall Mall Gazette*, 13 August 1889, p. 12.

290   **exclusive interview**: *Liverpool Mercury*, 14 August 1889, p. 6.

290   **Brierley had not been seen**: *Pall Mall Gazette*, 14 August 1889, p. 4.

290   *I was going away*: Interview repeated widely, e.g. *Sheffield and Rotherham Independent*, 14 August 1889, p. 5.

291   *I am a woman*: The Baroness's interview was reprinted in the *Liverpool Weekly Post*, 17 August 1889, p. 5.

292 **monstrous!**: *Liverpool Weekly Post*, 17 August 1889, p. 5.

292 **passionate response**: Ibid.

292 **held fast on the wheels**: Maybrick, *Mrs Maybrick's Own Story*, p. 59.

CHAPTER 29: THE BENEFIT OF DOUBT

294 **eight female convicts had been hanged**: Morris, *Women, Crime, and Criminal Justice*, p. 30.

294 **not the kind of man**: Ibid., p. 31; Nott-Bower, *Fifty-Two Years a Policeman*, p. 130.

294 **In the press**: *Liverpool Mercury*, 16 August 1889, p. 6. See also Whorton, *The Arsenic Century*, p. 93ff.

294 **Public memorials**: *The Times*, 15 August 1889, p. 5.

294 **The Lancet**: Vol. 134, no. 3442, 17 August 1889.

294 **In the House of Commons**: *Pall Mall Gazette*, 9 August 1889.

294 **three thousand people**: *Liverpool Weekly Post*, 17 August 1889.

295 **Alexander MacDougall**: Hartman, *Victorian Murderesses*, points out in her note 117 that MacDougall had previously involved himself in the perceived injustice of the 'Penge' case twelve years earlier, after the death of Harriet Staunton.

295 **Swamped**: *Liverpool Mercury*, 14 August 1889, p. 6.

295 **popular clamour**: *Pall Mall Gazette*, no date, clip in Home Office file HO 144.1638.A506778.

295 **obdurate**: Obituary of Henry Matthews, *Oxford Dictionary of National Biography*.

295 **a stubborn man**: *Liverpool Review*, 17 August 1889, p. 4.

296 **highest medical authorities**: Letter from Judge Stephen to Henry Matthews, 11 August 1889, HO 144.1638.A50678. The remainder of detail in this chapter about the deliberations and actions of Henry Matthews is taken (unless otherwise noted) from the records in this Home Office box.

296 **practically arrived at**: 'The Maybrick Case', *Daily News*, 14 August 1889.

296 **Two days later**: Letter from Richard Cleaver, 14 August 1889, HO 144.1638.A50678.

297 **Had this suspicion**: Letter from Judge Stephen to Henry Matthews, 14 August 1889, HO 144.1638.A50678.

298 **'alienist'**: From the French *aliéné*, or insane; an early psychologist or 'mind doctor'.

298 **twenty-one irritant poisons**: Winslow, *Recollections of Forty Years*. See also Molly Whittington-Egan, *Dr Forbes Winslow: Defender of the Insane* (Great Malvern: Capella Archive, 2000), pp. 95–7.

299 *What I want to know is*: Folder of minutes of the Home Office Conference, 16 August 1889, HO 144.1638.A50678. This document informs the rest of the description of the meeting and all quotations are taken from it unless otherwise indicated.

299 *The thing's a farce!*: *Liverpool Citizen*, 14 August 1889, p. 3.

300 **Cleaver's memorandum:** HO 144.1638.A50678.

300 *I believe* [her]: 'Comic Songs ... ', *Liverpool Weekly Post*, 17 August 1889, p. 5.

301 **Gore was summoned to Whitehall:** According to the *Liverpool Daily Post*, 21 August 1889. There is no note of this meeting in the surviving Home Office files.

301 *Yapp's present statement*: 23 August 1889, HO 144.1638.A50678.

301 **Dr Poore's vast report:** 15 August 1889, received at the Home Office 19 August, HO 144.1638.50678.

302 *from all quarters*: Godfrey Lushington's handwritten notes, 20 August 1889, HO 144.1638.50678.

303 *this is a case*: Ibid.

CHAPTER 30: THE INEXORABLE PASSING OF THE HOURS

304 **growing number of women:** Hartman, 'Crime and the Respectable Woman', p. 38ff. See also Morris, *Women, Crime, and Criminal Justice*, p. 47, on Mary Pearcey. Morris makes the point, too, about Stephen's prejudice altering the public's view of Florence Maybrick.

304 *if Mrs Maybrick is executed*: *Liverpool Weekly Post*, 17 August 1889, p. 5.

304 **Her fashionable silks:** *New York Herald*, London edition, 21 August 1889

304 **Mr Fletcher Rogers:** 'Battlecrease House', *Liverpool Citizen*, 21 August 1889.

305 *What the public feel*: Letter and editorial, *The Times*, 17 August 1889, p. 9.

305 *a pretty little cottage*: 'Important Interview with Mr Maybrick', *Evening Express*, 21 August 1889.

305 **Arrangements had been made:** Florence Maybrick, petition from Aylesbury about the welfare of her children and a report of interviewing Dr Fuller, 23 August 1896, HO 144.1640. Also, the 1891 census lists the Fullers at 33 Albany Street, Regent's Park.

305 **Michael finally spoke to the press:** 'Mr Michael Maybrick talks', *New York Herald*, 21 August 1889.

305 **Alfred Schweisso interview:** *Liverpool Weekly Post*, 17 August 1889, p. 5.

305 **Alice Yapp interview:** 'Alice Yapp Defends Herself', *New York Herald*, London edition, 21 August 1889.

306 **Mary Cadwallader interview:** 'Mr Michael Maybrick talks', op. cit.

306 **hundreds of letters a day:** *Liverpool Mercury*, 19 August 1889, p. 6.

306 *agonising distress:* The Baroness's interview with the *New York Herald* was reprinted, e.g. in *Liverpool Mercury*, 14 August 1889.

307 *logically any middle course:* *Liverpool Echo*, 22 August 1889, p. 3.

307 *British Medical Journal:* 24 August 1889.

307 **wound up his partnership:** *Pall Mall Gazette*, 14 August 1889, p. 4.

307 **beard grow long:** Reported in Boston newspapers, 30 August and 2 September 1889.

308 **chaplain sat with her:** 'Chaplain Fears the Worst', *Liverpool Echo*, 22 August 1889.

308 **Ten minutes later:** Christie, *Etched in Arsenic*, p. 175ff; Maybrick, *Mrs Maybrick's Own Story*, p. 60.

309 *hard to bear:* Maybrick, op. cit.

309 **advised the Queen:** Letter dated 22 August 1889, in Buckle (ed.) *The Letters of Queen Victoria*, vol. 1, p. 527ff.

309 *This decision:* HO 144.1639.A50678.

310 *singular:* *Daily News*, 23 August 1889.

310 *case of terribly strong suspicion:* *The Times*, 23 August 1889.

310 *parody on legal procedure:* 'Why Didn't Matthews Hang Her?', *Liverpool Citizen*, 28 August 1889.

311 **Maybrick Committee:** *Liverpool Mercury*, 23 August 1889, p. 6.

311 **Reports multiplied:** 'The Maybrick Case', *Pall Mall Gazette*, fourth edition, 23 August 1889.

311 **payments:** 15 September 1889, HO 144.1639.A50678.

311 **Sitting in a chair:** *Liverpool Mercury*, 28 August 1889, p. 5.

312 *Save me:* Ibid.

CHAPTER 31: A COLONY OF DEAD HOPES

313 **The monarch wished:** Buckle (ed.), *The Letters of Queen Victoria*, vol. 1.

314 **half her original size:** 'Removal of Mrs Maybrick', *Liverpool Echo*, 29 August 1889.

314 *living tomb:* Maybrick, *Mrs Maybrick's Own Story*, p. 62.

314 **conceal her emotion:** *Liverpool Mercury*, 30 August 1889, p. 6.

314 *colony of wasted lives:* *Graphic*, 31 August 1889.

315 **Her cell:** *Illustrated Police News*, 14 September 1889.

315 *nothing to say:* *Boston Herald*, 13 September 1889, p. 3.

315 *escape from his past existence:* Thomas Hardy, *Tess of the d'Urbervilles* (1891), chapter 49.

316 **Surrounded by former charwomen:** Trades from 1891 census; psychological suffering from Emsley, *Crime and Society*, p. 279; description of the tiers from Maybrick, op. cit., p. 61ff.

316 **Critics called it:** Zedner, *Women, Crime and Custody in Victorian England*, p. 104; Mayhew and Binny, *The Criminal Prisons of London*, p. 100.

316 **most raw and sensitive:** The three-stage system has been described by many, including Morris, *Women, Crime and Criminal Justice*, p. 105ff.

316 *memories and thoughts:* Maybrick, op. cit., p. 74.

316 **size of her cell doubled:** Scougal, *Scenes from a Silent World*, chapter 1.

316 **gruel ... tea:** Convict diets for the three classes from a Prison Commission report quoted in *Daily Chronicle*, 13 August 1904, p. 5.

316 **level of greatest prisoner freedom:** Four-stage system described in Maybrick, op. cit., p. 106ff.

316 **longed for and dreaded:** Ibid., p. 110.

317 *smallest compass:* Ibid., p. 104.

317 **'Maybrickmania':** For example, *Liverpool Review*, 14 March 1891, p. 3.

317 **lengthy petition:** Dated 23 May 1890, HO 144.1639.

317 **Michael Maybrick claimed the money:** 'Mrs Maybrick's Insurance', *New York Times*, 9 December 1891.

317 *New York World:* Reported widely in US newspapers, e.g. *Chicago Inter Ocean*, 19 October 1891, p. 4.

317 **mortgage:** 'Mrs Maybrick gives a Mortgage', *New York Times*, 23 October 1889.

318 *funds ... insufficient:* Letter from Richard Cleaver, dated 28 March 1894, HO 144.1639.

318 **James' arsenic addiction:** For example, Captain Irving; see 'The Maybrick Case', *Liverpool Daily Post*, 9 September 1889.

318 **thought-provoking pamphlet:** Sent to the Home Office with a letter dated 30 July 1890, HO 144.1639.A50678; Tidy and MacNamara, *The Maybrick Trial*.

318 **adding tinder:** For Judge Stephen's mental illness see Knelman, *Twisting in the Wind*, p. 238; also Martin L. Friedland, *The Trials of Israel Lipski* (London: Macmillan, 1984).

319 *matters proper:* Lumley & Lumley brief, 22 June 1892, HO 144.169.A50678.

319 *settle her business affairs:* For example her official request, 23 October 1889, HO 144.1639.A50678.

320 *fictitious:* HO 144.1639 contains multiple reports of Florence's malingering, including 7.12.1892; 23.12.1892; 18.1.1893; 26.4.1893; 15.10.1896; 27.7.1898.

320 **kitchen knife:** Report for Home Office from Woking Prison from Dr Gover, 5 December 1892, HO 144.1639.

320 *miscarriage of justice*: 27 May 1892, HO 144.1639.A50678.

321 *continually weeping*: 11 January 1894, HO 144.1639.A50678.

321 **Blake's sworn statement:** 11 April 1894, in folder sent to Home Office by solicitor J. E. Harris, HO 144.1639.A50678.

321 **Crossing its broad yard:** Maybrick, op. cit., p. 128.

322 **more enlightened:** Du Cane's leadership of the prison system ended in 1895, ushering in a new era of improvement. See, e.g., Brodie, Croom and Davies, *English Prisons*, p. 160.

322 **Wardresses in fresh Holland uniforms:** X.Y.Z., 'England's Convict Prison for Women'.

322 **Women's demands:** Zedner, op. cit., p. 126.

322 **despair and broken nerve:** For women's calls for prison reform see also Eliza Orme, 'Our Female Criminals' (*Fortnightly Review*, May 1898), and 'The Prison Treatment of Women', the reply by Sarah Amos in *Contemporary Review* the following month.

322 **Senate:** *London Standard*, 2 May 1896, p. 7.

322 **US government's efforts:** Recorded in HO 144.1639.A50678 (e.g. 1 May 1891; 22 Sept 1891; May 1892; 27 May 1892; 22 July 1892; 9 November 1894). Also HO 144.1638.A50678 (23 October 1891) and HO 144.1640 (19 June 1897 and April 1899).

323 *blundering stupidity*: *Chicago Daily Inter Ocean*, 17 October 1896, p. 16.

CHAPTER 32: CHANGED UTTERLY

324 *One great advantage*: Memo from Mr Byrne, 30 September 1895, HO 144.1639.A50678. in folder 'Memos on the case of FEM September 1895'.

325 *the adulteress and angry wife*: Letter from Lord Chancellor to Sir Charles Russell, 15 February 1896, HO 144.1640.A50678.

325 *so much agitation*: Kenelm Digby, 10 November 1895, HO 144.1639. A50678; correspondence December 1895, HO 144.1640.A50678.

325 **Diamond Jubilee:** Telegram from US President, 19 June 1897, HO 144.1640.A50678.

325 **served four times:** Irving, *The Trial of Mrs Maybrick*, p. xliii.

325 **Dreyfus:** See Piers Paul Read, *The Dreyfus Affair: The Story of the Most Famous Miscarriage of Justice in French History* (London: Bloomsbury, 2012).

326 **proper system of criminal appeal:** Levy, *The Necessity for Criminal Appeal*.

326 *beautiful woman*: Florence Aunspaugh letters folder, Christie Papers.

327 **leave the country and not return**: Kenelm Digby to Mr Ritchie, 10 July 1901, HO 144.1638.A50678; also Home Office memo, 21 October 1901, HO 144.1640.A50678.

327 **right to sidestep**: Memo from Aylesbury to Home Office, 26 October 1903, HO 144.1640.A50678.

327 **secret of her true identity:** In fact, the *Daily Mirror* soon discovered her whereabouts and broadcasted them to the nation but she seems not to have been bothered by journalists and there were none there when she departed. *Daily Illustrated Mirror*, 15 February 1904, p. 5. Home Office orders from HO.144.1640.A50678, 26 October 1903, arrangements – memo from Aylesbury Prison to Home Office.

328 *mundane things*: *New York Times*, 7 February 1904.

328 **Leaving the convent:** What she was wearing, her movements and intentions, the geography are all recorded. Her feelings, of course, are not.

328 **Mrs Morehouse:** *New York Times*, 24 July 1904; also 13 April 1910.

329 *pleasing-looking little lady*: *Daily Chronicle*, 13 August 1904, p. 5.

329 **the model:** Knelman, *Twisting in the Wind*, p. 119ff.

330 *little woman in white*: *New York Times*, 6 August 1906.

330 **small scar:** *Brooklyn Eagle*, 24 August 1904.

330 *pushed into a world*: *New York Tribune*, 18 November 1905, quoted in Christie, *Etched in Arsenic*, p. 252.

330 *Sad-faced, gentle-voiced*: *Sunday News*, 1 May 1927, p. 3.

331 *lose all hold*: 14 April 1905, HO 144.1640.

331 **never able to find them:** *Liverpool Mercury*, 7 January 1890.

331 **died penniless:** *New York Times*, 13 April 1910.

331 **Laura Withers:** Florence Maybrick's October 1896 petition to the Home Office alleges that Michael cohabited with Laura for fifteen years and that she was uneducated and immoral and not a proper guardian for her children. Florence may not have known that the children were by then with the Fullers. HO 144.1640.A50678.

332 **Edwin ... married:** Births, Marriages and Deaths, Marylebone, October, November, December 1892, vol. 1a, p. 1228. See also web article on Stephen Adams, <www.revolve.com.au/polemic/adams_profile.html>.

333 **ability to express herself:** Letters in the private collection of Richard Whittington Egan.

333 **lifeless body:** South Kent folder, Christie Papers.

333 *swore to keep it a secret*: Ibid.

333 *A time will come*: Maybrick, *Mrs Maybrick's Own Story*, p. 222.

333 **An old scrapbook:** *New York Times*, 26 October 1941.

AFTERWORD

335 **Oscar Wilde:** *An Ideal Husband* (1895), Act 2.

335 **girlish dreams:** Generally (though not specific to Florence Maybrick) this idea is Rachel Brownstein's. See *Becoming a Heroine*, introduction.

336 **no murder:** Letter from Sir Charles Russell to Matthew White Ridley, quoted in Irving, *The Trial of Mrs Maybrick*, p. xlii.

336 **Styrians:** *Chambers' Journal of Popular Literature, Science, and Art*, vol. 3, no. 79, July 1885.

336 *It is not merely:* Dr William Carter, post-trial manuscript notes, New Scotland Yard Crime Museum.

336 **not completely soluble:** There is, throughout, a lack of clarity about whether the poison under discussion was elemental arsenic or arsenic compounds. Irving, op. cit. (p. xxxv), points out that J. Dixon Mann's *Forensic Medicine and Toxicology* asserts that half a grain of solid arsenic is capable of being completely dissolved in meat juice. He also points out that there were three bottles of Valentine's in the house though only two were listed by the police.

337 **never made public:** Central Police Station, Liverpool, Mr Bower Head Constable of Liverpool to Secretary of State, 10 February 1890, HO 144.1639.A50678.

337 **discovered:** *Atlanta Constitution*, 20 November 1904.

337 **defining breach:** Christie, *Etched in Arsenic*, p. 35.

338 **one was noted as bearing the label:** Irving, op. cit., p. xxix.

338 **What happened to the third?:** Ibid.

338 **the letter she wrote:** 14 April 1889, HO 144.1639.A50678.

339 **had not menstruated:** Dr Hopper's statement, HO 144.1639.A50678.

340 **female sexuality:** Knelman, op. cit., pp. 232 and 255.

340 **unequal conventions:** Hartman, *Victorian Murderesses*, chapter 6.

340 **Jack the Ripper:** The contention rests on a diary attributed to James Maybrick and pointing to him as the Ripper. Much has been written on the subject. The diary has not been authenticated and there is a strong (though contested) conviction among many Ripper specialists that it is a fake.

340 **the fatal dose:** Emsley, *The Elements of Murder*, p. 179.

340 **too childlike:** Letter from Florence Aunspaugh to Trevor Christie, Christie Papers.

340 **Gissing:** Quoted in Pykett, *The 'Improper Feminine'*, introduction.

341 *based on fact:* Letter to James Osgood, 4 August 1889, in Purdy and Millgate (ed.), *The Collected Letters of Thomas Hardy*, vol. 1.

341 *kill the situation:* Quoted in Morris, *Double Jeopardy*, p. 131.

341 *liberal education:* Thomas Hardy, *Tess of the d'Urbervilles* (1891), chapter 15.

341   *vessel of emotion*: Ibid., chapter 2.

341   *arbitrary law of society*: Ibid., chapter 41.

342   is often claimed: For example, Boumelha, *Thomas Hardy and Women*; Ledger, *The New Woman*; Brownstein, *Becoming a Heroine*.

342   *rigid conditions*: Brownstein, op. cit., p. 239ff.

343   youthful mistake: Altick, *Victorian Studies in Scarlet*, p. 253.

343   snare: Brownstein, op. cit.

343   driven to violence: Hermann Mannheim, *Comparative Criminology: A Text Book* (London: Routledge, 1965), p. 702.

343   happy marriage: Morris, *Double Jeopardy*, introduction, discussing Hartman's thesis in 'Crime and the Respectable Woman'.

343   made such good criminals: Hartman, 'Crime and the Respectable Woman', 55.

343   *society was getting tired*: Wharton, *The Buccaneers*, p. 241.

343   literary interest: For more on this see Trodd, *Domestic Crime in the Victorian Novel*.

343   *on tiptoe*: Henry James, *The Golden Bowl* (1904), chapter 30.

344   damaged, distorting and dangerous: Trodd, op. cit., p. 11.

344   *victim of intrigue*: Letter from Baroness von Roques to Henry Matthews, 2 October 1889, HO 144.1639.A50678.

344   She would claim: Letter from Baroness von Roques to Henry Matthews, 4 August 1892, HO 144.1639.A50678.

344   *generally botched*: Quoted in Knelman, op. cit., p. 119.

344   *the only case*: James Fitzjames Stephen, *A General View of the Criminal Law of England* (London: Macmillan, 1890, second edition), p. 174.

345   *imprisonment* [was] *an injustice*: Letter from Sir Charles Russell to Matthew White Ridley, 21 November 1895, HO 144.1640.A50678.

346   a barometer of the shifting pressures: Hartman, *Victorian Murderesses*, pp. 215 and 263–5.

Index